RICHARD HOOKER
AND
CONTEMPORARY POLITICAL IDEAS

Ætat: suæ 50

RICHARD HOOKER, FROM AN ENGRAVING IN THE
1672 EDITION OF SPARROW'S "RATIONALE."

[Frontispiece.

RICHARD HOOKER

AND

CONTEMPORARY POLITICAL IDEAS

BY THE REV.

F. J. SHIRLEY, M.A., Ph.D., F.S.A.

*Canon Residentiary of Canterbury and Headmaster of the King's School,
sometime of the Honourable Society of Lincoln's Inn,
Barrister-at-Law*

Published for the Church Historical Society

LONDON

S · P · C · K

1949

RICHARD HOOKER

CONTEMPORARY POLITICAL IDEAS

Hooker, Richard

S.P.C.K.

PRINTED IN GREAT BRITAIN

PREFACE

ALTHOUGH much of this book was written earlier, the chapters on
the Reformation, on Hooker's life and subsequent influence, and
that entitled the Final Assessment, together with some examination
of Bishop Gauden's writings, were completed during the recent war,
in evacuation conditions in the south of Cornwall remote from
libraries. The book as a whole was finished by 1944; but even
since then important contributions have been made to the history
of political science, while the life of the Church of England has not
ceased to develop significantly. Thus a few remarks in the text may
seem to be " dated ". Moreover, the writing of this book has
been constantly interrupted by the busy and exacting duties of a
head master and residentiary canon. To undertake this task was
suggested to me originally by my friend and tutor, the late Sir
William Holdsworth, and I am grateful for this opportunity of
expressing my affection for that marvellous man, as humble in
character as he was distinguished in learning. I also record my
gratitude to another departed friend and former colleague, Captain
John Anthony of the Grenadier Guards, a very gallant Christian
gentleman, but for whose constant encouragement I should never
have persevered in this study. If the book had been worthy of a
Dedication, I should have dedicated it to these two splendid friends.

I hope that in respect of political theory and of Church history
this book may be of some service to those interested in the problems confronting Church and State during a most influential period
in our affairs. I set out from the Anglo-Catholic position in which
I had been brought up, but I confess I became obliged to conclude
that Hooker is not properly to be regarded as a High Anglican.
Thus, I cannot accept the Seventh Book as genuine Hooker, though
doubtless much of it is. In the text I have ventured to suggest, by
way of example, some passages which seem to me suspect: others
may not regard them so. None the less, the fact remains that the
Seventh Book cannot be squared with the first Five Books in
certain material points. Further than that it is dangerous to go;
but that conceded, we must go to the Books published in their
author's lifetime, and not to Book VII, to discover certainly what
Hooker believed about the Church.

The last Chapter, which may be felt to be provocative, is at all events a genuine, if inexpert, attempt to put myself into Hooker's place, and to deduce from his premisses what he would think of the Church of England to-day in regard to its inherent character and such questions as Parliamentary control, Disestablishment, and relationship with other Reformed Churches. I set out from my own standpoint as an advocate of Disestablishment, and I end as an upholder of the Establishment, converted by the judicious author of *The Laws of Ecclesiastical Polity*, whose words I would repeat, " By the goodness of Almighty God and His servant, Elizabeth, we are ", with the substitution of " the State " for Elizabeth, since it is of the essence of every Christian state that it is part of God's order and in consequence divine in origin and purpose as it ought to be in function. England is still a professedly Christian State, and it is the duty and high privilege of the Church to direct the Government to the will of God.

Recently, and some two years after this book went to the publisher, one or two historical studies have been published which tend to correct our ecclesiastical perspective—for example, Professor Norman Sykes' pamphlet on the English Church in the sixteenth and seventeenth centuries. It is hoped that the present study will have the effect of underlining Dr. Sykes' thesis, and in its own small way perhaps help to lead—as the Swedish historian Bishop Brilioth asks in an interesting review of Dr. Sykes' work—to some change of emphasis and attitude on the part of official church leaders especially in regard to such questions as intercommunion and re-union with the non-Episcopal Churches.

It remains for me to thank my friend the Rev. Stanley Poole for his great help in proof-readings and in compiling the index and for his constant interest; my secretary Miss M. E. Milward for having typed the pages of this book during crowded and anxious years; and Dr. R. W. Hunt, Keeper of the Western Manuscripts at the Bodleian, for his unfailing help and kindness.

F. J. S.

Precincts 15,
Canterbury.

CONTENTS

LIST OF ILLUSTRATIONS

CHAPTER I

THE ENGLISH REFORMATION AND ELIZABETHAN SETTLEMENT

" The one definite thing which can be said about the Reformation in England," writes Professor Powicke, " is that it was an act of State." [1] With equal truth it can be described as an act of the laity, not in the sense of the culmination of a deep-seated spiritual unrest (as on the Continent), but a lay revolt against clerical domination. [2] The accomplishment of the Reformation was the work of Parliament and the " godly prince " who was able and willing to step into the Pope's shoes, and represented at that time, at all events, as much the triumph of laity over clergy as a victory of State over Church. [3]

Two centuries earlier the rights of the State and of the laity had been emphasized by Marsiglio of Padua in his *Defensor Pacis*. [4] Nor is it without significance that during the life of the Reformation Parliament (1529–36) William Marshall drew Cromwell's attention to the existence of this work and to his own translation of it. There was no better book, he said, to suit the purposes they had in mind. It is not altogether fanciful to contend, therefore, that Marsiglio played his part in shaping the English Reformation: though Marshall omits and interpolates, as he thinks fit, in order that what in the original was a republican and democratic thesis should be twisted to fit the conditions of Tudor England by affirming the superiority of hereditary succession and placing the Prince as the heart and soul of the State, without whom no kingdom can stand.

Marsiglio published his *Defensor* in 1324 to make a case against the Pope on behalf of the national State, and for the laity against the clergy. Having seen the havoc wrought in Northern Italy by clerical interference, in his bitter resentment he set out to prove

---

[1] *The Reformation in England* (Oxford, 1941), p. 1.
[2] Froude, *H.E.*, XI, 102.
[3] Which had been won, in effect, by William I, Henry I and Henry II. It has been pointed out that Henry II's victory in the matter of Advowsons was of utmost importance for after ages, distinguishing England from other countries, and providing a basis for anti-papal Statutes (Pollock and Maitland, *H.E.L.*, I, 126).
[4] Ed. C. W. Previté-Orton (Camb., 1928).

that neither papal supremacy nor independent ecclesiastical jurisdiction rested on any divine basis, and further that the State was the
only " perfecta communitas ", and could tolerate no rival power
within or without. For there was then emerging into Italian history
that type of National State which, though at the moment anti-
clerical only in so far as this was dictated by the Imperialist alliance,
was to be the forerunner of the omnicompetent States of the sixteenth century.[1] In his purpose to destroy both papal pretensions
and the ecclesiastical system of the Middle Ages, with its buttress,
the Canon Law, Marsiglio argues that this political State is divine
because it is natural, while the clerical State, so far from being
divine, is but a natural function inherent in the political State.
The clergy are simply citizens, performing a State function, and
that function is purely moral and spiritual. Marsiglio seems to
admit that ordination confers a spiritual gift,[2] but allows to the clergy
no greater rights or privileges in respect of their " spiritual character " than other men may enjoy whose natural gifts or inclination
of mind take them to, say, medicine or the law. They constitute a
department of State, the " pars sacerdotalis ", in which all, laity as
well as clergy, have a vital interest. In short, they are a professional
body functioning like the medical profession, living in subjection to
the secular power, as did the first Apostles.[3]

It is difficult to think that the men who composed the Preamble
to the Statute of Appeals were unacquainted with this, the most
formidable and the most revolutionary and " modern " writer in
the anti-papal camp.[4] Their own indignation was doubtless
heightened by the unflattering pictures which he drew of the abuses
of the ecclesiastical system and the corrupting influence of Rome.
They echoed what he declared, that the system is a real disease,
weakening the Church; [5] it is the pest of States, the root and origin
of Italian (*mutatis mutandis* English) tragedy,[6] and must not be allowed
to continue. Reason unites with Nature, as divine with human
Law, in demanding that this ecclesiastical jurisdiction shall cease.[7]

As far back as 1515 (in Standish's case) Henry had reminded
Wolsey that he was King of England and would brook no superior.[8]

---

[1] Cf. Toynbee, *Study of History*, V, 668 *et seq.*
[2] Marsiglio, op. cit., Dictio II, xv, 2.
[3] Op. cit., Dictio II, xv, xvi.
[4] Certainly Hooker knew the *Defensor Pacis*—cf. (e.g.) *E.P.*, VII, xi, 3, 8, and
consider the subject-matter of the *D.P.*, Dictio II, chaps. 9, 10, 15. When Hooker
defines Natural Law as "the dictates of right Reason" he may be translating
Marsiglio's own phrase, " *dictamen rectae rationis* ".
[5] Op. cit., Dictio II, xxiv, 11.
[6] Op. cit., Dictio II, xxxiii, 12.
[7] Op. cit., Dictio II, xxiv, 17.
[8] Gairdner, *Lollardy*, I, 283.

No doubt he had in mind the successful stand made against the Pope by Ferdinand and Isabella, as Wolsey recalled the reforms of Archbishop Ximenes. But for the divorce,[1] it is probable that King and Cardinal would have worked together for some reformation in the Church and, as has been suggested,[2] the future history of the Church in England might not have been dissimilar to that of France. It is conceivable that Henry had in mind some concordat on the lines of that agreed between Francis I and Leo X in 1516. But a breach was inevitable once Henry had determined to put away Catherine.

In his *Obedience of a Christian Man* [3] (1528) Tyndale provided extravagant encouragement to Henry. Kings are God's vice-gerents, and may not be resisted; they are free from restraint of laws and are to God alone answerable.[4] He advises Henry not to share his power, to rule his realm himself with what expert advice he sees fit, but not that of prelates.[5] Simon Fish followed hard after in 1529, arguing in his "Supplication for the Beggars"[6] that the clergy have sapped the royal power to the extent of half the kingdom.

The series of assaults on the ecclesiastical system which were to culminate in severing the Church in England legally and constitutionally from Rome opened when, in November 1529, Parliament attacked clerical fees and pluralities. "Now with the Commons is nothing but down with the Church."[7] The King proceeded to secure the submission of the clergy—rendered liable to the penalties of praemunire for having recognized Wolsey as Legate—and their acceptance of himself as the Supreme Head of the Church, on the petition of the Commons, and Convocation was inhibited from legislating without royal licence and assent. His sovereignty over the clergy established, and the Church's independence at an end, Henry put forward the official case for the English Nation and English Church in the Preamble to the Statute of Appeals 1533.[8]

The Preamble, however, somewhat colours history [9] in asserting,

[1] This conventional term is retained, though, strictly, Henry sought a decree of nullity.
[2] Holdsworth, *H.E.L.*, I, 588.
[3] Parker Soc., 1848.
[4] Op. cit., p. 178.
[5] Op. cit., p. 206.
[6] Printed in Arber's *Tracts*.
[7] Bishop Fisher: quoted Constant, *Reformation in England*, I, 22.
[8] 24 Henry VIII, c. 12.
[9] There was precedent for this. In the Preamble to XXV Ed. III, Stat. 4, it is declared that the Church was founded in this country by the King and his progenitors, with the counts, barons and nobles of the realm and their ancestors. This Preamble of the Statute of Carlisle was also recited in XXV Ed. III, c. 6 (Provisors).

" By divers sundry old authentic histories and chronicles it is
manifestly declared . . . that this realm of England is an Empire
. . . governed by one supreme head and king . . . unto whom a
body politic, compact of all sorts and degrees of people, divided in
terms and by names of spirituality and temporality be bounded and
owe to bear next to God a natural and humble obedience; he being
also institute . . . with plenary whole and entire power, pre-
eminence, authority, prerogative and jurisdiction to render and
yield justice and final determination to all manner of folk, residents,
or subjects within this his realm in all causes . . . happening to
occur . . . within the limits thereof without restraint or provoca-
tion to any foreign princes or potentates of the world. The body
spiritual whereof having power when any cause of the law divine
happened to come in question or of spiritual learning, it was
declared . . . by that part of the said body politic called the
spirituality (now being usually called the English Church) which
. . . is sufficient and meet of itself, without the intermeddling of
any exterior person . . . to declare and determine all such doubts
and to administer all such offices and duties as to their rooms
spiritual doth appertain . . . : and the laws temporal for trial of
property of lands and goods for the conservation of the people of this
realm in unity and peace . . . was and yet is administered . . .
by sundry judges and administers of the other part of the said
body politic called the temporality, and both their authorities and
jurisdictions do conjoin together in the due administration of justice
the one to help the other: and . . . the king his most noble progenitors and the nobility and commons of this said realm at divers
and sundry Parliaments as well in the time of King Edward I,
Edward III, Richard II, Henry IV and other noble kings of this
realm made sundry . . . laws . . . for the entire and sure conservation of the said imperial crown of this realm, and of the jurisdictions Spiritual and Temporal of the same, to keep it from the
annoyance as well of the See of Rome as from the authority of other
foreign potentates."

Finally in 28 Henry VIII, c. 10—an Act extinguishing the
authority of the Bishop of Rome—it is stated that " the King's
Majesty, the Lords spiritual and temporal, and the Commons in this
realm, being over-wearied and fatigated with the experience of
the infinite abominations and mischiefs proceeding of his [sc. the
Pope's] impostures and craftily colouring of his deceits, to the great
damages of souls, bodies and goods, were forced of necessity for the
public weal of this realm to exclude that foreign pretended power,
jurisdiction and authority, used and usurped within this realm ".

Particular anti-papal legislation proceeded apace. Annates and first-fruits and other impositions were no more to be paid to Rome; the King would nominate bishops; appeals should be heard by the King in Chancery; licences were to come from Canterbury, not Rome; royal commissioners would visit monasteries. The coping-stone to all this was placed by the Act of Supremacy [1] 1534, which affirmed the authority of the Crown over all persons and causes in the realm, and gave to the Crown every power of ecclesiastical visitation and control. It finished thoroughly the work of the Reformation Parliament and exemplifies the doctrine " cuius regio eius religio ".

The Act of Supremacy afforded Gardiner, Bishop of Winchester, an opportunity of encouraging loyalty to the new Supreme Head. He promptly published his book, *De Vera Obedientia*,[2] arguing in favour of a " Gallican " Church, and written with an eye on the Preamble to the Statute of Appeals. Scripture teaches that the Prince is God's representative, to whom obedience is due from every subject. The entire nation has consented to the King's supremacy, which, grounded in Scripture, must be defended against the Pope's pretended power. The supremacy is grounded in Reason, too, since those who compose the Church of England also compose the Realm. To acknowledge the Prince head of the Realm but not of the Church would reduce him to Kingship over unbelievers only! All Scripture, from Moses onwards, shows the subordination of the ecclesiastical to the secular power. In the spirit of Marsiglio, he ridicules the papal claim to succeed to Peter's primacy; if Peter had a primacy, it was not of the nature of lordship at all, but service and example. " All manner of people receiving and embracing the truth do with one whole consent acknowledge honour and reverence the King for the Supreme Head of the Church on earth. They bid the Bishop of Rome farewell."

Gardiner's defence of the supremacy is typical of the sixteenth-century attitude towards this question. Thirty years later it was followed by Jewel, and it is difficult to over-estimate the importance of the " godly Prince ", whose claim to supreme jurisdiction is justified by Nature, Scripture and Reason. The Prince had re-gathered to himself his lawful " Imperium ", which had been usurped from him by the Pope, and all spiritual jurisdiction conse-quently emanated from him. So the Canon Law of the Church appropriately yielded place to the " King's Ecclesiastical Law of the Church of England ".[3]

[1] 26 Henry VIII, c. 1.
[2] Ed. with introduction by P. Janelle (Camb., 1930). Cromwell gave many copies away, to ambassadors in England and to useful people on the Continent. (Constant: op. cit., I, 352.)
[3] 27 Henry VIII, c. 20, s. 1.

Thus when Henry died in 1547 legal and constitutional revolution had taken place, not only in severing the Church of England from the Western Church, but also in placing it in subjection to the State. The ease with which it was achieved goes to prove a disposition as to its reasonableness. As Freeman says,[1] the nation, as a whole, went heartily with Henry at least in getting rid of the Pope. Only one bishop met martyrdom for his Holiness' sake, and the Pilgrimage of Grace was the sole mass protest. The King maintained no standing army and, as Froude points out,[2] the fact that all classes were armed proves the mutual confidence between King and people. But religious or doctrinal revolution was yet to come.

The short reign of Edward VI is important because, in the first place, there is a notable development of the Royal Supremacy and, secondly, doctrinal changes were made which were to become the basis of the future Elizabethan Settlement. The Supremacy had been to Henry intensely personal. The right of the Council to exercise it was therefore challenged by Bonner and Gardiner; they claimed that further change ought to await the King's coming of age. Their view could claim support from the fact that the Act 28 Henry VIII, cap. 17, permitted a Sovereign who was a minor to repeal by Letters Patent any laws passed in his minority when he should reach the age of twenty-four. But this Act was, in fact, repealed in the beginning of this reign, and the two bishops found a prison their reward. The Council at once went beyond even Henry's exercise of the Supremacy by ensuring to the Crown in 1547[3] that bishops should be appointed by Letters Patent. The capitular right of election being abolished, bishops became obviously State officers, liable to summary deprivation whenever the Crown should see fit to withdraw its Letters Patent.

The First Doctrinal Reformation occurred in 1549, when the Act of Uniformity[4] legalized a Book of Common Prayer. It was written in English, and ousted all local "uses". Moderate reformers regarded this Liturgy as scriptural, though extremists like Hooper[5] flatly refused to join in its Eucharistic worship. But Henricians such as Gardiner found it capable of Catholic interpretation. It was probably intended by the Government as a first instalment in doctrinal and liturgical reform,[6] while they felt the pulse of the nation on the matter.[7] The same year saw priests per-

---

[1] *Historical Essays* (London, 1892), Vol. IV, Essay 14.
[2] *H.E.*, I, 162.
[3] 1 Edw. VI, c. 2.
[4] 2 & 3 Edw. VI, c. 1.
[5] *Original Letters* (Parker Soc., 1847), p. 79.
[6] See *Original Letters*, pp. 535 et seq.
[7] Kennedy, *Studies in Tudor History* (London, 1916), p. 83.

mitted to marry. " Superstitious " books and images were abolished in 1550, and a general destruction of altars was ordered in the King's name, to be replaced by " honest tables ". But the high (or perhaps low) water mark of doctrinal changes was reached in 1551, when the Second Act of Uniformity [1] imposed a revised Book of Common Prayer (1552). No Henrician could find Catholic elements in the new Communion service; it was simply a commemorative rite, and suggests both the purpose of the Government to bring Anglican doctrine and worship into conformity with the tenets of the Reformed Churches generally (for example, the Council, without the consent of Parliament, appended the " Black Rubric " denying the Real Presence) and the extent to which Cranmer's own views had moved in an extreme Protestant direction. Convocation was not consulted, but Parliament doomed to imprisonment any who should attend services other than those in the Book of Common Prayer.[2]

Elizabeth, " that bright occidental Star ",[3] succeeded her sister Mary on the throne in 1558. Mary, the zealous daughter of the Catholic Church, had abolished the previous anti-papal legislation, but had not dared to undo the spoliation of the monasteries, which had created vested interests in which both Catholics and Protestants shared. The new Queen moved to the constitutional position of Henry VIII by the Act of Supremacy,[4] and to the doctrinal position of Edward's reign by the Act of Uniformity.[5] Whatever her private views, necessity dictated this step. Elizabeth could not be a Catholic, for she would have had to admit herself a bastard; [6] on the other hand, Calvinism would have made her less than a Queen, and that no Tudor could have tolerated. Consequently, papal power was removed, the Church again made national and placed under the State, the Crown provided its Church with officers and declared its doctrine and belief. The Church of England was built upon these two Acts, and the foundations of the relations of Church and State were thereby laid. It is of the utmost importance to remember that these laws were the work of the laity alone. Convocation was ignored throughout. In the House of Lords all the bishops opposed the Act of Supremacy, as they did the Act of Uniformity, though in this latter opposition

---

[1] 5 & 6 Edw. VI, c. 1.
[2] For an excellent account of the Prayer Books, see the Essay on Christian Worship and Liturgy, by E. C. Ratcliff, in *The Study of Theology* (ed. K. E. Kirk, London, 1939).
[3] Dedication of A.V. to James I.
[4] 1 Eliz. c. 1.
[5] 1 Eliz. c. 2.
[6] Maitland in *C.M.H.*, vol. II, ch. 16, p. 559 (though he notes that Rome would have been ready to remedy this defect). Cf. Meyer, *England and the Catholic Church under Queen Elizabeth* (Kegan Paul, 1916), p. 15.

they had the support of some temporal peers, and only missed defeating it by a majority of three. "If His Holiness proceed against the Queen and the realm", wrote the Spanish Ambassador to his master in 1559, " he must exempt the bishops and Convocation, who have been loud in their protests of allegiance to the Church. The majority of the people out of Parliament are innocent also."

The Act of Supremacy [1] claims to restore to the Crown its ancient jurisdiction over the State ecclesiastical and spiritual, thus emphasizing that the Supremacy was no new thing—it was inherent in the Crown. It revives most of Henry VIII's ecclesiastical legislation; asserts England's independence of any external authority; assigns complete powers of ecclesiastical visitation to the Crown, and declares Elizabeth Supreme Governor over all causes, ecclesiastical or temporal. Forfeiture of office is the penalty for refusal of the oath.[2] In any fashion to maintain the jurisdiction of any foreign Power renders the offender liable to forfeiture of goods for a first offence, praemunire for a second, a third offence constituting treason.[3] The Queen is empowered to delegate her ecclesiastical jurisdiction to Commissioners,[4] and the oath is to be taken by all clergy and laymen holding office under the Crown,[5] by ordinands and by candidates for University degrees.[6] The Act further endeavours to establish Christian doctrine by definition that nothing shall be adjudged heresy except such heresies as have already been condemned by the canonical Scriptures, the first four General Councils of the Church, " or such as hereafter shall be . . . judged . . . to be heresy by the High Court of Parliament of this realm with the assent of the Clergy in their Convocation." [7]

The Act of Uniformity [8] defined the doctrinal position, decided upon by Queen and Parliament. It recited that the new Prayer Book should be in use by June 24th next.[9] This book was largely the second Edwardine Prayer Book, modified to embrace as many as possible. Thus the " two sentences only added in the delivery of the sacrament to the communicants, and none other or otherwise " suggests a deliberate conflation of the 1549 and 1552 words of administration, so as to move away from a solely commemorative view of the Eucharist. Again, the " Ornaments Rubric " would sanction the use of the customary eucharistic vestments. Further, the Black Rubric disappeared. It was hoped that this attempt to blend the old and the new would be to such a degree acceptable that all except the extremists in the Papist and Puritan camps might use it, and thereby produce that outward unity in religion

---

[1] 1 Eliz. c. 1. [2] s. 10. [3] s. 14. [4] s. 8. [5] s. 9.
[6] s. 12. [7] s. 20. [8] 1 Eliz. c. 2. [9] s. 2.

without which it was (rightly for the times) deemed there could be no unity in the State. The new Queen dared not permit dispute in religion, " an apple in the eye of Government," as Francis Osborne wrote, " which if once suffered to roll and grow wanton, will render the people's minds unsteady betwixt the obedience they owe to God and their Prince, fondly imagining the first may be gratified at the prejudice of the latter ".[1] Consequently the use of any other form of worship was proscribed under threats of punishments ranging from forfeiture of a year's profit with six months' imprisonment for a first offence to perpetual imprisonment for a third.[2] Attendance at the parish church on Sundays and holy days was compulsory, enforced by a fine of 12 pence.[3] Anything done or spoken in derogation of the book brought penalties ranging from 100 marks for a first offence to life imprisonment for a third.[4] Cognizance of offences could be taken by ecclesiastical courts, by Justices of Oyer and Terminer and of Assize, while bishops could sit with the Justices if they chose.[5]

In this manner the Settlement was established, and the secular arm utilized to strengthen it. Further, the second Parliament of the reign (1563) came severely to the support of the Settlement by passing the Assurance of Supremacy Act,[6] and an " Act for the due Execution of the Writs de Excommunicato capiendo ";[7] the measure of severity is some indication of the state of feeling in the country. The Assurance of Supremacy Act attempted a sterner repression of papal sympathy; the crime was still only praemunire, but it was the duty of all Justices of the Peace to seek out offenders, remitting them to King's Bench for final verdict. The second purpose of the Act was to cause the oath of allegiance to be taken more widely and recusants to be punished more severely. All graduates of universities, lawyers, and schoolmasters had now to swear, in addition to all clergy and State officials.[8] Instead of forfeiture of goods, the penalty for a first offence was now praemunire; for a second offence the penalty became death as a traitor. Five classes of people were enumerated to whom the oath was to be tendered again, three months after a first refusal. The trial of offenders was in King's Bench, and the penalty that for treason.

At the same time Parliament passed [9] an Act for the due execution of the writ to remedy the weakness of the old procedure. The return was to be made to King's Bench, and a *capias* issued as often as needed, if the excommunicate could not be found. If and

---

[1] *Memoirs of Queen Elizabeth* (1658), p. 76.   [2] s. 2.
[3] s. 3.   [4] s. 3.   [5] ss. 4-6.   [6] 5 Eliz. c. 1.
[7] 5 Eliz. c. 23.   [8] As in 1 Eliz. c. 1.   [9] April 10th.

B

when found, he was to be forthwith imprisoned. But the bishop who pronounced the sentence was empowered to receive the offender's submission. These two Acts were plainly intended *in terrorem*, but largely through Parker's hatred of persecution were not pressed to any severe extent.[1]

Thus was the Settlement accomplished, and Mary's work undone. It marked again the complete triumph of the State over the Church; it was the action of the laity in Parliament. It was indeed an " Act of State ". As events were to show, however, the Settlement was enduring for Tudor England, but no later than the next dynasty were the problems set by the Supremacy and unsolved by Elizabeth to be the downfall of kings. The bridge built by Elizabeth was in reality a temporary structure. Its strength at the time lay in its anti-Roman and nationalist character (for Rome was identified with Spain); its principle was " cuius regio eius religio ".

Romanist historians insist that the Settlement erected a Church entirely distinct from that of Mary and Henry VIII; a fresh creation, a State-devised and Parliamentary system of religion; its bishops possessing no other orders than by the grace and favour of the State. The evidence adduced [2] for this position is that the first Convocation of the reign and the two universities were un-doubtedly Romanist; that the Acts of Supremacy and Uniformity were passed in a packed Commons and jockeyed through the Lords; [3] that the Settlement was entirely the work of laymen, by whose efforts a Church was set up six months before it had an archbishop. It is impossible to deny that there is truth in these statements, but they do not of necessity lead to the conclusion drawn. In the first place, it is argued, great care was taken, as in Parker's consecration, to show that the new line of bishops was one with the old. Further, although the help of Parliament was essential to establish some sort of Church *order* at this critical juncture, yet the Supremacy was a real and personal thing to Elizabeth, who had no intention of allowing the Church to be Parliament-ridden or administered. In any case, Gibson maintains, the very words of the Ordinal " do plainly carry in them an acknowledgement of a Power annexed to the office [*sc.* of a bishop] by Divine Right ".[4] To each bishop-elect the Archbishop puts the question, " Will you

---

[1] Parker, *Corr.*, p. 174 (Parker Society, 1853). Letter to the bishops. They are to be prudent in administering the oath; refusal to swear it to be reported to him, and the oath not to be tendered twice without his written authority.

[2] E.g., Dom Birt, *The Elizabethan Religious Settlement* (Bell, 1907), p. 93.

[3] Cf. Robert Parsons, writing in 1596 (*Jesuits' Memorial*, ed. Edward Gee, 1690, p. 109): " Again, it may be considered whether the first Parliament holden in this Queen's days were a good and lawful Parliament or no, by reason of the want of Bishops, and of the open violence used unto them by the Laity."

[4] *Codex* (London, 1713), p. xvii.

maintain and set forward . . . quietness, love and peace . . . and
. . . within your diocese correct and punish, according to such
authority as you *have by God's word*, and as to you shall be committed
by the Ordinance of this Realm? " This, the form by which all the
Elizabethan bishops were consecrated, is held sufficient of itself to
prove that, though the power of jurisdiction " in foro exteriori "
was a legal power given by the State, yet in religious matters the
bishops exercised spiritual authority. It is worth while remember-
ing, too, that Parliament itself, in 1566, in legalizing the Ordinal,
recognized this particular authority. The same writer further
remarks that, though the legislature often affirmed that all ecclesiastical authority is in, or derived from, the Crown's Royal Supremacy, this was an over-statement [1] due to the fact that the main
purpose of the laws passed to establish the Elizabethan Church was
to exclude the power of the Pope.

What in fact the Settlement amounted to in the eyes of contemporaries may be seen in two articles ordered by the Commissioners in February 1561 to be read by the prebendaries of Hereford.[2]
" First I am in conscience persuaded that the Church of England
is a true member of the Holy Catholic Church. And that the
Queen's Majesty is by right and just title the supreme governor of
the same Church of England next and immediately under our
Saviour Jesus Christ, both in matters ecclesiastical and temporal
. . . also . . . that the order of administration of sacraments, the
common prayers and other rites and ceremonies prescribed by the
book of Common Prayer are sincere, true and good, and consonant
to the doctrine of Holy Scriptures, and the ancient usage of the
Holy Catholic Church of Christ."

On the other hand, Protestant historians have asserted that the
change of religion was decidedly popular. It is, however, impossible to calculate what degree of welcome, what genuine acceptance, was accorded to the work of Elizabeth's Parliament, Commissioners, and bishops, for the reason that thousands must have
waited to see how far the change was to be permanent, and in the
meantime prudently conformed.[3] That there was a general and

---

[1] This is questionable. Neither Henry (probably; but see Dixon's *Church
History*, II, 311) nor Elizabeth claimed " *potestas ordinis* ", but fully claimed
" *potestas jurisdictionis* ". The Divine " impress " of episcopal character would be
given in consecration, but the right to put forward one to receive that impress
belonged to and derived from the Supreme Head, and nobody else.

[2] *A Collection of Original Letters* (ed. Mary Bateson; Camden Misc., 1895),
IX, 22.

[3] Anglican writers generally estimate about 200 deprivations for non-conforming
(e.g., Gee, *Elizabethan Clergy*, 1898, Chaps. 12, 13); Dom Birt, op. cit., p. 203, puts
the total at 2,000, including those who abandoned livings for conscience' sake.
Undoubtedly, the new episcopate had to ordain on wholesale scale, and to be

cordial welcome with open arms for the " new religion " is unlikely and certainly undemonstrable; for the restoration of the old ritual under Mary appears to have definitely approved itself to the majority. It is easy, as Freeman says,[1] " to scoff at the way in which the nation followed its rulers backwards and forwards—but it did follow them,[2] and for the most part willingly even if tardily ". Many would doubtless be inclined to the Elizabethan Settlement who, having approved the return to the old religion in 1553, yet deplored the re-establishment of the Papacy and the dread persecutions. But this is not to say that the new religion was popular at the outset—though it may well have become so within a reasonable time, or perhaps custom rendered the majority of the people used to it and indifferent to further change. In October 1564, for example, the Council asked the bishops for returns of J.P.s who were favourable and unfavourable to the Government in its religious policy. On a rough calculation the returns exhibit 431 as favourable, 157 hostile, while 264 are indifferent.[3] Yet it seems undeniable that for many a long year some people were tenacious of the old paths and hostile to innovation. Otherwise it is difficult to understand how remnants of " popery " could have endured in many parts, for as late as 1590 the Visitation Articles of bishops lead us to suppose, from their interrogatories, a considerable survival of furniture, vestments, and other things deemed popish.[4] At all events the machinery which was to establish the Settlement had to be manipulated with care, skill, and speed. Convocation, Oxford, and Cambridge were all hostile; the Commons may have been packed, but, if so, the Government had short time in which to do it; had the prelates and the Catholic lords been fully present in their House, the Supremacy and Uniformity Bills would have been wrecked; but, partly by fortune and partly by chicanery, the Romanist element was sufficiently weakened.

---

content with many unlearned men (cf. Hooker, *E.P.*, VII, xxiv, 7). The Visitation Articles and Injunctions of the bishops reveal this (cf. C. W. Foster, *The State of the Church*, Vol. I, Lincoln Record Society, 1926; and Froude, *H.E.*, XI, 66, 471 *et seq.*).

[1] Op. cit., p. 292.

[2] Most of the clergy seem to have done so at all events, e.g., Wotton held benefices from 1517 to 1566, including the Deanery of Canterbury from 1540 and that of York from 1544; Raphael Keene held the living of Brent Pelham, Herts, from 1539 to 1614 (Add. MSS., B.M., 5806, fol. 25). These examples are, of course, remarkable, and few can have been beneficed so long. But it does seem reasonable to conclude that most clergy conformed.

[3] Edited for the Camden Soc. by Mary Bateson, published in Camden Misc., Vol. IX (1895).

[4] See Kennedy's *Elizabethan Episcopal Administration* (1924), III, 261. In 1681 Thoresby was " amazed " at the ornaments, tapers, copes, and vestments at Durham. *Diary and Correspondence*, I, 75.

Elizabeth intended to restore the constitution of the Church as it was in the days of her father, though toned down in external worship, and in doctrine ambiguously phrased (a " midge-madge ", as Burleigh called it), so that it might be a home for all save those who could not reject papal supremacy; a continuation, not a creation; a restoration, not an innovation. Hence the care exercised in the consecration of Parker, and the *supplentes* clause to remedy any legal defects.[1] But it was not intended as a blend of Rome and Geneva.[2] The Elizabethan Church was an attempt to conserve individual liberty as against a didactic Rome with its emphasis on the corporate life, and yet to retain the corporate life of the Church as against the individualism of Protestant and Sectary. Antagonism to both extremes was necessary, for Rome crushed the individual in favour of the body, while the Protestant centre and left wing had no use for the conservation of the corporate life of the Church as a living and historic reality. The Anglican Church could make its appeal to Scripture and tradition that it was a truer Church than Rome, since, recognizing that God had willed His Church, it yet grasped the prime purpose of the Church, the salvation of the individual soul. Ideally it aimed at a balance, not a blend, but tragically shrouded its lofty spiritual designs by secular weapons and State machinery. Rome had only half the truth—the body was everything; Protestantism had the other half—the individual was all: each was complementary to the other. The Church of Jewel, Parker, and Hooker claimed to have the whole truth, and to be a middle way between the extremes.[3] It insisted that the religious world was divided not into two parts, the friends and foes of Rome, but into three, machine-like Romanism, Separatist licence, and Anglicanism, the home of true spiritual liberty, in which men of varying opinions could live together without shedding each other's blood. But neither Roman nor Puritan could understand this *via media*. To the Papist the Anglican Church was a State creature born and bred, having no connection with the historic Church. The Puritan held it a valid enough Church, but in further need of purging. His quarrel was not so much with the Church as with the State for maintaining it; for the basis of all Puritanism was that Church and State were not one and the same; they were two

---

[1] By some oversight the Ordinal was not included in the 1559 Act of Uniformity, and was therefore not passed by Parliament. Hence the difficulty that no ordinal had legal power when Parker was consecrated, the elaborate care exercised on that occasion, and the " *supplentes* " clause designed to meet any lack of legality.

[2] This is admirably brought out in Kennedy's *Parker* (London, 1908), Chap. I.

[3] " Keeping the middle way, between the pomp of Superstitious Tyranny, and the meanness of Fantastick Anarchy " (*Eikon Basilike*: King Charles' *Works*, 1687, p. 714).

separate kingdoms—a position in direct conflict with the Tudor theory. On this the Puritan erected his platform, and opposition to the Elizabethan Settlement was to come mainly from Geneva, not Rome.

The Royal Supremacy was as real in Elizabeth's as in Henry's reign. It is true that the title was softened from Supreme Head to Supreme Governor, but history was to demonstrate that there was small difference consequent on the change of name. It is also true that the passage through Parliament of the Act of Supremacy was a matter of months. Cecil must have foreseen trouble, for in the writs summoning the first Parliament the title " Supreme Head " did not appear, an elastic " etcetera " being deliberately substituted.[1] Long before Tudor days the Crown had had a vague but effective supremacy, exercising it at times in ordering and prohibiting visitations,[2] and in insisting on respect for royal wishes in the matter of ecclesiastical appointments.[3] The Catholic monarchs of Spain and France had determinedly exercised a similar ecclesiastical jurisdiction. The last years of Henry's reign, and the whole of Edward's, saw episcopal authority for visitation entirely inhibited by royal authority.[4] Mary herself had to carry through her early reactionary legislation by virtue of the Supremacy and by use of the title " Supreme Head "—a state of things ironical enough. Without the help of Parliament the new system of religion could never have been established,[5] and the aid of the Commons had been furnished as generously in 1559 as to Elizabeth's father in 1529.[6] The argument was logical; since Church and nation are one and the same, the King in Parliament can amend and establish the ecclesiastical constitution, declare doctrine, and be the supreme judge of appeal. The official view was as stated by Sir Thomas Smith: " The Parliament abrogateth old laws, maketh new, giveth orders for things past, and for things hereafter to be followed . . . establisheth forms of religion . . .", for Parliament " representeth and hath the power of the whole realm both the head and body ".[7] Yet Elizabeth was no doubt as much aware of possible accusations

[1] Maitland (*E.H.R.*, 1900, XV, 120–4) proves the title to be deliberate. Note p. 122: " He who knows what faith is ' the ' faith will be able to make a good guess touching the import of ' and so forth ' " (reprinted in *Collected Papers*, 1909, Vol. III).

[2] Frere, *Visitation Articles* (Alcuin Club), I, 119–20.

[3] Cf. *The Register of Archbishop Chichele*, Vol. I (ed. E. F. Jacob, Oxford, 1943).

[4] Frere, op. cit., pp. 133–6.

[5] For a discussion on the legality of the first two Acts of Elizabeth's reign, see Frere's *History of the English Church* (Macmillan, 1924, p. 39).

[6] So much so that Francis Osborne says, " The Doctrine professed most generally in England bore in foreign nations the name of Parliament-Faith ". (Op. cit., p. 77.)

[7] *De Rep. Angl.* (ed. Alston), p. 49.

that her Church was a mere State-creation as she was alive to the danger that lawyers and laity might attempt limitations on the royal supremacy. She therefore steadfastly adhered to a policy of keeping Parliament's hands off the Church. She alone would be its Governor, the Supremacy was not to be shared; delegated it might be, as to Commissioners, but nothing further. Thus, rather like an Anglican Pope, she " supplies " whatsoever legal requirements may have been defective in the form of consecration of the first Archbishop. She would legislate for the Church by herself, or through the Episcopate or the Commissioners, or by means of Convocation; and any method seems to have provided good law.[1] Parliament might assist when necessary, as in the Act of 8 Eliz. cap 1,[2] which declared the consecrations of the Elizabethan episcopate " good, lawful and perfect ", but it might not interfere. Thus, for example, in 1563 the Commons passed a Bill giving statutory force to the Articles of Religion; the Lords had read it once when, in December, Parker notified Parliament that the Bill was " stayed by her Majesty's special commandment ". Again, in 1572, the Speaker signified " that Her Majestie's pleasure is, that from henceforth no Bills concerning religion shall be preferred or received into this House, unless the same should be first considered and liked by the clergy ". Later, in 1575, the Commons were anxious to proceed to a reformation of discipline in the Church. They had to remain satisfied with the rejoinder that " she had already had conference with some of the Bishops about it, and had given them in charge to see due Reformation; and that if they should neglect or omit their duties, Her Majesty, by Her Supreme Power and authority over the Church of England, would speedily see such good redress therein, as might satisfy the expectations of Her loving subjects ". Nor was this policy of " prudent restraint " looked upon with any great reluctance, if Osborne's statement is accurate, by any except Cartwright and " some such other addle heads "; and he points out the Queen's cleverness in utilizing the menace of the malcontents' " distempered passions " so as to keep the Church humble and quiet, whilst she " gelt their sees by exchanges, and other mortifications of their power and estates, which during her life were not suffered to blaze out in their *Ecclesiastical Offices* as since they did ". [3]

---

[1] Some readers may consider inadequate attention is given in this brief summary of the Elizabethan settlement to the activity of Convocation in drawing up Canons during the reign, and the presence of Canon Law as part of the " King's Ecclesiastical Law." All the draft Canons could be easily enumerated, but since none of them received the royal assent they remained without coercive authority. From the Submission of the Clergy to 1604 *no* new Canons properly were enacted: i.e. with the royal assent and consequent coercive power.

[2] 1566.   [3] Osborne, op. cit., pp. 77–8.

In the first ten years of the reign there was no active persecution of
Romanists. The Queen's desire was to comprehend within the
national Church all possible subjects. The task of publishing an
explanation of the Church of England was entrusted to Jewel,
Bishop of Salisbury. In 1562 his famous *Apology for the Church of
England* [1] appeared, running on lines not very dissimilar to Gardiner's
De Vera Obedientia.

He deals with the vices of Popes, the intrigues of Rome, the
falsity of the whole papal position, with a thoroughness reminiscent
of Marsiglio of Padua. " We have indeed put ourselves apart, not
as heretics are wont, from the Church of Christ, but as all good men
ought to do, from the infection of naughty persons and hypocrites ". [2]
The Reformed Church is no novelty, but is founded on the Gospel
and the practices of primitive Christianity. " We are come, as
near as we possibly could, to the Church of the Apostles and of
the old Catholic bishops and fathers . . . the original and first
foundation . . . whence the ground of religion was first taken." [3]
In each country superiority over the Church properly belongs to the
Prince, God's representative, and therefore whoever withstands
the Prince withstands the ordinance of God. [4] In this country
the Prince had established the Reformed Church " in open Parliament, with long consultation, and before a notable synod and
convocation ". [5] A General Council would have been useless, since
Reformers would have been silenced, and the Council's decisions
subjected to papal ratification or rejection . . . " madness to think
that the Holy Ghost taketh his flight from a General Council to run
to Rome ". [6] The English Prince wields the same powers in ecclesiastical matters as the godly kings of the Old Testament. He
concludes, in manner reminiscent of the Statute of Appeals, " For
of very truth, we have departed from him, who we saw had blinded
the whole world this many a hundred year . . . to whom we were
not bound. . . . For our Kings . . . have long since found and felt
well enough the yoke and tyranny of the pope's Kingdom. For the
bishops of Rome took the crown off from the head of our King
Henry the Second, and compelled him . . . to come unto their
legate with great submission and humility, so as all his subjects
might laugh him to scorn. . . . Besides this, they excommunicated
and cursed King Henry the Eighth, and . . . put in adventure our
realm, to have been a very prey and spoil. Yet were they but fools
and mad, to think that either so mighty a prince could be scared
with bugs and rattles; or else, that so noble and great a Kingdom
might so easily, even at one morsel, be devoured and swallowed

---

[1] *Works* (Oxford, ed. 1848), Vol. VIII.   [2] p. 323.
[3] p. 373.   [4] p. 322.   [5] p. 357.   [6] pp. 358-9.

up." [1] As a final remark he points out that if Kings of England, of their own liberality, gave tribute and tax to Rome in the darkness of former times, for the sake of religion, the successors of those kings may most properly take back their gifts, " when ignorance and error is espied out ".[2] For all subsequent anti-papalist writers Jewel's is the standard work.

But external events were too strong for any policy of comprehension. The Council of Trent (1545-64) had for its main object the suppression of heresy everywhere, primarily in Lutheran Germany, in France and the Netherlands, then in England and Scotland. The presence of Mary Stuart in England from 1568 did not make things easier for English Romanists, and was the cause of the Northern Rebellion in 1569. In the next year the Papal Bull, " Regnans in Excelsis ", excommunicated and deposed Elizabeth, and " rendered treason a necessary part of the religious duties of every English Romanist ".[3]

The latter had to choose between Sovereign and Pope. Small wonder that when Queen and Archbishop surveyed the state of things they felt encompassed on the one side with " sedition, privy conspiracy and rebellion " and on the other with " false doctrine, heresy and schism ". Hitherto, as Fuller says, the English Papists had " slept in a whole skin; and so might have continued, had they not wilfully torn it themselves".[4] Quickly Parliament replied to the Pope by the Act against Bulls from Rome in 1571,[5] whereby it became treason to publish a papal Bull in any way; to conceal knowledge of any design to publish was misprision of treason; while to introduce any " vain and superstitious things from the Bishop or See of Rome " rendered the introducer liable to the dangers of praemunire. At the same time a strongly-worded homily, composed by Parker, against the wickedness of rebellion was assiduously preached from Anglican pulpits.

Meanwhile seminaries were being established for English Romanists, at Douai in 1568, at Rome in 1579, to which young men resorted from England, and in 1580 the Jesuits began an active mission in England. These factors seriously checked conformity. Hence in 1581 an Act against Reconciliation to Rome [6] was passed,

---

[1] p. 383.
[2] Ibid.
[3] Pollard, *Political History*, p. 377 (Longmans, 1910). For a Romanist view, see P. Hughes, *Rome and the Counter-Reformation in England* (Burns & Oates, 1942), and especially p. 189. " Never since 1570 has any pope excommunicated a Sovereign in such a way as to declare the subjects free from their allegiance and bound to rebel."
[4] *Church History* (ed. 1842), II, 497.
[5] 13 Eliz. c. 2.
[6] 23 Eliz. c. 1.

which made attempts at reconciliation treason, imposed heavy fines on those who celebrated or heard Mass, and on all over the age of sixteen who absented themselves from the services of the Anglican Church. The fine for non-attendance became £20 a month for each person, as against a shilling under the Act of Uniformity. It was a crippling penalty. "Twenty pounds a month!" exclaims Fuller; "a vast sum . . . enough to shatter . . . a rich man's estate . . . paid severally by every recusant for himself and as much for his wife (which though one flesh in divinity yet are two persons in law) . . ." [1] The Throgmorton Plot in October 1583, and the murder of William the Silent in July 1584, further alarmed Englishmen, and caused, in 1585, an Act to be passed against Jesuits and Seminary priests; they were given forty days in which to leave the country, and for any such ever to return was to be guilty of treason; to assist them was felony; and no children were to be sent abroad at all without leave from the Council. The year 1593 (heavy alike to Romanists and Puritans) saw the last blow delivered against the former, in the Act against Popish Recusants, who, if over sixteen years of age, were not to move more than five miles from their usual abode, disobedience to which brought banishment in its train.

But Hooker's purpose in writing his *Laws of the Ecclesiastical Polity* [2] was to justify the Anglican Church, as established by Parliament and upheld by the Queen, not against the Romanists, but against the attacks of the Puritan party. Their discontent with the Establishment ranged from the Vestiarian Controversy of 1560 to the hanging of Penry, Barrow, and Greenwood in 1593. Discontent, indeed, hardened into anger, and anger into a practical platform of opposition in that interval of time. A mass of literature was provoked, of which the most weighty contributions were:

> *The First Admonition to Parliament* of 1571.
> *The Second Admonition to Parliament* of 1572.
> *Whitgift's Answer to the Admonition*, 1573.
> *Cartwright's Reply to Whitgift's Answer*, 1574.
> *Whitgift's Defence of his Answer*, 1574.
> *Travers' Full and Plain Declaration*, 1575 (preface and translation by Cartwright).
> *Bancroft's Dangerous Positions*, 1593.

The first four books of the *Ecclesiastical Polity* appeared in 1593, the fifth in 1597, surveying the whole field of the quarrel, evoked

---

[1] Fuller, op. cit., III, 20.

[2] The *Ecclesiastical Polity* is "related to the Disciplinarian controversy as Shakespeare's plays are related to the Elizabethan drama" (Bayne: *The Ecclesiastical Polity, the Fifth Book*, Macmillan, 1902, p. xl).

by the success of the platform, the strength of Puritanism in Parliament and the political menace of this developed Puritanism. Some examination of this literature and its background and of the evolution of Puritanism is essential in order to appraise the task which Hooker set before him and the measure of success which attended his efforts.

In 1559 Fifty-three Injunctions were approved to be used in episcopal visitations, presumably to show that in administration the Act of Uniformity was not to be interpreted as an inclination towards Switzerland. The retention of kneeling for prayer and bowing at the Holy Name, the regulation of clerical outdoor dress, were indications of a conservative attitude. And in the statement as to the nature of the Royal Supremacy which Cecil appended to the Injunctions, an attempt was made to render it compatible with the conscience of those who might so escape becoming " recusants ". For this statement expressly excluded the Sovereign from an authority that could be deemed sacerdotal, while confirming his magisterial supremacy.[1] Within something like a twelvemonth the Episcopate framed a joint policy, known as the *Interpretations of the Bishops*;[2] the clergy were to wear outdoors " seemly habits, garments and square caps ", a cope at Communion and a surplice at other services. But to those who regarded such garments as symbols of idolatry, " habits of the Stage ",[3] and " relics of the Amorites ",[3] nothing but their extirpation could be satisfactory.[4] This Vestiarian controversy became acute, and the Queen was displeased with the lack of uniformity, which Parker endeavoured to secure by his *Advertisements* of 1565. Opposition remained as bitter as ever and, as Pilkington of Durham remarked, the only choice was to bear these things or break the peace of the Church.[5]

It may be said that from this time men either conformed or else decided upon the latter course—to break the peace of the Church. The Elizabethan Puritans might theologically look to the Continent, but politically drew their inspiration no longer from Luther and Calvin, but from a class of writers—of whom Ponet, Knox and Goodman are the outstanding examples—embittered by persecution to encourage resistance, approve the removal of rulers, and justify the murder of tyrants.[6]

[1] Strype, *Annals*, I, 236.

[2] Ed. W. M. Kennedy (Alcuin Club, 1908).

[3] So described originally by Jewel himself (see Neal, *History of the Puritans*, I, 159). The Vestiarian Controversy endured, here and there, throughout the reign. On 5 May, 1602, complaint was made to Cecil that the Bishop of Chester was compelling Lancashire ministers to wear cope, surplice, and tippet (*Salisbury Papers*, XII, 142). I owe this reference to G. B. Harrison's *Eliz. Journals*, iii. 274.

[4] Strype, op. cit., I, 257.

[5] Neal, *History of the Puritans* (London, 1822), I, 159.

[6] As to the leading Puritans see further; Knappen, *Tudor Puritanism*, Chapter 4.

Luther, the father and theologian of the Reformation, having repudiated the Roman Church, had been compelled to look for authority somewhere. Doubtless he regarded himself as adequate authority in theology, but a political reinforcement was essential. Having nothing in common with those who found their authority in the " inward light " of their own souls, he turned to the territorial State and its " godly prince ", into whose control he put the care of the Church. The temporal power existed by Divine Right to punish the bad and protect the good, and properly exercised its power over the whole Christian body without respect of persons.[1]   It was thus that he " saved the Reformation by cutting it adrift from the failing cause of the peasants and tying it to the chariot wheels of the triumphant princes ".[2]   Circumstances compelled this view, for a strong central authority was as necessary a weapon against Rome as against believers in the inward light.   He dared not affront the secular power, dared not appear a political revolutionary; indeed, he cordially hated those who had by their private views spoiled his godly reformation.   As he looked round his world, he could see little but evil.   Men are wicked—they need law and government— it is the Law of God which the magistrate enforces, and he must be obeyed without question.   Subjects may never resist—the utmost they may do is to refuse to obey if the magistrate acts against divine or natural law.   The ruler can never be deposed,[3] and if he prove bad and unjust he must be regarded as a punishment from God to wicked people.[4]   The Gospel teaches Christians to suffer wrong and pray to God in all their troubles : other remedy is none,[5] and he refuses to have his name coupled with and his authority cited by malcontents.[6]

Calvin also had taught that the magistrate is God's lieutenant, not because of the perversity of men (as Luther held), but because it is God's will that men should be governed.   This sanction should both support the magistrate in trouble and preserve him from injustice.[7]   Subjects must obey, must esteem their ruler, and endure all ills, if only for conscience' sake.   Even bad rulers serve a divine purpose—they are " God's anger " on the earth.[8]   The only exception to this general law of obedience is if the magistrate should command subjects contrary to the Law of God; then they may not

---

[1] *Address to the Nobility* (Eng. Trans., 1883), p. 23.
[2] *C.M.H.*, II, vi, 194.
[3] *Ob Kriegsleute* (Weimar ed)., XIX, 634.
[4] Op. cit., p. 637, and *Widder die sturmenden Bawren* (Weimar ed.), XVIII, 360.
[5] *Ermahnung zum Frieden* (Weimar ed.), XVIII, 320.
[6] *Treue Vermahnung* (Weimar ed.), VIII, 671.
[7] *Institute* (ed. Lefranc, Paris, 1911), pp. 756–8.
[8] Op. cit., p. 776.

obey, but Calvin does not counsel they shall resist.[1] Yet if the State is thus divine, how much more so is the Church? Church and State are not to be confused: " le royaume spirituel de Christ, et l'ordonnance civile, sont choses fort différentes ".[2] The ecclesiastical power is one of teaching, found only in Scripture. It is not the Church of Rome, which has sold itself for the kingdoms of the world.[3] Prophets and Apostles were infallible only when God dictated their thoughts: " voilà la puissance ecclésiastique ".[4]

Yet in the Church Militant there must be order,[5] and on the principles enunciated Calvin erected his theocratic State in Geneva. It was an aristocracy in practice, since the real power was in the hands of the Council of Pastors and Consistory of the Genevan Church; and the Council was able to impose on the nominal government submission to God as interpreted by Calvin, his prophet. Even in Geneva there were spirits who rebelled against this clerical tyranny, for " not only in taverns and lurking-places do the ungodly clamour when their sins are severely reproved, but they also go forth publicly and complain that too much liberty is allowed to the Ministers of the Word ".[6] It is easier for us than for Calvin to see that his State resembled a police system to enforce the will of the ministers. Thus princes were to accept the reproof of the clergy, encourage the latter's domination where Calvin's gospel was already accepted, and establish it everywhere else.

In 1556 John Ponet,[7] sometime Bishop of Salisbury, then in exile, had published his *Short Treatise of Politique Power*.[8] He discusses the origin and purpose of political power, and whether kings have absolute authority or less; whether they are subject to Divine and Positive Law; how far obedience of subjects is due, and whether it is lawful to depose an evil ruler and slay a tyrant.

God furnished corrupt man with rule first by the Law of Nature " planted and graved only in the mind of man ",[9] clarified later by the decalogue, and still later by Christ's teaching of man's duty to God and to his neighbours. This compendium of Divine Law is the stay of the commonwealth,[10] and the touchstone to try every man's doings, be he king or beggar.

---

[1] Yet in the second edition he certainly wavers on this question when the persecution of the Huguenots had begun.
[2] Op. cit., p. 753.
[3] Op. cit., p. 743.
[4] Op. cit., p. 725.
[5] Op. cit., p. 749.
[6] Calvin, *Lectures on Amos* (Edin., 1846), p. 195.
[7] *Vivebat* 1514 (?)–1556.
[8] Quotations from 1642 ed.
[9] p. 3.
[10] p. 4.

Political authority originated when God perceived that his lenity had been abused; yet the form of authority he left to the discretion of the people. Ponet himself prefers the " mixed " form—that is, by king, nobility, and Commons—for where that was exercised, " there too the Commonwealth longest continued ".[1] He insists that rulers represent God, and should be obeyed in honour and reverence, but no ruler is able to plead that in acting against God or the State he erred in ignorance.[2] He cannot break or dispense with Divine or Natural Law, for he himself is entirely subject to them; nor, save for trifling matters, can he make positive laws without authority from the whole State and body of the country,[3] still less dispense with them.[4] The King is as much bound by Positive Law as anyone else.[5]

Subjects must obey, but " if obedience be too much or too little in a Commonwealth, it causeth much evil and disorder ".[6] The Anabaptists would give too little, but others are too slavish in obedience, not weighing commands to see if they are repugnant to God's laws and justice.[7] Rather than obey in such a case, men should suffer a thousand deaths.[8] The Pope may certainly be deposed, and so may any other sort of king or governor.[9] " Here ye see the body of every State may yet and ought to redress and correct the offences of their heads and governors." [10]

Knox [11] had already, in 1554, asked Bullinger whether subjects are bound to obey their rulers in all things. This had elicited a careful reply that they must not obey when the ruler's commands are opposed to God and his lawful worship, but should rather hazard their persons, lives, and fortunes; but, adds Bullinger, " as other objects are often aimed at under the pretext of a just and necessary assertion or maintenance of right, and the worst characters mix themselves with the good, and the times are too full of danger; it is very difficult to pronounce upon every particular case ". [12]

In 1558 Knox became busy. He wrote his *First Blast of the Trumpet against the Monstrous Regiment of Women*, and addressed the nobles of Scotland in an " Appellation " and the commonalty in a " Letter ". He saw his native land and England both governed by women, a sight " detestable and damnable ". The nobility ought to rectify this evil. In the " Appellation " he regards them as having in their power the means to remedy evils (akin to Calvin's concession that the Princes of the blood *might* move against the King). It is Satan who teaches rulers they have no concern with the feeding of Christ's flock and that the reformation of religion is purely the duty

---

[1] p. 6.   [2] p. 9.   [3] p. 13.   [4] p. 14.   [5] p. 22.
[6] *Ibid.*   [7] p. 24.   [8] p. 36.   [9] pp. 48–9.   [10] *Ibid.*
[11] *Vivebat* 1505–72.   [12] Knox: *Works* (ed. Laing), III, 224–5.

of the spiritual people.[1] It is by the nobles that things repugnant to God's word should be corrected,[2] and the punishment of idolatry is particularly theirs; thus the English nobility should have put Mary Tudor to death.[3] Somebody must purge the Commonwealth; if the King will not, the nobles must; if they fail, the whole people are bound to do it. Thus in the " Letter " he states, " Neither would I that ye should esteeme the Reformation and care of Religion lesse to apertaine to you, because ye are no Kings, Rulers, Judges, Nobils nor in auctoritie ".[4]

In the same year Christopher Goodman [5] published his book at Geneva, *How Superior Powers ought to be Obeyed of their Subjects*, the matter of which is identical with that of the " Appellation ". Both Calvin and Beza were anxious to prove to the English Government that they had known nothing of the " Blast " or of Goodman's book. The importance of the latter lies in the fact that similar ideas of the duties of subjects and monarchs were held by English Puritans as well as Scottish. Both Goodman and Knox regard the consent of the people as a necessary element in creating a king, and hold the nobles as ordained to be defenders of true religion and a bridle to the licence of princes.[6] Kings are amenable to punishment for ill-ruling, and subjects must do more than refuse to obey—they must actively resist, if they would be guiltless before God.[7] " The people " (to whom Goodman appeals more than to the nobility, therein differing from Knox) " are charged to see the laws of God kept."[8] The clearest trumpet-call comes later, " when the magistrates or other officers cease to do their duty, they [i.e., the people] are, as it were, without officers, yea worse than if they had none at all, and then God giveth the sword into the people's hand, and He Himself is become immediately their head ".[9]

The mantle of Ponet, Knox, and Goodman fell in England on Cartwright.[10] He had become in 1569 Lady Margaret Professor of Divinity at Cambridge and, " whether it were out of some disgust for not being hitherto preferred, or out of admiration of the discipline practised in the Church of Geneva, or both, he set himself, with some other young men in the University, to overthrow the government of this Church. . . ."[11] Cartwright was then a Fellow of Trinity College, of which Whitgift was Master. He was forbidden to lecture and, proving intractable to the " Christian means " used by the Vice-Chancellor and Heads, was deprived and retired to Geneva.

---

[1] III, 485–6.   [2] III, 495.   [3] III, 507.   [4] III, 526.
[5] *Vivebat* 1520 (?)–1603.
[6] Goodman, op. cit. (ed. 1558), p. 35.
[7] p. 43.   [8] Chap. xiii.   [9] p. 185.
[10] *Vivebat* 1535–1603.   [11] Strype, *Annals*, II, 373.

The Admonitions to Parliament [1] were the first avowed manifestos of the Puritans; they exhibited something of a constructive
policy, hostile to the existing system of the Church of England and
designed to supplant it. But their platform was never really
popular with the bulk of Englishmen, less affected than Frenchmen
by its clear-cut system, and still preferring objectivity in religion
rather than the inner light. This is not to say that a good deal
of sympathy was not aroused for men who had suffered as martyrs
at the hands of the bishops; for a time feeling in the Commons
was undoubtedly in favour of relaxing the requirements of Uniformity, but there is no evidence that England welcomed the
platform.

The First Admonition (1571) furnished the marks of the true
Church : [2] (1) preaching the pure Word; (2) ministering the
Sacraments; (3) the existence of ecclesiastical discipline. It condemns what it regards as abuses in the Anglican Church, such as
ordination of unlearned men, "sixty, eighty or a hundred at a
clap"; the union of benefices; absence of election of ministers by
the congregation; the "lordship" of bishops; [3] the non-existence
of a real excommunication, and such-like.[4] The present Anglican
ministry is "bastard, idle and unpreaching"; the Universities
filled with cormorants, no one of whom should have more than
one living, where he should reside; the Statutes authorizing the
present ministry must be repealed and episcopacy abolished; the
only rightful calling of a minister lies with the parishioners, and he
can be ordained only by the elders; to read the Book of Common
Prayer, its services, homilies and so forth, "boys and senseless
asses" are sufficient; that book knows nothing of real prayer; in
every congregation must be a consistory, comprising the ministers
and elected representatives of the congregation, to control the
religious and moral life of the people, and to see to the relief of the
poor; members of each consistory will attend provincial and
national councils; the Anglican ministry is not that which God
erected in his Church. The claims that the entire regiment of

---

[1] Printed in *Puritan Manifestos* (ed. Frere and Douglas, 1907).

[2] Op. cit., p. 9.

[3] The Elizabethan Episcopate does not show up too well. It is known that
some amassed great wealth (Parker left a fortune) partly by alienating estates in
which they had only a life-interest (see Froude, *Hist. of Eng.*, X, 410), partly by
sale of dispensations to minors to hold cures. Horne's treatment of Bonner leaves
an unpleasant taste (Strype, *Annals*, I, ii, 3–8). Hooker laments their neglect
of Confirmation, none being held for twenty-nine years (*E.P.*, V. lxvi, 8). On the
other hand, nobody seems to have loved them much, and Elizabeth herself
("Greater than man, less than woman", as Essex said) viewed them with some
contempt; if they favoured Protestantism, like Grindal, she would suspend them;
and zeal against Romanists earned her rebuke (Strype, *Aylmer*, p. 89).

[4] Op. cit., pp. 10–14.

the Church should be in the ministers, elders, and deacons, by whose instructions, admonitions, corrections, and punishments men may frame their wills and lives according to the law of God. If such reformation is good for France and Scotland, is it not good for England?[1] The Popish abuses that remain should be abolished, such as the Archbishop's Court,[2] that "filthy quagmire and poysoned plashe", and the Commissary's Court,[3] "that is but a pettie little stinking ditche, that floweth out of that former great puddle".

The authors of this—said to be Field and Wilcox—having been sent to Newgate, "next dore to hanging", Cartwright issued the Second Admonition (1572). The First Admonition had protested against any intention to take away the authority of the civil magistrate, and the second professes heartily, plainly, and faithfully "that the chefe governors in civill matters, have chefe authoritie over all persons . . . and are the foster fathers and nurses of Christes Church".[4] But as no inferior magistrate may usurp the office of a superior, so may no magistrate usurp God's;[5] yet the Admonition implies that this has happened in England, since it is more dangerous to offend against the Prayer Book, injunctions, articles, or advertisements than against the Bible.[6] The test of everything is God's Word, and the Church of England must be examined thereby; wherein if offence is made against any law, then that law must be reformed, not the Puritans punished. Anglican prelates have usurped the civil magistrates' powers by their laws and prisons;[7] no punishment in spiritual causes by spiritual persons should be possible except admonitions and excommunication of the obstinate.[8] But now Church prelates can command all mayors, bailiffs, and constables. "All prisons are open to them, all jailors obey them."[9]

Two years later Cartwright's *Full and Plain Declaration*,[10] the handbook of English Puritans, finally constructed the platform, advocating the establishment of Calvin's Genevan Church, and attacking the Royal Supremacy. The Church and the State are distinct societies, otherwise why does not an excommunicate lose his citizenship and a banished man become *ipso facto* excommunicate?[11] Therefore all purely spiritual functions belong to the ministers, and

[1] Op. cit., p. 19.   [2] Op. cit., p. 32.   [3] Op. cit., p. 33.
[4] Op. cit., p. 85.   [5] Op. cit., p. 93.   [6] Op. cit., p. 91.
[7] It is fair to state that Grindal of London and Coxe of Ely suggested to the Council the torture of a priest to extract evidence. (Froude, op. cit., VI, 576.)
[8] Op. cit., p. 120.
[9] Op. cit., p. 127.
[10] Travers wrote it in Latin; Cartwright made the English translation and published it with a preface.
[11] A question that Hooker was hard put to answer. (*E.P.*, VIII, i, 6.)

C

to no secular persons, and clerical people ought not to hold civil offices. Scriptural history shows this distinction; the nature and end of the two States prove it. The Church is spiritual and divine, the State secular and temporary. The Church is the foundation of the State, which must be framed in accordance with it. Since the Church is indwelt by the Spirit of God, as God cannot change, so Church government must be immutable, but civil government can be established in any form as circumstances require. Scripture contains this immutable form of government, which is Presbyterianism; hence the latter must be of divine right, while civil government is not necessarily so. But though the Societies be distinct, they are yet composed of the same men and women. Who is to be the final arbiter of troubles arising in the debatable land?

Anglicans answered, "The magistrate"; Cartwright replied that there would be no trouble if the ministry were consulted. Nurse and foster-father of the Church though a king might be in Presbyterian theory, it was clear that he would have to submit his sceptre to the Church, becoming in effect its mere servant; which, after all, was the Hildebrandine claim. A king, in the Puritans' view, had only duties towards the Church, not rights; he must execute God's laws, after the ministers had interpreted them. He might set on foot a religious reformation, and establish the true Church; but who should decide what is the true Church? Clearly, for Presbyterians, some infallible Calvin alone would be capable. The nature of such teaching as this made it apparent that the authors were working for a limited monarchy, in which the sovereign should be amenable to the Discipline, involving as great a danger of clericalism as ever had been in the strongest days of Romanism. Philander, the Jesuit in Bilson's [1] *True Difference*,[2] is in exact company with Cartwright; he answers concerning the Royal Supremacy, "This Sovereignty gives the Queen power to confer on others what she has not and may not do herself. . . . It makes the body above the soul, the temporal regiment above the spiritual; it makes the Queen free from Ecclesiastical Discipline, from which no true child of God's family is excepted."[3]

A familiar line with the Puritans is to explain that Elizabeth herself does not wish for this supremacy; the true state of things is concealed from her by evil advisers, who tell her that the new reformation is only "a new-fangled and seditious attempt, proceeding from the factious and discontented brains of those who are slandered to desire thereby nothing else, but the alteration of the

---

[1] Thomas Bilson, Bishop of Winchester, *vivebat* 1546–1616.
[2] *True Difference between Christian Subjection and Unchristian Rebellion* (Oxford, 1595).
[3] Op. cit., p. 214.

present state, dangerous to her royal crowne and person, and ruinous unto the whole Kingdome ".[1] That the Queen and Council should, in fact, have taken this view is not surprising, in the light of contemporary Scottish history and the violent language of Puritan writers. Penry [2] was second to none in this accomplishment, although the logic of Cartwright was not his. Thus, in his *Humble Motion* of 1590, he admits the Anglican Church to be a true Church, but wishes it had also " certaine things of very good moment ",[3] which had not yet obtained their due authority; nevertheless, on the very next page he proceeds, " I understand the Church government of discipline, not to be in small and trifling ceremonies . . . but in the very swaye and frame of the Church, the pillars, foundations, building and builders thereof ".[4] He, like others, might lavish high-sounding epithets on the Queen's power, but that such should appear no more than lip-service astonishes us little.[5]

Whitgift,[6] who in years gone by had " watched and withstood " Cartwright, had at once proceeded to reply to the Admonitions in his *Answer*, but his *Defence of the Answer* in 1574 is more important. He reminds Cartwright that in the earlier years nothing except the cap, the surplice, and the tippet was in question—the Puritans contended for nothing else; but now a far graver situation has arisen, " for he that in heart and deed misliketh the religion, cannot like well of such as maintain the same ".[7] He has already pointed out the political danger of the Puritan position—" Your opinions . . . tend indeed to confusion . . . bring such in contempt as be in authority . . .",[8] and later, " in defacing this present State of religion, that is, the Order of Common Prayers, the ministry, the Sacraments, the kind of government, you join with the papists . . . and in disquieting the Church for external things, you join with the anabaptists ".[9] Subsequently he adds, " And, certainly, if it were well examined, I believe it would fall out that the authors of this book have conspired with the papists to overthrow . . . the state both of this Church and realm, however subtilly they seem to detest papistry ". [10]

Whitgift sees danger in the power of the individual minister,

---

[1] Penry, *Public Wants* (ed. 1861), p. 10.
[2] *Vivebat* 1559–1593. Hooker refers to him in *E.P.*, Preface, viii, 1; V, xxii, 17, 19; VII, xxiii, 11.
[3] Penry, *Humble Motion* (ed. 1590), p. 11.
[4] Penry, op. cit., p. 12.
[5] E.g., Penry, op. cit., pp. 23, 32, 33.
[6] *Vivebat* 1530(?)–1604; Archbishop of Canterbury, 1583–1604. Fuller (*Church History*, Book X, p. 218) says Whitgift's finger moved more in Church matters than the hands of all the rest of the Privy Councillors together.
[7] Whitgift, *Works*, II, 7.
[8] Op. cit., I, 19.   [9] Op. cit., I, 57.   [10] Op. cit., I, 291.

" Let every minister be king and pope in his own parish . . . and you shall have as many kinds of religion as there are parishes. . . . Princes, nobles and magistrates were never brought into greater servitude and bondage than these men seek to lay upon them." [1] He notes that the Puritan Church is to be popular in the strict sense, but accuses Cartwright of using this as a catch-party slogan, fraught with danger to the body politic. " Popularity you cannot avoid, seeing you seek so great an equality, commit so many things to the voices of the people, and . . . so greatly magnify them; than the which three what can be more popular ? " [2]

Indeed, he points out, the whole Puritan system is anti-monarchical. They deny to the Prince his natural supremacy over the Church, for who else, if not he, should be its head ? [3] Then, in order to disaffect people, they " ignorantly or wilfully confound monarchiam with tyranny ". They make protestations of obedience to the Prince, but abridge his authority, for when faced with a command which they wish not to obey, the Puritans claim it is not commanded " in the Lord ", and is against their " conscience ". [4] If Cartwright had his way, Elizabeth would be overthrown, for his principle is that " the government of the Commonwealth must be framed according to the government of the Church ", in such fashion " as the hangings are made fit for the house ". [5] Whatever might be the form of polity, indeed, Cartwright would not allow any ecclesiastical supremacy to the chief magistrate, for all such authority he permits only to " ministers and ecclesiastical governors ", subjecting the Prince or magistrate to them, requiring the magistrate to execute those laws which the clergy prescribe, and so far from the magistrate handling ecclesiastical matters at all, " the Church may be established without him ". [6]

These Puritans, he writes, are restless and seditious people, anxious to stir up trouble, " busily devising and working . . . to overthrow the State both of religion and the realm ",[7] whereas all their supposedly Scriptural platform rests on two false foundations: (i) that a Church must necessarily be in form exactly what it was in Apostolic time, and that the form is defined in Scripture; (ii) that nothing may be retained in a Church that has been abused under the Pope.[8] But " this I dare boldly affirm ", says Whitgift, " that all points of religion necessary to salvation . . . are as purely and perfectly taught, and by public authority established, in this Church of England at this day, as ever they were in any

---

[1] Op. cit., III, 9–10.   [2] Op. cit., I, 42.   [3] Op. cit., II, 85.
[4] Op. cit., I, 82, and II, 239.   [5] Op. cit., III, 192.
[6] Op. cit., III, 296.   [7] Op. cit., I, Preface, p. 5.
[8] Op. cit., I, Preface, p. 6.

Church since the apostles' time, or now be in any reformed church
in the world ".[1]

The Puritan position did not "stand with the truth and with
learning ". He sums up the position thus: "That any one
kind of government is so necessary that without it the Church cannot be saved, or that it may not be altered into some other kind
thought to be more expedient, I utterly deny; and the reasons
that move me so to do be these: The first is, because I find no one
certain and perfect kind of government prescribed or commanded
in the scriptures to the church of Christ; which no doubt should
have been done, if it had been a matter necessary unto the salvation
of the church. Secondly, because the essential notes of the church
be these only: the true preaching of the word of God, and the right
administration of the sacraments. . . . So that, notwithstanding
government, or some kind of government, may be a part of the
church, touching the outward form and perfection of it, yet is it
not such a part of the essence and being, but that it may be the
church of Christ without this or that kind of government, and
therefore the ' kind of government ' of the church is not ' necessary
unto salvation '." [2]

The work of Whitgift was to be the chief Anglican weapon
until the publication of the *Laws of Ecclesiastical Polity*. Plain, un-
adorned, and vigorous, it prepared the way for the greater and
more dignified work of Hooker. Erastian through and through,
it served well to point to all who would read it the grave political
issues involved in the Church controversy, and is a definite land-
mark in the history of the alliance of Church and Crown against
Puritan and lawyer.

From Whitgift's efforts in 1574 till the appearance of Hooker's
Laws, Bancroft deals more lucidly than any other Anglican with the
Puritan position. The situation had grown in danger, for wide
experiments in Presbyterian government had been made. About
1570 ministers had met for religious discussion in " exercises ",
not without some episcopal sympathy.[3] Despite royal order for
their suppression in 1577, they hardened into the " Classis "
system, the core of the Discipline. This " Classis " system con-
sisted in a hierarchy of district assemblies, beginning with an
executive for each parish, composed of minister, elders, deacons, and

---

[1] Op. cit., I, Preface, p. 3.
[2] Whitgift, *Works*, I, 180–1, 184–5, 187.
[3] Osborne notes that the Hierarchy " connived at *Lecturer* and *Weekly Preaching*,
through which they let in more by the Posterne, than they could crowd out at the
Great Gate " (op. cit., p. 83). See Grindal's *Letter to the Queen* (1576) quoting the
approval of himself and nine other bishops for the " exercises " (Strype, *Grindal*,
ed. Oxford, 1821, pp. 330–2 and 558–74).

widows, and culminating in a National Assembly. The ministers of twelve parishes formed a " classis "; delegates from twenty-four of these " classes " made the Provincial Synod, and the National Assembly was chosen from the Synods. The Minute Book of the Dedham Classis suggests, however, that little of public opinion supported the ministers, and there is evidence that ministers could not remedy disorders in their parishes.[1] Nor were the petitions of the people necessarily spontaneous. Still, they could be stirred up and worked upon, and they were. For example, at a meeting at Barfolde in 1585–6,[2] the " classis " advised a minister who was likely to be ousted by the patron to " signify to the people of his parish his mind, and stir them up to labour with my Lord Chancellor for the preventing of it ". The loquacity and rank of a few Puritans probably, as has been suggested,[3] gave the movement a wider publicity and an appearance of greater numerical force than was in fact the case.[4] Yet honest Anglicans cannot be blamed if they tended to identify the followers of Calvin with those of the Papacy as a political menace; while the tyrannies of minister and priest bore surprising similarity. Consequently in his sermon at Paul's Cross in 1588 Bancroft, lamenting " the presumption which is everywhere to be found in these days ", points out that their congregationalism is not proved in Scripture, and has not been heard of in the Church for 1,500 years,[5] while bishops have had the care of the Church from the days of St. Mark.[6] The Puritans complain that England has substituted a temporal Pope, in the shape of the Queen, for a spiritual Pope; a seditious position, as he demonstrates syllogistically,[7] which puts them in alliance with Papalists against the throne.

Dr. John Bridges, Dean of Salisbury, also rallied to the defence of the Church of England, but in a lengthy and ponderous work [8] which might easily be taken in enfilade by a nimble and unscrupulous opponent. Martin Marprelate [9] jumped to his chance in the same

---

[1] *Minute Book of the Dedham Classis*, 1582–9 (ed. R. G. Usher; R. Hist. Soc., 1905), pp. 61–2.

[2] Op. cit., p. 55.

[3] Op. cit., p. xxv.

[4] But Strype, writing to Thoresby in 1716, says that though Elizabeth twice suppressed the " Exercises " (under Parker and Grindal) yet they were revived, and " had the countenance of the Council, so well were they esteemed of in those days ". (Thoresby, *Diary and Corr.*, IV, 344.)

[5] Bancroft, *Sermon* (ed. 1588), p. 10.

[6] Op. cit., p. 14.

[7] Op. cit., p. 67.

[8] *A Defence of the Government Established* (London, 1587).

[9] Hooker refers to Marprelate in *E.P.*, Preface, viii, 1, and III, 10, viii. Essex used to carry a copy with him (see Codrington's *Life and Death of the Illustrious Robert, Earl of Essex*, 1646, Harl. Misc., Vol. I, p. 217, 1808).

year, with his " Epistle " [1] designed " for the behoofe and over-throw of the Parsons . . . that have learnt their Catechismes and are past Grace ". Scurrilous and humorous, he objects to his opponents' " wainscot-faces " as to their doctrines. His swash-buckling attack moved Bancroft [2] at much greater length in his *Dangerous Positions* to identify Geneva with Rome as a political danger, " both of them labouring with all their might, by rayling, libelling and lying, to steale away the people's harts from their governours, to bringe them to a dislike of the present state of our Church, and to drawe them into parts-taking ".[3] He makes great play with the treatment afforded by Presbyterianism to the Scottish throne; and quotes at length from Knox and Buchanan [4] to show how the Calvinistic Church would limit the powers of monarchs and elevate those of the people. He admits that their first attack is on the bishops, but significantly reminds his readers that the Anabaptists in Germany began with the bishops and ended with the civil magistrate.[5] A sound point is certainly made when he shows that not until Beza and Calvin did any Reformers claim that the Genevan Discipline was an essential feature of a Church,[6] but now " they doo bragge in their bookes, that they will not sticke to dye in the cause ", yet as late as 1585 the Form of Discipline was not perfected, and had to be sent to Travers to be amended.[7]

This acute observer thus sums up the position: " Lastly, in all this whole booke of Discipline, there is not once mention made of any authority, or office, in or over the Church, belonging to the Christian Civile Magistrate. Hee hath not so much, as either voyce or place, in any of their Synodes, as a member thereof; except he be chosen to be an Elder." [8] Later he adds, "What with the pretence of God's law, of man's law, and (I know not) of what law, they have been suffered to go so farre against all lawes: that now they have taken such heart, as that some of them are not afraid to affirme . . . that there is no authoritie, which may lawfully suppresse their foresaid proceedings. No Magistrate . . . may lawfully mayme or deforme the body of Christ, which is the Church: no lawfull Church government is changeable, at the pleasure of the Magistrate: of necessitie all Christian magistrates are bound to receive this government.

" And thus hitherto you have seen the proceedings of our English reformers according to their ringleaders' actions in Scotland: they have had their draughts of discipline, they have subscribed a

---

[1] Printed in Arber's *Tracts*, No. 11 ; and in Pierce, *The Marprelate Tracts* (London, 1911).
[2] Richard Bancroft, *vivebat* 1544-1610: Archbishop of Canterbury, 1604-10.
[3] Ed. 1593, p. 2. [4] E.g., op. cit., p. 15. [5] Op. cit., p. 29.
[6] Op. cit., p. 42. [7] p. 75. [8] p. 97.

particular book for England . . . they have, by their false gloses, seduced many of her Majestie's subjects: they have combined themselves together into a strange brotherhood. They challenge to their unlawful and seditious assemblies, the true and most proper name of the Church. They say their doings are according to law." [1]

But it remained for Hooker to put his finger, more gently and yet as firmly, on the real core of the danger, appalling to a man whose philosophy and patriotism alike demanded unity in all things. " Our wisdom in this case," he writes, " must be such as doth not propose to itself τό ἴδιον, our own particular, the desire . . . whereof poisoneth wheresoever it taketh place; but the scope and mark which we are to aim at is τό κοινόν, the public and common good of all." [2]

Thus was the Church of England settled, attacked, and defended during the reign of Elizabeth; and as those who defend a city are apt to be intimate with the outworks and bastions of the fortifications rather than with its heart, so there remains to this day a doubt as to the nature of that jealously guarded establishment. To set theory aside, there is no reason to suppose that the Civil Power which was able to establish the Settlement could not have settled it otherwise than it did. Certain institutions were retained, which might equally have been rejected, and Sir Francis Knollys was not alone in maintaining that if the Queen and Parliament had set up, for example, a non-episcopal Church, none could have complained of any defect.[3] Here surely is no controversy. Elizabeth and Parliament had the power to break all historic and spiritual continuity by removing the ancient and customary marks of a " Catholic Church ".

From piety or expediency they did not, in fact, do so; and it is a matter only of historical and cautionary importance that the Anglican Church might have lost these marks. Roman Catholicism did not lose anything of its essential nature in the England of Mary's reign by the fact that it was re-instituted by the use of the royal prerogative. That the existence of that royal prerogative was compatible with a truly reasonable, doctrinally sound, fundamentally primitive and Catholic Church, and that the Church of England possessed these qualities, it was the work of Hooker, in the *Laws of the Ecclesiastical Polity* to endeavour to demonstrate.

---

[1] pp. 126–7.   [2] *E.P.*, V, Dedication, ix, 8.
[3] Strype, *Whitgift*, III, 222.

CHAPTER II

LIFE AND WORKS OF HOOKER

IT was an odd chance perhaps that pushed Richard Hooker—" a poor obscure English priest ", as the Roman hierarchy described him [1]—to the forefront of the stage at a critical juncture in the English Reformation and purchased for him enduring renown, both as the greatest apologist that the Church of England has ever enjoyed, and as a student of political and ecclesiastical matters who has wielded considerable influence, and is still readily quoted as a principal authority in the realm of political philosophy.[2]

The accepted description of his person scarcely prepares us for his fame, for he is depicted as " an obscure harmless man; a man in poor clothes, his loins usually girt in a coarse gown, or canonical coat; of a mean stature, and stooping, and yet more lowly in the thoughts of his soul; his body worn out, not with age, but study, and holy mortifications . . . of so mild and humble a nature, that his poor parish-clerk and he did never talk but with both their hats on, or both off, at the same time ".[3] It is such a delightful and charming portrait that we are tempted to conclude it is, in some degree, an idealization, to wonder if possibly Walton has unconsciously identified his own attractive and simple character with Hooker's. Yet there is no doubt Hooker was that simple, meek, and saintly man. There is better evidence than Walton's for it. William Covel was moved to publish in 1603 his *Just and Temperate Defence of the Five Books of the " Ecclesiastical Polity " written by Mr. Richard Hooker*, in reply to the *Christian Letter*, and provides us with a contemporary view of the author.   " He was truly of a mild spirit," he wrote, " and an humble heart, and abounding in all other virtues; yet he specially excelled in the grace of meekness: for the gravity of his looks . . . was cleared by them that did sit, or converse with him; lest he should be burdensome unto them; but a full laughter, few ever discerned in him." [4]   But over against the note of " childish simplicity ", which Walton emphasizes, must be set the

---

[1] Walton's *Life*, Keble's ed. of *E.P.*, I, 171.
[2] Holdsworth, *H.E.L.*, IV, 212 *et seq.*
[3] Walton, op. cit., p. 77.
[4] Ed. 1603, p. 9.

fact that Covel compares him with Cato for resolution of character
and control of passion.   Though prone to no boisterous humour or
gaiety, Hooker had a real sense of the ludicrous and absurd, as
may be seen in various places in the *Ecclesiastical Polity*,[1] and we
smile with him—for laughter is out of the question—when he
exclaims, " Safer to discuss all the Saints in heaven than M. Calvin!"
For the most part his humour is ironic, dry, and biting, as when in
the margin of the *Christian Letter* he notes of his opponents, who
insist on their charity towards him in the midst of vituperation,
criticism, and abuse, " As if Cassius and Brutus, having slain Caesar,
they should have solemnly protested to his friends, they meant him
nothing but mere good-will and friendship."   Other notes of his
written on the pages of the *Christian Letter* are blunt, it may be
thought, to the degree of offensiveness.   " Your godfathers and
godmothers ", he tells the author of the *Letter*, " have much to
answer unto God for not seeing you better catechized."   Or again,
in sardonically encouraging strain, " I doubt not but if you once
attain to understand the rudiments and principles of Christian
religion, which with good helps may be done in reasonable time,
those other gifts of speech and writing . . . may do good for the
edifying of poor country people."   Marked features of his character
though humility and self-control may have been, once touched on
the raw, as by criticism of his prose style or his logical reasoning,
Hooker did not bear such slights with that degree of patient suffering
and innocent acceptance which Walton would have us see as invari-
able in him.   " I must look as nature," he writes, " speak as custom,
and think as God's good Spirit hath taught me, judge you how-
soever either of my mind or of my style, or if you will of my look
also."   Irritation, not humility, is surely in the note, " I must tell
you whether I have not as bad an opinion of myself and mine own
writings, as you have of both."   Is he whimsical or exasperated in
writing, " What a misery is it to be troubled with an adversary
into whom a man must put both truth and wit! "?   His great task
of the *Laws of the Ecclesiastical Polity* completed, he could not or
would not consent to be further troubled to publish any reply to the
Puritan criticisms contained in the *Christian Letter*.   Covel notes
that by then (1599) his health was beginning to give way (partly, he
implies, because the Puritans had " set him upon the rack "), and
we have his authority that Hooker said it was unfit that a man
who had a long journey before him should turn back to beat every
barking cur.[2]

It is true that most of these foregoing quotations are taken not

[1] E.g., V, lxxi, 6.
[2] Covel, op. cit., p. 13.

from the pages of the *Ecclesiastical Polity*, but from Hooker's own marginal notes in the copy of the *Christian Letter* [1] now in the library of Corpus Christi College, Oxford. That *Letter* was published in 1599, two years after the appearance of the Fifth Book. It is a sharp and querulous examination of the Five Books from the Puritan angle. It was apparently the work of one author—whose identity was known to Hooker, but is unknown to us—and, on Covel's evidence, it was translated into other languages. It clearly irritated Hooker, but Covel denies that its unfairness hastened his end. Hooker condemns it, he says, and would have answered it had he lived. But in these marginal notes, if anywhere, is to be seen the real Richard Hooker—Hooker the man. He was grave in church, grave in company, grave in his published writings; but here, with the copy of the *Letter*, he is alone, and there is no public to be shocked by the realization that the grave and reverend Mr. Hooker had faults like other men, that wanton ignorance annoyed him, and ill-founded criticism roused him to contempt and anger.

Throughout the long pages of the *Ecclesiastical Polity*, Walton's gentle, simple, child-like Hooker reveals himself as notable for his shrewd common-sense grasp of the problems of his day, for his unerring insight into the weak positions of his opponents, for his capacity for irritation, irony, and quiet fun at their absurdities, as for his unsurpassed mass of learning, eloquence of style, breadth of intellectual culture, and depths of religious feeling.

He ruled no city, like Calvin, nor did he appear defiant before an Emperor, like Luther, much less perish in battle, like Zwingli. Half of the twenty years of his active ministry were spent in the shelter of a University Fellowship or the tranquil retreat of a country living. His brief spell of public life as Master of the Temple (1585–91) was on the whole distasteful to him, and he was glad to quit the limelight of public controversy for peaceful seclusion. He was no magnificent prelate, like Wolsey; no ecclesiastical statesman, like Gardiner; no archbishop, like Parker; and certainly no fanatic, like Pole, or martyr, like Cranmer. Even amongst scholars, where he naturally takes a first place, he did not distinguish himself, as Melancthon, by writing a Confession or, like Colet, by founding a School, nor did he translate the Scriptures. His love of culture and reason earned him no reputation among the great humanists, for his talents were not of the aggressive, sceptical kind that distinguished

---

[1] Keble gives considerable extracts from the *Letter* and Hooker's notes in his edition. Benjamin Hanbury reprints the *Letter* in his (1831) edition of the *Ecclesiastical Polity*, as does also R. Bayne in his edition of the Fifth Book (Macmillan, 1902). There is a copy in the Cathedral Library at Canterbury, bound up with Covel's *Just and Temperate Defence of the Five Books* (1603).

Erasmus. He was simply the judicious Hooker,[1] the poor country parson, more suggestive at first sight of Arnold's Scholar Gipsy than of a consummate philosopher.

His career is not, in point of fact, of paramount importance, for it is by his *Laws of Ecclesiastical Polity* rather than by his life that he is remembered; a work which stands out, as has been well said, in a magnificent isolation among the lesser writings of the day, which, belonging to no school, influences all, and is an abiding possession, for it has " given to our Anglican theology a tone and a direction which it has never lost ".[2] It is true that his mode of life was possessed of moral worth, and it has been held up as " singularly well worth studying ", illustrating " the best way to live in a time of much controversy and confusion ",[3] not least for his single-hearted devotion to his great work and his absolute disinterestedness.

Nevertheless he had to wait over half a century to find a biographer, and many of the facts are still uncertain. Fuller [4] mentions him in his *Church History* (published 1655) and again in his *Worthies* (1662), but his entries are not satisfactory, for in the former he asserts that Hooker was a bachelor,[5] and in the latter he retracts this only to state that Hooker's wife and children " were neither to his comfort when living, nor credit when dead "! [6] Fuller was followed by Gauden,[7] Bishop of Worcester, the soi-disant author of the *Eikon Basilike*, who had secured the manuscript of the Seventh Book of the *Ecclesiastical Polity* and published it in 1662, together with a short life of its author.

This biography was so badly written and inaccurate that the Archbishop of Canterbury (Gilbert Sheldon) intervened to commission Izaak Walton,[8] the famous author of the *Compleat Angler*, to produce a better account. Doubtless Walton was chosen because, apart from his literary reputation, which would give whatever he produced eminent authority, he had special sources of information, as he was a nephew of George Cranmer (great-nephew of the Archbishop), the lifelong friend and pupil of Hooker. Moreover, Walton's aunt, the sister of Cranmer, married Dr. Spenser, who had been an undergraduate with Hooker at Corpus Christi College, Oxford, and a trustee under Hooker's will, to

---

[1] This epithet was first applied to him in an epitaph by Sir William Cowper, who in 1635 caused a monument to be erected in Bishopsbourne Church to Hooker's memory. The date thereon is incorrect.

[2] Barry, *Masters in English Theology* (London, 1877), pp. 7, 59.

[3] F. Paget, *An Introduction to the 5th Book of Hooker's Treatise of the Laws of Ecclesiastical Polity* (Oxford, 1907), p. 7.

[4] *Vivebat* 1608–61.

[5] Vol. III (ed. Nicholls, 1842), p. 155.

[6] Vol. I (ed. Nuttall, 1840), p. 424.

[7] *Vivebat* 1605–62.   [8] *Vivebat* 1593–1683.

whom the unpublished books of the *Ecclesiastical Polity* came after their author's death.

Walton's *Life*, which was published in 1665, became the accepted biography, and remained virtually unchallenged until 1940, when Professor Sisson, using new information found in the Public Records, was able to demonstrate the inaccuracies contained in it.[1]

From these sources the life of Hooker can now be more accurately constructed. Born of middle-class parents at Heavitree near Exeter in March 1553-4, Hooker was educated at Exeter Grammar School, where his prowess was sufficient to secure the patronage of Bishop Jewel—himself a native of Devon and at that time Bishop of Salisbury—who, in 1568, secured for him a clerk's place in his old College, Corpus Christi, Oxford.

In 1573 Hooker was elected a Foundation Scholar (perhaps the most distinguished member of the College in all its history [2]) of his College, proceeding B.A. in January 1573-4, and becoming M.A. and Fellow in 1577. His learning was deep both in Greek and Hebrew, although his Oxford fame rested principally on his lectures in logic. For some years he delivered lectures in Hebrew to the University as deputy for the Regius Professor—" And for his behaviour, among other testimonies, this still remains of him, that in four years he was but twice absent from the chapel-prayers ".[3] He appears to have been in Holy Orders before 1581, since in that year he was chosen to preach at Paul's Cross.

Quiet student as he was, nevertheless Hooker became mildly involved in the vortex of Elizabethan College politics, for in October 1579 he and some of his colleagues were temporarily expelled for opposing the nomination of Dr. Barfoot, a moderate but a Disciplinarian, to the post of President of the College. At this time Hooker was probably not without some Puritan sympathies. Possibly these sympathies were inherited from his uncle, John Hooker,[4] who may have sat in Elizabeth's third Parliament of 1572, and who certainly had been a Marian exile at Strasbourg, where he had studied under Peter Martyr. It was this uncle who had been instrumental in introducing Richard Hooker to Jewel, himself also a Marian exile. However, Hooker was reinstated after a month, and continued to hold his Fellowship until December 1584, when he was presented to the living of Drayton Beauchamp in Buckinghamshire. But it is doubtful if he ever went there, for it appears to have been a

[1] Sisson, *The Judicious Marriage of Mr. Hooker and the Birth of the Laws of the Ecclesiastical Polity* (C.U.P., 1940).
[2] Fowler, *History of C.C.C.* (London, 1898), p. 82. See also *Milne, Early History of Corpus Christi College, Oxford;* Chapter 3.   [3] Walton, op. cit., p. 15.
[4] For further details of John Hooker's life, see *D.N.B.*

stop-gap until his appointment as Master of the Temple could be definitely settled in February 1585.[1]

At the Temple Hooker found a very difficult situation. The post had been secured for him by the Archbishop of York (Edwin Sandys), who had succeeded Jewel[2] as Hooker's patron at the University, and whose son was Hooker's pupil there. There had been two other candidates for the Mastership. Walter Travers,[3] the more important of these, was already Reader in the Temple, but had been passed over by Queen Elizabeth because he was an extreme Puritan without episcopal ordination, although he enjoyed the support of Burleigh, to whom he had acted as chaplain, and was also supposed to be the choice of the late Master. As Travers stayed on, the position for Hooker was far from easy. The Reader had been a regular and attractive preacher at the Temple, and Hooker was anything but a popular preacher. Travers was a leading Presbyterian, the friend of Cartwright (" a younger Cartwright ") and author of the book, *De Disciplina Ecclesiastica*, advocating the establishment of the Calvinistic Church. " Now began the heat and height of the sad contest betwixt Mr. Richard Hooker, Master—and Mr. Walter Travers, lecturer—of the Temple . . . the public champions of their party . . . both sides being glad they had gotten two such eminent leaders ",[4] though Fuller admits that Hooker's pen was " a better bucket than his tongue "[5] to draw out his depth of learning. Travers had the advantage in oratory, for " Hooker's voice was low, stature little, gesture none at all . . . the doctrine he delivered had nothing but itself to garnish it ".[6] " He may be said to have made good music with his fiddle and stick alone, without any resin." [7] In the morning Hooker preached, and in the afternoon Travers discoursed to a larger audience; so that " the pulpit spake pure Canterbury in the morning, and Geneva in the afternoon ".[8] Benchers and students attended in numbers, including men like Sir Edward Coke, and were as assiduous in taking down notes as in compiling facts for their briefs.

Travers was horrified that Hooker should maintain the Church of Rome, though containing abuses, to be yet a true Church, and its members, living and dead, capable of salvation. " Give me a Pope or a Cardinal . . . whose heart God hath touched with true sorrow for all his sins . . . shall I think, because of . . . error, such men touch not so much as the hem of Christ's garment? " asks

---

[1] Sisson, op. cit., pp. 20–1.
[2] Jewel died in 1571, before Hooker graduated.
[3] *Vivebat ?*1548–1635.
[4] Fuller, *Church History*, III, 125.
[5] *Ibid.*   [6] *Ibid.*
[7] Fuller, *Worthies*, I, 423.   [8] *Ibid,*

Hooker.[1] "Surely," he adds later, " I must confess that if it be an error to think that God may be merciful to save men even when they err, my greatest comfort is my error." [2] Similarly he writes, in the Fifth Book, " To say that in nothing they may be followed which are of the Church of Rome were violent and extreme. . . . Where Rome keepeth that which is ancienter and better, others whom we much more affect leaving it for newer and changing it for worse; we had rather follow the perfections of them whom we like not, than in defects resemble them whom we love." [3] Fifteen points of difference and discussion between the rival preachers are enumerated by Walton, and though traces of Calvinism are apparent enough in Hooker, we see a liberality and breadth of view, a deep sense of law, a grasp of principle, a love of man, a profound respect for the power of human reason, markedly absent in the narrowness of his opponent. When Hooker claims that " the assurance of things which we believe by the Word, is not so sure as of those which we perceive by sense ",[4] we seem once more to be listening to the reasoning of Bishop Pecock.[5]

However, Travers was silenced by Whitgift in peremptory fashion, because he had received ordination from an Antwerp presbytery and had no licence to preach. Subsequently he proceeded to Dublin, as Provost of Trinity College, and died in London in 1635 at an advanced age. Yet all the bickering and partisanship had made Hooker unhappy, for he esteemed Travers as a good man; " it turned to his extreme grief ".[6] The trouble gave birth to a great desire to examine and set down in writing the principles of the establishment of the Church of England. Consequently he besought Whitgift to release him from the Temple, that he might have freedom to study and write. In 1591, therefore, he exchanged his post for the living of Boscombe in Wiltshire, to which in the same year was added a minor prebend in the Cathedral of Salisbury, but it appears probable that he discharged his duties by deputy. In all likelihood he lived on in London with the Churchmans, his wife's parents, in Watling Street and worked on the first four books of the *Ecclesiastical Polity*, which he had begun probably as early as 1586. His sermons dealing with the Travers controversy, 1585-6, show that his mind was even then occupied with the plan of such a work. In 1593 the first four books were published, intentionally following the execution of the Puritan extremists, Penry, Barrow, and Greenwood.

---

[1] " Sermon on Justification," *E.P.*, III, 541.
[2] *E.P.*, III, 543.
[3] *E.P.*, V, xxviii, i, 127.
[4] Walton, *Life*, I, 60.
[5] *Repressor of Overmuch Blaming of the Clergy* (c. 1449).
[6] More particularly as in 1580 Travers' brother had married Hooker's sister.

Hooker clearly had access to the most important and recent contemporary books, and all the circumstances warrant the conclusion that he had the approval and support of the Government. In point of fact, this is suggested by Covel as early as 1603. In his *Just and Temperate Defence* he writes that Hooker " hath laboured in a weighty cause, with reasons, against those whom the Magistrate's severity could not easily suppress . . . (and) hath undertaken it by appointment ".[1]

In 1595 the Crown presented Hooker to the living of Bishopsbourne, near Canterbury, where he was to end his days. Here he completed the Fifth Book, which was published in 1597. At Bishopsbourne Hooker formed a great friendship with Dr. Adrian Saravia (they are said to have acted as confessors to each other), a learned minister of the Dutch Reformed Church, lately become a prebendary of Canterbury. This friendship was the chief earthly solace of Hooker's few remaining years. He died, a worn-out man, on November 2, 1600, and was buried in his own chancel at Bishopsbourne. When Walton wrote, " It is thought he hastened his own death by hastening to give life to his Books," [2] he is but echoing Covel, who had said the same thing sixty years before, as he moved to the peroration of his *Just and Temperate Defence*. " Death . . . hath taken from us, and from the Church of God, a sweet friend, a wise counsellor and a strong champion. . . . Others fit enough to live in the midst of error, vanity, unthankfulness and deceit, but he too good. For he was as the morning star in the midst of a cloud, and as the Moon when it is full: and as the Sun shining upon the Temple of the Most High, and as the rainbow that is bright in the fair clouds; when he put on the garment of honour, and was clothed with all beauty, he went up to the holy Altar, and made the garment of holiness honourable." [3]

During his Mastership, in 1588,[4] Hooker had married Joan, the daughter of John Churchman. She came from a well-known family of Merchant Taylors, of which Company her father was Master in 1594. The family bore arms, and Joan brought Hooker a dowry of seven hundred pounds: an admirable and judicious connection. It is likely that Hooker lived with his father-in-law until he departed to Kent.

For some reason, Hooker's University friends—notably the young Edwin Sandys and George Cranmer—disapproved of Mrs. Hooker, and through them the legend grew up, repeated by Fuller, Gauden, and Walton,[5] that she was an unattractive and common shrew

---

[1] Covel, op. cit., p. 11.
[2] Walton, op. cit., p. 84.
[3] Covel, op. cit., p. 13.
[4] 13 February (Register of St. Augustine's, Watling Street).
[5] Walton, op. cit., I, 22.

PAGE FROM THE BISHOPSBOURNE REGISTER SHOWING MARRIAGE ENTRY.

[To face page 40.

foisted by scheming parents upon an innocent scholar when he was a lonely young priest lodging in London for the first time. Such a story had been felt by many to involve a grave reflection on Hooker's judgement,[1] but not till Professor Sisson's researches came to light was it seen to be demonstrably false. Hooker, in his will, dated October 26, 1600, affectionately refers to his wife as "well-beloved" and appointed her his residuary legatee and sole executrix, and her father (" my well-beloved father ") as one of the overseers. The fact that she married in less than six months Edward Nethersole of Canterbury, and that her father later became bankrupt and her daughters subsequently involved in litigation with Sandys, may probably go far to account for the odium in which she later stood.

The same obscurity that has till recently prevailed over some of the more important facts of Hooker's life has similarly rested over his writings, notably the *Laws of Ecclesiastical Polity*. This was originally planned to include eight books, as the Preface and the title-page of the 1593 edition show, but at the time of Hooker's death only five books had appeared. Book VI, which deals with the authority of ministers in the matter of Penitence, Confession, and Absolution, and Book VIII, on the Royal Supremacy, did not appear until 1648, whilst Book VII, devoted to an examination of Episcopacy, did not see the light of day until 1662.

This long delay in publication inevitably gave rise to doubts about the authenticity of the three books. They contain—particularly Books VII and VIII—much vital and controversial matter, and with our present knowledge it is impossible to pronounce to what precise extent they are completely genuine. Book VI is perhaps slightly less important. Keble thought it " the most perplexing " of the three, and whilst ready to accept it as the work of Hooker, maintained that it was never meant to form part of the *Ecclesiastical Polity*, because it " marked an entire deviation from its subject ".[2] Possibly part of it has been lost, but Professor Sisson argues that " nothing could be more germane . . . to the general question of the jurisdiction of the ministry as against that of lay elders" than the discussion of Penitence, Confession, and Absolution.[3] He is prepared, in fact, to accept it not only as " authentic Hooker ", but probably " the complete Hooker of Book VI ",[4] against the judgement of the *Dictionary of National Biography*,[5] which flatly

---

[1] See Church's *Introduction to Hooker*, Book I. He points out that Walton's story " exalts Hooker's simplicity at the expense of his good sense and good feeling in a way which provokes suspicion ". (Ed. 1882, pp. viii, ix.)
[2] Keble, Editor's Preface, pp. xxxiv, xxxviii, Vol. I.
[3] Sisson, op. cit., p. 105.   [4] Sisson, op. cit., p. 102.
[5] Article by Sidney Lee.

D

asserts the present Sixth Book has no right to its place in the *Ecclesiastical Polity*.

What appears to have occurred is that, on the death of Hooker, John Churchman, his father-in-law and overseer of his will, collected all the manuscripts from Bishopsbourne and handed them over to a committee consisting of Sandys, Dr. Spenser (a trustee under the will) and Dr. Parry, later Bishop of Worcester. They were given to Sandys to sort out, and were subsequently distributed between Spenser, Parry and Lancelot Andrewes (who had now been added to the committee). Spenser took all those bearing on the *Ecclesiastical Polity*, and Parry and Andrewes took care of the sermons and minor works.

Most of the sermons were published within a few years,[1] but almost half a century was to elapse before any more of the *Ecclesiastical Polity* was published. According to Spenser, Books VI and VII were virtually ready for publication, but Book VIII was in the form of notes and a rough draft, and would require considerable editorial attention.[2] In 1604 he republished the first five books with a preface of his own announcing his intention of giving the others to the world in their defaced condition. But Spenser's time was then occupied with the translation of the Authorized Version of the Bible. He therefore employed a young scholar living in Oxford, named Henry Jackson, to transcribe the three remaining books. The Authorized Version appeared in 1611, and Jackson published some of the sermons in 1612, but still the *Ecclesiastical Polity* made no appearance. The real reason for delay appears to have been a disagreement between Sandys, still somewhat of a Calvinist, and Lancelot Andrewes, who was definitely an Arminian, about the doctrinal contents of Book VI. " It is difficult ", writes Professor Sisson, " not to suspect some deliberate suppression of the material left by Hooker." [3]

In 1613, in the course of a lawsuit brought by Hooker's daughters against Sandys about payment for the publication of the *Ecclesiastical Polity*, Spenser declared that with the permission of the

---

[1] Five sermons were published in 1612, and the two sermons on the Epistle of Jude in 1613. There is reason to believe Sandys retained some of the sermons, for it was his agent, Eveleigh, and not Lancelot Andrewes, who released the sermons on Jude for publication in 1613. Walton published one sermon in 1678, which he described as being " found in the study of the late learned Bishop Andrewes ". And in 1836 Keble published part of a sermon found in the library of Trinity College, Dublin. The rest of it had been published in 1612.

[2] Covel says Hooker stated they were completed (op. cit., pp. 149-50), but Covel was ignorant of their whereabouts, and was obviously in doubt whether they would ever be published.

Hooker himself suggests Book VIII was virtually finished (*E.P.*, Preface, sec. 8).

[3] Op. cit., p. 98.

court he would rather not say why the manuscripts of Books VI and VII could not be printed at the moment. In 1614 he died, leaving his manuscripts to Dr. King, Bishop of London, in the care of whose family they remained for twenty years or more, till Archbishop Abbott [1] ordered them to be placed in the Lambeth Palace Library.[2] It seems strange that Laud did nothing with them, since he was obviously a great admirer of Hooker, and built much of his own arguments on the earlier books.[3] On his fall in December 1640 they passed into the possession of Parliament, and finally, in 1643, that body permitted the Archbishop's library to go to Hugh Peters.[4]

After the first reprint of 1604, editions followed in 1611 and 1617. The years 1632 and 1638 saw further reprints, and in 1641 the Oxford Press issued an edition under the sanction of Archbishop Ussher.[5] The Sixth and Eighth Books were first printed in 1648, but not till Gauden published what purported to be the complete work in 1662 was the Seventh Book ever seen.

A convenient way of accounting for this chequered history, and at the same time of preparing the world not to accept Books VII and VIII as entirely genuine, was to suggest that they had been tampered with by Puritans. The legend thus grew up that Mrs. Hooker—who is again made the villain of the story—had allowed her son-in-law, a neighbouring Puritan minister named Ezekiel Charke, from Harbledown near Canterbury, with the assistance of another, to enter her husband's study and to work his will on the manuscripts he found there. There is, however, a total lack of evidence to prove it, and it may well have been entire invention. Walton confesses his evidence for this is hearsay, forty years old at that, and originating from a friend of Hooker. But if any minister of the name of Charke committed the outrage, it was certainly none named Ezekiel. The date would permit the perpetrator to be the famous Puritan, William Charke, Fellow of Peterhouse, and Preacher at Lincoln's Inn from 1581 until Whitgift silenced him in 1593, for nothing is known of his activities from that time until his death in 1617. But he is not known to have lived in or near Canterbury. It seems very probable that he had a son Ezekiel, but at the time of Hooker's death Ezekiel was only a boy of sixteen. It is a fact that this same Ezekiel became Rector of S. Michael's, Harbledown (*not* S. Nicholas, as Walton says, which was a leper hospital), but not until Parliament put him there in 1643, where three years later he died.

[1] *Vivebat* 1560–1633.
[2] Keble's Preface to *E.P.*, I, xxxii.
[3] See his *Conference with Fisher* (Parker, 1844).
[4] Laud's *Life and Trial* (London, 1695), p. 365.
[5] *Vivebat* 1581–1656.

If any Charke married Margaret, Hooker's youngest daughter, it can only have been this Ezekiel, as Margaret was certainly not born earlier than 1593, and was co-plaintiff in her own name in lawsuits of 1610 and 1613. No Charke can have been Mrs. Hooker's son-in-law at the date of the alleged outrage. This Ezekiel undoubtedly did marry, but not till 1617, when he vacated his Fellowship at King's College, Cambridge; and there is recorded the baptism in 1618 of a small Ezekiel at St. Dionis, London, the church where the celebrated William lay buried. This Ezekiel II is he whom Walton mentions as the Rector of Waldron in Sussex, and calls the son of Ezekiel I and Margaret. But this legend of Puritan outrage, based on the hearsay of nearly half a century before, can hardly be accepted as authentic history.

Indeed, another conspiracy to destroy the MSS. was suggested as early as 1614, again on hearsay evidence only. Edmund Parbo, a witness in a Chancery suit of that date, declared he had heard that three men—Edward Nethersole, Roger Raven, and Francis Aldrich, all Canterbury men—burnt the papers of Hooker after the marriage of Nethersole and Mrs. Hooker. Again there is no tittle of supporting evidence. It is true that Nethersole seems to have been a tricky fellow, but Raven and Aldrich must have been men of character, and were Anglicans in religion. These two were close friends. Raven was the Headmaster of the King's School, Canterbury, from 1591 till his death in 1614, and Aldrich was probably a boy at the school, whence he proceeded to Clare Hall, where Raven had been an undergraduate. Raven was Whitgift's own nominee to the Dean and Chapter for the Headmastership, and cannot therefore have been even suspected of Puritan leanings. He was an extremely successful Headmaster, and on his death was buried in the Cathedral cloisters, while in due time his son became the Lower Master of the school. Aldrich appointed his friend overseer of his will and bequeathed to him his *Works of St. Bernard*. At the early age of thirty-three Aldrich died in 1609, having reached the dignity of the Mastership of Sidney Sussex College. His father, also named Francis, had lived in Canterbury for many years, practising as a Notary Public and Registrar of the Consistory Court. If he were alive at the time of Hooker's death—as appears likely, since he was giving evidence in a Consistory Court case of 1596— he would be about fifty-five; and it is inconceivable that he should allow his son to jeopardize his own career and his father's public position by such a rash act as the destruction of Hooker's last books. All that is known of the characters of Raven and Aldrich, coupled with their public offices and the fact that Nethersole became Mayor of Canterbury for the second time in 1604, permits this unsupported charge to be dismissed. In fine, the subject-matter of these two books being Monarchical Episcopacy and Royal Supremacy, it is reasonable to conclude that tampering—if any there were—may with as much probability be charged against the enemies of Puritanism.

The 1648 edition, which included for the first time the so-called Sixth and the Eighth Books, laments the complete disappearance of the Seventh. Nothing was known of it until, like a bolt from the blue, it was launched on the world by Gauden, Bishop of Worcester, in 1662, by whom it was placed after the Eighth Book. This editor maintained that he possessed the manuscript, which lacked only Hooker's " last polishing "; but he omits all mention of its history, or of the manner in which it had come into his own hands. Hence, pending further discoveries, it is by the internal evidence alone and by consideration of Gauden's character that readers can endeavour to satisfy themselves whether it be Hooker or no.

Keble considers it scarcely possible that Gauden forged it, since it was unskilfully edited and contained palpable blunders. A sentence in Gauden's *Life of Hooker* (prefaced to his edition of the *Ecclesiastical Polity*) is not, however, without suggestive influence. He remarks that it is not easy to counterfeit Hooker's style, method, or notions.[1]

This Gauden is a perplexing person. His ecclesiastical career was ambiguous. In 1641 he secured the Deanery of Bocking [2] through the good-will of Parliament, and was chosen to be in the Assembly of Divines, but by some " sleight of hand was shuffled out " of it.[3] He apparently took the Covenant, though in later years he denied having done so; at any rate he contrived to retain his preferments while conforming to the Presbyterian requirements of the Commonwealth: yet in 1653 he was bold enough to publish a long, learned and outspoken *Defence for the Ministry of the Church of England*, calling for its reinstatement, and ridiculing the sectarianism of the times. Presumably he remained on friendly terms with Parliament, for otherwise his possession of the MS. of Book VII at any time before 1660 can hardly be accounted for. His Church history in the *Defence* runs along the lines of Jewel and Hooker, whom he often mentions, and he treats Episcopacy as primitive and apostolic.

---

[1] Ed. 1662 (London), p. 26.

[2] Laud states that Gauden was made Dean of Bocking at the pressing request of the Earl of Warwick, and by order of the House of Lords. The Archbishop's first reply was that he could not gratify Dr. Gauden with Bocking (Laud's *Life and Trial* (ed. 1695), pp. 194-5).

Gauden admits that at his interview with Laud he was " under some prejudice with him, as to some relation I then had " (*Eccl. Ang. Susp.*, p. 632).

[3] *Ecclesiae Anglicanae Suspiria* (London, 1659), p. 377.

His arguments are much the same on this subject as those of the *Eikon Basilike* (1648), the authorship of which he claimed at the Restoration. " Paternal Episcopacy " he defends, but not " Pontifical Prelacy ", the former of which " looks very like an immediate *institution* of Christ, either preceptive and explicit, or tacit and exemplary ",[1] though he admits reformation of the Order may be desirable,[2] and implies that King and Parliament could establish the Church without it.[3] With the death of Oliver and the incompetence of Richard Cromwell, and a consequent restoration of the Monarchy in prospect, Gauden published, in 1659, his largest work, the *Ecclesiae Anglicanae Suspiria*. Here he comes out strongly for episcopal government in the pontifical sense,[4] although, characteristically, he now and then refers to the abuses and dangers of Prelatical Episcopacy, and cautiously suggests that the paternal and presidential type is advisable.[5]

Nevertheless, suspicion has often questioned the genuineness of this Seventh Book, for it certainly appears in places at variance with Hooker's teaching of Episcopacy in the earlier books. For example, writing in 1661, Stillingfleet does not hesitate to call Hooker to his aid, on the strength of the Third Book alone, to prove that bishops need only be State creations. Hallam,[6] therefore, rightly and reasonably raises the question whether Anglicans were not as likely as Puritans to corrupt the last books of Hooker.[7] This can only, of course, be a matter of surmise, and it is difficult to conceive that any of the Carolines would be guilty of such forgery; while also it has been argued that the passages at variance can, to a certain extent, be reconciled. Andrewes certainly had the manuscripts of some sermons and of Hooker's Sixth and Eighth Books, but he did not ever possess the Seventh, as far as is known; nor is it conceivable that a man of such unblemished life should stoop to flagrant literary dishonesty. If ever such corruption were made, it would have to be perpetrated either by a man whose zeal for Episcopacy was so great as to make him consider that the end justified the means, or by an unscrupulous rogue for his own ends. The only Caroline divine of sufficient literary skill, who was equally resolute against Prince and Independent for the divine right of bishops (far more strongly than Hooker or Andrewes), was Thorndike.[8] But, zealous High Churchman as he was, he was not the man to descend

---

[1] See his *Loosing of S. Peter's Bands* (1660), p. 19.
[2] Op. cit., p. 13.
[3] Op. cit., p. 21.
[4] E.g., pp. 23 *et seq.*
[5] E.g., op. cit., pp. 448, 459, 465, 477.
[6] Coleridge was of the same opinion (*Literary Remains*, 1818, III, 19-20).
[7] *C.H.*, I, iv, 220 (n.) (1867).   [8] *Vivebat* 1598-1672.

to literary forgery. Quite apart from the fact that most of his published works were written or appeared before 1660—i.e., before the Seventh Book ever saw the light of day—he would have encountered great difficulty in successfully copying a style so unlike his own.

But the fact that John Gauden, of all people, had possession of the MS. cannot but give rise to a feeling of insecurity when the personal character of the man is brought into consideration. His character is of material importance in the question before us. Gauden was a thoroughly unscrupulous and ambitious man, and the evidence for this comes from his own hand. He wrote letters to Clarendon [1] in 1660 and to the Earl of Bristol,[2] in which he un-blushingly pressed his claims first for a bishopric and then for translation from Exeter to a more profitable See, on the ground that he had written the *Eikon Basilike*—a secret from the world, " that great arcanum " known only to Charles, James, Clarendon, Morley and himself—" a rare service in those horrors of times ", and one " which will never be equalled " for the reputation it begot for Charles I and its influence in rallying Englishmen again to Monarchy and Restoration. He virtually threatens blackmail, and laments, " True, I played this best card in my hand something too late ". Exeter was " banishment ", a prison rather than a palace, worth only £500 a year.[3] He had written the book " to buoy up the honour of the Royal Family, the Church and *Episcopacy* ", and bluntly continues that while no man is more devoted to serve God, the Church, and the King than he is, " I only expect that if I do my work I may have honourable wages ". He invites Clarendon to " make me see those effects which may assure me, that my loyalty, pains, care, hazard and *silence*, are accepted by the King and Royal Family ". The outcome was a speedy translation to Worcester, though he had set his heart on Winchester.

This is the man who, a twelvemonth before, wrote, " Ambitious vanities are never seasonable or comely for any humble Christians, and least for the Ministers of Christ (who ought to be crucified to the world, and the world to them), especially at my years, and in my condition." [4] This is the potential blackmailer who could exhort his hearers to " take heed of setting thy heart on anything

---

[1] Clarendon, *State Papers*, Vol. III, Supp., pp. xxvi–xxxii, xcv–xcvi.

[2] Op. cit., pp. xcvii–c.

[3] There is a MS. list of the revenues of Exeter in the Sheldon papers (Bodl. Add. MS. C.302, ff. 108–9) in contemporary writing, according to which his figure would not be very inaccurate. Seth Ward, who followed him at Exeter, wrote to Sheldon that Gauden never paid a farthing for dilapidations when he quitted Exeter (Bodl. Add. MSS. C.305, f. 277).

[4] *Eccl. Ang. Susp.*, Pref., p. 13.

which may leave thee whether thou and it will or no. . . . O lay hold thyself, and help others to fasten on eternal life . . . the only entertainment worthy of thy immortal soul. . . . Take heed life be not done before we think of ' living ' or ' dying ', as we should. . . . Remember upon this moment depends eternity. . . . Let us so live here . . . that we may not be ashamed to see one another at the last day." [1] Similar sentiments are uttered in plenty in his *Funerals Made Cordials*—and indeed in all his sermons—preached in 1658 at the funeral of the Earl of Warwick's son; such as, "Ask thy soul . . . not what goods thou hast laid up . . . not what honours thou enjoyest, not what lands thou possessest or expectest, but what preparation thou hast made to meet thy God! "

But there is further first-hand evidence of roguery. Bishop Wordsworth deals at great length with Gauden's character in his *Who Wrote Eikon Basilike?* [2] and proves him completely untrustworthy—a man capable of writing and saying anything that favoured his chance of preferment. Thus Wordsworth establishes, for example, that Gauden's *Just Invective* is a forgery, in the sense that, so far from being written—as Gauden affirmed—in 1649, it was, in fact, compiled with the Restoration in immediate prospect. [3] In this century S. R. Gardiner has proved a similar forgery, that Gauden published just before the Restoration a *Remonstrance* which, he declared, he had presented to Cromwell on behalf of the clergy ejected from Royalist houses by the Declaration of November 24th, 1655. A serious confusion which Gauden made in the all-important dates of this Declaration, and the actual Expulsion which was its consequence, convinces Gardiner that Gauden never, in fact, presented his *Remonstrance* to the Protector. [4]

Nor does the evidence that Gauden possessed few principles cease with this. Baxter relates that in May 1660 he and Gauden with two others held conference in Gray's Inn as to some possible concordat in religion. " But whereas I told Dr. Gauden, That for the *Doctrinal Part* of the Common Prayer Book, though I knew that there were many Exceptions against it, yet I remembered nothing which I could not assent to, allowing it but the favourable Interpretation which the Writings of all Divines are allowed : He took advantage from these Words, [5] to praise my Moderation in the next Book which he printed, as if I had spoke this of the Liturgy in general, as a Frame of Worship, leaving out the first Words, ' *As to the Doctrinal*

---

[1] *Sermon at the Funeral of Dr. Brounrig, Bishop of Exeter*, 1660, pp. 120–1.
[2] London, 1824.
[3] Op. cit., Letter II.
[4] *History of the Commonwealth and Protectorate* (Longmans, 1901), III, 192 (n.).
[5] As he does also by inserting his own parentheses in a quotation from the Preface of the *Ecclesiastical Polity* (*Eccl. Anglic. Susp.*, p. 183).

Part' to which only I limited my assent: so that I was put in print so far to vindicate myself, as to set down the true Words; which he never contradicted." [1] This " next book " of Gauden was entitled *Considerations Touching the Liturgy of the Church of England*, where he shows his customary opportunism and suppression of the truth thus: " I cannot but commend the candour, justice and ingenuity of Mr. Baxter, who lately professed to me, that he saw nothing in the Liturgy which might not well bear a good construction if men looked upon it as became Christians." [2] It has already been stated that, according to Gauden, his edition of the Seventh Book was almost as it left Hooker's hand; it lacked only the author's " last polishing ". This he wrote in 1662. Yet, writing in 1659, he says, concerning the last three books, " I have been credibly informed, that some of the then dissenters from the Church of England had the good (or rather evil) fortune, utterly to suppress those (now defective, but by him promised and performed) books touching the vindication of the Church of England." [3]

Wood [4] contains a reference to Gauden's character as given in the Appendix to the *Life of Dr. John Barwick*, from which White Kennet also quotes. [5] It is contemporary evidence, and unflattering. Peter Barwick, the author, says that Gauden was extremely fond of popular applause; that he had joined himself to the sworn enemies of the Church and Crown; that he became Bishop of Exeter, though he had before abjured the whole Episcopal Order and was reputed to have advised Charles II in a " Letter " to abjure it in Scotland. Happily he had failed to obtain the See of Winchester, " yet I know not by what ill destiny he gained that of Worcester ". Barwick sees him as " that false apostate Gauden ", " that most vain man ", that " unhappy blemish and reproach of the sacred order ", [6] who lived and died despised by the King whom he had so much flattered. [7]

Burnet states that James, Duke of York, assured him in 1673 that Gauden wrote the *Eikon Basilike*, and for that reason was given a bishopric, although Sheldon opposed his promotion on the ground that he had taken the Covenant. [8] Kennet ascribes to him the draft of declarations of liberty of conscience in 1662 both for

[1] *Reliquiae Baxt.* (London, 1696), Lib. I, p. 218.
[2] London, 1660, p. 33.
[3] *Eccl. Ang. Susp.*, p. 84.
[4] *Ath. Ox.* (ed. Bliss, 1817), III, 618.
[5] *Register* (London, 1728), p. 773.
[6] *Vita J. Barwick* (London, 1721), pp. 247–56.
[7] The amiable Ralph Thoresby who, once he became a Churchman and increasingly intimate with the Episcopate, could hardly think ill of any Anglican bishop, suggests that the author is perhaps too unkind to Bishop Gauden (*Diary and Corr.*, II, 411).
[8] *History of His Own Times* (ed. 1724), I, 50–2.

Papists and Quakers, from no better motive than the sordid hope of currying further favour with the Court.[1] Finally, the writer of the *Lives of the Bishops* remarks that " he never would have thriven as he did, if he had appeared to the world a Non-covenanter. . . . In 1660 he was ready trimm'd for Sailing, and took the advantage of the gale of Oblivion ".[2]

Whether Gauden wrote the *Eikon Basilike* or not is immaterial in this question of the genuineness of Book VII of the *Ecclesiastical Polity*, but his character is vitally important. If he wrote the *King's Book*,[3] he was doubly unscrupulous, first because he had taken the Covenant a few years earlier, and next because his letters are plain blackmail. If he was not the author, he is a liar. In either case, an unreliable person to possess Book VII, and, concealing its origin, to publish it so appositely. It is enough for us that he held some secret through which he could bring pressure on the Court, and did not shrink from using it; enough that he lied about his own publications; enough that he could twist Baxter's words. Baxter was alive and could protest. Hooker was dead—the state of the MS. was secret from all—no protest could be made if, at the restoration of monarchy and prelacy, it should have suited the editor to vary the author's sentiments. Keble admits that for the genuineness of Book VII " our only direct testimony is the affirmation of Dr. Gauden. In other words, we are left to make up our minds by internal evidence only." [4] He goes on to say that there may be suspicion that forgery, or at least interpolation, may have been practised to promote the sale of the work. That would certainly be a reason commending itself to Gauden, but we may be more ready to look for the prime motive in his episcopal ambitions. The best summary of his character may well be found in his own words, in the advice which he says he gave to Laud. " I added that people were not taken generally so much with grand and severer virtues, as with things more plausibly and seasonably . . . adapted to their capacity . . . that it was possible to serve *the times*, and yet to serve *the Lord*." [5]

When and from whom did the Essex doctor acquire the MS.? It had remained in the Lambeth Library from Abbot's time until Leighton and Hugh Peters ransacked Laud's papers and books in 1643 [6]—and why had the prelatical Laud made no use of it? As

[1] Op. cit., p. 775.
[2] 1731, p. 353.
[3] Almack's *Bibliography of the King's Book* (London, 1896) summarizes the writings for and against Gauden's authorship.
[4] Editor's Preface to *E.P.*, p. xli.
[5] *Eccles. Angl. Susp.*, pp. 632–3.
[6] *Archbishop Laud*, H. Trevor-Roper (Macmillan), 1940, p. 416.

early as 1641 Smectymnus remarked, " It is worth the enquiring, whether the three last books of Hooker's *Ecclesiastical Polity* be not suppressed by him that hath them, because they give the Prince too much power in Ecclesiastical matters, and are not for the Divine Right of Bishops." [1] It may be the full truth will never be known, but we know something. Hugh Peters had lived some time in Essex; his wife's home was at Pebmarsh, some six miles only from Bocking. Gauden was a protégé of the Earl of Warwick, as whose private chaplain he functioned. Warwick and Peters were undoubtedly closely connected with each other in the fortunes of the New England Colonies. Peters, moreover, was Warwick's Naval Chaplain and personal agent in the early years of the Civil War. Gauden and Peters were well acquainted with one another, and no doubt met often at Leighs, Warwick's estate in Essex. In fact, Gauden refers to one meeting with Peters in 1641 " at a noble Earl's table ".[2] Reason concludes that they, servants and chaplains of the same Parliamentarian Lord, were more than acquaintances. Parliament had granted Laud's Library to Peters,[3] and it is possible he gave or sold the Hooker MS. to his friend and colleague, Gauden, who—it may well be—waited for the appropriate instant to use it, as he waited with his own *Just Invective*, and his *Remonstrance*, and that momentous secret known to so few. But it is not impossible that the MS. passed to him only in 1660, perhaps as a legacy from his former fellow-chaplain on the eve of his execution as a regicide. Certainly in 1659 Gauden professed his belief that the MS. of the last three books had been destroyed, and if this profession were true, he must have acquired the MS. in 1660 or thereabouts, in order to publish it by 1662.

The Eighth Book had frequently been copied, as we may well understand, and is the least complete of the whole. It is quite impossible to say how much, if anything, has been interpolated, though accusations in plenty have been made. Keble's conjecture is that Jackson was so angry at having to hand over Hooker's papers to Bishop King that he retained the completed copy, giving up only the rough draft. That copy, or a transcript, might have come into Ussher's hands, and thence to Trinity College, Dublin— since the Dublin MS. is corrected, and larger than the other three MSS. in existence. If that is true, and transcriptions were made from the rough draft, it would help to account for any uncertainties in the political teaching of that book.

[1] *A Vindication of the Answer to the Humble Remonstrance*, pp. 9–10.
[2] *Anti-Baal-Berith* (1661), p. 179.
[3] See his *Dying Father's Last Legacy* (1660), p. 104, where he says his share of Laud's books was valued at £140, but he had often tried to sell them and his own for £150 without success.

Nevertheless the weight of evidence seems to point in the direction of the genuineness of the book. Its own subject-matter appears to refute the accusation of gross interpolations. The principles of civil government, which Hooker lays down in the First Book, are the same, expanded, in the Eighth. The purpose of the book is to vindicate the Royal Supremacy, which he does by identifying Church and Commonwealth. In accordance with his theory of the origin of society and of civil government, " contract " and " consent " and the ultimate sovereignty of the people are no more and no less apparent in the last than in the early book. This was Baxter's opinion, according to Anthony à Wood. " The reason why the said Mr. Baxter contends so earnestly for their genuineness ", he writes, " is because the said three books, but more especially the eighth, do contain certain popular and false principles, concerning the true nature of the legislative power, the Original of Government and the Office of Kings itself, as derived from the people. . . . And that he may charge these destructive assertions home on our author, he saith, ' If any do causelessly question whether the eighth imperfect book be in those dangerous passages above-mentioned his own, let them remember that the sum of them is in his first book, which is old, and highly honoured by the prelatists.' " [1]

The above space has been given to the history of the *Ecclesiastical Polity* because it is a document of the first importance. Not only does it represent a thorough-going defence of an institution which is still in existence and still constitutionally very much what it was in Hooker's own day, but it also deals with the fundamental political and ecclesiastical issues of the sixteenth century, which have been, in fact, the main problems of political thought and practice since the days of Plato and Aristotle, and which modern democracy and the totalitarianism of the twentieth century have revived in acute form.

Hooker's place is high amongst all sixteenth-century writers. Pope Clement VIII said, after Dr. Stapleton had read the First Book of the *Ecclesiastical Polity* to him, "There is no learning that this man hath not searched into: nothing too hard for his understanding: this man indeed deserves the name of an author: his books will get reverence by age; for there is in them such seeds of eternity, that if the rest be like this, they shall last till the last fire shall consume all learning." [2] A modern writer acknowledges that " for breadth of view, combined with intellectual honesty and detachment, he had no serious rival save Bodin. For fairness and courtesy in controversy only Cardinal Bellarmine was his equal. Among learned or controversial or philosophical books, no literary

[1] Wood, op. cit., I, 697.   [2] Walton's *Life*, I, 71.

style is comparable in excellence to his, save the totally dissimilar
style of Calvin." [1]   In the troubles of his century he mingled, says
Hallam, " like a knight of romance among caitiff brawlers, with
arms of finer temper and worthy to be proved in a nobler field ".[2]
And it is with the double authority of a contemporary and an expert
that Ben Jonson brackets Sir Philip Sidney and Mr. Hooker as
masters of literature and of wisdom.[3]

APPENDIX TO CHAPTER II

The Seventh Book as it stands contains passages difficult to
reconcile with each other, and its tone is frequently not that of the
first five books.   It is perplexing that Hooker should change his
views on the origin of Episcopacy,[4] particularly if Covel is right,
who says in his *Defence* of the *Ecclesiastical Polity* (1603) that he had
it from Hooker's own mouth that Books VI–VIII were finished,
and *if* the Gauden MS. did indeed lack only his " last polishing ".[5]
For he does not reveal the Seventh Book's " Monarchical and
Prelatical " tone in Book V (published in 1597)—and he died in
1600.   Timothy and Titus appear in Book V as missionary-presby-
ters, but in Book VII as monarchic bishops with power to ordain,
censure, and judge the inferior clergy.   The Newport divines,
indeed, felt they could quote Book V as authority on their side
against Charles.[6]   Hugh Peters [op. cit., pp. 3, 31] could commend
the study of Hooker to his daughter with other definitely Protestant
writers.   Again, if Book VII is genuine Hooker—if the institution
of bishops was from Heaven and the Holy Ghost the Author of it,[7]
if Episcopacy is of the *esse* of the Church—why did Hooker employ
Saravia as his confessor, a Dutch Reformed pastor with no episcopal
ordination?

The characters of Hooker and Gauden being known, some
examination of their respective literary styles may warrant readers
in concluding that the MS. was freely and carelessly edited and
suffered interpolations.   The book cannot have lacked only
Hooker's " last polishing ".   It is not improbable that Gauden
patched insertions into it from time to time—this would account
for any passages that are suggestive of the early years of the Long
Parliament (e.g., VII, i, 2)—while as the Restoration appeared

---

[1] Allen, *Political Thought in the Sixteenth Century*, p. 184.
[2] Hallam, *Constitutional History*, I, 214.
[3] *Discoveries* (ed. 1641), p. 102.
[4] *E.P.*, VII, xi, 8.
[5] As to this, contrast, *Eccl. Angl. Susp.*, p. 84.
[6] *Works of King Charles*, p. 625.
[7] *E.P.*, VII, v, 10.

more and more likely, he finally, and quickly perhaps, sharpened up the " Prelatical " tone, even as he was not averse from publishing the *Just Invective* and the *Remonstrance* in 1660, pretending they had been issued years before.

Be the truth what it may, there are features worth consideration. For example:

1. It may be thought that the tone of Book VII is predominantly " Prelatical " in the seventeenth-century sense; the terms prelate and prelacy abound, whereas they do not occur at all in Books I–IV, and in the Fifth Book only in the Dedication and some six or seven other places (e.g., xix, 1; xxx, 4; xli, 2; xlii, 2, 11; xlvi, 5, 8), where for the most part the term is applied to the Fathers. An examination of Books I–V warrants the conclusion that Hooker regarded Episcopacy as of the *bene esse* of the Church and no more; Book VII asserts it is the *esse*.

2. There are passages which appear to display qualities of character unlike Hooker's, e.g.:

(i) VII, i, 2; i, 3 (" this most unkind world "; and the Puritans' Lord is the Devil).

(ii) i, 4. " O nation utterly without knowledge, without sense."

(iii) v, 10, p. 168. " bold and peremptory "—could Hooker so write (and again on p. 260) as to the *absolute* " *ius divinum* " of Episcopacy, when a few pages earlier he admits ancient custom might well be a sufficient origin? (Against this must be admitted that he dare not " peremptorily and boldly " affirm anything (V, lxxii, 7).)

(iv) xxiv, 3, p. 303. " Amongst the manifold accusations . . . courteous acceptation." A cringing servility and false humility of which Hooker surely was not capable.

(v) xxiv, 7, pp. 307–8. Unqualified abuse of patrons, which might have been inserted in xiv, 12, p. 232, if these are Hooker's words. His reference to patrons in V, xxxi, 4, does not suggest they deserve such abuse, though some are condemned in V, lxxxi, 16. He calls unsuitable clergy " refuse ", in contrast to III, xii, 20.

(vi) xxiv, 7, 8, 9, pp. 306–9. If these lists of episcopal evil practices are correct, the bishops must have been *very* corrupt. But would not Hooker have placed his finger more gently on the sores? In any case, he has already dealt with the major abuses here mentioned (see V, lxxxi), and it does seem that the original and genuine Book VII was even then written complete (see V, lxxx, 13).

(vii) xxiv, 12, p. 310. " The souls of men are not loved "—a severe and sweeping condemnation.

(viii) xxiv, 15, p. 313. Returns to attacks on the bishops.

(ix) xxiv, 18, 19, 20, pp. 316–21. Lamentations over wealth, unlike Hooker. There seems in places a grudging and avaricious ring. In V, lxxix, 5–17, he deals with much the same topics, but not in this tone, which seems unfitting to his dignity, and suggests a self-pity foreign to him—but not to the writer of the blackmailing letters to Clarendon. The passage on p. 317 beginning, " The travels and crosses . . . many thereunto " appears written by one of the Episcopate, and Hooker was incapable of the sneer in the last sentence.

(x) xxiv, 24, 25, pp. 322–24. The same spirit of personal grudge and self-commiseration is displayed.

(xi) xxiv, 26, p. 324. A flattering eulogy on the bishops, contrasting sharply with pp. 306–9.

(xii) xxiv, 26, p. 325. The peroration invokes a curse on the writer's opponents, contrary to Hooker's precept and practice.

3. Some passages suggest the ornate style of Gauden rather than the majestic, calm prose of Hooker, e.g.:

(i) Many, if not all, of those recited in 2 above.

(ii) Fairly frequent rhetorical modes of expression, which are hardly ever to be found in Books I–V.

(iii) xvi, 9; xviii, 10. (" O that there were for the encouragement of prelates. . . ."); xviii, 12; xxi, 1; xxii, 2, 3; xxii, 7; xxiv, 1, 2, 3, 4.

4. Passages suggestive of seventeenth-century conditions (e.g., VII, i, 2; i, 4; vii, 2; xv, 7; xxiv, 25). True, Hooker does indicate (Dedication to Book V) the gravity of danger likely to arise from civil strife engendered by religious discord, but it reads rather as a warning than as a statement of tragic result already experienced; and we read the warning with the feeling that the Government has grasped the dangerous situation firmly and has it in hand.

5. Other items of interest:

(i) VII, i, 3, p. 143. Christ directly appoints bishops. This does not cohere with the main theme of Book VII in so far as it is on all fours with Books III and V. But it is reminiscent of the treatment of Episcopacy in *Eikon Basilike*, Tit. xvii.

(ii) ii, 2, p. 148. The phrase " lame and impotent " occurs

in *Othello*, Act II, Sc. i, published in 1611; though it may have been in current use.

(iii) v, 2, pp. 156, also 208. The " Angels " of the Churches in Revelation. These passages recall the argument between Charles I and the Newport Divines.[1] If Gauden did write the *Eikon Basilike* he defines *use* as " the great arbitrator of words and master of language ";[2] and on p. 617 is the definition, " usage, which is the best master of words ".[3]

(iv) vi, 4. Hooker does not seem to limit Confirmation to bishops. Contrast V, lxvi, 3, 6.

(v) xiv, 12. Suggests churches have been destroyed in quantity, whereas V, xii, 1, implies that building and consecration of churches is a familiar incident. Certainly V, xxii, 17, and lxxi, 17, suggest the National Church is in vigorous life.

(vi) xi, 8, p. 209. Hooker changes his view, *very late in life*. It is difficult to understand this, and still more so if Book VII was already in existence when he was writing Book V (see V, lxxx, 13).

(vii) xiv, 11, pp. 230-1. Episcopacy is not *absolutely* essential; and the second example of " extraordinary kind of vocation " would suit Gauden's times better than Hooker's.

(viii) xxiv, pp. 302 *et seq.* These pages dealing with " sacrilege " are very reminiscent of Gauden's treatment of the same subject in, e.g., his *Hieraspistes*, pp. 464, 484-6.

(ix) xxiv, 21, p. 319. " The cup of cold water " figures not very dissimilarly in *Hieraspistes* at p. 505. The cup appears in *Eikon Basilike* at p. 690, where the " sacrilege " argument is treated in similar fashion.

A final word. Throughout the Commonwealth and Protectorate, Gauden conformed. He took the Covenant, but wrote now and then in defence of the Church. Where he touches on Episcopacy— as, e.g., in *Slight Healers of Public Hurts*, a sermon preached before Monk and the Lord Mayor in February 1659—as in *Hieraspistes*— it is primitive and presidential, not monarchical and prelatical. In that sermon—at a time when the future was still uncertain—he proposed a concordat between the Episcopal, Presbyterian, and Independent parties. The Episcopate was to be simply presidential, assisted by the Presbytery (" that the whole clergy of a Diocese . . . might not be exposed to one man's sole jurisdiction "), as safest for bishops, presbyters and People; since the last have from ancient times their rights: " that Church-Government might not seem to be

---

[1] See King Charles's *Works*, pp. 614, 618.   [2] See op. cit., p. 688.
[3] Charles' *Answer to the Newport Divines.*

a tyranny, or an arbitrary and absolute domineering over the faith and consciences of Christ's flock, but a mutual and sweet conspiring of the shepherds with the sheep ".[1] This is the spirit of the first footnote on p. 179 of the *Ecclesiastical Polity*, Book VII. Unhappily, Gauden remained a server of the times, and thoroughly endorsed the Church policy of the Cavalier Parliament. As White Kennett succinctly put it, " He was capable of Under-work ".[2]

[1] *Slight Healers*, p. 105. [2] *Register* (London, 1728), p. 775.

E

CHAPTER III

HOOKER'S GROUNDS OF DEFENCE: THE PREFACE

EMILY BRONTË, in *Wuthering Heights*, puts into the mouth of Mrs. Dean words which might adequately describe the Calvinist of the type with which Hooker had to contend. " He was, and is yet most likely, the wearisomest, self-righteous Pharisee that ever ransacked a Bible to rake the promises to himself, and fling the curses on his neighbours." [1] True, Hooker laughs at the element of childishness in his opponents' position, but he realizes such men are dangerous. Their self-confidence attracts the weak, who prefer to receive categorical assertions than to remain in the condition of uncertainty where thought is necessary. The Calvinistic appeal is of the same psychological nature as the Romanist. Hooker himself notices its effect upon women, and sagely observes on the power and persuasive qualities of that sex, remarking on its faculties of exact observation and comment upon neighbours, " through a singular delight which they take in giving very large and particular intelligence, how all near about them stand affected as concerning the same cause ".[2]

Catholicism had never permitted the unfettered use of reason. The result of this limitation had been to confine the attention of dialecticians to, and concentrate it upon, certain allowable grounds of controversy. The essentials of faith were received uncritically by those who valued their lives or places; the intellect remained in bondage, and only a relative few maintained the claims of reason. For reasoning is unnecessary where conclusions are already certainly arrived at; the rational faculty of the soul must rest content as far as these matters are concerned. But the emotional and intuitional faculties were, as ever, able to attempt to apprehend what reason's substitute declared as truth. As Spinoza so well understood, the mystical intuition of the divine lies at the end of a path beaten out by reason, not at its beginning. But since in important matters a dogmatic substitute for reason was employed, the power and desire of reasoning grew weak, while the emotions grew strong. The

---

[1] An almost identical passage occurs in the Preface to the *E.P.* (ed. 1888), I, viii, 10.

[2] *E.P.*, Preface, iii, 13.

psychic process of the Reformation may therefore be regarded as an over-toppling, due to the top-heaviness of the emotional faculties. Faith was, as before, accepted on trust, but from a different source— namely, the Bible—in the light of what was believed to be each individual's illumination, but was, in fact, each individual's emotion without sufficient basis of reason. The old hierarchy of the Church falling, in its place could only be erected whatever kind of spiritual dominion could be proved to be appointed by Scripture. The words of Scripture that might be taken as ordaining ecclesiastical regiment were few and doubtful to the unelect reader; but to the individual illumined by the direct light of Heaven their paucity was amply atoned for by the certainty of their purport. So the Discipline arose under the strong, albeit predestined, hand of Jean Calvin, " incomparably the wisest man that ever the French church did enjoy ".[1] Against the assertion by his followers of the infallibility of Calvin's interpretation of Scripture, Hooker sets his reason to justify the position of the Church of England, as being a part of the Church universal. His first care, in the Preface, is to destroy by exposition and by ridicule the exclusive claims of his opponents, and then in the remainder of the *Ecclesiastical Polity* to justify the nature and accidents of Anglicanism by an appeal to basic principles.

Therefore, the general grounds of Hooker's position are to be found in the Preface [2] to the *Laws of Ecclesiastical Polity*. Had no more than this ever been written we should have had an answer vital and pragmatically complete to the Puritan criticism of Elizabeth's Church Settlement. For in it Hooker outlines the plan of the eight books of his *Laws*, and provides a general sketch of the philosophical and logical basis for the constitution of the Church of England.

It was part of the genius of Hooker that he saw more clearly than most of his contemporaries that the reformation and establishment of religion were fundamentally a question of authority. From the outset the Reformers had seen that they must have an authority somewhere. The excesses of the Anabaptists, if nothing else, had brought home to them the perils of anarchism or complete individualism. For sixteenth-century Protestants the great authority, which superseded Pope and Church, was of course the Bible. But the Bible as the ultimate seat of authority for all Protestants soon presented obvious difficulties. It provided an answer varying according to what a man wished to find and Anabaptists could claim Scriptural authority for many of their beliefs and practices no less than Lutherans. The practical genius of Calvin had been quick to see this, and he organized and perfected a system at Geneva

[1] *E.P.*, Preface, ii, 1.   [2] *E.P.* (ed. 1888), I, 125–96.

which not merely claimed the sanction of the Bible, but insisted that itself was the only legitimate Protestant authority. Thus most Protestant roads, although leading at first to the Scriptures, tended finally to converge on Geneva.

That briefly was the situation when Hooker took up his pen to write the *Laws of Ecclesiastical Polity*. It imposed upon him a three-fold practical task—first, to vindicate the necessity for authority; secondly, to find some more adequate basis for it than the Scriptures; and thirdly, in examining the authority claimed by Calvin to demonstrate its faults, imperfectibilities, and unreasonableness. The first involved an attack on the extreme Protestant individualists, such as the Anabaptists; the second drove Hooker back to the mediaeval scholastics, notably Aquinas, to extract from them a basis for authority in Law; the third was marked by a sustained attack on the prevailing ideas of the Puritan party.

Hooker is not greatly concerned with opposition coming from Rome.[1] Jewel in his *Apology* had effectively dealt with their attacks. The issue between Rome and Canterbury, it is true, like that between Canterbury and Geneva, was basically the same conflict between two rival authorities, but in the case of Rome the position was at first purely political, even legal in its aspects. Moreover, by his time the Catholics represented a minority of the population who were very much on the defensive, and whose power and popularity were gravely prejudiced by the alliance between the Papacy and Spain. The general effect of the Roman controversy on Hooker was to make him an Erastian, for the obvious defence against the claims of Rome was the anti-papal legislation of Henry VIII and Elizabeth. The denial of the papal authority was found most patently at hand not in the New Testament, but in various Acts of Parliament. The best counterblast to the theory of Papal Supremacy was the Royal Supremacy. England was an Empire, supreme and independent. And until the development of the later High Anglican theory of the divine right of Episcopacy the apologists of the Church of England were all Erastians, as Hooker's predecessors —Jewel and Whitgift—had been. They could hardly be anything else, for they believed in the identity of Church and State.[2] And

[1] All eight books of the *Ecclesiastical Polity* are directed against Puritan not Roman objections to the Church of England, as the titles themselves show. But Hooker was quite capable of highly forceful language and weighty argument, tinctured with irony, in denouncing Rome's pretensions. (See Sermon V, Keble, III, 659–80.)

[2] " I perceive no such distinction of a Commonwealth and the Church that they should be counted, as it were, two several bodies "; and, " In respect of the external Society of the same (i.e., the Church), and the supreme authority that is given of God to the prince over his people in all causes, he may be also in that respect called the head of the Church." Whitgift's *Defence of the Answer*, I, 21, 391.

they were most anxious to emphasize their antipathy to Rome, for they were mainly Calvinists in theology, and were friendly with many of the most famous Continental reformers.

Thus the principal antagonist whom Hooker had to meet was not the Jesuit from Douai, but the Puritan fanatic imbued with the ideas of Calvin, and desirous of making Canterbury a second Geneva. But the essence of the defence will be the same—the Empire of England could not tolerate the claim of a part to be independent. Hooker therefore makes it his first task to give an historical account of the origin and evolution of the Puritan Discipline, intending thereby, as he candidly observes, to " rip up to the very bottom, how and by whom your Discipline was planted. . . ." [1]

Above all things, the first essential was to break the magic of all that the name of Calvin somehow or other cast over Protestant opinion. Most of the Preface is devoted to this. Hooker admits that Calvin, the founder of the Church of his name, was " incomparably the wisest man " that ever the Huguenots had. He had come to Geneva in 1536, when the Government was democratic and power in the hands of officers annually chosen by the people. But in ecclesiastical matters there was no uniformity of government, and individual pastors had to depend on what they could accomplish by their personal influence. Having become one of their ministers, and perceiving the danger that the welfare of the Church should be at the mercy of the fickle and ignorant populace, Calvin, aided by Farel and Couraut, persuaded the people, not without difficulty, to take an oath: first, never to admit Romanism again, and, secondly, to obey a form of Church government drawn up by these ministers and vouched by them to be in accordance with Scripture. But it was not long before the Genevans regretted this oath, and began " irefully to champ upon the bit they had taken into their mouths ", [2] since they were becoming estranged from the other Swiss Churches. Hooker points out that the Swiss Churches had only one fundamental thing in common—hatred of Rome. [3] Each Church was independent, and made strides to get as far from Rome as possible, and the farther it was removed, the more perfect a Church it considered itself; so that between them jealousies, jars, and discords sprang up. Every such Church declared the entirety of its own way to be necessary to salvation, which, from the great differences

[1] *E.P.*, Preface, i, 3. Bancroft, likewise perceiving the value of this method, gives a similar account in the second chapter of his *Survey of the Pretended Holy Discipline*.

[2] *E.P.*, Preface, ii, 2.

[3] Cf. also *E.P.*, V, 5, i, 28: " As that, In outward things belonging to the service of God, reformed Churches ought by all means to shun conformity with the Church of Rome."

existing between them (since they had only one fundamental in common and that a negative), effectively prevented any union. Not one of them could admit error, " and therefore that which once they had done, they became for ever after resolute to maintain ".[1]

In 1538 the Church of Geneva mustered courage to banish Calvin, together with Farel and Couraut, for refusing the Communion to those who would not live according to their oath of obedience, but in 1541 the Senate clamoured for him to return. They hoped Calvin would be more complaisant, and in any event " it was not unlikely but that his credit in the world might many ways stand the poor town in great stead ".[2] His reputation among other countries had certainly been " the best stake in their hedge ". But his price was no longer a tenancy-at-will under the people; they were obliged to accept by sworn oath a complete form of discipline to bind them and theirs for ever.

The scheme of the Discipline was the erection of a standing ecclesiastical court, the ministers being perpetual judges; but the people were to choose annual representatives, at the rate of two for each minister, to sit as judges; the court had power over all men's manners, and all ecclesiastical causes, with authority to punish, as far as excommunication, any one, great and small. A convenient device, Hooker admits, in the particularly unsettled state of Geneva, and a frank offer, two laymen to one minister.[3] But many, especially among the ministers, were not in favour of the Discipline, since other Reformed Churches managed to live orderly without it, and it seemed little better than Popish tyranny in a new form. Frank as the proposal appeared, Hooker cleverly shows that it was in effect very much a " one-man " scheme; for the people's representatives were annual, and would therefore be in awe of the ministers' learning and perpetual authority, while the latter themselves would be dominated by Calvin. Some could see this, but had either to accept it or banish Calvin again and appear foolish; so " they thought it better to be somewhat hardly yoked at home, than for ever abroad discredited ".[4]

This in itself would go far to prove the Discipline had no divine origin; but still better evidence remained. In 1553 these " twice-sworn " men in their Senate made a last assault on the Discipline by relaxing from the Elders' excommunication one named Bertelier, claiming to be themselves the final appeal in cases of excommunication. Calvin at once threatened to leave Geneva, whereupon the Senate suspended their decree until the judgement of the other Swiss

---

[1] *E.P.*, Preface, ii, 2. [2] *E.P.*, Preface, ii, 3.
[3] *E.P.*, Preface, ii, 4. [4] *Ibid.*

Churches could be taken. There is no doubt that Calvin wrote urgently and earnestly to the latter that things would go ill at Geneva unless he and his fellow-ministers were supported by strong approval; their answer *must* contain " an absolute approbation of the Discipline of Geneva as consonant unto the word of God, without any cautions, qualifications, ifs and ands ", and should *not* contain any suggested innovation.[1] Such earnestness was displayed, according to Beza, " for that he saw how needful these bridles were, to be put in the jaws of that city ". Hooker's comment is " that which by wisdom he saw to be requisite for that people, was by as great wisdom compassed ".[2]

Hooker next charges Calvin with wresting the Scriptures for the purpose of maintaining his Discipline. " Wise men are men, and the truth is the truth." Calvin had acted adroitly in establishing the Discipline, but his effort to that end was more praiseworthy than " that which he taught for the countenancing of it established ". He was in love with his own counsels, his own device, to such an extent that every passage in Scripture, if it was in the least degree possible, he interpreted as intending his Discipline. By virtue of his influence as the author of the " Institute ", and as the foremost exegetist, he enjoyed an enormous advantage and could do this; if other scholars interpreted Scripture after him in contrary direction, Calvin had the advantage of prejudice against them; if their explanations were the same as his, then of " glory above them ".[3] Hence it followed that " the perfectest divines were judged they which were skilfullest in Calvin's writings. His books almost the very canon to judge both doctrine and discipline by." [4] Consequently, just as Papalists believed that the Church of Rome could not err, Calvinists in Switzerland, France, and Scotland held the Church of Geneva was infallible. In this fashion spread that Discipline which of itself at first was so weak that, without the approbation of the other Swiss Churches, it could not have been established, yet now challenged universal obedience, including those very Churches that had come to its support.[5]

Hooker then proceeds to explain the reasons for the wide acceptance of the Genevan Discipline, and here his touch is remarkably sure. First, the faults of those in authority have been " ripped up" with severe reproof in the hearing of the multitude—a task which easily earns a man the credit of virtue. Then every fault and corruption in the world is attributed to the kind of ecclesiastical government established—which secures a reputation for wisdom. Hooker illustrates this attitude again later, pointing out the mischief

[1] *E.P.*, Preface, ii, 6.   [2] *E.P.*, Preface, ii, 7.
[3] *E.P.*, Preface, ii, 8.   [4] *Ibid.*   [5] *Ibid.*

that must ensue to Church and State alike. "The best stratagem that Satan hath, who knoweth his kingdom to be no one way more shaken than by public devout prayers of God's Church, is by traducing the form and manner of them to bring them into contempt, and so to shake the force of all men's devotion towards them."[1] The natural sequence is to propose the Genevan Church as a sovereign remedy for all these evils—as in sickness some men put faith in remedies frequently commended, but infrequently tried. Lastly, the minds of men have been so worked upon that whatever they approve of in Scripture they make refer to the Discipline; while their leaders flatter them that it is by special illumination of the Holy Ghost that they can discern the Scriptures and others cannot; their opinions are framed by their affections, a mental state which always makes men more earnest in defence of error. This sense of special illumination furnishes to the "faithful" a conviction of being *sealed* as God's children, so that they and they alone are "the brethren", "the Godly", while all others are "worldings, time-servers". Lest the spirit be quenched, they try to inflame it by meetings and conferences with one another, and not least by their propaganda. Women, weaker in reason and judgment than men, play a large part in influencing their relatives and friends and comforting the preachers; but, be they women or men, they will listen to no reasoned argument, and annoyingly clinch matters by calmly stating, "We are of God; he that knoweth God heareth us. . . . Ye are of the world".[2] They are no whit different in all this from the Anabaptists; unamenable to logic or reason, they defame magistrates as bloodthirsty when the latter are compelled to punish them in the interests of law and order.

He challenges[3] the leaders, those "whose judgment is a lantern of direction for all the rest", to prove by their learning the necessity for the Discipline. "A very strange thing sure it were, that such a discipline as ye speak of should be taught by Christ and his Apostles in the word of God and no church ever have found it out . . . till this present time";[4] whereas the form of government they attack has in fact existed universally since the first days of Christianity. He invites them to name a single Church, from Apostolic times, established on the Genevan model and not on Episcopacy. The Puritans maintain, indeed, that their model is the most ancient, but this is for fashion's sake; it is not seriously intended, for Cartwright's own book denies it to be safe to follow the precedents of any age from

[1] *E.P.*, V, 26, i, pp. 121–2.
[2] "Which cloak sitteth no less fit on the back of their cause, than of the Anabaptists." (*E.P.*, Preface, iii, 14.)
[3] *E.P.*, Preface, iv, 1.
[4] Cf. Bancroft's *Sermon*, 1588, pp. 10, 11.

the Apostles onwards. In so far as they commend the Apostolic pattern, it is with an ulterior motive—namely, they yawn for Anglican clergy to experience Apostolic poverty, in order to take of the spoils! But if clerical poverty is the sign of the truly Primitive Church, then Rome alone can be that Church, which abounds in poor mendicant Orders. But, he drily continues, the poverty of the early Christians was not confined to the clergy—the laity were included. Bring *that* state of things about " and in this reformation there will be, though little wisdom, yet some indifference ".[1]

But the cry, " Back to the Apostles ", is an absurdity, for nowhere is the full polity of the then existing Church revealed in Scripture. There were developments even in Apostolic, and certainly in sub-apostolic, times (and the Puritans anyhow discredit precedents of antiquity); and since they insist that the foundations of " anti-Christ " were laid in those very Apostolic times, it is difficult to know " wherein we are to keep ourselves unto the pattern of their times ". The appeal to antiquity cannot be sustained, for one might fetch a love-feast as well as a deacon from that source.

Failing the appeal to antiquity, the only other authority they boast is the judgements of certain foreign Reformers.[2] This is not particularly weighty evidence, for some of them are in quality " very near the dregs "; nor are the best so infallible that the laws of the Anglican Church should yield to them. In any case, not all the eminent Reformers agree that the Discipline is necessary, and the majority of those who do so only follow Calvin. If the Discipline is now universal, there is no necessary cogency in that.[3] It was set up at Geneva at a critical time in that town's history, when something had to be done; this device was speedily produced, and it attracted the multitude by the power apparently given to them. Other Churches later copied the material points of the Genevan, but this fact is no additional *argument*. " Though ten persons be brought to give testimony in any cause, yet if the knowledge they have . . . appear to have grown from some one amongst them . . . they are all in force but as one testimony. Nor is it otherwise here where the daughter Churches do speak their mother's dialect; here where so many sing one song, by reason that he (i.e., Calvin) is the guide of the choir." [4] Whatever degree of admiration may be felt for Luther and Calvin by their uncritical disciples, these men are not infallible; and he ironically concludes, " Yet are we not able to define, whether the wisdom of that God . . . might not permit those worthy vessels of His glory to be in some things blemished with the stain of human frailty." [5]

[1] *E.P.*, Preface, iv, 3.   [2] *E.P.*, Preface, iv, 6.
[3] *E.P.*, Preface, iv, 7, 8.   [4] *E.P.*, Preface, iv, 8.   [5] *Ibid.*

Anglican and Puritan being in diametric opposition, there can be no peace until the rival positions are submitted to an arbiter, but it is unreasonable to expect the laws to be suspended " till some disputer can persuade you to be obedient ". A final authority there must be, as Nature, Scripture, and experience alike teach. There are only two possible judges :[1] either the Government of the country or a General Council of the Church. Scripture abounds in precedents for bringing disputes to magistrates and judges; their sentence is definitive, and thereby controversy ends. God Himself appointed such judges, though He knew they were fallible men and would not always decide correctly; but better that sometimes an erroneous verdict should be given than that strifes be permitted to grow.[2] A judicial decision is " ground sufficient for any reasonable man's conscience to build the duty of obedience upon ".[3] But all England knows what the Puritans think of her ecclesiastical Courts—therefore a General Council, which Beza [4] (" in his last book save one ") himself desired, may be their preference. However, until such time come the Puritans are advised to re-examine their case, and to consider what it is they purpose to overthrow, " sith equity and reason, the law of nature, God and man, do all favour that which is in being, till orderly judgment of decision be given against it ".[5] They had better weigh their reasons well for attacking the established Church, in order to discover if they are so logically cogent that the mind is compelled to assent. If they are less than this they cannot be more than probabilities, and nothing was ever established in the world but that some " probable show " might be made against it.[6]

Having demonstrated the nature and origin of the Genevan Discipline and the method of its establishment and propagation, Hooker turns in detail to the question of authority. He emphasizes that in all things in life—laws or anything else—Nature teaches man to discern good from evil by the force of his discretion. In all matters of plain right and wrong this is relatively simple. But many other things that enter into Christian men's lives are too obscure, too intricate, to be thus easily judged; hence God has given to certain men special faculties for discovering the truth, so that their understanding may be a light to direct others.[7] God

---

[1] *E.P.*, Preface, vi, 2.
[2] *E.P.*, Preface, vi, 3.   [3] *Ibid.*
[4] " That in some common lawful assembly of Churches all these strifes may at once be decided." (Beza: *Praefatio de Presbyteris et Excommunicatione*, London, J. Norton, 1590.)
[5] *E.P.*, Preface, vi, 5.
[6] *E.P.*, Preface, vi, 6.
[7] *E.P.*, Preface, iii, 1, 2. Cf. Pecock's *Repressor*, Part I, caps. 9, 16.

is the God of peace and order, not of confusion; and the matters which simple Puritan minds discuss are too deep for them. Indeed, their own Calvin denies to private men the right of discussing the best form of civil policy; are simple people, then, the wisest judges of what ecclesiastical government in this country is most fitting? The recently executed Penry is appositely quoted as stating, "With whom the truth is I will not determine, for I know not"; [1] if a leader writes thus, how can the mass of his followers expect to have precise knowledge by the light of their mere private judgement? That the ignorant should trespass in fields which are of necessity reserved to those equipped to find the path is always to Hooker intolerable. "It behoveth generally all sorts of men to keep themselves within the limits of their own vocation. . . . They that in anything exceed the compass of their own order do as much as in them lieth to dissolve that order which is the harmony of God's Church." [2] This is akin to Plato's statement of the nature of justice, which is simply that everyone should mind his own business; [3] that the whole should be perfect it is necessary that the parts perform their proper motions. This conception of wholeness, of symmetry, is a trait of Hooker's mind common with the Greeks.

He then carries the war into the enemy's camp by pointing out that there were divisions even among the English Puritans, as the Brownist schism showed very plainly. The more wary Puritans do not commend their hastiness, and "with merciful terms" reprove their error, calling them "poor brethren", only to have "false brethren" flung back at them, and the superior logic of the Brownists' position pointed out. George Cranmer had, in a letter to Hooker, indicated that the Brownists were more logical. [4] He wrote, "Here come the Brownists in the first rank, their lineal descendants, who have seized upon a number of strange opinions; whereof although their ancestors the reformers were never actually possessed, yet by right and interest from them derived, the Brownist and Barrowists have taken possession of them. For if the positions of the reformers be true, I cannot see how the main and general conclusions of Brownism should be false." [5] The Brownist argues against the Puritan, "For adventuring to erect the discipline of Christ without the leave of the Christian Magistrate, haply ye may condemn us as fools, in that we hazard thereby our estates and persons further than

---

[1] Penry, Petition directed to the Queen, p. 3: Bancroft's *Survey*, p. 342.

[2] *E.P.*, V, 62, xii, 29.

[3] *Republic*, Book IV (ed. Jowett, Oxford, 1921).

[4] Cf. Kennedy's *Elizabethan Episcopal Administration* (1924), I, clx. "It was little wonder that the conscientious and logical sectaries, like the Brownists, despised them as trimmers." (Cf. *E.P.*, Preface, viii, 1.)

[5] *E.P.*, V, App. II, pp. 602, 603: letter from George Cranmer to Hooker.

you . . . but . . . with what conscience can you accuse us, when your own positions are that the things we observe should every one of them be dearer unto us than ten thousand lives? . . . When God commandeth shall we answer that we will obey, if so be Caesar will grant us leave? Is discipline an ecclesiastical matter or a civil?" This last question, after all, puts the Puritan position in a nutshell, and when the Independent continues, reminding Cartwright and his friends that they had applauded the action of Reformers abroad in establishing the Discipline against the will of the magistrate, we feel with Hooker that the Brownist has correctly drawn his schismatic conclusion from Puritan principles. "Him therefore we leave to be satisfied by you from whom he hath sprung."[1]

The need for authority demonstrated, Hooker seeks to find a more adequate basis for it than Scripture. According to the Puritans, Scripture contained, not merely the principle of Church government, but the form itself. "The discipline of Christ's Church, that it is necessary for all times, is delivered by Christ, and set down in the Holy Scriptures. Therefore the true and lawful discipline is to be fetched from thence, and from thence alone. And that which resteth upon any other foundation ought to be esteemed unlawful and counterfeit."[2] Therefore, in doctrinal or institutional religion, to add to or to deviate from Scripture was impossible.

On the contrary, Hooker would reply that life must be directed and governed by "all the sources of light and truth with which man finds himself encompassed", and that Scripture deals with only a definite field in man's experience of life.[3] He asks (as Pecock before him) how can it "stand with reason to make the bare mandate of Sacred Scripture the only rule of all good and evil in the actions of mortal men"?[4] For example, the Puritans omit natural law, to which all human institutions, civil and religious, must conform, for "obedience of creatures unto the law of nature is the stay of the whole world".[5] As Natural Law is discoverable by the light of human reason, reason therefore itself is one of the guides of man's life.[6]

---

[1] *E.P.*, Preface, viii, 1.
[2] Cartwright's *Admonition*.
[3] Cf. Dowden: "The liberal spirit of the Renaissance, which does honour to every human faculty, reacts in Hooker against the narrower spirit of the Reformation." *Puritan and Anglican*, p. 89.
[4] *E.P.*, II, viii, 5.
[5] *E.P.*, I, iii, 3.
[6] The point is well put by Sanderson in the Preface (1657) to his sermons (London, 7th ed., 1681). "When God gave us the light of His holy word, He left us, as He found us, reasonable creatures still; without any purpose, by His gift of that greater and sublimer light, to put out the light He had formerly given us (that of reason) or to render it useless and unserviceable."

Therefore he proceeds to defend the Elizabethan Church as conformable not only to Scripture, but also to Reason, and argues that any reasonable being who is not an extremist can accept it. He declines to wrest Scripture in order to find the polity of the Church precisely within it, but sets out to prove, by appeal to first principles and to history, that the Church of England is the same Church as primitive Christians knew, and membership of it consequently rational.

Now for Hooker, as for most other contemporary thinkers and all mediaevalists, Church and State were one and the same, two aspects of one society. "We mean by the Commonwealth, that society with relation unto all public affairs thereof, only the matter of religion excepted; by the Church, the same society, with only reference unto the matter of true religion, without any other affair besides." Therefore, if certain people refuse to obey the laws of the Church, presided over by the Sovereign, they equally refuse to obey the State; and that is sedition. Clearly the real issue is that of authority. But authority is a product of law; hence he discusses at once and at length the nature of law and the problems of sovereignty and obedience. Hooker was, in fact, one of the few people who, from roughly 1550 to 1800, saw that the real core of the problem of government, the harmony of sovereignty and obedience, is the element of consent. This, indeed, constitutes one of his chief claims to greatness; here, as in the limitations placed by him on the power of the sovereign, he seems an original Whig, and the direct forerunner of Sidney, Locke, and Rousseau; while also he seems to found a school of philosophic conservatism of which later the ornament was Burke. We might be reading the *Ecclesiastical Polity* when, in his *Reflections on the French Revolution*, Burke says, "A disposition to preserve, and an ability to improve, taken together, would be my standard of a statesman,"[1] insisting that where we cannot immediately improve we must venerate. But Whig or Conservative, Hooker, in his defence of the Elizabethan Settlement, is going beyond question to move towards the modern Sovereign State.

Law being the basis and source of all authority, institutions, whether in Church or State, have their sanction and justification in their adequacy and reasonableness to allow life and development according to law. These institutions are expressions of a corporate life, and, the form being of less importance than the matter, have the right to develop according to their needs. This separates Hooker at once from the Puritans, whose conception of institutions and of law was static. Rightly enough, therefore, Hooker begins

[1] Everyman ed., p. 153.

CHAPTER IV

LAW AND AUTHORITY

" In heaven ", I replied, " there is laid up a pattern of it, methinks, which he who desires may behold, and beholding may set his own house in order." [1] It is for ever upon the heavenly pattern that Hooker's eyes are fixed; all laws that are good are comprehended within the Law Eternal; all true laws are therefore in a sense divine, all good laws rational, since men " seem the makers of those laws which indeed are His, and they but only the finders of them out." [2] Plato voices a similar opinion at the beginning of *The Laws*:

" Athenian Stranger: ' Tell me, Strangers, is a God or some man supposed to be the author of your laws? '

" Cleinias: ' A God, Stranger; in very truth a God: Among us Cretans he is said to have been Zeus, but in Lacedaemon, whence our friend here comes, they would say that Apollo is their lawgiver. Would they not, Megillus? '

" Megillus: ' Certainly.' " [3]

It is significant that Jowett, in commenting on this passage, uses Hooker's own words as indicative of Plato's conception of law, " Her seat is the bosom of God, her voice the harmony of the world." [4] And Hooker goes on, " All things in Heaven and earth do her homage, the very least as feeling her care, and the greatest as not exempted from her power, both Angels and men and creatures of what condition soever, though each in different sort and manner, yet all with uniform consent, admiring her as the mother of their peace and joy." [5]

But though law breathes the majesty of God, and is the noblest fact of the universe, it possesses for Hooker a very practical importance as well as mystical beauty. It lay at the heart of the controversy between the Puritans and himself. Their quarrel resolved itself for all effective purposes into a struggle concerning the constitution and government of the Church, and nothing could be more germane to such an issue than the idea of law.

[1] Plato, *Republic*, Book IX, 591D (Jowett's trans.), Oxford, 1921.
[2] *E.P.*, I, viii, 3.
[3] *Laws*, Jowett's trans., Book I.
[4] Op. cit., Intro., lxxvi; *E.P.*, I, xvi, 8.
[5] *Ibid.*

Indebted as he undoubtedly is to Greek philosophy, Hooker goes to the scholastics—despised by Reformers and persecuted by Authority—for his ideas of law and nature. He expresses himself in agreement with Scotus, " the wittiest of the School-divines ",[1] whose name the bitterness of Protestant thought was destined to equate with Dunce.[2] St. Thomas Aquinas he declared to be " the greatest amongst the School-divines ",[3] and takes to his own use the Saint's categories of laws, though with original modifications. This is not surprising, for it is doubtful if all the efforts of authority had succeeded in replacing Aquinas with Calvin in that University which is noted for its loyalty to the hallowed past.[4] He therefore deliberately turns to them when he bases his theories of law and society on the Law of Nature. Thereby he earns the scorn of his opponents, who accuse him in the *Christian Letter* of exalting reason against Scripture on the authority of Aristotle and the Schoolmen; but he is equal to the occasion. " If Aristotle and the Schoolmen be such perilous creatures, you must needs think yourself an happy man, whom God hath so fairly blest from too much knowledge in them."[5] Thus it was that Hooker ensured the continued existence of ideas on law, nature, and the individual which, notwithstanding the changes such terms would undergo, left lasting traces and exercised profound influence on English political thought.

The Puritans maintained in essence the existence of two laws: the divine, as revealed in the Scriptures, and the purely human law of the world. The first was the touchstone for all human activity, the latter had no real place in a Christian community. They therefore distinguished Church from State, as two separate kingdoms; the Church enjoys a rigid, immutable government, divine in origin, function, and purpose, while the civil State is a purely human affair, alterable according to circumstances, and in no sense divine. The civil State should therefore be ordered according to the Law of God (as interpreted by the Puritans), which in effect would ensure a supremacy to the Church over the State. The Bible, not legal statutes, is the criterion of human rights, and an ample guide to political and civil life. Thus human reason had nothing to do with the question. They were here following the orthodox Protestant teaching about Original Sin. The early Reformers had taught that man is a being, now bruised and stained

[1] *E.P.*, I, xi, 5.
[2] Croce remarks (*Aesthetic*, p. 207, London, 1922) that the works of Scotus were reprinted and widely read in the seventeenth century.
[3] *E.P.*, III, ix, 2.
[4] Cf. Mallet: *History of the University of Oxford* (Methuen, 1924), II, 62 *et seq.*
[5] Paget, *Introduction to Book V*, p. 266, note; Bayne, op. cit., p. 627.

with sin, fallen from his primitive bliss; his will, therefore, has no quality of goodness, his intellect no light, his whole being is deprived of all power of right living. Nay, more, of the illumination, the goodness, the rectitude that once were his, he desires the opposites. Man in the strength of his human nature can therefore play no great role. Weighed down with sin, he has no freedom, except in the trifling things of material life.[1] Luther could say man is the devil's prisoner, the human world is Satan's kingdom; "liberum arbitrium per sese in omnibus hominibus est regnum Satanae". On this foundation the great Reformers built their notions of law, moral, natural, and positive.

The Catholic view was that divine justice differs from human not really in kind but in degree; it is, of course, infinitely sublime, and beyond man's comprehension, but nevertheless there is a harmonious relation between God and man, between God's justice and the attempts of man to fulfil His moral law, between God's will and man's free will. Such teaching horrified the Reformers, who maintained that God has set His moral law in Scripture; it is complete, perfect, eternal; God Himself cannot abolish it. It is an image of perfect justice, composed not of many laws for right living, but of one only. It is *the law*. But, they added, however much men may strive for the perfection of that law, they can never accomplish it. The Catholic, of course, would point out the gravity of the implication—to subject man to living under a law which he knows he can never fulfil is to make him despair or presume; in judging his life by the standard of that law he can find only damnation for himself. The Calvinist will answer that here is justification by faith; man is a debtor to God, and cannot pay, but as he abases himself and accepts the free gift of pardon and grace through Christ, he, if he be of the elect, will be raised to God Himself. There can be no question of legal relationship between God and man, of working or atoning for wrong; no idea of a balance as between parties can be entertained, for God alone is the author of man's bliss. Justice is a balance of harmony which can exist only in the thought of God—for man it has no meaning. "On cherchait une équation. On trouve une identité." [2]

Man can play only that part in life which God wills. He chooses His elect; He fills them with His works or not. The core of the moral law is the free will of God directing the unresisting hand of man as seems good to him. Little need we wonder at the rigidity of the Puritan mind with such notions of an inflexible Deity, with

---

[1] *E.g.*, " De Servo Arbitrio " (*Werke*, ed. Weimar, XVIII, 707, and cf. pp. 627, 658, 749–50).

[2] Lagarde, *Recherches sur l'esprit politique de la Réforme* (Douai, p. 165, 1926).

F

whom justice is scarce different from caprice. "Justice effroyable d'un Père qui engendre des enfants pour les vouer à la mort éternelle." [1]

Such being the conception of the Reformers of the nature of law in its moral sense, and of the utter worthlessness of man and all things belonging to him, we cannot expect much place being given, or dignity ascribed, to either natural or positive law. The Law of Nature had always been, even among pagan writers, a grand conception, while Catholic theology taught that it was a reflection of the light of God in the mind of man, a link between God and man simply as man.

Luther admitted the existence of some degree of conscience in man, but it was scarcely perceptible (a "paltry desire") [2] amid the passions for sin that all men know. He would not allow that by the light of natural reason man could attain to the principles of right living. [3] Such ideas he dismissed with contempt as belonging to mere philosophy. Zwingli, humanist though he was, also showed little favour to human reason as a guide to life; if the so-called Law of Nature could be called a law at all, it could gain no force or value from the corrupt nature of man. Man's reason was a slave to emotions and passions, and the Law of Nature could owe nothing to man. In grand phrase he defines law as nothing else but the Eternal Will of GOD, but proceeds at once to narrow down his conception. He has not "civil laws" in mind, he says, laws which touch the "outward man"; the only true law is that which governs the inner man. Therefore when the heathen fulfil the law—promulgated to them by no tables—this obedience derives not from the light of natural reason but from the direction of GOD. GOD and He alone is the direct source—"At in corda nemo scribit nisi solus deus "—for men were ignorant as to the nature of sin and as to what ought to be done or refrained from except by the instruction of GOD. [4] Calvin agreed that some spark of the divine image must remain in man, separating him from brute creation, but though his will had not completely perished, it had reached such a depth of evil that it could not desire good, and was almost extinguished. [5]

The consensus of belief, then, among these teachers was that natural law could owe nothing estimable to human nature; it might

---

[1] Lagarde, op. cit., p. 168.

[2] " Parvulus motus animi."

[3] " Commentary on the Epistle to the Romans" (*Werke*, ed. Weimar, LVI, 271-7).

[4] See e.g. *De Vera et Falsa Religione* : Zwingli, Opera. Tom. II, pp. 182 et seq. (1581). Zürich.

[5] *L'Institution de la Religion Chrestienne*, ed. Lefranc, 1541 ed., Paris, 1911, I, ii, pp. 64-8, 85-6.

appear to come from man, but was nothing else than the will of God in action. Nature was only a projection of God, having no independent existence, hence no qualities of its own. God was all and in all: " un Dieu qui gouverne et conduit sans cesse ".[1] The Law of Nature could have, as law, no independent existence; to emphasize its natural character was to elevate human reason, which could only compass iniquity; to insist on its qualities as a law was to limit the absolutism of God, and was blasphemy. In so far as it might be a law, it could only be as contained within the Mosaic Law or the Gospel, part of the revelation of the divine will.

Hence, however freely the Reformers might use the term, they denied to the Law of Nature any existence in the reason of man, any character of law, any value as a source for positive law. Law for them was the Jewish Law,[2] which included the moral within it—a confusion of the civil and moral spheres logically resulting from their doctrine of justification by faith. Positive Law was for brigands, bandits, and sinners, compelled by its sword to be outwardly virtuous, but the Christian had no need of it. Law was robbed of its spiritual element, and stood only for command as naked as the sword that, in the hands of the law-giver, should avenge every breach of it: " lex coactiva, non directiva ". But the Catholic world had held that, while law was physically coercive, it was also morally obligatory; hence positive laws must be founded in reason: the force of law must come from its own virtue, not merely from the constraint of the law-giver; from its matter as well as from its form.

But defenders of the true character of the Law of Nature, and of law, were to arise even in the ranks of the Protestants. Contrary to the teaching of their masters, these disciples maintained that natural law did exist as good and pure law. It was natural because the light of man's reason taught it, and by his own strength he could fulfil it. Moreover, this law by its own light revealed the measure and purpose of man's life on earth. Hence, fifty years later, against the Calvinist Puritans in England, as Arminius against Gomarus in Holland, Hooker constituted himself the defender of the Law of Nature, teaching that it was a light of the human reason, which man might know apart from revelation; that the Bible does not contain the sum of all political and moral life.

The task that Hooker set himself was to demonstrate that, in refusing the law of the Church, the Puritans refused their obligations as members of a political society. He saw that in this task, and in

---

[1] Lagarde, op. cit., p. 173.
[2] See Scott Pearson: *T. Cartwright and Elizabethan Puritanism* (Cambridge, 1925), p. 90.

the complement of proving the lawfulness of the Tudor Supremacy, he must first get to the foundation of the problem, and study the true nature of law itself and the ground of political obligation. First, therefore, he defines law, passing on to a classification of laws (in categories similar to St. Thomas'), insisting that all true laws have an eternal character. They are founded on *Law*, which is itself eternal, being, at its highest, the counsel of God; therefore all laws must partake of this character too. With Hooker law is almost entirely *directiva*; we read little of the *vis coactiva*. In the divine order of the universe God has appointed a law for Himself; man, being in the image of God, must live a life of law if he is to retain that image; the essence of man's life must be law, akin as he is to God in intellect and soul.

Hooker then proceeds to a detailed examination of law. Everything that exists must function towards its natural purpose; its functioning is neither violent nor casual, but is performed in obedience to a directive power which appoints to anything its function, force, form, measure, and purpose. That which so appoints, Hooker defines as a law. All things exist for a purpose, and if that purpose is to be fulfilled, actions must be regulated by some canon or law; if not, all existence would be aimless and capricious. In this sense, indeed, the operations of God Himself are lawful. Thus everything that exists according to its nature is subject to law, and law implies an author. Of His works God is both the Author and the Law, for His own perfection is given to His works. But "dangerous it were for the feeble brain of man to wade far into the doings of the Most High . . . our safest eloquence concerning Him is our silence. . . . He is above and we upon earth; therefore it behoveth our words to be wary and few ".[1]

God is a law to Himself for the operations which He does; such operations have their purposes, and those purposes are a reason for His will to do them. "That and nothing else is done by God, which to leave undone were not so good." [2] This, God's law or counsel, is perfect, incomprehensible to man, and eternal; because it is eternal, therefore it is immutable. This is the *first Eternal Law*, " That order which God before all ages hath set down with Himself, for Himself to do all things by ".[3] Elsewhere, in a magnificent passage, Hooker enlarges this when he says, " All things which God in their times and seasons hath brought forth were eternally and before all times in God, as a work unbegun is in the artificer which afterwards bringeth it unto effect. Therefore we do now behold in this present world, it was enwrapped within the bowels of divine Mercy, written in the book of Eternal Wisdom, and held in the

---

[1] *E.P.*, I, ii, 2.   [2] *E.P.*, I, ii, 3.   [3] *E.P.*, I, ii, 6.

hands of Omnipotent Power, the first foundations of the world being as yet unlaid." [1]   It is divine reason governing the universe, and this *ratio gubernationis* has the character of law; the purpose of this divine government is God Himself, hence His law is none other than Himself.

But, Hooker proceeds, there is a second Eternal Law, and here he emphasizes that his definition of law is " any kind of rule or canon, whereby actions are framed ", differing from those who define law as a " rule of working which superior authority imposeth ".[2]   This second Eternal Law embraces all true laws, all the laws of God's creation, natural (for non-human agents), celestial (for spirits), moral, scriptural (or supernatural), and human positive law (for men), for all are laid up in the counsel of God.   In short, everything that is true to its nature and purpose conforms to this second Eternal Law.[3]   As Aquinas puts it, " Id omne, quod in rebus creatis fit, est materia legis aeternae "; and again, " Sic igitur legi aeternae subduntur omnia, quae sunt in rebus a Deo creatis, sive sint contingentia, sive sint necessaria." [4]

He then takes the first of these classes of law—the operation of the " starry firmament above "—before he proceeds to the " moral law within ".   By the *Law of Nature* [5] Hooker means the orderly existence of creation, its uniform working.   " The end why the Heavens do move, the Heavens themselves know not, and their motions they cannot but continue." [6]   It is the law for non-voluntary natural agents, " who keep the law of their kind unwittingly ".[7] Although it chances now and then that some part of creation swerve from its law, yet " no man denieth but those things which nature worketh are wrought, either always or for the most part, after one and the same manner ".   These natural agents fulfil their functions, since God in his first Law Eternal has willed their purposes.   So man can speak of God's Providence in appointing such law for created nature, and of natural destiny when that nature fulfils its purpose.   " Nature therefore is nothing else but God's instrument."   In this treatment Hooker is original, for with St. Thomas, as with most other philosophers, the Law of Nature is what Hooker will call the Law of Reason, that participation which *rational* creatures have in God's eternal law by virtue of their reason.   This, of course, was the crux of the whole matter.   An examination of the Eternal Law, the Law of Nature and the Celestial Law was necessary to him simply as part of Hooker's

---

[1] *E.P.*, V, 56, vi, 248.   [2] *E.P.*, I, iii, 1.   [3] *Ibid.*
[4] *S.T. Prima Sec.* Qu. 93 Art. 4.   [5] *E.P.*, I, iii, 2-5.
[6] " Sermon on Pride," III, 599.
[7] Harrington, in his *Oceana*, makes a basic use of this.   See pp. 208, 209 *infra.*

system, but the real controversy raged round the type of law connected with human life.

Passing over the second division, *Celestial Law* [1]—the law for spirits, such as angels—we come to God's law for man, divided into moral (the Law of Reason), human positive law (*i.e.* State laws and International Law), and Supernatural Law, or Scriptural. Before dealing with these particulars of laws for men, Hooker has much to say of man's natural capacity for living according to law. It is of God's Eternal Law that man should seek Him—that is, what is good—since this is so, and since man is an effect of God, he is like his Maker, and will therefore imitate Him. Hence man, striving *ever* after an eternal ideal, procreates his species. Sensible capacity man shares with beasts, but he alone is able to reach higher than sensible things, and to struggle towards divine perfection. Consequently the history of man is a history of gradual progress and improvement, due to education, experience, and instruction, by which processes his natural faculty of reason is abler and quicker in judging rightly between truth and error.

By his reason man comes to know of things both sensible and not sensible, but even his reason needs some spur to its working towards unsensible things. Being like his Maker, he works freely and wittingly, having knowledge of the end of his operations, and will to choose his course of action. [2] Therefore where understanding and knowledge are lacking, reason directs man's will to discover what particular action is good, " for the Laws of well-doing are the dictates of right Reason ". [3] His will is free to choose or refuse, but man chooses *good* or what appears his good, since " evil as evil cannot be desired ". [4]

Everything naturally and necessarily desires the greatest good and utmost perfection of which Nature makes it capable, and so man. Man covets happiness, and his will inclines him to anything that makes for this, if reason judges well of it. Should reason err, he is to that extent deprived of the perfection he seeks. [5] But the basis of all choice is the knowledge of goodness—that is, straightness, rightness, beauty; evil is that which is crooked. Goodness may be known by its causes (but this is too deep a matter for " this present age, full of tongue and weak of brain ") or by its effects. The

[1] *E.P.*, I, iv.
[2] Hooker notes that an inferior sort of will exists in Appetite, the object of which is mere sensible good, but Will seeks that good which Reason dictates. " Appetite is the Will's solicitor, and the Will is Appetite's controller " (*E.P.*, I, vii, 3). Cf. Aristotle: appetite partakes of reason " in so far as it is obedient to it, and capable of submitting to its ruler " (*Nic. Eth.*, Lib. I, xiii, 17).
[3] *E.P.*, I, vii, 4.
[4] *E.P.*, I, vii, 6.
[5] *E.P.*, I, vii, 6, 7.

surest such effect is "if the general persuasion of all men do so account it".[1] This is *vox populi, vox Dei*; for "the general and perpetual voice of men is as the sentence of God Himself", since Nature herself must have taught what men have at all times believed. Whatever is so learned from Nature comes from God, and can be vouched as good, apart from any other warrant; therefore laws, universally assented to, are clearly good. Thus when St. Paul says that the heathen are a law to themselves,[2] he means that God illuminates the reason of every man whereby he may learn good from evil, truth from falsity. "Under the name of the Law, we must comprehend not only that which God hath written in tables and leaves, but that which nature hath engraven in the hearts of men."[3] Yet man, having by natural reason this knowledge, deems himself the author of these laws, of which he is only the finder-out.

Now, law in general is a "directive rule unto operation of goodness",[4] and reason is man's rule, which pronounces on the goodness (or not) of any purposed operation. Further, because it is a natural law that "the best produces the best", the first law for every man is that his highest faculty, the mind, should require obedience from his other faculties;[5] the mind must be supreme over the will. Natural reason has revealed to the mind of man laws as to the existence of God, the necessity of love and reverence for Him, of love for his neighbour, and suchlike, that are axiomatic.[6]

This, then, is the Moral Law of Reason, declaring by command, or by permission, or by warning, what man shall or shall not do, "which men by discourse of natural Reason have rightly found out themselves to be all for ever bound unto in their actions". The Laws of Nature have distinctive marks,[7] so that those who live by them most resemble Nature in that their works are "behoveful, beautiful, without superfluity or defect"; they can be investigated by reason, without the aid of divine revelation (i.e. Scripture); the knowledge of them is general, "the world hath always been acquainted with them". Any such law "is not agreed upon by one, or two, or few, but by all . . . such that being proposed no man can reject it as unreasonable and unjust". The Law of Reason, which men usually have called the Law of Nature, "mean-

[1] *E.P.*, I, viii, 3.
[2] Rom. 2. 14.
[3] "Sermon on Pride," III, 600.
[4] *E.P.*, I, viii, 4.
[5] *E.P.*, I, iii, 6; cf. Aristotle, *Pol.*, i, 5.
[6] *E.P.*, I, viii, 7.
[7] *E.P.*, I, viii, 9.

ing thereby the Law which human nature knoweth itself in reason universally bound unto . . . comprehendeth all those things which men by the light of their natural understanding evidently know, or at leastwise may know, to be beseeming or unbeseeming, virtuous or vicious, good or evil for them to do ".[1] Its basis is " an infallible knowledge printed in the minds of all the children of men, whereby both general principles for directing of human actions are comprehended, and conclusions derived from them ".[2] That is, simply, man has intuitions, reasoning upon which he can deduce principles as to right and wrong, and this becomes the Moral Law of Reason. The cumulative effect of all the decisions that man has to make is, in fact, free-will whether to act as an animal or in the proper function of a man. As the angels, in their pride, arrogated to themselves a position in creation higher than was properly theirs, man may degrade himself below his station. The effect is similar, in that it tends to destroy the symmetry and perfection of the whole. A false note, out of harmony, wanders disconsolately in the air, and has no part in the symphony. Even as " the creation of the world is a victory of persuasion over force ",[3] so man's observance of right laws is a victory of order over chaos, of the higher over the lower principle in man, and is therefore creative. Man is of creatures alone able to choose whether he will take his due place in creation, and the essentially voluntary nature of his actions demands that the law which governs him shall be primarily directive and persuasive, not arbitrary and coercive. He may obey and disobey; " he doth not otherwise than voluntarily the one or the other ",[4] and these laws are incumbent upon him to keep simply as a man, whether or not he be a member of a commonwealth.

So, having shown that Nature itself furnishes moral laws " to men as men ",[5] and that men are able to discover and fulfil them, Hooker proceeds to discuss the character of those laws which bind men as members of a " settled fellowship "—i.e. Human (or Positive) Law. At this point he is bound to reflect upon the origin of political society.[6] Human needs, wants, and fellowship (life " fit for the dignity of man ") are the groundwork of political society, which is itself natural. Such a society is a Commonwealth which has two foundations, " the one a natural inclination whereby all men desire sociable life and fellowship; the other, an order

---

[1] He quotes Sophocles (Antig. V, 456) : " it is no child of to-day's or yesterday's birth, but hath been no man knoweth how long sithence " (*E.P.*, I, viii, 9).
[2] *E.P.*, II, viii, 6.
[3] Plato: quoted Whitehead, *Adventures of Ideas* (Cambridge, 1943), pp. 31, 105.
[4] *E.P.*, I, ix, 1.
[5] *E.P.*, I, x, 1.
[6] Cf. Aristotle, *Pol.*, i, 2.

expressly or secretly agreed upon touching the manner of their union in living together ".[1] The latter foundation is of importance in any discussion as to Hooker's political philosophy of a " social compact "; for the present it is sufficient to observe that he regards the resultant law of a Commonwealth (its " soul ") as intended to prevent inconveniences arising to the whole body by reason of the transgression of the law of their nature by individuals. Therefore it is that " laws politic are never framed as they should be, unless presuming the will of man to be inwardly obstinate, rebellious and averse from all obedience unto the sacred laws of his nature ".[2] This law of the Commonwealth, to be perfect, must realize that man, apart from civil society, would use his powers for evil. Government is necessary to escape the worse evil of anarchy. Means must be provided to frame men's outward actions so that they do not hinder others. (In passing, we cannot but notice that though Hooker's conception of government and law is infinitely finer, his account of the " state of nature " differs at this point from that of Hobbes only in being less explicit.) So it was that men, desiring true happiness (which is not primarily material, for " of earthly blessings, the meanest is wealth ")[3] and self-preservation, ordained a political society, agreeing to yield themselves subject to it, that " unto whom they granted authority to rule and govern, by them the peace, tranquillity and happy estate of the rest might be procured ".[4] Otherwise, each would have to live for himself, and neither life nor property would be safe, since " each man is towards himself . . . partial ".[5] A ruler of some kind is appointed by general consent,[6] without which consent no one ought to take upon himself any such supremacy, unless, indeed, by the immediate appointment of God. Probably in the beginning a ruler governed absolutely,[7] but since " to live by one man's will became the cause of all men's misery ", laws were made prescribing duties and penalties.[8]

Thus positive municipal law both teaches what is a man's duty and enforces it. In the devising of positive municipal law, there-

[1] *E.P.*, I, x, 1.
[2] *Ibid.*
[3] *E.P.*, V, lxxvi, 2.
[4] *E.P.*, I, x, 4.
[5] For Milton's similar view, see pp. 206–7.
[6] Cf. Aristotle, *Pol.*, I, V, lib. iii and iv. Hooker does not agree that one man is " naturally " a governor. Cf. also *Pol.*, 1, 2.
[7] *E.P.*, I, x, 5.
[8] Cf. Plato's *Republic*, II, 358c. (ed. Jowett, Oxford, 1921). (Glaucon's statement as to the common opinion of the origin and nature of justice.) " And so when men have both done and suffered injustice and have had experience of both, not being able to avoid the one and obtain the other, they think that they had better agree among themselves to have neither; hence there arise laws and mutual covenants."

fore, care must be taken that only wise men be employed,[1] for only the most fitting things should be ordered. Obedience will be the more readily obtained, for although bad men will pay no heed to good advice, they will respect that advice once it is embodied as a law; "for why? they presume that the law doth speak with all indifferency ".[2]

But the sanction of law lies not in the wisdom of its makers, but in that power which gives it the strength of law—that is, in the power of its imposer.[3] Now, by natural Law of Reason the power of imposing laws on a whole political society belongs to that same society; no prince of any kind can impose laws (except he reign as a tyrant) unless he is expressly commissioned by God, or else by authority derived at the first from those on whom the laws are imposed. Hooker seizes on the necessity for public approbation and consent as an essence of Positive Law; [4] so far from its being an edict of the ruler, law must be the work of the whole body. This most valuable contribution to political theory Hooker certainly qualifies by stating that this consent is given as well by representa-tion as in person—" qui facit per alium facit per se "—by means of Parliaments, Councils, Assemblies. Moreover, the consent of preceding generations is sufficient for their successors; " we do consent when that Society whereof we are part hath at any time before consented, without revoking the same after by the like universal agreement ", because " we were then alive in our pre-decessors, and they in their successors do live still ".[5] On the same reasoning, custom is good law, for it could never have arisen without consent, and the approbation of subjects to proposed laws need not necessarily be apparent. Thus a commonwealth is immortal, and each generation is, as it were, a competent committee of the whole.

The function of the State, we may therefore summarize, is largely that of enforcing the observance of the Law of Reason upon the recalcitrant, and in order to do this the Laws of Reason must be codified; virtue, the observance of them, must be made rewardable, and vice, their neglect, punishable. We have seen that the making of law was at that time widely regarded simply as the publication of what had always existed.[6] This doctrine is analogous with that of the Roman Church with regard to so-called " new " doctrines. Hooker himself notes a parallel in the English Common Law; Jowett gives a similar opinion regarding the Greeks. It was deemed impiety to alter the fundamental laws, and even " the additions which were made to them in later ages in order to meet the

---

[1] *E.P.*, I, x, 7.   Perhaps he is here glancing at the Parliaments of his time.
[2] *Ibid.*   [3] *E.P.*, I, x, 8.   [4] *Ibid.*   [5] *Ibid.*
[6] *E.P.*, I, viii, 3–5.

increasing complexity of affairs were still ascribed by a fiction to the original legislator ". [1]

But Hooker's final observation about Positive Municipal Law is of the highest importance. He points out [2] that laws are made for a definite nation in a definite set of circumstances, and that therefore such laws, although they will all be based on reason, will vary from country to country. Bodin and other political writers held the same opinion. Both geography and history enter into the picture as determining the positive law of countries. The recognition of this diversity provided for the ever-changing legislative scene, and was a conception alike fatal to the universalism of Rome and the claims of Geneva that every church should bear her exclusive pattern.

From Positive Municipal Law Hooker proceeds to the *Law of Nations*, or International Law.[3] This is not an important section for our present purposes, since it was not greatly involved in the central controversy with the Puritans [4] about the nature and extent of authority. Building on Aristotle's theory that man is a social animal,[5] Hooker shows that men desire as far as may be social relations with all mankind, and not merely with fellow-members of their own polity. " Which thing Socrates intending to signify professed himself a citizen, not of this or that Commonwealth, but of the world." [6] But Hooker does bring out a distinction with reference to International Law, which applies equally well to the Law of Reason where personal and political relationships are involved. All law is primary or secondary.[7] Primary law is that built upon sincere nature, which sufficed for individual man before he became depraved and for men in a society when they possessed the harmless disposition they had and might have retained. But Secondary laws, built upon depraved nature, had in each case to be superimposed. In international relationships Primary laws regulated all innocent relations, like embassies, the courteous entertainment of foreigners and " commodious traffic "; but Secondary laws " are such as this present unquiet world is most familiarly acquainted with: I mean laws of arms, which yet are much better known than kept ". The distinction agrees precisely

---

[1] Jowett, *Introduction to Republic*, p. 154 (Oxford, 1921).
[2] *E.P.*, I, x, 9.
[3] Yet one other and greater defender of the Natural Law, Hugo Grotius, was soon to publish his great work concerning the laws of international relations: 1625. *De Jure Belli et Pacis*.
[4] In the Preface Hooker regrets the Puritans' desire to abolish the law of the " Commerce of Nations " (*E.P.*, Preface, viii, 4).
[5] Cf. Aristotle, *Pol.*, i, 2.
[6] *E.P.*, I, x, 12.
[7] *E.P.*, I, x, 13.

with that in other branches of law; natural laws are the necessities of "perfection character"; positive laws are made necessary by the fall of man. And just as, in any State, the law (which is the act of all) overrides any several part of the State, so no one nation should to the prejudice of another "annihilate that whereupon the whole world hath agreed".[1] Hooker cannot help lamenting, with his main purpose in view, that relations between States are not more regulated; how much easier to have overcome religious differences if there had been more "correspondence" among nations, and, if, in particular, the custom of holding General Councils had not lapsed. The mere fact that Councils had at some time been worked for party reasons should not prevent the world from seeing their value for "spiritual commerce"; the renewal of the ancient Councils is much preferable to "these proceedings continued, which either make all contentions endless, or bring them to one only determination, and that of all other the worst, which is by sword".[2] There is actually some confusion in Hooker as to whether International Law is positive law or forms part of the natural law of reason. His language on the point is not at all consistent, but International Law was at this time only in process of development. Probably it would be subsumed under Natural Law, for in his day the disputes of nations were either founded upon or inextricably connected with the holding of different creeds. It is not without significance that two successive volumes of the *Cambridge Modern History* are named, *The Wars of Religion* and the *Thirty Years' War*.

More important for our purpose is the last division of law, the Supernatural [3]—that is, the law revealed by God in Scripture: Divine Law, which for the Puritan was the supreme authority. Man, a spiritual being, cannot be satisfied with finite happiness; [4] his last and chief good is infinite; what man "coveteth as good in itself towards that his desire is ever infinite. So that unless the last good of all, which is desired altogether for itself, be also infinite, we do evil in making it our end." [5] Such infinite happiness man cannot know in perfection on earth; he can only strive ever towards it, "the full possession of that which simply for itself is to be desired"—that is, perfect communion with God. But even on earth "capable we are of God both by understanding and will",[6] wherefore, since also all men possess it, this ideal of everlasting happiness is natural to man, and, further, is peculiar to him out of all creation; moreover, to some extent the ideal can be realized in this life, since no natural desire can be utterly frustrate,[7] although

---

[1] *E.P.*, I, x. 13.　　　[2] *E.P.*, I, x, 14.　　　[3] *E.P.*, I, xi, 1 *et seq.*
[4] Cf. Aristotle, *Pol.*, Libs. iv and vii.　　　[5] *E.P.*, I, xi, 2.
[6] *E.P.*, I, xi, 3.　　　[7] *E.P.*, I, xi, 4.

only hereafter can it be perfectly apprehended. But the way to this
happiness is not natural; it is a mystery, not susceptible of discovery
by reasoning, and only so far discovered as God has willed by
supernatural revelation. The means disclosed is threefold—of faith,
of hope, of charity; without these the way cannot be trodden, nor
the goal reached.[1] " Concerning Faith, the principal object
whereof is that eternal Verity which hath discovered the treasures
of hidden wisdom in Christ; concerning Hope, the highest object
whereof is that everlasting goodness which in Christ doth quicken
the dead; concerning Charity, the final object whereof is that
incomprehensible Beauty, which shineth in the countenance of
Christ the Son of the living God . . . there is not in the world a
syllable muttered with certain truth concerning any of these three,
more than hath been supernaturally received from the mouth of the
Eternal God." [2] It is on similar lines of reasoning, where he
points out the purpose of a State is to attain, through a life of
virtue, to the enjoyment of the divine, that St. Thomas Aquinas [3]
indicates the necessity for divine laws as well as human.

But God's law in Scripture is not concerned only with the way of
salvation; it comprehends also laws of nature and of reason.[4] It is
well that Scripture does so, for such natural laws as it enforces are
perhaps those which men would not easily have found out, and it
is a benefit to have them defined; in any case, obscure or not, they
are strengthened as laws by being incorporated into God's own
testimony. The Law of Scripture, moreover, is sharper than
Natural or Positive Municipal Law, piercing the closest corners of
the heart in a way that Natural Law can hardly, Positive Law
cannot possibly, do; so that men may know, for example, that
secret concupiscence is sin, and are fearful to offend even in a
" wandering cogitation ".[5] Again, it is a great benefit to have
God's Law written, in order to distinguish essentials from traditions,
and thus to have a complete answer to the claim of the Roman
Church [6] that her traditions be received on the same footing as the
venerable Scriptures.

But while the law in Scripture is sufficient for its purpose—that is,
to teach what is necessary for man to believe and know for his soul's
health—there are many things of which Scripture makes no
account; for example, the Puritan Discipline.[7] Man needs no
more than the knowledge of Nature and Scripture to attain to

---

[1] *E.P.*, I, xi, 6.   [2] *Ibid.*
[3] *De Reg. Princ.*, i, 14.   [4] *E.P.*, I, xii, 1.
[5] *E.P.*, I, xii, 2. The same point is emphasized by Marsiglio in his *Defensor
Pacis*, Dictio II, caps. viii, ix.
[6] *E.P.*, I, xiii, 2.
[7] *E.P.*, I, xiv, 2.

eternal bliss; those who add traditions as essential to salvation make a grave mistake, unless these traditions can be clearly shown to be of God.[1]

Supernatural or Scriptural Law, like Positive Municipal Law, contains both natural and positive laws.[2] Some people imagine that Positive Municipal Laws, being man-made, are of laws alone mutable. But many positive laws are changeable, whether they are municipal or Scriptural—it is their matter,[3] not their author that decides this. "Whether God or man be the maker of them, alteration they so far forth admit, as the matter doth exact."[4] Supernatural laws are all positive,[5] imposed on individual men, or else on the supernatural society, the Church, bidding men obey such duties as could not without revelation be found out, and prescribing to the Church that kind of service which God requires. If their subject-matter is constant, if they fulfil the original purpose of their institution, they are changeless, as, for example, the Gospel teaching of Christ; but if they were imposed for particular times or people, which in their original condition no longer exist, they are changeable, even if given by God himself, as happened with the Jewish Ceremonial Laws. The matter decides the eternal and immutable character of a law.[6]

At this point Hooker briefly summarizes his conclusions so far reached to show "how all this belongeth to the cause in question".[7] He has sought to show men a reason why just laws are of so great force and use; to encourage them to reduce to their first causes the laws "whereof there is present controversy". He apologizes for having considered the subject of laws in general at such length, "seeing that our whole question concerneth the quality of ecclesiastical laws"; but their principles are the same, their forcible operation the same. It is only wise and judicious men, he points out, that will set themselves to judge of a law.[8] But if men are bent upon inquiry, Hooker begs them to have always before their eyes that Eternal Law, which breeds in religious minds a dutiful estimation of all good laws, since laws obviously good have a divine course, "copied out of the very tables of that high everlasting law".[9] Then, too, laws may be good, although the goodness is not easily to be discerned; and men disgrace God by hasty and ignorant invective, not pausing to realize that human laws are derived from the Eternal Law of God.

[1] *E.P.*, I, xiv, 5.
[2] *E.P.*, I, xv, 1 and 2.
[3] Cf. "It is not the author which maketh, but the matter whereon they are made, that causeth laws to be thus distinguished" ("Sermon on Pride," III, 619).
[4] *E.P.*, I, xv, 1.   [5] *E.P.*, I, xv, 2.   [6] *E.P.*, I, xv, 3.
[7] *E.P.*, I, xvi.   [8] *E.P.*, I, xvi, 2.   [9] *Ibid.*

Further, men have different functions,[1] " some natural, some
rational, some supernatural, some politic, some finally ecclesiastical; which if we measure not each by its own proper law,
whereas the things themselves are so different, there will be in our
understanding and judgment of them confusion ". It is this
confusion which formed the ground of the first great error of the
Puritans.[2] Rightly contending that man must glorify God, and
cannot do so if his actions are not framed according to Divine Law,
they wrongly conclude that the only law which God has given to
men in that behalf is the sacred Scripture. But men glorify God
when they eat and sleep,[3] in the performance of all rational and
moral acts; [4] even the heathen, who have no written law of God,
but only the universal law of mankind, do this, while the Christian
has the advantage of performing religious acts as well.[5]

Most decidedly men glorify God as members of a society by obedience to its laws and government. Those laws are expressions of
Eternal Law, and obedience to them is definitely prescribed in
Scripture, which orders, " Let every soul be subject to the higher
powers ". The public power of a society is above every individual
member, and its chief purpose is to appoint laws for members,
which must be obeyed where they are not contrary to the Law of
Reason or of God. The ruler, once appointed, holds permanent
power to command, but to permit an individual to disobey on
private judgement is to deprive the ruler of his power, to destroy
unity and to frustrate the purpose of political society.

Over and over again Hooker emphasizes this danger of the
Puritan outlook. The claim of private judgement is never out of his
mind. Accordingly, he writes in the same strain later on, " The
patrons of liberty have here made solemn proclamation that all
such laws and commandments are void, inasmuch as every man
is left to the freedom of his own mind in such things as are not either
exacted or prohibited by the Law of God. . . . The plain contradictory whereunto is infallibly certain. Those things which the
law of God leaveth arbitrary and at liberty are all subject unto
positive laws of men, which laws for the common benefit abridge
particular men's liberty in such things as far as the rules of equity
will suffer. This we must either maintain, or else overturn the
world and make every man his own commander." [6]

Unless men defer to public authority, social life is impossible. If
this deference had been shown to ecclesiastical authority, and if
Puritans had realized by how many laws men's actions are controlled, the present contentions could not have arisen. Life in

---

[1] *E.P.*, I, xvi, 5.   [2] *Ibid.*   [3] *Ibid.*   [4] *Ibid.*
       [5] *Ibid.*   [6] *E.P.*, V, 71, iv., pp. 396–7.

society makes demands on men; their private judgements and pre-dilections must bow to the general good, as interpreted by public authority.[1] This deference is difficult for some men to pay; excellent in individual life as they are, as members of a society they are less praiseworthy. " Yea, I am persuaded, that of them with whom in this cause we strive, there are whose betters among men would hardly be found, if they did not live amongst men, but in some wilderness by themselves." [2] The reason of their unfitness is the same; whether the question is of Church Government in general, of conformity between Churches, or of the observances of the Anglican Church—whatever it be, they have framed the rule for themselves in despite of all the laws of public authority, the rule of private judgment.[3] He sums up, " Thus by following the law of private reason, where the law of public should take place, they breed disturbance ".[4]

This, then, is Hooker's theory of the origin and the sanctions of law. The first thing to note about it is its richness and variety. Law is something greater than sets of precepts or rules. Hooker's conception is hierarchic, and law is made to fulfil an essential func-tion in the universe as being a bridge from God to man and from man to God—a vital connecting link. The Puritan conception of Divine Law (found exclusively in the Scriptures) and Human Law is represented as but a fragment of the whole, bald and incomplete.

The second thing to note is the important part played in the scheme by reason. By equating *lex* with *ratio* Hooker is erecting an authority—the human reason—as a touchstone of judgment. This was some-thing to place beside the Bible as a Protestant court of appeal. All true law is derived from God and by reason is apprehended. Hooker does not, however, follow the Puritan error of making his authority complete and self-sufficient. He admits that the human reason cannot always penetrate the ways of God, the Fount of all law, and that it must be content to submit where it cannot hope to understand. But he provided new ground on which to meet the Puritans. All previous apologists, including Whitgift himself, had tended to meet the Puritans on their own chosen field—the Scrip-tures—and to pit one interpretation against another. Hooker, by vindicating the place of reason, translated the controversy to an entirely different level. Thus he managed to close the breach between reason and revelation, and he shifts the emphasis from the Fall and its unhappy consequences to champion the doctrine of

[1] *E.P.*, I, xvi, 6.
[2] *Ibid.*
[3] Cf. *E.P.*, V, 25, v, p. 121. " Where every man's private spirit and gift . . . is the only Bishop that ordaineth him to this ministry."
[4] *Ibid.*

Creation and all that is involved by it. His theological background, together with his strong conservative instincts and feeling for history, was sufficient to protect him from any purely rationalistic point of view. Nevertheless we cannot but be struck with the position in the universe which Hooker accords to the natural man, with his sense of belonging to a higher scheme of things than his immediate surroundings, with his dignity and consciousness of capacity for true greatness, even though he must admit that political society originated to curb natural depravity; the epithets of degradation applied by the Continental reformers appear harsher and more hopeless than ever, and with Hooker conscience, as the voice of God in man (though he does not expressly state this), is infinitely nobler than Luther's definition of it as a " paltry desire ".

The third great characteristic of Hooker's scheme of law is its provision for change. The trouble with the Puritans was that all their conceptions were rigid and static. They ignored the past and made no allowance for the future. They had no philosophy of progress. Hooker overcame this difficulty by allowing for mutability in his idea of law. The problem was not new, and had in fact never been satisfactorily solved by the mediaeval schoolmen themselves. Hooker provided for mutability in his distinction between natural and positive law. In the First Eternal Law there could, of course, be no scope for change, for that would involve contradictions in the Godhead and bring with it insuperable theological problems. Nor could there be change in the Law of Nature, for, like Nature itself, it was unalterable; only positive law was mutable, according to its subject-matter. In so far as any positive law contained coercive sanctions to conceptions of natural law (described as " mixedly human ", as distinct from " merely human " law, which had nothing of natural law within it),[1] it was unalterable. The legislative act which created " merely human " law had power to unmake or change it. The problem of how far Divine Law must be obeyed Hooker solves also by a new method—not by the old distinction between moral and ceremonial precepts. He insists that all divine laws affecting man in his supernatural capacity as a religious member of society are above Nature and, though positive, unchangeable; while those controlling him in civil and ecclesiastical life are alterable and must in fact vary with circumstance. This distinction exempted questions of faith from discussion, but justified changes in Church ceremonies, Church order, and Church discipline. This provision has been rightly described as " one of the elements of most permanent value in his [Hooker's] philosophy of law ",[2] which brought with it a regard for and belief in history unknown to

[1] E.P., I, x, 10.   [2] See D'Entrèves' *Ricardo Hooker* (Turin, 1932), p. 70,

G

the Puritans. "Wherein they mark not," Hooker writes, "that laws are instruments to rule by, and that instruments are not only to be framed according unto the general end for which they are provided, but even according unto that very particular, which riseth out of the matter whereon they have to work." [1] Hence even Apostolic rites and customs are not necessarily permanent,[2] and this foregoing argument forms Hooker's philosophic defence of the Thirty-fourth Article of the Church of England.

Finally it must be noted that Hooker's conception of law is not original, in so far as the basic fabric of his system was not the product of his own invention. He appeals to ancient philosophy, notably to Aristotle, and to the Fathers, while his conception of the Law of Nature owes much to Stoic influence. But it is from the mediaeval Scholastics that Hooker takes most.[3] His tenderness for the Scholastics is in marked contrast to most Protestant thought. To Luther they were mere sophists, and Calvin scornfully dismissed their works as " resveries des theologiens papistes "; and even some humanists, like Colet, had viewed them with an unfriendly eye. But to Hooker they were part of the essential philosophic tradition which he longed to see restored, and above all it is to Aquinas that he stands most indebted. Their systems of law are parallel, and there is much in the *Summa Totius Theologiae* that is reproduced in this section of the *Ecclesiastical Polity*, though Hooker has not hesitated to make some variation in the great doctor's scheme. Thus, although Aquinas discriminates between *Lex Aeterna* [4] and *Lex Divina*, there is nothing in him corresponding to Hooker's distinction between the First and Second Laws Eternal, the First being that Law which God Himself observes and the Second comprehending all laws which as Creator He gives to His creatures. Aquinas teaches that Law is inherent reason governing the universe. It is the *measure* or *criterion* of human actions, because it is the inner principle determining them and directing them to the fulfilment of their proper ends. He is influenced by St. Augustine's idea that law is the supreme reason and is therefore unchangeable and eternal. But Hooker and Aquinas stand together in contrast to St. Augustine as they place emphasis on the affinity between God and man. Aquinas explains [5] that the idea of God's government of the universe has the nature of an Eternal Law, and His Law is thus not distinct from Himself. But since man's being is directed to the end of eternal beatitude,

---

[1] *E.P.*, III, x, 3.
[2] *E.P.*, I, xiv, 5.
[3] For a full examination of the mediaeval sources of Hooker's juridical philosophy, see D'Entrèves, op. cit. Chapter 4.
[4] *S.T. Prima Sec.* Q. 91. Art. 2.
[5] *S.T. Prima Sec.* Q. 91. Art. 1.

which exceeds the capacity of natural human faculties, Divine Law comes to man's aid in addition to human and natural Law: for natural human judgments are diverse and uncertain, and every man must know without doubt what is the right thing for him to do in given circumstances. Moreover, Divine Law is essential to the control of inward dispositions and motives.[1] Hooker with similar outlook places all laws within the compass of God's Eternal Law, whether they be for celestial beings, or for inanimate nature, or whether they are the Moral Law of Reason or Human Positive Laws. The two philosophers walk together in essential agreement, and it seems fair to deduce that Hooker set out, in so far as he could, to restore the authority of St. Thomas to the world of Protestant belief and thought. To ignore Hooker's special (and purely logical) category of Celestial Law, the most important difference between them is that from the Law of Reason Hooker separates the Law of Nature, whereas Aquinas tends to identify them. For St. Thomas the Natural Law is the reflection in man's reason of the Eternal Law. We might say, perhaps, that Aquinas emphasizes the Divine Reason, while Hooker takes pains to elevate human reason, the limitations of which St. Thomas is careful to point out.[2] Hooker's Law of Nature, pure and simple, refers to inanimate creation; his Law of Reason belongs solely to human beings who, by use of their reason, can (unlike inanimate Nature) discover their own laws. Thus he identifies *lex* and *ratio,* and this constitutes the essence of his defence of authority and the decisive grounds of obligation.

What difference there is found between Master and Disciple is therefore principally difference in terminology, and perhaps in the scope of Law Eternal, but in all essence the two are as one. When Aquinas writes in the *Summa* that it is by natural law that man partakes of the Eternal Law (which is Eternal Reason) according to the capacity of his natural human faculties, for the Law of Nature is nothing else than the rational creature's participation of the Eternal Law, it is what Hooker means when he describes the Moral Law of Reason. It is by this, they both agree, that the rational creature (man) has share in the Eternal Reason; this participation (*Lex naturalis . . . est participatio legis aeternae in rationabili creatura*) in the Eternal Law by the rational creature the one may describe as Natural Law,[3] the other as the Law of Reason, but both are right, since a law is something pertaining to reason (*nam lex est aliquid rationis*). It is thus also that man shares in the divine providence, since he is provident both for himself and others; his natural inclination to his own act and end derives from this very share of the

[1] *S.T. Prima Sec.* Q. 91. Art. 4. [2] *S.T. Prima Sec.* Q. 91. Art. 3.
[3] *S.T. Prima Sec.* Q. 91. Art. 2.

CHAPTER V

HOOKER'S THEORY OF THE STATE

HOOKER's theory of the State proceeds from two basic conceptions, which are in marked contrast, though not necessarily at variance with one another—the idea of Nature (or spontaneous growth) and the idea of Contract. For most sixteenth-century political writers the State was a natural, and not an artificial, creation; and Hooker is in this no exception to the general rule. The two conceptions—Nature on the one side and Contract on the other—marked to some extent the distinction between Natural Law and Positive Human Law, and therefore it is not surprising that so ardent a champion of the Law of Nature as Hooker should place his emphasis on the former rather than on the latter.

In this he is following Aristotle, from whose *Politics* and *Ethics* he quotes. His view of the origin of society is in the first instance Aristotelian. Aristotle teaches that in the nature of man two aspects must be noted: his physical needs and his moral forces.[1] The State itself results from these two elements, for it is the result of a natural development of the family, and is the essential condition of all development, since man, to develop his nature, must fulfil that nature and live in a State. Thus the State is a complete organic whole, of which the individual is a part, and therefore posterior to the State. But the ethical value of the State is much more important than any mere assuring to men their material well-being: the State supremely exists as an instrument for achieving an ethical end. It is a community whose duty it is to enforce a particular character (ἦθος) on its members, and the creation of that character is its special function. The identity of the State—that which makes it what it is—is not race or language, but its " polity ", which he defines as " the system of government adopted by any State together with the end (τέλος) which the citizens propose to themselves ". The State is teleological, because Aristotle believes that Nature does nothing in vain; everything was created to subserve a purpose. If it has not this ethical end—the life of virtue—the State cannot rightly exist.

[1] *Pol.*, Lib. i.

Thus Hooker begins by asserting that life " fit for the dignity of man " [1] cannot be lived in isolation; human nature would be defective and imperfect—men are therefore naturally driven to seek communion and fellowship with others.   This natural inclination for social fellowship is the first basis of organic society; the second foundation is " an order expressly or secretly agreed upon touching the manner of their union in living together ".[2]   It is thus that a political society, a State, comes into being.   This open or secret order is the fundamental Law of the State, the ground of all its future existence.[3]   As with Aristotle and Aquinas, Hooker gives his State a teleological character—the Kingdom of God must first be sought in order of importance, but, " inasmuch as righteous life presupposeth life ", the first matter in time is the due provision of means of living.[4]

But Hooker had not derived his ideas merely from the most famous of pagan philosophers; he was also strongly imbued with the orthodox theological views of the Christian religion.   From the Christian Fathers came the idea that the State was a necessity in view of man's fall and of the sinful consequences of that unhappy act which were still being felt in the world.   The State was to such thinkers (notably St. Augustine) a direct consequence of the Fall, and their view of the part played by nature in the formation of political society was very different from that of Aristotle.

For them Nature was the Golden Age, the primitive state of man's innocence and bliss, from which he fell when he embraced sin. Hence Nature as such can have played no part in founding civilized societies.   Various pre-Christian agencies (notably Roman Law and Stoic philosophy) had also contributed to bequeath this thought as a legacy to the Middle Ages.   Thus, for example, Roman jurists [5] held slavery to be an institution against Nature; and Seneca looks

---

[1] *E.P.*, I, x, 1.

[2] *Ibid.*

[3] The American Colonists did embody their Fundamental Law in their written Constitution. Pollock and Maitland point out (*H.E.L.*, I, 173) that Magna Carta, with all its faults, was the nearest approach to a " fundamental law " England has ever had. Generations to come would demand its confirmation and appeal to it against oppression, even when some of its clauses were hopelessly antiquated. " For in brief it means this, that the King is and shall be below the law." This idea of " fundamental law " persisted for centuries, and is well illustrated, for example, in Henry Neville's *Plato Redivivus* (London, 4th ed., 1763). In that book of Dialogues the " English gentleman " says, " The people by the fundamental laws (that is, by the constitution of the government of England) have entire freedom in their lives, properties, and their persons." Magna Carta, the Petition of Right, and St. Edward's Laws are clearly the " fundamental laws " in his mind (op. cit., pp. 130–4). Later he repeats that these are the laws which " make the law and the judges the only disposers of the liberties of our persons " (op. cit., pp. 258–9).

[4] *E.P.*, I, x, 2.

[5] *E.g.*, Ulpian; Florentinus.

back to the Golden Age.[1] The Christian Fathers—as, for instance, Irenaeus and Augustine—combining this with the Pauline doctrine of the Fall of Man, placed the origin and purpose of political government in the depravity of man. If this were so, political societies have *conventional* and not natural bases, and are artificial structures, a view which dominated European theories of politics till nineteenth-century philosophy pointed men back to Aristotle's teaching that political society is natural, inasmuch as it is the aid by which man may attain to his true nature.

But in the thirteenth century, when the works of Aristotle became known to the mediaeval world, a new conception was added to the normal Christian view. This view, which was an attempt to reconcile Aristotle's ideas with contemporary political thought, found in coercive government both the result of man's evil and the means whereby that evil might be checked. St. Thomas Aquinas, going back to Aristotle's political theory, taught that political society is natural rather than artificial, because man must live in a society, as is evidenced by his physical weakness, material needs, and his faculties of reason and speech; but, living thus, he must be ordered. Consequently Government itself is natural, since it would be *inconveniens* for Society to be deprived of the natural excellence of justice and knowledge existing in one or more members. Therefore political society, having as its purpose and function the maintenance of righteousness, whereby its members may progress by a life of virtue to the enjoyment of God, is a divine institution.[2]

Christian thinkers still remained divided as to whether the State was created because of the Fall or whether it had simply existed in a purer form in the Golden Age before Adam's sin. Hooker himself is not absolutely consistent on the point, but it is clear that he accepts the fundamental Christian point of view about life after the Fall. On the one hand he can say, " Laws politic, ordained for external order and regiment amongst men, are never formed as they should be, unless presuming the will of man to be inwardly obstinate, rebellious and averse from all obedience unto the sacred laws of his nature; in a word, unless presuming man to be in regard of his depraved mind little better than a wild beast. . . ."[3] On the other hand, he remarks that there is " no impossibility in nature considered by itself, but that men might have lived without any public regiment ".[4] He has not reached the point of Hobbes that the life of " natural " men is " solitary, poore, nasty, brutish and

---

[1] *Ep.*, xiv, 2.
[2] E.g., *De Regimine Principum* (Venice, 1787), I, 14.
[3] *E.P.*, I, x, 1.   [4] *E.P.*, I, x, 4.

short ",[1] but he does accept much of the Christian belief in the depravity of man. He nowhere however identifies the origin of the State with sin; but, on the contrary, sees organized political life as a blessing, enabling members to fulfil the divine purpose.

To resolve the difficulty in reconciling what he has inherited from the Fathers with what he has inherited from Aristotle, Hooker goes farther than Aquinas, and adopts the view of the social compact. This theory was comparatively new, but it placed too much emphasis on the rights of the individual and not enough on those of the community to commend itself greatly to the mediaeval mind. There are, however, traces of the idea in Marsiglio of Padua, whose work was certainly known to Hooker,[2] and several of Hooker's own contemporaries were arriving at similar conclusions. He certainly knew of Sir Thomas Smith's *De Republica Anglorum* (published in 1583), which has a passing reference to the Social Contract in the Introduction, and Buchanan's *De Jure Regni apud Scotos*[3] (published in 1578), although he does not refer to either of them. The great name connected by Gierke with the doctrine is that of Althusius. However, he wrote ten years after Hooker, and his subsequent considerable influence was confined to Germany and the Continent, little affecting English political thought. On the whole, it may be safely stated that Hooker was the first Englishman systematically to formulate the idea of a social compact as the historical and legal basis of the State.

Hooker's own words on the subject are therefore worth attention. He says, " Two foundations there are which bear up public societies, the one, a natural inclination whereby all men desire sociable life and fellowship, the other, an order expressly or secretly agreed upon touching the manner of their union in living together. The latter is that which we call the Law of a Commonweal, the very soul of a politic body, the parts whereof are by law animated, held together, and set on work in such actions, as the common good requireth."[4] The next step, and an immediate one, was to set up a government. Having outlined the wickedness which flourished " with those times wherein there were no civil societies . . . wherein there was as yet no manner of public regiment established ",[5] Hooker goes on to explain, " to take away all such mutual

---

[1] Hobbes: *Leviathan* (Oxford, 1909), I, xiii, 97.
[2] Reference has been already made to Marshall's translation of the *Defensor Pacis*, published in London in 1535, and to Hooker's knowledge of the book. See Chapter I, p. 3, *supra*.
[3] Buchanan did not strictly teach a Contract Theory in any case; Nature, which he equates with Divine Wisdom, first taught men to seek society, and Utility reinforced Nature's urge (see pp. 153-158, *infra*).
[4] *E.P.*, I, x, 1.
[5] *E.P.*, I, x, 3.

grievances, injuries and wrongs, there was no way but only by growing into composition and agreement amongst themselves, by ordaining some kind of government public, and by yielding themselves subject thereunto; that unto whom they granted authority to rule and govern, by them the peace, tranquillity, and happy estate of the rest might be procured." [1] Thus Hooker passes on logically enough from his social compact to the idea of a contract of sovereignty. For this second conception there was a far more ancient history than for the idea of a social compact. The notion of a contract of sovereignty has been traced back to Greek political thought,[2] but it took real root in the early Middle Ages. The elective nature of so many mediaeval institutions, including the Empire and the Papacy themselves, and the whole contractual basis of feudalism furnished examples to mediaeval political thinkers, from Manegold von Lauterbach onwards. As early as 1095 he had raised the problem at the height of the Investiture contest, and vindicated the people's right both to expel a king who had degenerated into tyranny and to recover their freedom if the ruler had broken his contract. Such philosophers could and did defend the contractual basis of sovereignty further by pointing to the *Concessio* of the imperium from the Roman people, and to the Jewish conception of the Covenant. On this ground any social compact was properly separated from a contract of sovereignty, a separation first suggested by John of Paris.[3] As we shall see, the elective and contractual nature of sovereignty was to play a still greater part in Hooker's own day in the writings of the Huguenot and Catholic Monarchomachs. This view had, in fact, been previously discussed by William of Ockham on behalf of the Conciliar Movement, and by Sir John Fortescue to defend the Lancastrian Experiment. In Tudor times it was raised in England by Bishop Ponet,[4] who was anxious to show how Mary Tudor had broken the contract by her Catholic reaction, and in Scotland by Buchanan to justify the deposition of Mary Stuart. Briefly these writers argued that the people had surrendered their sovereignty to a prince who must rule for the public good. If he ceases to do this he can be deposed.

Hooker, with a clear eye to the realities of the English situation under the Tudors, is far from agreeing with this. It is true that there is some difference in attitude between Books I and VIII, for in Book I he is dealing with general theory, and in Book VIII, where

---

[1] *E.P.*, I, x, 4. Cf. Milton, *Tenure of Kings and Magistrates*, I, 30 (ed. 2 vols., London, J. A. St. John).

[2] E.g., Jellinek, *Allgemeine Staatslehre* (Berlin, 1905).

[3] Maitland's *Gierke*, p. 187.

[4] In his *Short Treatise of Politic Power*, 1556.

he is defending the Tudor Royal Supremacy, he is obliged to meet his opponents [1] on their own ground and to emphasize the constitutional aspects of the Tudor monarchy.

For Hooker the social contract and the contract of sovereignty are really two aspects of the same thing and are indissolubly mixed. Thus to take away the one is to dissolve the other. They cannot exist apart. He does not go beyond saying that every kind of government must have been started from " deliberate advice, consultation and composition between men ".[2] He goes no farther than this in definition, and does not postulate any formal contract. Any agreement between ruler and subjects imposes at best a moral obligation, and Hooker's view of it is therefore dissimilar to Locke's, although Locke took the idea of it from his master. When Hallam salutes Hooker as an original Whig, it is on the ground that he was the father of the theories of contract and consent. Hallam wondered why the Eighth Book in particular was ever allowed to be published without any toning down. " The popular origin of government and necessity of popular consent to its due exercise, laid down in Books one and eight, with a boldness not usual in Elizabeth's reign, and a latitude of expression that leads us forward to the most unalloyed democracy "[3] astonished him. But Hallam failed to allow for the differences between the sixteenth and eighteenth centuries. Moreover, it is very doubtful if Hooker was aware of what might later be deduced from his idealist principles. He pictured man originally in a state of nature; at some period in human history a political society must have been formed; reason dictates the belief that it suited men to agree to live in ordered life; somehow they recognized it was all for the best, and have ever since continued to recognize it— the original machinery of institution had long since perished—the entire process was natural, the authority arising from it legitimate; and therefore it is divine. Of any evidence in his book of an historical contract, in the legal and formal sense of Locke, there is little; in the sense of Hobbes, none whatever. His main concern is always the supremacy of law and order; his emphasis on duties rather than rights.

Hooker was certainly ready to agree with the Huguenot Monarchomachs that sovereigns should rule for the public good; but only by agreement (to which he admits the Prince is unlikely to consent) could any alteration in the basic system of government be

---

[1] In particular he is dealing with the *Vindiciae contra Tyrannos*, published anonymously in Latin in 1578. A French version appeared in 1581, and two in English before 1590.

[2] *E.P.*, I, x, 4.

[3] *H.L.E.*, II, 48. Cf. " I have indeed myself heard him styled the Father of the Whigs " (Hoadly, *Works*, 1773, II, 253).

allowed. There could be no question of getting rid even of a tyrant, still less his legitimate successors. Only when an entire dynasty came to an end might the situation be in any way reviewed and a contract of sovereignty be remade. It is clear that for Hooker, as for St. Paul,[1] the powers that be are ordained of God and that all legitimate authority is divine. He is not in the least teaching the seventeenth-century view of the divine right of kings, and he is equally far removed from the idea of popular sovereignty, but his position can be regarded (as the English Parliament of the sixteenth century can be so regarded) as representing a halfway house between the two ideas. He discusses his view at length when he comes to defend the constitution of the Tudor State in Book VIII.

All States must have constitutions. " Without order there is no living in public society, because the want thereof is the mother of confusion, whereupon division of necessity followeth, and out of division, inevitable destruction. . . . This order of things and persons in public societies is the work of polity."[2] But this constitution is not regarded by Hooker, as it is by Locke, as needing a separate contract. He then examines the three classical forms of government. He is naturally most concerned with monarchy, but admits that change and development may well occur. In fact, " the inconveniences of one kind have caused sundry other to be devised."[3] Elsewhere he repeats, " In these things the experience of time may breed both civil and ecclesiastical change from that which hath been before received, neither do latter things always violently exclude former, but the one growing less convenient than it hath been, giveth place to that which is now become more. That which was fit for the people themselves to do at the first, might afterwards be more convenient for them to do by some other."[4] Indeed, it was the constitutional nature of the English monarchy that appealed to Hooker. He had none of Aristotle's views about the natural right of some to rule and others to be ruled. In one remarkable passage he says that a ruler owes his position to the fact that men have of their common consent so chosen him,[5] " without which consent there were no reason that one man should take upon him to be lord or judge over another; because although there be according to the opinion of some very great and judicious men a kind of natural right in the noble, wise and virtuous, to govern them which are of servile disposition; nevertheless for manifestation of this their right, and men's more peaceable contentment on both sides, the assent of them who are to be governed seemeth necessary ".

---

[1] Rom. 13. 1.　　　[2] E.P., VIII, ii, 2.　　　[3] E.P., I, x, 4.
[4] E.P., VII, xiv, 7.　　　[5] E.P., I, x, 4.

The first form of government was probably monarchical. He uses Aristotle's patriarchal theory to indicate this; the idea of kingship is the most natural, as copying the fact of a father's natural dominion over his family. But however natural the father's authority may be, a king's is not. No one can take on himself the government of a State without the consent of the members, unless (like Moses) he is immediately appointed by God.[1] The necessity for government is natural, " the corruption of our nature being presupposed ", but the *kind* of government is entirely artificial. Men might have set up what forms of polity they pleased. After some one kind of rule had originally been established, he naïvely suggests, in all probability nobody thought anything more about the matter, but left government entirely to the ruler. He seems to mean that there was a period of arbitrary rule when there was no law but the ruler's will, and anything became a wrong that he chose to consider wrong. This proving no remedy, and " one man's will " causing all other men's misery, compelled the State " to come unto laws ".[2] The implication clearly is that these laws are to be the supreme Sovereign, and the ruler—himself bound by them—their protector and administrator: it is the mediaeval conception of the supremacy of law. We begin to think a firm contract between ruler and subjects is intended, but he goes no farther on this head. We note Hooker has developed his government, but he omits to state by what means; certainly he nowhere suggests that the original " one man " had broken a clear contract; all we can deduce is that people generally felt the time had come to curb tendencies to arbitrary rule, and clearly in his view, as here expressed, they have a residuum of power which may be invoked to set up a legal restraint upon the ruler, and at the same time impose legal duties on everyone, with appropriate rewards and penalties. Undeniably Hooker poses some kind of original contract, but there is no clear-cut development of his theory. The idea itself was to prove more useful to posterity than Hooker's explanation of its working. Indeed, his original government seems to commence—to use Hume's words [3]—" casually and imperfectly " and the mergence or ascendancy of the " one man " occurred in all probability, as the same writer suggests, during a state of war.

Bodin had written that the first and greatest mark of sovereignty—so great as to include all other marks—was " the power to give laws ".[4] To the State Hooker attributes its chief and necessary

---

[1] *E.P.*, I, x, 4.
[2] *E.P.*, I, x, 5.
[3] Hume's *Essays* (ed. Green, London, 1875), I, 115, Pt. i, Essay 5.
[4] *The Six Bookes of a Commonweal* (ed. Knolles, London, 1606), Book I, cap. x (Latin edition, Frankfort, 1609).

feature in the same power. The law of reason, of course, already binds, whether or no it is incorporated into the State law. Men deduce " certain more particular determinates " from the wide principles of the Law of Nature; and these determinations, being in accord with reason and fulfilling the conditions of establishment, become human laws.[1] But the State adds laws, imposing duties and obligations where there were none before.[2] The important point here is the source from which the Law-giver of the State received this power to bind. Beyond any doubt it is from the people. Reason itself teaches that " the lawful power of making laws to command whole politic societies of men belongeth so properly unto the same entire societies, that for any prince or potentate of what kind soever upon earth to exercise the same of himself" without either express Divine commission or authority originally derived from the people's consent " is no better than mere tyranny ".[3] This ought to mean that apart from some ruler immediately appointed by God, kings reign by virtue of original compact or agreement, and however much forgotten or buried in the past this fundamental is, and however ineffective the people's control, the King is the agent of the people, and properly should be answerable to them. But Hooker flatly denies that the people can resume their power. Whatever original contract there may have been must be apparently formally renewed for each occupant of the throne, if it is to be a live instrument. If the Fundamental Law does not provide for this renewal, the people have no remedy.[4] In the Eighth Book, where he is providing the philosophy underlying the Tudor despotism, he is obliged to be more realist than in the First Book, where he is at liberty to theorize. In fact, Hooker could not allow the people any control, other than in their representative assemblies; the sixteenth century could not afford it, and in England times were too dangerous. The people had the original right to form their Constitution—" Unto me it seemeth almost out of doubt and controversy, that every independent multitude, before any certain form of regiment established, hath, under God's supreme authority, full dominion over itself, even as a man . . . hath over himself the like power. God creating mankind did endue it naturally with full power to guide itself, in what kind of societies soever it should choose to live." [5] But this right of establishing a polity vindicated, and the theoretical claim of an ultimate residuum of power in the people acknowledged, Hooker insists that the machinery of the Constitution must be left to perform its functions. Chief among these functions is the power of law-making, which has

[1] *E.P.*, III, ix, 1, 2.   [2] *E.P.*, I, x, 10.   [3] *E.P.*, I, x, 8,
[4] *E.P.*, VIII, ii, 10.   [5] *E.P.*, VIII, ii, 5.

been transferred to the ruler. This did belong to the whole body, by natural reason—a fact which may be recognized in that the approbation of the people to proposed legislation must be in some way secured. Consent is of the essence of legislation, but this consent may be given by overt sign, by proxy, or by representation, or by implication. Individuals cannot stand out against authority established by their (or their predecessors') assent. Once he is established, the power to command must inhere in the ruler, or else social life is impossible.[1] Obedience to the dictates of the State is naturally to be given, since without it the State must fall. If positive laws are in accordance with the laws of God and of reason, so far from any individual possessing the right to disobedience, they are the very act of that individual. "A Law is the deed of the whole body politic, whereof if ye judge yourselves to be any part, then is the Law your deed also."[2] There can be no right to disobey a law which is not contrary to divine or natural law, merely because a private man or some party disapproves of it, for then no right to make law could subsist at all. Only general agreement can overthrow that which by general agreement has been established.

We have already mentioned the only limitations on the power of the ruler in his legislation. He, using the power of the whole body, must legislate in accordance with the law of reason and of God. This sovereign may be a king or any other kind of ruler. "That the Christian world should be ordered by Kingly regiment, the law of God doth not anywhere command."[3] But does he take office definitely on conditions expressed? Is there any kind of contractual agreement limiting the scope of his legislative powers? We are faced with ambiguity. Hooker ought on his principles to affirm a ruler's responsibility to the people; he denies the existence of any such responsibility unless a contract has been presented to a ruler, which cannot anyhow be done if the sovereign reigns by divine intervention, or hereditary right, or by conquest. It is as difficult for us to follow his reasoning as it was for him, in Tudor England, to square practice with his theory. It is clear that men came out from nature to form a social contract; they effected some kind of political government and set up a ruler; when he proved despotic they limited him by fundamental laws which formed the terms of agreement between ruler and ruled. But nobody can find from the *Ecclesiastical Polity* whether this despot had already broken his compact of government, or whether that compact was the system of fundamental laws established to prevent further acts of despotism. The general implication of Hooker's theory is that the Sovereign, being originally commissioned by the fundamental law, can legislate

[1] *E.P.*, I, xvi, 5.   [2] *E.P.*, Preface, v, 2.   [3] *E.P.*, VIII, ii, 6.

freely (with the help of representative assemblies) for the common good, in accordance with reason and divine will. He insists on a divine character for the Sovereign, and elsewhere makes it evident that the English Sovereign is not an elected monarch.[1] " Order " in the universe is divine in origin and purpose, and in human societies there must be those who order and those to whom it is ordered ; the Sovereign is limited by obedience to God and to the fundamental law. " Where the law doth give him dominion, who doubteth but that the King . . . must hold it of and under the law? " [2] Yet, once appointed, he is God's lieutenant,[3] and must confess his power to be God's, an echo of Bracton's " Corona est potestas delegata a Deo ".[4] Elsewhere Hooker states definitely, " The power of all sorts of superiors, made by consent of common-wealth within themselves, or grown from agreement amongst nations, such power is of God's institution in respect of the kind thereof ",[5] and, further, not only is their power of divine origin, but the actual " derivation of it *into their persons* is from him ".[6] Yet, perplexingly enough, he can say, " Touching Kings which were first instituted by agreement and composition made with them over whom they reign, how far their power may lawfully extend, the articles of compact between them must show ".[7] Perhaps the solution of the ambiguity is something like this : it matters not at all what kind of rule a State has, if it were lawfully instituted ; let it be a monarchy, limited in terms, then the monarch's power is unhampered within the scope of his limitation ; let it be an absolute monarchy, then the very will of the King, as expressed in his edicts, must prevail over all as true law, subject to its com-patibility with reason and God's law. Our author is only con-cerned to show that men must obey their rulers in all matters that they can be lawfully called upon to perform.

If the monarch exceed his prerogative (the nature and extent of which will have originally been defined presumably by the funda-mental law), then subjects may rightly refuse to obey should his

[1] " Is it not manifest that in this realm . . . where the tenure of lands is altogether grounded on military laws, and held as in fee under princes *which are not made heads of the people by force of voluntary election, but born the sovereign lords* of those whole and entire territories. . . .? " (*E.P.*, V, 80, xi, 507–8).
It is interesting to note that the principle of legitimacy was so strong in England that even Ponet opposed the attempt to make Jane Grey queen instead of Mary.
[2] *E.P.*, VIII, ii, 3.
[3] *Ibid.*
[4] Cf. Pollock and Maitland (*H.E.L.*, I, 181–2) : " That the King is below the law is a doctrine which even a royal justice may fearlessly proclaim " (ref. Bracton's *Note Book*, I, 29–33).
[5] Sermon on Civil Obedience, III, 458.
[6] *Ibid.*
[7] *E.P.*, VIII, ii, 11.

actions be against the general good—that is, against the law of reason or of God. But Hooker cannot tolerate any idea of actual rebellion: passive obedience is the maximum protest. In certain circumstances, as by failure of a line of kings where hereditary succession is the rule, the dominion exercised by the Sovereign escheats to the body politic. But can the body politic withdraw that dominion, wholly or in part, from the Sovereign back to itself, if they find his exercise of it " inconvenient "? [1] He considers that in such cases sovereigns would not oppose the general will, and " be stiff in detaining " that dominion; " but surely ", and here he speaks with no uncertainty, " without their consent I see not how the body should be able by any just means to help itself, saving when dominion doth escheat. Such things therefore must be thought upon beforehand, that power may be limited ere it be granted ".[2] Subjects have made their beds and must lie on them, till the Sovereign chooses to resign. This would definitely dispel any idea that Hooker regarded every Sovereign as a contractual officer, liable to forfeit his place, as Marsiglio taught; *it might be so* if the body politic had originally cared to establish their government in this way; otherwise they have handed over their power to the ruler, who must be borne with so long as he does not over-step the law of reason, divine law, or the bounds of that fundamental law which placed him on the throne, although nobody now knows what that law is.

Nevertheless all subsequent political philosophers of our country have been indebted to Hooker's ideas of the State. Confused and uncertain he unquestionably is; it could hardly be otherwise when a patriotic Englishman used all his resources to defend his country at its most glorious peak of history, confronted with the hostility of Spain without, and plagued with sedition and privy conspiracy within. Yet underlying his whole-hearted advocacy of the Tudor constitution there are to be discerned doctrines that will shake the world. On the one hand, men would come to believe in a social contract of some sort; a contract of Government would be a matter of natural reason and common sense; a fundamental law was to enshrine subjects' rights; political society would be felt to exist for the benefit of the governed, and not for the splendour of the Sovereign; and that being so, their consent—and a real consent at that—would be a vital necessity for all legislation. On the other hand, the doctrine of the unity of the State, its common conscience and common will, as expressed in its Representative Assemblies, will play its part in shaping the Sovereign, omni-competent State, the sole *persona* of days yet far off.

[1] *E.P.*, VIII, ii, 10.   [2] *Ibid.*

Thus it is true to say that Hooker helped to lay in this country the foundations of liberal development in politics and of the absolute supremacy of the State alike, even while he was wittingly defending a policy of another order, his English inheritance, to him of inestimable worth, and sacred as a divine dispensation. But his defence is appreciably different from the " divine right of kings ", which denies any reality to the popular will. He was not the forerunner of Filmer. Nowhere does Hooker make out a case for monarchy as the one divinely ordained form of government, nor does he regard the monarch as above all law.[1] It is quite clear that he has, in fact, the English situation ever before his eyes, and that his views are expressed accordingly. Parliament in Tudor times was not a strong body, and the initiative, even in legislation, lay with the Sovereign, but it did stand for some constitutional customs, if not rights. Hooker is prepared to side with the believers in divine right in stressing the need for proper succession (i.e., legitimism), and he is ready to preach the necessity for passive obedience, but that is as far as the agreement goes. Not until the seventeenth century, when Parliament became overwhelmingly hostile to the Church of England, did Anglicanism identify itself with the full doctrine of the divine right of kings, which in turn caused men of more liberal mind to turn over the pages of the Ecclesiastical Polity for the doctrines of contract and consent.

[1] Mediaeval doctrine gave a representative character to the monarch. "However highly his powers might be extolled, the thought that Lordship is Office had . . . always remained a living thought " (Maitland's *Gierke*, p. 62).

CHAPTER VI

RELATIONS OF CHURCH AND STATE

THE one thing common to most forms of Protestantism was the conviction within the believer of his faith and salvation. For many this subjective assurance was its own complete and absolute authority; others sought further an objective foundation and grasped it in the infallible Word of God. The last stage for countless numbers was the addition of the Genevan Discipline, claimed to be the primitive order of the Church.

Whitgift had attempted to deal with the Calvinist claim, but with only moderate success in his defence of the Establishment as a political compromise satisfactorily settled. Hooker, proceeding on a loftier plane of reason and first principles, shows the Elizabethan Settlement to be the expression of a national unity, and the Church itself primitive and Catholic. If he cannot provide a permanent answer to Puritan attacks, he at least proves his opponents guilty of a narrow, static, and irrational conception of law, and disturbers of the nation's peace and unity. Blind to the Divine Order in the world, they were blind to the light of reason in man. From the pride engendered by their conviction of an inward illumination they rejected the Church and its corporate life. Corporate life demands authority, and in refusing the authority of the Church they attacked the authority of the State, which itself is also divine.

As a matter of fact, Hooker himself was not without a touch of Puritanism. He admits that the only true Church is the invisible Church of the Elect, known to God alone, part of which is already in heaven, part on earth.[1] The visible Church, containing all baptized people who profess " One Lord, one Faith, one Baptism ",[2] is similar to Noah's Ark, the known and certain vessel of salvation. With this important difference, that all the inhabitants of the Ark were saved.[3] The Church, however, contains bad as well as good, and fell into corruptions, of which it was purged at the Reformation. That was the extent of Luther's Reformation—no new Church was

---

[1] *E.P.*, III, i, 2.   [2] *E.P.*, III, i, 3, 7.
[3] *E.P.*, V, lxviii, 6.

erected.[1] "We hope, therefore, that to reform ourselves, if at any time we have done amiss, is not to sever ourselves from the Church we were of before. In the Church we were, and we are so still." [2]

The Church is a Society, "the public Society of God",[3] no mere assembly of believers, but a real living entity, existing for the purpose of maintaining the good life, by public acts of worship and devotion. Each Church has its fixed place and geographical de-limitations, comprising in totality the Catholic Church, " as the main body of the sea being one, yet within divers precincts hath divers names ".[4] Every particular Church must possess a polity, " a form of ordering the public spiritual affairs " based on authority. The same kind of polity is not essential for all Churches, but if the polity is fit it will be divine.[5] A necessary form of polity is certainly not to be found in Scripture, which is concerned with matters of faith and doctrine essential to salvation, and forms of Church government are not included in such matters.[6] Individual Churches have power to establish and to vary their own forms of polity " as the difference of times or places shall require . . . we must note, that he which affirmeth speech to be necessary amongst all men throughout the world, doth not thereby import that all men must necessarily speak one kind of language. Even so the necessity of polity and regiment in all Churches may be held without holding any one certain form to be necessary in them all." [7]

This is the substance of Hooker's views on the Church up to the time of publication of the first four books in 1593: a touch of Puritanism; a challenge to show the Discipline set out in Scripture; a vindication against Rome and Geneva of the right of National Churches to be still Catholic and to provide themselves with their own system of government, adaptable as time and circumstance may require, as against any rigid and static form, universally binding —and an alignment with Luther, coupled with a lamentation that the Scottish and French Churches have not adopted an Episcopal government " which best agreeth with the sacred Scripture ", but they are not to be blamed on that account.[8]

Four years later the Fifth Book was issued, and in its Dedication

---

[1] E.P., III, i, 10. Cf. Sherlock: " The stabbing question, as the Church of Rome thinks, to the Reformed Churches is, Where was your Church before Luther? . . . a plain and easy answer to this, That the Church was before Luther, where it was afterwards; for they did not make a new Church . . . but only reformed . . . purged . . . which can no more make a new Church than a man's washing off the dirt makes a new Face" (*Discourse concerning the Nature and Unity of the Catholic Church* (London, 1688), p. 58).

[2] E.P., III, i, 10.   [3] E.P., V, iv, 3.   [4] E.P., III, i, 14.
[5] E.P., III, ii, 1.   [6] E.P., III, ii, 1; x, 7   [7] E.P., III, ii, 1.
[8] E.P., III, xi, 16.

Hooker states the authority for the polity of the Church of England. " By the goodness of Almighty God and His servant Elizabeth we are . . .'' There is some development in his Church teaching. He distinguishes the power of order from the power of jurisdiction.[1] The former power belongs to the ordained ministry by virtue of ordination when they receive the same Holy Spirit as did the Apostles at Pentecost. These ordained men constitute a separate order, and are commissioned by " the Church ", though at times God himself gives immediate commission to men.[2] The Sovereign's power is to control the ministry and appoint them to particular functions; he cannot give that divine grace which comes by ordination.[3]

The Church consists of clergy and laity, and the clergy are divided into presbyters and deacons.[4] A presbyter is defined as one who has power of " spiritual procreation ".[5] The Apostles, as well as others, were presbyters, but constituted a more " eminent " section, for the growth of the Church required them to possess a more extensive authority. The ranks of the ministry were then Apostles and presbyters, to which later were added deacons. In the course of the early days of Christianity, therefore, there emerged three degrees of ecclesiastical order: bishops, presbyters, and deacons; and those three orders are in the Church of England to-day.[6]

All the foregoing teaching would substantially be that which the Elizabethan Episcopate in general would accept. No particular " character " is stated to be of the *esse* of Church government; we do not so far read " ecclesia est in episcopo ", or that bishops are the sole direct and true heir of the Apostles. There is no theory of " monarchical episcopacy "; no doctrine of Apostolic Succession in the sense that a Church forfeits its validity if an historic and lineal descent is not preserved: on the contrary, it is the presbyter who is credited with power of " spiritual procreation ". The Elizabethan bishops were all Erastians, from the point of view that they rested the government of the Church on the civil ruler, believing that his relation to the Church was properly that which had existed between Old Testament kings and the Jewish priesthood. Not only did Scripture and reason fortify them in this position, but necessity dictated it as the only effective answer to

[1] *E.P.*, V, lxxvii, 2.
[2] *Ibid.*
[3] *E.P.*, V, lxxvii, 5.
[4] *E.P.*, V, lxxviii, 2. Hooker with deliberation uses the term " presbyter " in preference to " priest " (loc. cit.).
[5] *E.P.*, V, lxxviii, 3.
[6] *E.P.*, V, lxxviii, 5–12.

Rome's claim to supremacy and the Calvinist claim to the *ius divinum* of the presbytery. As Aylmer, Bishop of London, put it to Robert Cawdrey: " Are not we the Queen's servants? And is not the surplice the livery which she hath appointed to be worn? And do you think she will be content if we refuse to wear it? " [1]

It is the sixteenth-century position. The Elizabethans were compelled—as against the foreign enemy—to reject the imperial claim of the Papacy to be the vicegerent of Christ, and to refute the *ius divinum* claim of Presbyterianism, which split the Reformed front at home and threatened civil dissension, while yet they desired to maintain sympathetic and cordial relations with the Reformed Churches abroad. Keble regrets that they did not " take the highest ground, and challenge for the Bishops the same unreserved submission, on the same plea of exclusive apostolical prerogative, which their adversaries feared not to insist on for their elders and deacons. It is notorious, however, that such was not in general the line preferred by Jewel, Whitgift, Bishop Cooper, and others. . . . It is enough, with them, to shew that the government by archbishops and bishops is ancient and allowable; they never venture to urge its *exclusive* claim, or to connect the succession with the validity of the holy Sacraments ".[2] Thus it is that in the earlier books, while Hooker deliberately retains the historic and traditional ministry, he enters into no explanation of its doctrinal significance, and rivals neither Pope nor presbyter in claiming an exclusive *ius divinum* for Episcopacy. Herein he is representative of the Elizabethan Church, as may be seen, for example, by a consideration of the XIXth, XXIIIrd and XXXVIth Articles and the Preface to the Ordinal. So far from stating that episcopal government is the *esse* of a Church, Hooker insists—as Whitgift had—that matters necessary to salvation will be found expressly in Scripture or deducible therefrom, but that Church order and ceremonies are of less importance, are not prescribed in Scripture, and are within the competence of any Church to change and develop.[3] The former are " necessary ", the latter " accessory and dependent ",[4] and the form of Church government is " in the number of things accessory ".[5]

But the Seventh Book contains views which go considerably beyond and cut across this position. The Apostolic origin of the Episcopate is far more sharply asserted, and the Church is stated to have been governed by them for 1,500 years.[6] The first Apostles were bishops, and all bishops are their true successors.[7] The

---

[1] Brook: *Lives of the Puritans* (London, 1813), I, 433.
[2] Keble's *Preface*, I, lxvii (Ed. 1888).
[3] *E.P.*, III, ii, 2.   [4] *E.P.*, III, iii, 4.
[5] *Ibid.*   [6] *E.P.*, VII, i, 4.
[7] Cf. Marsiglio of Padua: *Defensor Pacis*, Dictio II, caps. vi and xv.

order was universal and the Holy Spirit was its Author [1]: and he quotes with approval, " Ecclesia est in episcopo ",[2] which confronts us with a new view—Episcopacy is of the *esse* of a Church [3]—" No Bishop, no Church "—and the poor presbyter *vis-à-vis* the Bishop has dwindled into a mere " light borrowed from the other's lamp ".[4]

It is difficult, indeed, to reconcile these passages of the Seventh Book with all that has gone before. These words never saw the light of day until 1662, amid the enthusiasm engendered by the restoration of the monarchy and the triumph of High Anglicanism. Are they, in fact, Hooker's opinions? None can say. He had plainly refused to oppose to the Puritans' claim of divine right and scriptural title for Presbyterianism a similar stand for Episcopacy, though aware of the value of such counter-argument. " The very best way for us ", he said, " and the strongest against them, were to hold, even as they do, that in Scripture there must needs be found some particular form of Church polity, which God hath instituted, and which for that very cause belongeth to all Churches to all times. But with any such partial eye to respect ourselves, and by cunning to make those things seem the truest which are the fittest for our purpose, is a thing which we neither like nor mean to follow." [5] Passages in the Seventh Book, however, are in direct contrast to this decision. Later in that book he admits that his views have undergone some change,[6] but if Books I–V represent his view up to 1597, and the learned author died in 1600, what can have happened in three short and occupied years to enlighten his mind on this matter after a life of study on it? A few pages farther on he acknowledges that in certain emergencies non-episcopal ordination is valid,[7] and flatly denies that continued succession of bishops is invariably essential.[8] But when he laments that the ruin of the prelacy will be the ruin of the nobility,[9] suspicion insists on entering the mind as to whether the Hooker who wrote the first five books could ever have adopted so utilitarian a view. Laud, in the course of his trial, raised the question whether temporal peers

---

[1] *E.P.*, VII, v, 10.

[2] *E.P.*, VII, v, 2.

[3] The *Christian Letter* accuses Hooker of advocating either Popery or Atheism under the guise of an attack on Puritanism. If in the first Five Books Hooker had dealt with the Church or Episcopacy in the manner of Book VII, his antagonist would have fastened on to it as further evidence of insinuating Romanism. Again, if his thesis anywhere in Books I–V contained the view " ecclesia in episcopo ", there would be no point in the question raised by the *Letter* how Hooker, in fact, discerns a congregation to be a member of the visible Church.

[4] *E.P.*, VII, vi, 3.

[5] *E.P.*, III, x, 8.

[6] *E.P.*, VII, xi, 8.

[7] Cf. Gauden, *Ecclesiae Anglicanae Suspiria* (London, 1659), p. 474.

[8] *E.P.*, VII, xiv, 11.

[9] *E.P.*, VII, xviii, 10.

would not share a like fate if bishops were abolished and Church lands confiscated.[1] Moreover, the Episcopate of the 1590's seemed in little danger of being ruined; their chief detractors had been hanged; they themselves were about to claim a divine right as well as kingly favour; in a few short years Episcopacy gathered such strength as to be planted in Scotland anew. The sentiment would hold good far more of the Commonwealth years, or even of the first two years of the Restoration, when the bishops were anxious to get their hands on manors and episcopal lands which had been alienated. The differences and confusion can hardly be explained: it is puzzling to think that the " judicious " Hooker could, between the years 1597 and 1600, write such contradictory views.

It has already been stated that the MS. of the last three books was for many years in the Lambeth Library. The sentiments of Book VII—which certainly are not wholly those of Books I to V— on Church government would have found ready acceptance with Laud. He knew and appreciated his Hooker as much as anyone.[2] In his " Conference with Fisher "[3] he relies with great frequency on Hooker in such topics as the place of reason, General Councils, the force and value of tradition, and misses no chance of exposing where Romanists have misquoted or unfairly cited from the *Ecclesiastical Polity*. But it is on Bilson, not Hooker, that he relies, when he argues for the divine right of bishops,[4] maintaining for the Anglican Episcopate a personal succession from St. Peter—the " Archbishop's Pedigree ", as Nicholas sneeringly called it at Laud's trial.[5]

It is strange that he never consulted, still less published, the MS., if, indeed, as Gauden said, it lacked only Hooker's " last polishing ". That he was ignorant of its existence is scarcely credible. Assuming that the Archbishop—that zealous defender of episcopal government —knew the MS., yet neither used nor published it, it would seem not unreasonable to conclude that its views were on all fours with what had been previously expressed in the five published books.[6]

---

[1] *Life and Trial* (London, 1695), p. 142. Richard Stretton writing to Thoresby, " Bishop Laud's Life is put out by his friends at 18s. price, and I think, to a considering reader, they expose him more than Mr. Prynne did " (Thoresby, *Diary and Corr.*, III, 183).

[2] Walton mentions that Laud had copiously annotated his own copy of the *E.P.* (*Life of Hooker*, p. 89).

[3] Laud's *Works* (Parker Soc., 1844), Vol. II.

[4] Laud's *Life and Trial* (London, 1695), p. 376.

[5] Op. cit., p. 393.

[6] This may be the explanation why defenders of the *ius divinum* of bishops do not quote Hooker until well after Gauden's edition. Indeed, it is more common to find him cited on the other side! Thus Thorndike, the deeply learned Anglo-Catholic—whose books were mostly published before 1660—never relies on him. Thorndike's Works were massively edited by A. W. Haddan (sometime Newman's

Ignoring uncertain and controversial matter contained in the Seventh Book, there is ample material to provide a summary of Hooker's doctrine of the Church. The influence of Marsiglio of Padua is to be discerned. For instance, ecclesiastical appointments are made by the civil ruler; the laity are as integral a part of the Church as the clergy, who differ from the laity solely in their ministerial function; the execution of Church censures and judgments belongs to the whole Church; while God in ordination impresses the priestly character on a man, it is for the civil ruler to appoint him to a particular task or office; presbyter and episcopus were originally synonymous terms, the latter having only a wider power of superintendence; when, with the growth of the Church, a senior presbyter was elected to preside, he retained the name of bishop, but possessed no greater sacerdotal authority than others; the civil ruler, acting on behalf of the whole Church (laity and clergy) is the source of coercive ecclesiastical jurisdiction; the Church and the State are aspects of the same thing; and much else might be paralleled.

Hooker teaches that the Church is a divine Society, originating from Christ and the Apostles. What was the unity of the *Respublica Christiana* of Europe has now been dissolved into the particular unities of National Churches. Hence in England the Church is the same Society as the State, differing only in function, organically one.[1] To preserve that identity and unity—the alternative is division and ruin—there must be a Supreme Head over both, the Source of law and authority. Scripture, reason, and history all agree that this Supreme Head must be the Sovereign. Present circumstances reinforce this need, for there are two rival claimants for ecclesiastical supremacy, the Pope and the Presbytery. The Church is not less divine by being organically bound with the State, but more so,

---

curate) and published in eight volumes by Parker, 1844–6. I can find Hooker mentioned only once—" Our Hooker " (IV, i, 174)—and that about baptism. In four other places Thorndike has him in mind, but disapprovingly: as to a National Church (IV, ii, 864), excommunication of kings (I, ii, 565), his views on the distinction between bishops and presbyters (on which Hooker merely disputed " curiously and ingenuously ") (IV, i, 376), and because he did not condemn the Puritans for the *crime* of schism by Divine Law (I, ii, 798). He nowhere quotes him to defend Monarchical Episcopacy, though the *Tractarian Editor* frequently inserts references to Book VII. It is worth noting, too, that Smectymnus, in his *Vindication of the Answer to the Humble Remonstrance* " (1641), nowhere includes Hooker among the upholders of the divine right of bishops. The author of *The Case of Ordination Considered* (3rd ed., London, 1717, by a presbyter of the Church of England) can hardly have believed the authenticity of Book VII, when he writes in his *Preface* that several very considerable writers have asserted " the *Episcopal Eminency* to be only an *After-Constitution* of the *Church* upon *Prudential Motives*," and he includes Hooker among them, quoting Book III.

[1] " The religious consecration of social life . . . at once a symbol and a reality " (Sturzo: *Church and State*, London, 1939, p. 68).

because the State itself is of divine origin and exists to a divine end. King and people constitute at once the Church and the State; the Anglican Church of the sixteenth century is as essentially the Church of the preceding centuries [1] as the realm of Elizabeth is the historic descendant of the realm of her predecessors. On its spiritual side the realm of England has put its house in order by appeal to Scripture and the precedents of history in the light of reason. But the Puritans insisted that " the discipline of Christ's Church, that is necessary for all time, is delivered by Christ, and set down in the Holy Scriptures. Therefore the true and lawful discipline is to be fetched from thence, and from thence alone. And that which resteth upon any other foundation ought to be esteemed unlawful and counterfeit ".[2] If Cartwright's contention was sound, Elizabeth—since the Anglican Church was founded on the Royal Supremacy (" Our Church hath dependency upon the chief in our commonwealth ") [3]—was acting *ultra vires*. The question of limitation upon regal rule would arise; limitation implies an authority who may set bounds; a further question is opened up: What are subjects to do when these bounds have been passed? We have already seen the quality of obedience Goodman considered to be due.[4] Knox, despite Bullinger's reminder that hazard attaches to attempts to oppose the laws,[5] had endeavoured to stir up first the nobles [6] and then the people [7] of Scotland " to punish idolatry ". They had militant descendants like Penry, who threatened Parliament in 1588 with " an heavie reckoning ",[8] on the ground that the Anglican Church was intolerable because there was no distinction between Church and State: holy and spiritual things were not the concern of the civil government.[9]

It was in answer to the Puritan claims to disobey the ecclesiastical laws of England that Hooker developed his view of the relations between Church and State. He had already shown that law is divine order permeating all parts of creation; that political society is natural and divine; that the supremacy in a State is therefore divine, and obedience part of the divine plan. Particularly he had demolished one main Puritan platform—that Scripture is an all-sufficient guide of life. Since Scripture does not, in fact, contain

---

[1] Cf. Pollock and Maitland: *History of the English Law* (Cambridge, 1923). " The oldest utterance of English law that has come down to us has Greek words in it: words such as *bishop*, *priest* and *deacon* " (Vol. I, p. 1).

[2] *Admonition.*

[3] *E.P.*, VIII, i, 7.

[4] See p. 23, *supra.*

[5] Bullinger to Knox, Knox's *Works*, III, 224.

[6] Op. cit., p. 504.

[7] Op. cit., p. 506.

[8] *Public Wants and Disorders*, p. 14.

[9] *Humble Motion*, 1590, p. 15.

the precise form of Church government, reason dictates that Church rites and order belong to the sovereign power. The real battle-ground, therefore, between Anglican and Puritan was the Royal Supremacy. Hooker's immediate task is to establish the reasonable-ness of the Supremacy by proving the identity in England of Church and State. This identity—blasphemy to the Puritans—had already been asserted by Gardiner [1] to defend Henry VIII's settlement, and by Whitgift [2] to defend Elizabeth's. But it sprang readily from Hooker's view of law and his passionate and overwhelming desire for unity.

Church and Commonwealth are distinct by nature, but not (as the Puritans say) in essence; [3] the Puritan purpose is to destroy the Supremacy in order to elevate the ministers and make a distinct Society. Any Commonwealth which possesses the Christian religion " in gross " (one Lord, one Faith, one Baptism) [4] is a Church; in its political aspect it is a State, in its ecclesiastical a Church. The difference is solely one of function. As a matter of fact, Elizabethan England did mostly look like this. Englishmen were not Jews, Saracens, or infidels, and were therefore Christians, however impious, even excommunicable, and consequently within the Church. They held at least the faith " in gross ", and where they differed it was in negligible particulars. To Hooker this identity was a fact, not a legal fiction. Reason dictated it, the times demanded it, the Government intended it. Without unity the country's future was precarious; the Church was the spiritual side of the State, and religion alone was the vital force that could bind all Englishmen together for security and well-being, but most of all for the pursuit of God, the true purpose of the State. If, two centuries later, Burke could say that the people " do not consider their Church establishment convenient, but as essential to their State . . . the foundation of their whole constitution . . . an indissoluble union ",[5] we may estimate the conviction with which Hooker and all good sixteenth-century Anglicans held their view. He could not be, therefore, an advocate of toleration; atheists, for example, are a " wicked brood " who ought to be kept in subjection,[6] for, " With us," he declares, " one Society is both the Church and the Common-wealth . . . whole and entire . . . under one chief Governor ",[7] and proudly boasts, " In a word our estate is according to the pattern of God's own ancient, elect people." [8]

Having asserted, in the interests of national unity, the essential

---

[1] *De Vera Obedientia*, 1525.   [2] *Defence of the Answer to the Admonition.*
[3] *E.P.*, VIII, i, 2.   [4] *E.P.*, III, i, 3.
[5] Burke, *Reflections* (Everyman ed.), p. 96.   [6] *E.P.*, V, ii, 2.
[7] *E.P.*, VIII, i, 7.   [8] *Ibid.*

identity of Church and State, as against the disintegrating Puritan doctrine that they are separate corporations, Hooker proceeds to vindicate the Royal Supremacy, the symbol of that unity. Historical precedents exist in plenty. "The power of ecclesiastical dominion" was not denied to Jewish civil rulers.[1] Simon Maccabeus was, for example, both King and High Priest. David, Asa, Josiah and others all made, by virtue of their civil power, laws concerning religion, regulating Temple services and ecclesiastical affairs in general. This power was not an extra gift to the King, but belonged to him *officii natura*. The nation's religion, moreover, often depended on the personal worth of the King; his piety or impiety would change the face of public religion, and no priest's ever did. History is full of his regulations, "the deeds of the King", illustrating a supremacy to be his that never adhered to the High Priest, unless he were also King. Between England and Israel there is, in Hooker's opinion, a marked likeness.

In every public society there must be order, the absence of which is "the mother of all confusion"; there must be those who order and those who obey, for "order is a gradual disposition", to which, indeed, the order of the whole universe, divine in origin and purpose, gives testimony. The arranging of people and things in their "order" is the work of the polity, and the instrument is power; power being the ability which already resides in us or is given to us to perform actions. Spiritual power, therefore, arranges religious order, and civil power (or "dominion") all else. The plain meaning of the spiritual supremacy of the Sovereign in England is that he has power in his territory to command in religious affairs, nor does any power exist superior to his in this respect [2] ("the highest uncommanded commander"). Supremacy here means simply "highest"; it does not mean unlimited, since a three-fold limitation there may well be. God is superior obviously; so is the law, where his "dominion" is given to any Sovereign by the law; so too are "all the States . . . conjoined"[3] (presumably a genuine union of the whole people by representation). Apart from these higher powers, Hooker defines the Royal Supremacy as "that ruling authority, which neither any foreign state, nor yet any part of that politic body at home . . . can lawfully overrule".[4]

Whether the source of this power is from God or men is immaterial, since if from men, it is none the less ratified by God, and is therefore of right divine. Romanists hold that this supremacy is the Pope's by divine right; Puritans claim it for the clergy.[5] Both refuse it to a layman. To meet this objection Hooker reverts

---

[1] *E.P.*, VIII, i, 1, 2.   [2] *E.P.*, VIII, ii, 3.   [3] *Ibid.*
[4] *Ibid.*   [5] *E.P.*, VIII, ii, 4.

again to his theory of the origin of political societies, showing that, whatever the means of their establishment, Sovereigns are approved by God, are his lieutenants and " confess their power His ".[1]

Passing from the question of its origin, Hooker then proceeds to further consideration of limitations on sovereign power in the State. Beyond allowing that the King is " major singulis, universis minor ", he shows himself a firm supporter of the lawfulness of hereditary succession,[2] and an abhorrer of the limited and conditional monarchy of the *Vindiciae contra Tyrannos*. When the son succeeds his royal father, the former does not enter on " an estate in condition " by the voluntary act of the people; the latter have no right to ignore the heir, for it would be against all law and equity, since they originally agreed to the stock whence this branch has sprung. That in such a State the Crown is elective, or that coronation is the sign whereby the people invest a man with the kingly power, is strange and untrue, " set abroad by seedsmen of rebellion ".[3] Birth gives right, and " the death of the predecessor putteth the successor by blood in seisin ".[4] Coronation is a mere induction into the powers he is already possessed of; and, conversely, one without hereditary right is a usurper despite coronation. The first King took his powers from the whole people as a gift, but " not as if such dependency did grow ".[5] The people cannot at each subsequent succession further limit the new King. Once and for all they parted with their power, and the sovereign authority is ever since indefeasible, except by way of escheat. Fundamentally and theoretically, power resides in the people; derivatively and practically it is in the King. Further, if limitation be impossible, still more is complete withdrawal. The kingly power cannot be forfeited save by consent of the wielders, who, presumably, would not be " stiff in detaining that, the use whereof is with public detriment ".[6] Cold comfort is it for the followers of a Hotman, a Mornay, a Cartwright, to be told that their remote ancestors should have thought of all this first! [7]

So far Hooker has delineated the Royal Supremacy as the " highest " authority, of divine origin, derived from the people at some earlier date, yet not of itself unlimited; the absolute monarch, whose power rests on conquest, must not transgress the bounds set by natural and divine law, while those monarchs whose ancestors were " first instituted by agreement and composition " are bound by " the articles of the compact " between the original ruler and

---

[1] *E.P.*, VIII, ii, 7. It is worth noticing that Hooker seems to consider that the English sovereignty originated in conquest (V, lxxx, 11; VIII, vi, 1).
[2] *E.P.*, VIII, ii, 8.   [3] *Ibid.*   [4] *Ibid.*
[5] *E.P.*, VIII, ii, 9.   [6] *E.P.*, VIII, ii, 10.   [7] *Ibid.*

people.[1] But these articles are completely or partially forgotten, and therefore the measure of the prerogative is to be found in the existing positive and customary laws. These are " after-agreements ",[2] by means of which the would-be absolute monarchs among the earlier Sovereigns were forcibly taught lessons of moderation; their descendants, wiser in their generation, adapted themselves to " that most sweet form of Kingly government ", a limited monarchy " with chiefty of power in the greatest things ".[3]

But it is clear that king with limitation of power may be to Hooker no more than a titular sovereign. The English form of monarchy, where power is not " most limited ", but " best limited ", has his complete approval; no person or party is beyond the King's power; he is supreme to command in all departments of public life, but his power is measured by the laws.[4] He quotes admiringly, " Lex facit regem "; " Rex nihil potest nisi quod jure potest ". " Happier that people whose law is their King in the greatest things, than that whose King is himself their law." [5] Where the King guides the State, and the law guides the King, then the Commonwealth is as a harp or melodious instrument.[6] In defining royal dominion in ecclesiastical affairs Hooker concludes there can be no limitation of subject-matter; [7] " religion whole " is under regal authority and subject to the temporal sword, although nobody pretends that the King can minister sacraments, or perform spiritual functions; [8] whilst it is agreed that, even in the matter of his lawful ecclesiastical dominion, there should be a certain rule, by which a King is bound, and to which he should be tied in all ecclesiastical proceedings. Unhappily there has been no uniformity of agreement as to what this rule should be. In describing his view of it Hooker gives a picture [9] of the working of the English Monarchy of his day [10] as the most reasonable rule.

The " best-established dominion " is where the King rules according to law, with supremacy in both religious and secular spheres. By virtue of his supremacy the King can do many things

---

[1] *E.P.*, VIII, ii, 11.

[2] *Ibid.*

[3] *Ibid.*

[4] Thus Hooker would have been one of the " Episcopal party ", who protested against Charles II's Declaration of Indulgence, on the ground that " the King's power was bounded by the law; and that these proceedings were the trampling of law underfoot " (Burnet, *History of Own Times* (1724), I, 283).

[5] *E.P.*, VIII, ii, 12.

[6] *Ibid.*

[7] *E.P.*, VIII, ii, 15–16.

[8] Cf. No. XXXVII of the XXXIX Articles.

[9] Said by Holdsworth (*H.E.L.*, IV, 212) to contain the best statement of the actual constitutional position of the Tudor monarchy known to exist.

[10] *E.P.*, VIII, ii, 17.

of his own will, such as making war and peace and regulating relations with other States, but in much he is powerless without Parliament; for example, he can make no alterations in the legal system, " no, not so much as restore blood ".[1] His prerogative, controlled in secular affairs by positive law established by Parliament or custom, is by the same controlled in religious matters. Ruling according to the laws and liberties of the Church, the King can exercise his ecclesiastical supremacy, but against those laws and liberties he is powerless. He is as much restrained by positive law in the Church as in the State. For example, the law, by the Act of Supremacy, has denied to the royal prerogative the right to define heresy, referring that power for the future to Parliament and Convocation.[2]

The prerogative rule of the monarch is a wise measure, making for expedition [3] in public affairs; it prevents that dissipation which occurs in unregulated society, where every man seeks his particular gain; the *bonum publicum* which is the end of all government can only be achieved by the subordination of the natural powers of all to the control of one. Thus the supremacy is as rational as it is wise. " A gross error it is, to think that regal power ought to serve . . . for men's temporal peace, and not for their eternal safety; as if God had ordained Kings for no other end and purpose but only to fat up men like hogs, and to see that they have their mast." [4] Moreover, although the Church has her spiritual discipline, she stands as much in need of the civil sword as ever. " Will any man deny that the Church doth need the rod of corporal punishment to keep her children in obedience? " [5] Indeed, as Hooker slyly points out, some Christian Churches are always running to the magistrates to coerce those who will not otherwise be reformed.

Since the Supremacy itself is lawful, the title of Supreme Head is lawful, and it is idle for Cartwright and others to object to it on the grounds that no mortal man may be so entitled, lest he place himself on an equality with Christ. " But," says Hooker, " if I term Christ and Caesar lords, yet there is no equalling of Caesar with Christ. . . . Not in the communication of names, but in the confusion of things is error." [6] The two supremacies are different things. Earthly royal supremacy differs from Christ's Headship in order,[7] since His is ὑπερ πάντα; in measure,[8] for a King's is strictly limited; in the very kind of their power,[9] for the King's headship " is altogether visibly exercised, and ordereth only the

---

[1] *E.P.*, VIII, ii, 17.   [2] I Eliz. Cap. 1, s. 36.   [3] *E.P.*, VIII, ii, 18.
[4] *E.P.*, VIII, iii, 2.   [5] *E.P.*, VIII, iii, 4.   [6] *E.P.*, VIII, iv, 3.
[7] *E.P.*, VIII, iv, 5.   [8] *Ibid.*   [9] *Ibid.*

external frame of the Church's affairs ". The Puritan objection that there is no need for a substitute, since Christ is never absent from His body, Hooker retorts, is a confusion of the visible with the invisible Church. Admitting this spiritual unity in the invisible Church, yet for the visible Church visible government is necessary; [1] " and it doth not appear how the exercise of visible government over such multitudes everywhere dispersed throughout the world should consist without sundry visible governors." [2] The fact is the Puritans condemn the name of Supreme Head because they dislike the power. [3] " In truth the question is, whether the Magistrate, by being Head in such sense as we term him, do use or exercise any part of that authority, not which belongeth unto Christ, but which other men ought to have." [4]

So far Hooker has defined the nature of the Royal Supremacy, explained its limitations, established its divine right and vindicated its title. In the sixth chapter—much the most important that remains—he examines the working of the Tudor Constitution in spiritual matters, and especially the necessary and close connection between King, Parliament and, to a less extent, Convocation.

The welfare of a commonwealth depends to such an extent upon the making of good laws that the body politic does not " clean resign " this power into the hands of a single person. Similarly, the law-making power for the Church is the whole body of the Church. Nobody can have spiritual dominion " otherwise than derived from the body of the Church ". [5] No single person (such as the Pope) can impose ecclesiastical canons on a Church, nor can any other Church (such as the Genevan) impose laws upon another. It is this necessary derivation of authority from the whole body of the Church that the Romanists most hate. [6]

Hooker makes it clear that he is concerned with external behaviour in religion; no sensible person can deny that to be within the province of government, " but the reason is not so plain wherefore human laws should appoint men what to believe ". [7] Admittedly human law cannot order beliefs, but " it may for public unity's sake require men's professed assent, or prohibit contradiction to special articles ", [8] where otherwise controversy, harmful alike to

---

[1] *E.P.*, VIII, iv, 7.
[2] *Ibid.*
[3] *E.P.*, VIII, ii, 8. Here he refers to Calvin's *Commentary on Amos*, VII, 13. See especially pp. 349–50 Calvin's *Commentaries*, II (Edinburgh, 1846).
[4] *E.P.*, VIII, iv, 8.
[5] *E.P.*, VIII, vi, 2.
[6] *Ibid.* Another echo of Marsiglio: *Defensor Pacis*; e.g., Dictio I, xvii, 13; Dictio II, v, 9; Dictio II, xv, 1; Dictio II, xvii, 8–12.
[7] *E.P.*, VIII, vi, 5.
[8] *Ibid.*

the souls of men and to the State, might continue. This would seem a plea for State religion undisguised, and puts Hooker in line with those who would prosecute under the Act of Uniformity. It is not easy to see how he squares his view of human law with the freedom of conscience. Human laws are made to restrain outward actions, he admits, and have no concern with a man's private thoughts. Yet he plainly abhors men who simulate obedience in order to comply with the laws,[1] though on his own premisses he ought to be content with outward conformity. None the less, he clearly wishes to scrutinize their motives and penalize them when they are unworthy. His real position appears to be that a worthy man will obey the human law worthily, partly because of the threatened penalties, but also in part because he recognizes that there is natural justice embodied in the law. While, therefore, Hooker would persecute, we have to acknowledge that there is also here to be found a germ of the idea of toleration; liberty of conscience is to be permitted, since it is a natural right, and in any event the State cannot prevent it. But this is not the same as religious liberty, which is destructive of national unity. The State cannot compel men to think and believe in their innermost souls at its dictation, but must oblige to external professions of belief of that which is not believed, for public unity, that all may in outward conformity be one.[2] State-preservation is the all-important end of State religion; or, conversely, and perhaps more correctly, the principal aim of the State is the maintenance of true religion.

Therefore, precisely as the State makes laws for its secular well-being, so it can legislate for its spiritual side. " What authority as touching laws for religion a Commonwealth hath simply, it must of necessity, being Christian, have the same as touching laws for Christian religion." [3] Now the Puritans would restrain this legislative activity to the clergy, on the analogy of the Council of Jerusalem, but this example is not in point. That Council was divine, not human—" it seemed good to the Holy Ghost and to us . . ."—it was for all Churches, nor has its like ever since met.[4] The Church in any place was then but a persecuted handful; now it is a Commonwealth, and the King its foster-father. Seeing, then, Hooker concludes, that the condition of the Church is so utterly different from what it was originally, and kings are now its protectors who were its persecutors, " and the clergy not now that which then they were ",[5] unless the Puritans can show a special law of Christ annexing this legislative power to the clergy alone,

---

[1] *E.P.*, V, lxviii, 7.   [2] *Ibid.*   [3] *E.P.*, VIII, vi, 6.
          [4] *E.P.*, VIII, vi, 7.   [5] *E.P.*, VIII, vi, 8.

the only reasonable deduction is that in a Christian State the consent of the laity, clergy, and King must be obtained for the making of any ecclesiastical laws. No king would enforce on his subjects laws of which he is ignorant; and the laity must be joined, since what touches all should be approved by all.[1]

There is, indeed, in antiquity no evidence that Church laws were imposed without a Sovereign's assent, and contemporary proof is afforded of a Sovereign's power over ecclesiastical legislation. For example, the decrees of the Council of Trent are not recognized everywhere as binding, since even His Most Catholic Majesty of Spain, Philip II, in publishing them in the Low Countries, expressly excepted his prerogatives and the rights of any of his vassals.[2] If Philip could *limit* the Tridentine decrees, he could refuse them. Either, therefore, you must make the King's authority over the clergy less in the greatest things—less, relatively, than that of the Rector of a University or Corporation—*or* you must conclude that it is indecent for clergy to impose laws, " the supreme governor's assent not asked ".[3]

Puritan and Romanist would agree that King and Parliament cannot legislate for the Church, any more than they can for the angels. In Hooker's reply there is an irresistible logic, once the identity of Church and State be granted. " The Parliament of England, together with the convocation annexed thereunto, is that whereupon the very essence of all government within this Kingdom doth depend; it is even the body of the whole realm; it consisteth of the King, and of all that within the land are subject unto him; for they are all there present, either in person or by such as they voluntarily have derived their very personal right unto. The parliament is a court not so merely temporal as if it might meddle with nothing but only leather and wool." [4]

Romanists cannot have it both ways. Did not the kingdom in the person of its Parliament submit in Mary's reign once more to the Papacy, obtaining absolution on condition of repealing the anti-papal laws of Henry VIII and Edward VI? " Had they power to repeal laws made, and none to make laws concerning the regiment of the Church? " [5] " Somewhat belike they [i.e., Romanists] thought there was in this mere temporal court, without which the Pope's own mere ecclesiastical legate's dispensation had taken small effect in the Church of England." Nor, he drily remarks, did any of the Papal party charge Parliament in so acting to be contrary to divine or natural law.[6] Wherefore, Hooker concludes that the English Parliament has competent authority to define and determine

---

[1] *E.P.*, VIII, vi, 8.   [2] *E.P.*, VIII, vi, 9.   [3] *Ibid.*
[4] *E.P.*, VIII, vi, 11.   [5] *Ibid.*   [6] *Ibid.*

I

ecclesiastical affairs " by way of assent and approbation "; and by its inherent power to declare its findings as laws.[1]

It is surprising that Hooker, having raised the question, should not have discussed the position and powers of Convocation as distinct from Parliament.   There can be no doubt that he must have regarded Convocation as a valid legislature, acting with the royal assent, for the Church.   Elizabeth had made it abundantly clear that the Supremacy was her personal possession, whereby she would protect the Church from any stranglehold by Parliament. Anglicanism was to provide a State Church, in the sense of a Church fit for the genius of the nation, not in the sense of a State-ridden Church.   In adopting this attitude she was, of course, emphasizing the position taken up by the Statute of Appeals (1533) that the " body politic called the spirituality . . . is sufficient and meet of itself, without the intermeddling of any exterior person . . . to declare and determine all such . . . duties as to their rooms spiritual doth appertain ".[2]   Hooker was fully alive to all this, and his omission of this question is possibly due to the delicacy of the situation. Perhaps he found it not easy to formulate any theory by which Convocation could be said to represent the laity of the Church, since the consent of her *whole* people by way of representation is the core of Hooker's teaching on legislation.   Moreover, to discuss Convocation's legislative powers may have been impolitic in one who accused the Puritans of desiring to control all religious and moral life by and through the Assemblies of Clergy.   As a political theorist, at all events, Hooker seems to regard Convocation as no other than the Clerical Estate, part and parcel of Parliament, unable to legislate for the other Estates without their consent.

In all legislation the King's power lies directly in his right of veto;[3] whatever the form of polity, that party is ultimately sovereign which possesses this veto.   It belongs to kings as kings. It was exercised by Christian emperors in Church affairs throughout history, who therefore must be condemned as presumptuous, unless opponents admit the reasonableness of " quod principi placuit, legis habet vigorem ", since the people derived their whole legislative power into the Emperor.[4]   Nor does it follow that, as a private individual, the King is not spiritually subject to pastors, which " may stand very well without resignation of supremacy of power in making laws ".[5]

Having vindicated (against the Romanists) the place of Parlia-

---

[1] *E.P.*, VIII, vi, 11.
[2] Cf. Sykes: *Church and State in the XVIIIth Century* (Cambridge, 1934), pp. 298-9, and Gibson's *Codex*, Intro. Discourse (1713), p. xxix.
[3] *Ibid.*   [4] *Ibid.*   [5] *Ibid.*

ment in Church and nation, and again reminded them that Church laws do not receive their force from power given by King to Parliament, but from the power which the whole realm originally possessed by nature, and by free assent derived to the Sovereign, Hooker returns to further Puritan objections.   They deny that civil magistrates may meddle with Church laws, any more than ecclesiastical governors may with municipal laws.   Again, he drily points out, Puritans hate ecclesiastical persons to be lords, yet should wish to restrain to them ecclesiastical legislation " which thing is of all others most proper unto dominion ".[1]   They would not argue like this if they realized the actual process of law-making.   A law must be first devised, then sifted, lastly authorized.   Granted ecclesiastical people are most fit to devise and sift Church laws,[2] but the power of dominion alone can establish them as laws.[3]   Again, Hooker repeats his challenge to the Puritans to produce even one law of Christ which forbids this power of dominion, this royal supremacy, to earthly kings.

The Puritan position is altogether illogical.   Even they themselves admit the King must have this supremacy in cases of necessity,[4] as, for example, where there is no lawful ministry, that is—according to Puritans—when the ministry is wicked.   But what if the King be also wicked?   Then, he points out, they must have recourse to Brownist logic, and admit the supremacy to devolve " unto the godly among the people "; " some Knipperdoling with his retinue must take the work of the Lord in hand ",[5] and make laws, the wise and great having failed.   Apparently in order to further their position, the Puritans insist that the Anglican ministry is wicked— here is a case of necessity, and the King may do something.   He may oust the Anglicans by his Supremacy till the Puritans enter in, who " will disburden and ease him of it ".[6]   Thereafter he is to see that all Church affairs are observed and executed, and to punish ecclesiastical persons who fail in their duty.   All sides—Anglican, Roman, Puritan—acknowledge this power of *maintenance* of Church laws, but only the Anglican party allows the King supremacy in ecclesiastical legislation; yet the Puritans have admitted that in the Christian Empire no canon or council had the force of law unless approved by the Emperor.   On their own showing he had a veto on Church legislation, which, after all, is only what Anglicans claim for their King.[7]

Since the Puritans have heaped abuse upon the lawfulness of episcopal and commissary courts under the Royal Supremacy,

[1] *E.P.*, VIII, vi, 12.
[2] Cf. Marsiglio of Padua, *Defensor Paçis*, Dictio II, vi, 12.
[3] *Ibid.*   [4] *E.P.*, VIII, vi, 14.   [5] *Ibid.*   [6] *Ibid.*   [7] *Ibid.*

some examination of their nature is essential. Part of the abuse
arises from a deliberate misconception of the Anglican position,
which in no wise permits sacerdotal functions to the King or allows
him to sit as an ecclesiastical judge. There are two sorts of ecclesiastical judges: the " Ordinary ", who by the law of the land
must be the diocesan bishop—his jurisdiction extends to purely
spiritual causes; it is exercised by him " natura officii ", and
cannot be exercised by a layman—and, secondly, Commissionary
judges, who may be lay or spiritual. Besides these " there is
required an universal power which reacheth over all . . . all
courts, all judges, all causes ",[1] to maintain their particular jurisdictions and to remedy their deficiencies. Formerly this power was
in the hands of the Pope, but " was for just considerations by public
consent annexed unto the King's royal seat and crown ".[2] Now
it is this universal power which the Puritans wish to transfer to
their national synod, embracing as it does powers of visitation and
reformation in the whole or any part of the Church, deliberately
given to the Crown by law.[3]

The King, too, has the supreme appellate jurisdiction. Who else
if not he? Puritans may possibly admit appeals to their synod,
and Romanists, of course, to the Pope, but neither tolerate the royal
claim to it.[4] The Puritans, by their division of England into
parishes of equal standing, must make the King far less indeed than
many subjects.[5] As a member of his parish, he perhaps would not
even be an office-holder,[6] and could be called to account by the
parish consistory; but even if he had so much preferment as to
be made a parish officer, he would still be incapable of supreme
appellate jurisdiction. Neither upon Scriptural support nor on
the argument of personal unfitness can the Puritans debar the King
from his supreme jurisdiction, exercised personally or by delegation.
" All men are not for all things sufficient," therefore must there be
udges and jurisdictions, yet one transcendant authority.[7] It is
authority, not a licentious tyranny. The laws of England have
prescribed fixed bounds to each kind of power, civil and ecclesiastical; neither prince nor prelate can judge at his own discretion,
" but law hath prescribed what both shall do ".[8] " What power
the King hath he hath it by law, the bounds . . . of which are
known." [9] General direction as to the administration of public
affairs is given to the community by law; particular application
to causes is given by the King, as head of the community, by the same
law. " The whole body politic maketh laws, which laws give

[1] *E.P.*, VIII, viii, 4.   [2] *Ibid.*   [3] *Ibid.*   [4] *E.P.*, VIII, viii, 5.
[5] *Ibid.*   [6] Cf. Bancroft, *Dangerous Positions*, p. 97.
[7] *E.P.*, VIII, viii, 7.   [8] *E.P.*, VIII, viii, 9.   [9] *Ibid.*

power unto the King, and the King having bound himself to use according unto law that power, it so falleth out, that the execution of the one is accomplished by the other in most religious and peaceable sort." [1]   Civil and ecclesiastical jurisdictions are entirely separate.

The last aspect of the question of the King's supremacy is whether he personally, as a man, is exempt from ecclesiastical jurisdiction. [2] Hooker admits that for gross sin the King may be rebuked, and even debarred from Communion, but may not be punished as an evil-doer by excommunication or any other method. But the Puritans, from Calvin onwards, would call the magistrate to account as a member of the Church. This, to Hooker, seems illogical and dangerous. In every State there must be some supreme power of which the whole community should stand in awe. Consequently this supremely empowered person can never be in subjection to any part of his kingdom. This maxim may lead at times to harmful results, but it is none the less necessary to maintain. Justice is a fountain which must spring from some source; there must be a superior to whom inferior magistrates are obliged to answer; kings are answerable only to Heaven, " on earth they are not accountable to any ". [3]

Similarly, the King is not subject to laws in a sense: that is to say, he cannot be punished, as subjects are, for breach of the laws, since there is no person superior to him to order process and punishment. [4]   None the less, he is bound by the Law of Nature and of God, not only as all men are, but morally much more, inasmuch as the greater the sinner the greater is the sin. [5]   Presumably, too, the King is bound by the fundamental and original law establishing the *State*, but Hooker says nothing of that in this place. His limitations on the royal power are vague, procedure against him undefined. Indeed, on the question how far the King is " legibus solutus ", Hooker is very far from clear. Where positive laws prescribe definite powers, the King is tied to them, though we are left uncertain what is to happen if he oversteps the limits. The original law of the State contained " articles of agreement ", but Hooker elsewhere confesses they are probably long since forgotten and can scarce be expected to bind generations of successive kings. Outside the limitations fixed, therefore, by the Laws of Nature, of the State and of God, the King is bound to have a vast latitude, and for his actions within this scope the King is responsible only to his Maker: a practical position, when examined, not so much unlike Bodin's or Hobbes's, for all we read of law, consent, compact and agreement.

---

[1] *E.P.*, VIII, viii, 9.   [2] *E.P.*, VIII, ix, 1.   [3] *E.P.*, VIII, ix, 2.
[4] *E.P.*, VIII, ix, 3.   [5] *Ibid.*

But attack on the Royal Supremacy was destined to come from elsewhere, too. The Elizabethan bishops cannot have had a very happy time, and some did not deserve it anyhow. Treated on the one hand by the Council as mere officials, as holding office by virtue of a commission, and removable at the Sovereign's pleasure, on the other hand regarded by the Puritans as the last rag of Popery, without adequate help from their employer, and no possibility of sympathetic understanding from their opponents, they began to assert their courage and to claim some measure of *ius divinum* as the sanction of episcopal office. At least they ventured to retort, in reply to the continued attack of the Cambridge Movement, beginning from 1570, that there is more in Scripture to warrant episcopacy than the Discipline, of which " no age ever had knowledge of it but only ours ".[1]

As time passed Anglicans grew bolder, and in his sermon at Paul's Cross in 1588 Bancroft made an *ad hoc* reply that Episcopacy had endured since Apostolic times, a view on the whole shared by Hooker. " I may securely therefore conclude that there are in this day in the Church of England . . . Bishops [2] . . . which had their beginning from Christ and His Blessed Apostles." [3] Before long it would dawn on Anglicans that a safer basis for Episcopacy must be found than the royal fiat. The High Anglicans of the seventeenth century could not accept, even if Jewel, Parker, Whitgift and Hooker could, the position of the " learned man " who wrote to Sir Francis Knollys, " The Bishops of this realm do not . . . nor must not claim to themselves any greater authority than is given them by the Statute of the 25. of K. Henry VIII revived in the

---

[1] *E.P.*, III, x, 8.

[2] In all these arguments concerning Episcopacy everything turns on the definition of the term. All Protestant Churches admitted that bishops were primitive in the sense of " senior presbyters " for regional administration. Calvin agreed to this, and had the thing, if not the title. When learned Reformed ministers, like Saravia, defend Episcopacy, they have this conception in mind. So had Jewel and Whitgift, and Hooker seems to mean this except in places in Book VII. What Protestants attacked was monarchical episcopacy, prelacy, hateful because of its " lordship ", arrogating itself as the only channel of Divine Grace for a Ministry. As Baxter in the next century said, " If Episcopacy in general were proved part of the Protestant Religion, the English Accidents and Corruptions are not so; They, that say that episcopacy is *Jure Divino*, and unalterable, do yet say, that National, and Provincial Churches are *Jure Humano* " (*Reliquiae Baxterianae*, London, 1696, Pt. III, p. 169). Elsewhere in the same book he distinguishes between the genus of episcopacy and its species prelacy (op. cit., II, 426). Or, as Smectymnus put it earlier still, " It is well observed by Gerhard, that a Bishop, ' phrasi Apostolica ', that is, a Bishop that is the same with a Presbyter, is of fifteen hundred years' standing; but a Bishop, ' phrasi Pontificia ', that is, a distinct Order superior to a Presbyter invested with sole power of Ordination and Jurisdiction, is but a novel invention " (*An Answer to a Book entitled an Humble Remonstrance* (1641), p. 19).

[3] *E.P.*, V, lxxviii, 12.

first year of her Majestie's reign; or by other Statutes of this land. Neither is it reasonable that they should make other claims. For if it had pleased her Majesty, with the wisdom of the realm, to have used no bishops at all, we could not have complained justly of any defect in our Church. . . . But sith it pleased Her Majesty to use the ministry of Bishops, and to assign them this authority, it must be to me, that am a subject, as God's ordinance." [1] Their claim to divine right was an attack on the Royal Supremacy from another angle, and was the foundation of the future alliance between Crown and Church exemplified in Stuart times by the epigrammatic " No Bishop, No King ".

The core of all Hooker's argument on the relations of Church and State is obviously " unity ". The conception of unity, the " argumentum unitatis ", which distinguished mediaeval thinking, whether of the Guelphic or the Ghibelline party, informs every aspect of Hooker's thought, and his application of this same standard to national State and national Church is an outstanding mark of continuity between him and his Scholastic predecessors. " Plato's Republic has been said to be a church and not a state, and such an ideal of a city in the heavens has always hovered over the Christian world." [2] Gierke gives perhaps the most illuminating account of the basis of this profound and all-pervading belief. " Thus every particular Being . . . is a Microcosmus or Minor Mundus in which the Macrocosmus is mirrored. Thus the theory of Human Society must accept the divinely created organisation of the Universe as a prototype of the first principles which govern the construction of human communities." [3] " Credo unum Deum ", and therefore I believe in one law, and in one human society governed by it, so far as is possible for unity to be. But unity in the mediaeval sense, in the sense of the world society, had suffered a shattering blow, and had been splintered into fragments.

England was one of those fragments, and the contest was between those who believed that the fragment retained a characteristic of unity within itself from the whole and those who proposed to carry on the process of disintegration. England, Church and State united, was open to double attack from those—the Roman Catholics —who were the champions of a larger unit, and those who, like the Puritans, wished for a separation of powers and further division. Hooker's position is that the nation is a spiritual society, and therefore its head a spiritual head, who is competent to rule in matters

[1] Strype: *Whitgift*, III, 222.
[2] Jowett: *Introduction to the Republic* (Oxford, 1921), pp. 160-1.
[3] Gierke: *Political Theories of the Middle Ages* (trans. Maitland, Cambridge, 1938), pp. 7 *et seq.*, and cf. Barker's *Gierke* (Cambridge, 1934), I, cap. 1.

other than the commerce of the citizens, just as " the parliament is a court not so merely temporal as if it might meddle with nothing but only leather and wool ".[1] That a nation is a spiritual society scarcely stands in need of demonstration; the common accidents of life are sufficiently articulate. Sir Ernest Barker has urged with considerable force the advantages arising from the fusion of " the spiritual tradition of the old and Christian society " with " the spiritual tradition of the new and secular nation ",[2] and this belief, though in other words and in another form, is the basis of the Eighth Book of the *Ecclesiastical Polity*. It explains, moreover, its contradictions. The advantages which 300 years later can so shortly be summarized by Professor Barker were too close and too new to Hooker to take upon themselves the simplicity with which the lapse of years allows us to see them. But Hooker possessed an overwhelming belief, an intuition, that Ecclesia Anglicana possessed a vast potentiality and that his opponents continually missed the point when, for instance, they argued about excommunication.[3] He was compelled to answer their arguments, but more in order to clear difficulties out of their way than to justify the Church to which he belonged. It would certainly not have affected Hooker personally if, instead of being able only partially and unsatisfactorily, even contradictorily, to answer the argument about Excommunication, he had not been able to answer it at all.

This is not to say that the main thesis of Book VIII was not vital to Hooker, but simply that it was so vital that small and incidental trifles were powerless to affect the whole. We must not, he says, " be carried up and down with the waves of uncertain arguments, but rather positively to lead on . . . till the very nature of the thing itself do make manifest what is truth." [4] And the truth to Hooker was that Church and State were one society, called the Church " with only reference unto true religion, without any affairs besides ",[5] and called the State " with relation unto all the public affairs thereof, the matter of true religion excepted ". This was so because a like double relation existed in every member of the Commonwealth; he was a Churchman and a citizen, and might be thought of analogously with a triangle, of which any side is, from another angle, the base.[6] It is but another example of macrocosm and microcosm upon another step in the order of

---

[1] *E.P.*, VIII, vi, 11.
[2] *Church, State and Study* (London, 1930), p. 139 and *passim*.
[3] *E.P.*, VIII, i, 6. Cartwright posed the case of a man excommunicated but not civilly punished; or civilly punished and not excommunicated.
[4] *E.P.*, V, xxi, 2.
[5] *E.P.*, VIII, i, 5.
[6] *E.P.*, VIII, i, 2.

creation. It accords with the mighty plan which Hooker believed to be conceived in the mind of the one God and, ultimately, a deduction from the fact of his existence; and a deduction which man, by virtue of his reason, was able to make.

The gulf, therefore, that separates him from his opponents is not only one of conclusion, but one of method. It is in reality the same gulf that separates them when they contend upon any subject. " The discipline of Christ's Church, that is necessary for all times, is delivered by Christ, and set down in the Holy Scriptures. Therefore the true and lawful discipline is to be fetched from thence, and from thence alone." When Cartwright wrote that, he and his brother Puritans fully believed that one thing they could with certainty " fetch from the Scriptures ", and that was that Church and State were not one society. Penry, indeed, as we have seen, regarded Queen, Parliament, and prelates as " wicked and intolerable, because they make no difference between that which belongeth to the true worship of God, as ecclesiastical government doth, and that which appertaineth unto civil policie ".[1] Here was that division of " the whole and making it into several impaled societies " against which Hooker contended.[2] Its corollary was, of course, a division between the government of the two societies, the one purely spiritual and the other merely temporal, a return to that duplicity which the mediaevalists had always endeavoured to reduce to a unity, and which was the starting-point of the controversy of Empire and Papacy.[3] In claiming the independence of the ecclesiastical organization, the Puritans were in fact standing in the shoes of the Papalists, who claimed independence as a first step towards securing supremacy—they were demonstrating that " new presbyter is but old priest writ large ".

Neither the party of the Empire nor the party of the Papacy had been wholly successful in the Middle Age. The scope of their claims was, for one thing, too large; the geographical extent of Christendom was too wide to allow an effective sovereignty of Pope or Emperor. But now in our smaller island a centralized single government was in force, and ideals of government appear more attainable in small States than in large. Aristotle limits the size of the State, and Rousseau, too, while More chooses an island as the scene of political perfection. But though neither Clement nor Marsiglio did, nor could, realize their ideal, the struggle was now which of their conceptions would in very material fact be realized in this smaller sphere; if indeed it might not be said that Marsiglio's

---

[1] Penry, *Public Wants and Disorders*, p. 37.
[2] *E.P.*, VIII, i, 4.
[3] Maitland's *Gierke*, op. cit., p. 11, and *passim*.

system was already on the throne, and Clement's, in Puritan guise, an ineffectual thunder at the gates.

For, as Maitland pointed out,[1] we are in danger of forgetting the revival by Elizabeth in 1559 of 37 Henry VIII, c. 17, and particularly so if we lay stress on the removal of the phrase " supremum caput " from the Act of Supremacy, and upon Hooker's Eighth Book as a picture of the working of the Tudor Constitution, as we are advised by Sir William Holdsworth to do. With particular reference to the Act which we mention as having been revived, Maitland wrote, " Surely Erastianism is a bad name for the theory that King Henry approved ; Marsilianism seems better, but Byzantinism seems best." [2] The particularly relevant words are these, that his, or, when revived, her, " most royal majesty is, and hath always been, supreme head in earth of the Church of England, and hath full power and authority to correct, punish and repress all manner of heresies . . . and to exercise all other manner of jurisdiction usually called ecclesiastical jurisdiction ". Moreover he, or she, " is the only and undoubted supreme head of the Church of England, and also of Ireland, to whom by Holy Scripture all authority and power is wholly given to hear and determine all manner of causes ecclesiastical ".[3] Such was the legal position of Elizabeth. It differed from Marsilianism not in any imperfection of the supremacy of the temporal ruler, but in the absolute position of the monarch. That is why Maitland spoke of it as Byzantinism, as being influenced by the civilian conceptions which England so desperately fought with the Gothic armament of the Lancastrian Constitution. But again, it differed from Byzantinism because it was ultimately based upon the consent of the people ; and it was only when James II lost their consent that the desperate fight to which we have referred took place—and Marsilianism triumphed.

If, therefore, Hooker's apology for Elizabethanism is not wholly consistent, if he seems at one moment to be defending absolutism and at another asserting constitutionalism, we may observe that that is actually what he is doing. He is defending a system which was effective, but of which the actual basis was somewhat uncertain ; it was not for nothing that all, or nearly all, English works appearing at the time were submitted to the judgement of authority, either in a note at the beginning or at the end. Hooker was eminently an authoritarian ; his philosophic position demanded above all things a

[1] Maitland, *Collected Papers* (Cambridge, 1911), Vol. III, pp. 203–4.

[2] Maitland, *English Law and the Renaissance* (Cambridge, 1901), p. 14. For full significance of " Byzantinism " see Runciman, *Byzantine Civilization* (London, 1932), pp. 61 *et seq.*, and Sturzo : *Church and State* (London, 1939), Chap. 2.

[3] 37 Henry VIII, c. 17.

submission to the higher powers, just because he regarded order as " a gradual disposition ", and the whole creation as hierarchical in form. The great and distant outlines of the Major Mundus were sufficiently clear, as with Plato the greater the abstraction the clearer the truth, but in the Minor Mundus, of proximate human experience, the clarity and consistency were bound to be far less.

Even those whose daily duty it was to administer the law of the realm, and who occupied high office of State, betrayed in their writings the greatest uncertainty as to the actual constitution. Sir Thomas Smith's *De Republica Anglorum* [1] is an eminent example, and particularly relevant to Hooker because it is supposed that he had a foundation in Smith's book.[2] At least Smith wrote with great authority, even though, as he told a friend, he wrote entirely from memory and had with him no books. Professor Maitland delighted to call him " the Rev. Professor Sir Thomas Smith, Kt., M.P., Dean of Carlisle, Provost of Eton, Ambassador to the Court of France and one of the Secretaries of State to Queen Elizabeth ".[3] But, despite his titles, it would be exceedingly difficult to extract from the *De Republica Anglorum* any statement as to who is Sovereign; although Sir Thomas, with greatest care, defined at the very outset just what sovereignty is. " To rule," he wrote, " is under-stoode to have the highest and supreme authoritie of commaunde-ment. That part or member of the commonwealth is said to rule which doth controwle, correct, and direct all other members of the commonwealth." [4] So much, as Sir Frederick Pollock suggests, may be influenced by Bodin; [6] the remainder belongs far more to the stream that bore Locke and Rousseau than to that which carried Hobbes and Austin. We shall later suggest an extension of this opinion. Meanwhile the difficulty of ascertaining any particular doctrine of sovereignty may be exemplified by two extracts from the *De Republica*. " To be short the prince is the life, the head, the authoritie of all things that be doone in the realme of England ",[7] and, secondly, " . . . the parliament of Englande, which representeth and hath the power of the whole realme both the head and the body ".[8] It would be possible to produce a large number of hardly reconcilable quotations, but we are not likely

[1] Prynne makes frequent reference to it in his *Sovereign Power of Parliaments*, 1643.

[2] Cf. Holdsworth: *H.E.L.*, IV, 212.

[3] Maitland, *English Law and the Renaissance*, p. 10.

[4] *De Repub. Angl.* (ed. Alston, Cambridge, 1904), p. 9.

[5] *Hist. Sci. of Politics* (1919), pp. 57, 58.

[6] As Sir Thomas wrote the book while he was Ambassador in France, he may have come into some contact with Bodin.

[7] *De Repub. Angl.*, p. 62.

[8] *Op. cit.*, p. 49.

to come to a more apparently unshakeable conclusion than did Mr. Alston. " The contrast upon which Smith's attention is focussed is not the contrast between the powers of the Prince and of the Parliament, but between the powers of Parliament and of those other courts which he describes in later chapters, and describes without any feeling of essential difference between them and this the highest court." [1] When he makes mention of the wide powers vested in the Prince, and distinguishes the ruling body in peace from that in war,[2] he is expressing the existence of a strong government, adaptable to the circumstances in which it might be placed. His book might, indeed, very probably be supposed to be one of the bases of Hooker's work, though the divine nature and purpose of the State do not appear to have concerned Her Majesty's Secretary any more than the theory of contract, which he mentions, but upon which he does not insist.[3]

We have therefore the man of affairs and the theorist writing to exalt the Elizabethan Constitution, without complete knowledge of what it was; both of them making serious omissions. Neither lays any stress upon the Council or the Convocation, but both have the same drift, conditioned by the State and the time in which they lived, in their belief in the unity and omnicompetence of government. Smith in his chapter on the Ecclesiastical Courts,[4] and Hooker wherever he deals with the relations of Church and State,[5] are of one mind in this connection. Now, Sir Thomas Smith was a Civilian, and lectured upon Civil Law at Cambridge, and although the *De Republica Anglorum* was largely a favourable comparison of the working of English Common Law with that of the countries of the Reception, the very completeness of the national State was the outcome of the triumph of what Gierke called the antique concept of the State—" the drift of theory set incessantly towards an exaltation of the Sovereignty of the State which ended in the exclusive representation by the State of all the common interests and common life of the Community ".[6] " The mediaeval ideal of the organic articulation of mankind " [7] was weakening, the all-powerful and absorbing State was taken as a premiss in argument as to whence came that authority—namely, in the later contest between the Contractual and Divine Right theories of government. Hooker, then, had reached this position, which was fraught with danger for the Church of which he wrote. For, as Gierke pointed out, " If . . . the Individual just in so far as he belongs to the Community is

[1] Alston, Intro. in *De Repub. Angl.*, p. xxxiii.
[2] *De Repub. Angl.*, Book II, Chap. 3.
[3] Op. cit., p. 20.   [4] Book III, Chap. ix.
[5] Principally, of course, Books III, V and VIII.
[6] Maitland's *Gierke*: op. cit., p. 98.   [7] *Ibid.*

fully and wholly absorbed into the State, so, on the other hand, there is a strong tendency to emancipate the Individual from all bonds that are not of the State's making."[1] The path is open to what Figgis deplored,[2] the omnicompetent State over against the isolated individual, and the purely fictitious personal and spiritual non-existence before this law of all corporations, including alike the established and disestablished Churches. In the field of political theory Figgis points to the works of Professor Dicey;[3] in that of legal action to the case of the Free Churches of Scotland.[4] From both he deduces that Churches established and disestablished are free neither from the higher Hegelianism of Lord Haldane nor the Parliamentary judgements of free-thinkers. And he establishes that this is not a phenomenon confined to England, but common to Europe. Had he lived to see the effects of the interesting and all-pervading efforts of Fascist enthusiasm he would have been provided with further evidence.[5]

It is at this point that we must revert to Hooker and Sir Thomas Smith, and the extension of the opinion which we there foreshadowed. In that both Smith and Hooker emphasized the mixed nature of the Constitution, the existence of " checks " in the Constitution and, moreover, that they allowed the free rights of the individual committed in some manner to the State as the basis of its power—in both these matters we may claim them in some true and real measure as precursors of Locke. But in so far as they exalted the omnicompetence of the central Government they are equally precursors of Hobbes and Austin, pointing towards the realization of the Great Leviathan in the Parliamentary Government of our day.

Hooker's conception was, indeed, involved in one great and increasing fallacy, namely that every member of the Church was likewise a member of the State. We are reminded of a Whig comment on the Social Contract: " To establish the throne upon a notorious untruth is to establish it upon Mr. Milton's Vacuum, where it must fall ten thousand fathoms deep, and know no end of falling." [6] In Hooker's day it was not a notorious untruth that the

---

[1] Op. cit., p. 94.

[2] *Churches in the Modern State* (London, 1913).

[3] *Law of the Constitution.*

[4] *United Church of Scotland Appeals* (ed. Orr, 1903).

[5] It is perhaps not without significance that in the heyday of Fascism both Germany and Italy produced books on Hooker (1933). The Dean of St. Paul's related to me that in 1936 at Marburg a Professor of that University attempted an *apologia* of Hitler in the course of conversation, somewhat thus: " There's something to be said for Hitler. After all, he is only trying to do what your Queen Elizabeth did."

[6] Quoted Maitland, *Collected Papers*, I, 76.

State was a single " persona " with a temporal and a spiritual aspect, but it was rapidly to become so. It is true that Burke could echo Hooker's " with us one Society is both the Church and the Commonwealth . . . whole and entire . . . under our chief Governor " [1] by his own statement that Church and State are ideas inseparable in English minds,[2] that, in fact, " in a Christian Commonwealth the Church and the State are one and the same thing, being different integral parts of the same whole ".[3] This is due to Burke's fear of " red ruin and the breaking up of Laws ". He clung to the ancient constitution of the Church and State and has been compared very closely with Hooker by Dr. Murray; [4] but the problem of the " bondage " of the Church in England had not been raised in the comfortable days of eighteenth-century English Christianity.

The problem, then, that has been left us by the ages is how to provide spiritual freedom for spiritual societies, to recognize the Church as a group " in which the natural authority over its members extends to the provision of a social atmosphere ".[5] With regret we must turn our backs upon the Eighth Book of the *Ecclesiastical Polity* as envisaging a condition which has long ceased to exist; but we must retain from it the ideal, the lively hope, the dream of unity, of the synthesis of the spiritual and the temporal, which has ever inspired and animated Christendom, till a day shall dawn when Cavour's cry becomes the truth, " Libera chiesa in libero stato ".

---

[1] *E.P.*, VIII, i, 7.
[2] Burke, *Reflections on the French Revolution*, p. 96.
[3] Speech, May 11th, 1792.
[4] *Political Consequences of the Reformation* (London, 1926), pp. 279–80.
[5] Figgis, op. cit., p. 90.

CHAPTER VII

THE RIGHT TO RESIST: THE HUGUENOT ANSWER

VOLTAIRE, in his *Essai sur les Moeurs*, dismisses religious strife as " une maladie de plus dans l'esprit humain ",[1] but he does less than justice to the human mind when he regards the Reformation as a quarrel over the Mass between Papists who " mangeaient Dieu pour pain, les luthériens du pain et Dieu, les calvinistes mangeaient le pain et ne mangèrent point Dieu ". In fact the struggle was also political. On the one hand was the genesis of the " omnicompetent State ", on the other the claim of corporations to act freely within it. It was characteristic of the century that the corporations which took up the struggle were religious, and so, as Figgis put it, " political liberty is the residuary legatee of ecclesiastical animosities ".[2] It is surely no accident, as Professor Allen has pointed out, that the author of the *Vindiciae Contra Tyrannos*[3] sees France divided into separate communities, each one of which would appear to have the right to resist a tyrant. " The Empire ", writes Professor White-head,[4] " was faced with the claim for freedom of corporate action. Modern political history, from that day to this, is the confused story of the strenuous resistance of the State and of its partial concessions." He sees the theories of Divine Right and of the Contract, the one as the " ghost of the ' divine Emperor ' ", the other as a rationalizing fiction. The Contract theory, although based largely upon the contracts of feudalism,[5] was new in so far as it was of an " *original* " contract. It is suggested that this new conception may be traced to the knowledge of primitive races which the adventurous spirits of the Renaissance had " discovered ", and whose existence was a new object of study. Now there can be no contract without law. This law is, therefore, to the Contractualists, anterior to political association; it is, in fact, the Law of Nature. Positive law was frequently regarded as being simply a revelation to the legislator of a principle already comprised in this unwritten *Corpus Juris*

[1] Quoted Croce: *On History* (London, 1921), p. 258.
[2] *From Gerson to Grotius* (Cambridge, 1923), p. 118.
[3] Allen, op. cit., p. 323.
[4] *Adventures of Ideas* (Cambridge, 1933), p. 70.
[5] Figgis pointed out that the *Liber de Feudis* was appended in every complete copy of the *Corpus Juris Civilis* (Figgis, op. cit., pp. 130-1).

Naturalis. But what is unwritten is also unreadable, and if we admit with Hooker that " that which all men have at all times learned, Nature herself must needs have taught ",[1] we should estimate very lowly the didactic powers of Nature in politics. Yet, though the " Law of Nature " is so uncertainly knowable that Professor Whitehead is able to trace four distinct conceptions of its nature,[2] and though, as so many commentators on Rousseau have pointed out, the contract theory is historically untenable, there is a sense in which both would seem to exist; that is, as the instinctive bases of human thought. That which was contentious became instinctive by its triumph over the other conception of the sole and absolute sovereignty of the State—" a mere way to provide policemen for the counting-houses of merchants ".[3]

We have seen, therefore, the indefinable Law of Nature and the non-existent contract as conceptions contributory to political liberty and as bases of that political thought which is termed " liberalism "; but it would be inaccurate, indeed ridiculous, to picture either Huguenot or Jesuit Monarchomachs as fighting for liberty or toleration for the generality of mankind. That was an incidental result of a process carried on with particular interests in view. The duty of tolerance has been magnificently defined as " our finite homage to the abundance of inexhaustible novelty which is awaiting the future, and to the complexity of accomplished fact which exceeds our stretch of insight ".[4] This duty of tolerance was acknowledged by very few in the sixteenth century. The " prodigiosi errores " of Michael Servetus may be reduced to the single error of believing Calvin fallible, and that was why Servetus was burned. Calvinist no less than Papist was guilty of the conclusion set down by Castellion [5] that " we consider all as heretics who do not agree with us in our opinion ". Professor Allen truly remarks that a Protestant doctrine of toleration might have provided a basis for rebellion,[6] but such a doctrine was to be its result rather than its cause.

The conclusion to be drawn from a theory of contract is, of course, that the Sovereign has no irrevocable authority—(he is not, in fact, Sovereign, for very few definitions of sovereignty would permit of such a limitation)—and there remains to the people the right of reclaiming their authority and doing away with the ruler who breaks the contract. But in whom does the people consist? The answers given by the Huguenot Monarchomachs are circumstantial for, to justify their own right of rebellion (and why else did

---

[1] *E.P.*, I, viii, 3.
[2] Whitehead, op. cit., Chap. VII.
[3] Whitehead, op. cit., p. 76.
[4] Whitehead, op. cit., p. 65.
[5] *Vivebat* 1515–63.
[6] Allen, op. cit., p. 224 *et seq.*

they waste paper?), the Huguenot minority must be proved to be sufficiently the people to have a right to power usurped in fact by someone else. This explains why they define " the people " not as the " bellua " but the " maior ", in the sense of the " melior pars ", " gens du bien et d'honneur ", Luther's " untere Obrigkeit ", Beza's " sanior pars ". It is true that the numerical majority has not for them obtained the stature with which it has since become endowed ; but by allowing a part of the people to act for the people they laid the foundation of this result, inescapable in later ages when arithmetic is considered a more important part of education than values, and when two are distinguished from one not only by " partaking of duality ", but of greater sanctity.[1]

The whole contradictory, but suggestive, pile of books that had been compiled and plagiarized was hastily put away so soon as the succession of Henry of Navarre to the throne appeared possible ; but as ever " the moving finger writes, and having writ, moves on ". As Castellion's plea for toleration availed nothing in his time, but helped, when he was dead, to provide a harbour in Holland for Spinoza, so the Huguenot writings helped to produce revolution in seventeenth-century England and in eighteenth-century France.

The Massacre of St. Bartholomew let loose again the dogs of war and the pens of angry men. The first contribution to Huguenot political theory in order of time was the *Franco-Gallia* of Hotman. Francis Hotman,[2] born in Paris in 1524, was a learned jurist, having held professorial chairs in Lausanne, Strasbourg, Valence, and Bourges. One of the foremost Huguenots, he narrowly escaped death in the massacre at Bourges, and in 1572 took refuge in Geneva. In this year and the next, in the bitterness of the memories of St. Bartholomew, he set himself to write what was afterwards his favourite book. Published in 1573, a second edition of the *Franco-Gallia* appeared in the following year, and a Latin text in 1576. Contrary possibly to our expectations, the book was of sufficient interest to be published in English in 1711, followed by a second edition in 1738. Some authors have found the *Franco-Gallia* a manifesto of the Huguenot party, but it has been pointed out[3] that as a manifesto the book would have better appeared in 1568, after the Second Civil War, when its constitutional theory might have rallied supporters to the Huguenot as to the patriotic cause. But, written in passion and anger, as we may see from outbursts here and there in the text, it was probably intended

---

[1] Plato, *Phaedo* (Loeb ed.), 1914, pp. 347-9.
[2] *Vivebat* 1524-90. Hooker refers to an earlier work of his in *E.P.*, VII, viii, 9, but not to the *Franco-Gallia*.
[3] J. W. Allen, op. cit., p. 309.

K

to serve as a trumpet-call to the Huguenot party as a whole; quite possibly its main thesis was, at the time, of less importance than the deduction that Hotman himself did not draw, but presumably left for his readers as plain and unmistakable. The Huguenots were Frenchmen and were Calvinists, much governed by their ministers. The unspoken proposition of the overthrow of the existing tyranny could not be reconciled to Calvinistic political teaching, since Kings were God's Vicars and might not, without sin, be resisted. In some way Calvinistic theology must be made to accord with the political needs of the moment. Thus to restore to France its original constitution, and thereby preserve it from all its miseries, was not to rebel, but to defend. But to win support from all Huguenots this political theory must have theological support, which Beza proceeded to give in his *De Jure Magistratuum* of 1576.

The *Franco-Gallia* was written, therefore, with a definite purpose to suit the needs of the moment. It was a *livre de circonstance*. It has not the usual contemporary mixture of theology, ethics, and politics; it claims to be not philosophic, but purely historical. In the book we find no analysis of law, no theory of State, no origins of political society, no discussion on the individual rights of men. It is so far from profound, in spite of countless quotations, that we feel a conviction of sketchiness; the author skates over the surface lightly, cutting figures in such fashion and profusion that they may pass for historic certainties. Hotman uses the historical method to prove that the Valois tyranny was no more than one hundred years old. His main thesis is that, in the beginning, and up to the reign of Louis XI,[1] the French Constitution was a limited monarchy, controlled by the States-General; and, since what was original must necessarily be right, France ought to return to her own.

Opinions differ as to the value of the *Franco-Gallia*. Sir William Holdsworth dismisses [2] the effect of its argument as academic, since the Estates-General were dead and the " Parlements " enfeebled. Professor Allen considers [3] the book much overrated, a fantasy of history and in no other sense original. Labitte, however, regards [4] it as clever, learned and of importance. It was the first important manifesto of Calvinistic radicalism; for the first time, democratic doctrines were applied to French history and the *droit populaire* justified by appeal to tradition. Weill thinks [5] the value of the *Franco-Gallia* lies really in its being the counterpart of the *Vindiciae*. " Hotman fait appel aux traditions, à l'histoire; c'est

---

[1] 1461–83.
[2] *History of English Law*, IV, 197.
[3] Allen, op. cit., pp. 308–11.
[4] Labitte, *De la Démocratie* (Paris, 1865), p. 58.
[5] Weill, *Pouvoir Royal en France* (Paris, 1892), Chap. V.

de la loi divine et naturelle que Mornay deduit la légitimité de la résistance.   La *Franco-Gallia* se borne à décrire les libertés passées; l'autre ouvrage donne les moyens d'arrêter la tyrannie présente et à venir." [1]   More recently, however, a learned author has found the *Franco-Gallia* to have had a definite importance.[2]   It was the book of and for the moment. Showing easily its German origin and dislike of Latin–French civilization, and scarcely built at all on Reformation principles, it nevertheless did provide for none-too-scrupulous Huguenots a theory justifying open rebellion in so far as they were Frenchmen, and for the scrupulous made further " halting between two opinions " less possible, since the letter of Calvinistic theology had to be interpreted in a wider spirit by the ministers; it marked the beginning of the turning-point when Protestant theology had to bow to the stern necessity of Protestant politics, and the *Réveille-Matin* completed the transition.[3]   A brief survey of the book is necessary if we are to see where precisely it takes its place among the political writings of the time that may have influenced English opinion.

The *Franco-Gallia*, dedicated to Frederick, Elector Palatine, consists of a preface and twenty-one chapters. The author states in his preface that he has collected out of French and German historic records a true state of the Commonwealth, as it flourished from pre-Roman times to the reign of Louis XI, except for the short, unnoticeable period of Roman government. No remedy for present evils can be found except by going back to the wisdom of those ancestors who first framed the constitution of France. The cause of its present wreckage is the reign of Louis XI.

The *Franco-Gallia* is expressly an attempt to prove constitutionalism to be rightful in the government of France because historically the French people have been free. It is an attempt to prove a right without having recourse to first principles, but rather to early conditions. In feudalism there had been a variety of contracts, but also numerous customary rights,[4] and both had acquired sanctity, so that the argument of the *Franco-Gallia* was probably as intelligible to its contemporary readers as, say, that of the *Vindiciae*. Both relied upon history, both perverted it, but in different ways. The title is significant: " Franco " is construed as " free ", and the deduction made that France is, or should be, peculiarly free.[5]

---

[1] Weill, *Pouvoir Royal en France* (Paris, 1892), Chap. V.

[2] Lagarde, *Recherches sur l'esprit politique de la Réforme* (Douai, 1926).

[3] Lagarde, op. cit., pp. 126 *et seq.* and 250 *et seq.*

[4] See Pollock and Maitland, *History of English Law* (Cambridge, 1923), I, 106–7 and 185–8; and Coulton, *The Mediaeval Village* (Cambridge, 1931), pp. 33, 76, 293.

[5] *Franco-Gallia*, cap. 5.

This freedom consists, of course, in the supremacy of the people over the King, who is no more than a " magistrate for life ",[1] and even during his life deposable for bad behaviour.[2] There was no law of succession, for the King was elected[3] by the supreme body, which was the National Assembly.[4] To this assembly the King was subject and the royal ministers responsible, and we seem near the conclusion that the early Franks were the most laudable constitutional democrats when we discover that it is not the common people, but the *regni proceres* once more, who are to possess this supreme power. The barons of Runnymede would have gladdened the heart of Francis Hotman, and the savage lords who deposed " Richard of Bordeaux "[5] might be represented as following a devout constitutional practice of the early Franks. The appeal was to early German history, before the influence of the Roman Civil Law, which Hotman hated, had made itself felt.[6] He tried to prove the continuance of those institutions and constitutional conceptions through the French Middle Age, and saw in the Valois those absolutist tendencies which he combated. It was the work of Louis XI and the Valois that he wished undone, and he appealed to a largely imaginary past to arouse the feelings necessary to undo it. Yet perhaps one of the greatest results of Hotman's favourite book, and surely the bitterest of all to him, is that he unwittingly furnished the Guises and their League with the arguments of elective monarchy and the sovereignty of the people.

Hard on the *Franco-Gallia* came *Le Réville-Matin des François et de leurs Voisins*.[7] It was published, ostensibly at Edinburgh, in two parts in 1574, though probably the first part was issued first in 1573, that being the date of the dedicatory letter to Elizabeth, Queen of England. Each part of the *Réveille* is called a Dialogue, and mostly it makes poor reading. It has been suggested that several authors had a hand in it, which may well be believed, when its tediousness, lack of arrangement, want of connected purpose, and its plagiarism are considered. It deals freely in the contemporary history of France, of England (with frequent flattering references to Elizabeth), and of German States. From the point of view of political theory the first Dialogue is worthless. The second (between a Politique and an Historian) consists mostly of a drawn-out history of the religious wars and troubles of the Huguenots, interlarded, as is the other Dialogue, with lengthy prayers. If it were not for the twenty or so pages beginning roughly at page 75, the *Réveille* would be but a

---

[1] Op. cit., cap. 1.   [2] Caps. 5 and 6.   [3] Cap. 7.   [4] *Ibid.*
[5] Gordon Daviot's modern play of that name gives a remarkable picture of *regni proceres*.
[6] See Maitland, *C.M.H.*, II, Chap. XVI.
[7] Refs. to French ed. (Edinburgh, 1574).

dull epitome of contemporary history revealed by yet duller dialogue. In those few pages lies all the political theory that the *Réveille* can boast, nor does it reveal anything startingly new.   The last pages are a denunciation of tyranny and of the cowardice of subjects in enduring tyrants.   The authors of the *Réveille* have unblushingly stolen the very words of the *Contr'un*.   They must have had a manuscript copy—since the *Contr'un* was not printed till 1576—and have transcribed, without apology, pages of La Boëtie's essay.   In fact the only reward of ploughing through the *Réveille* is to light on these two pieces of political theory, the first section of which is unquestionably owed to Hotman, the second purloined bodily from the *Contr'un*.

If the argument of the author of the *Réveille-Matin* is confused and invalid, at least his conclusion is clear.   "Je dis . . . avec l'ancien peuple romain: que d'entre tous les actes genereux, le plus illustre et magnanime est, d'occire le Tyran." [1]   For a tyrant is one who, "increasing with the decreasing of his people ", [2] abuses power not his own, but wielded as the vicar of God, who alone remains absolutely sovereign. [3]   Moreover, the Prince holds his vicariate by contract with the people as well as by the permission of God, and he has therefore obligations to those under him as well as they to him. [4]   They would not, he concludes, have been so foolish and ill-advised " de donner à aucun tant de souveraine puissance, qu'ils ne se soyent tousjours reservez de tenir comme par les renes une bonne et forte bride, de peur que la Royauté . . . ne tombast tost en tyrannie ". [5]   There was, in fact, a definite check on the royal authority in the form of the power given to the inferior magistracy.   Here again we encounter the " regni proceres ", the " untere Obrigkeit ". [6]   Moreover, we find the same apparent duality in the repository of sovereign power.   God remains sovereign, but the people, acting through the magistracy, are ultimately his vicar, and not the Prince.   This may be explained by the belief, recorded by Professor Allen, [7] that the people could give a government force, but not authority.   The question then remained as to when God might be supposed to withdraw His authority from a bad government, and so bring into play the force of the people to set up a new one, to which in turn He might give His authority. For the actual " force " of the people is emphasized in the *Réveille-Matin* as much as in La Boëtie's Essay, and for sufficiently stressed reasons.   The people have not actively to exert themselves, they have but to withdraw their support and the prince falls.   " Je ne

---

[1] *Le Réveille-Matin*, p. 75.   [2] Op. cit., p. 74.
[3] Op. cit., pp. 76–80.   [4] p. 80.
[5] pp. 85–6.   [6] p. 88.   [7] Allen, op. cit., p. 318.

veux pas que vous le poussiez, ou estranliez : mais seulement ne le soustenez plus. . . ." [1] The question for such an author is simply as to when this becomes lawful; when is the authority of God withdrawn so that the force of the people may rightfully be re-asserted ?

Un discours de la Servitude Volontaire was written probably before 1550. It has therefore no connection in time and none deliberately in argument with the Huguenot quarrel. It was published in 1576 among the tracts of *Mémoires de l'Estat de France sous Charles IX.* It is, in reality, an essay directed against all forms and persons of monarchy, and the argument is finally based upon a doctrine of the natural equality of man. La Boëtie's [2] work is therefore full of scorn for the people who submit themselves to a man precisely like themselves if they dared but recognize it; he addresses them contemptuously as " accomplices of the murtherer who kills you and traitors to yourselves ".[3] Nor does it greatly concern the author how the Prince obtained his power—whether by election or succession—" their manner of reigning being still the same ".[4] In other words, he does away with the distinction of " tyrannus absque titulo " and " tyrannus in exercitio " by classing all monarchs, including Julius Caesar, as tyrants simpliciter. This is very dashing and refreshing, and inspired the dull brains of the authors of the *Réveille-Matin* to copy, for the conclusion of La Boëtie with regard to the overthrow of tyrants rings familiarly :—
" I do not advise you to shake or overturn him, forbear only to support him, and you will see him like a great Colossus . . . fall . . . and be broken in pieces." [5] Here indeed was revolutionary doctrine, not specifically Huguenot, with all the violence and completeness of a purely academic essay. Figgis points out that, in regarding monarchy *per se* as an evil phenomenon, and without regard to the conditions that surround it, the author followed a very definite principle of much Renaissance thinking.[6] But in the particular controversy with which we are dealing, the *Contr'un*, as it is sometimes called, could have only an incidental effect; something the same kind of effect, we may surmise, as the publication of Rousseau's *Contrat Social* might have had in the same century. It provided arguments in a quarrel other than its own. Much paper

---

[1] *Le Réveille-Matin*, p. 190.
[2] Stephen de la Boëtie, *vivebat* 1530–63. Montaigne (Essay XXVII) says he knew no man comparable to la Boëtie in natural ability; that the author never saw the MS. again after it went out of his hands ; and that the work was published by those who had obtained the MS. with the " mischievous design " of changing the condition of the government.
[3] 1735 translation, p. 16.
[4] Op. cit., p. 26.
[5] Op. cit., p. 17; cf. *Le Réveille-Matin*, p. 190.
[6] Figgis, op. cit., p. 108–9, and Notes to Lecture IV (15), pp. 214–15.

and many lives were to be spent in political controversies before the people of France overthrew the "tyrant" and ceased to earn La Boëtie's contempt for those who submit to monarchies.

But the most famous of all the Huguenot writings, and a book which our own Hooker unquestionably had often in mind,[1] was the *Vindiciae contra Tyrannos* of Junius Brutus. The authorship of the book is uncertain.[2] It has been attributed to Hubert Languet,[3] and again to the Huguenot nobleman Duplessis-Mornay,[4] nor does the disputed question seem ever to have been settled. Many are inclined to regard the book as the work of both. It was, however, published anonymously in Latin in 1579,[5] over the name of Junius Brutus, a French version following in 1581, with two English editions before 1590. Its influence was even greater in the succeeding century, English translations appearing several times, notably in the significant years 1648 and 1689.[6] In the circumstances it is perhaps better to adhere to the author's *nom de plume*.

This book is entirely different from the *Franco-Gallia*. In the first place, as Weill has pointed out,[7] it was written with an eye on present and future history, whereas the *Franco-Gallia* grounded itself in the past, leaving merely its implications for the present. Again, the *Vindiciae* is a philosophical work, glancing only occasionally at historical backgrounds: it is a discussion of the theory of political sovereignty, Hotman's book purporting to be a constitutional history of France. Analytical though it is, the *Vindiciae* shares with the *Franco-Gallia* to an extent the same ideal—namely, that of restoring those institutions which could bridle the Valois kings: an ideal perfectly unattainable, since those institutions had been shattered by the growing absolutisms of the Kings of France. The States-General did not exist, and the "Parlements" were but shadows of their former selves. Unlike as they are, however, in method and treatment, the two books are, in a way, each the counterpart of the other, rather as the *Ecclesiastical Polity* provides the theory underlying the political facts of the *De Republica Anglorum*. Analytical and philosophical, the *Vindiciae* has been described as "the first work in modern history that constructs a political philosophy on the basis of certain inalienable rights of man",[8] proving

---

[1] E.g., *E.P.*, VIII, 2, vii, viii.
[2] For the question of the authorship, see Barker, *Church, State and Study* (1930), pp. 80, 96; and also the same writer in the *Cambridge Historical Journal*, 1930.
[3] *Vivebat* 1518–81.
[4] *Vivebat* 1549–1623.
[5] Refs. to Latin ed. (Amsterdam, 1660).
[6] 1689 edition reprinted with valuable introduction by H. J. Laski (London, 1924).
[7] Weill, op. cit., Chap. V.
[8] Gooch, *English Democratic Ideas in the Seventeenth Century* (ed. 1898), p. 16.

subsequently of enormous usage in Holland and in the England of the Stuarts. It is of the utmost interest to see how it links the democracy of the future among the contractualists, and particularly Locke, with the rationalist philosophy of mediaeval scholasticism and St. Thomas Aquinas, and with the political theories expressed in the Conciliar Movement.

The *Vindiciae* was a book widely considered as founding the sovereignty of the people. That is its professed theme, including the necessary corollary that kingship is a delegated office, held on conditions. " Inter reges et populum mutua obligatio est, quae . . . nullo pacto tolli, nullo jure violari vi rescindi potest." [1] But its author quite clearly has no use for the people as a whole; he refers to them as " bellua ". He has, however, the " popular " idea, but weds it to the aristocratic; but so strongly is the latter emphasized, and so prominent is the feudal notion, that the author must be suspect of forwarding the interests of his own aristocratic class disguised under the sounding name of the People. One learned writer, indeed, indicts Hotman and Brutus of the " hypocritical democracy of Protestantism ", on the ground that it was simply a weapon against the monarchy, and a cuirass whereby the nobility might keep their fiefs intact.

Equally interesting is the breakaway from pure Calvinism, which taught that passive obedience was by divine command.[2] But Brutus, while basing his fabric on the Scriptures and Jewish history in the true spirit of the early Reformers, nevertheless, held that active resistance was of right divine. Professing Scripture as the greatest guide of life, he none the less, under cover of it, goes back to fifteenth-century natural philosophy for justification of this doctrine, which outraged scrupulous, earnest Calvinists.

Brutus is not a democrat; he is a feudal noble, anxious to curb an over-mighty Prince; he is not a Calvinist, he is a militant Protestant of the new order; he is neither nationalist nor patriot, since (as we shall see) he would prefer the good of a part to that of the whole; yet, for all that, he gave to his own generation and to posterity food for thought when he taught that rulers are answerable to some power on earth; and that men's consciences are their own, not to be controlled by kings' commandments, and when he claims freedom of religion for town or province, he comes near to the vision of the only practical solution of the problem, toleration,

---

[1] *Vindiciae*, p. 232. "Between King and people there is a mutual obligation which cannot be destroyed by bargain, by any law be abrogated or by force made void."

[2] In Britain, Ponet, Goodman, and Knox were the first to break away.

which might have been the perfect vision could he have dissociated his religion from his feudal politics.[1]

The teaching of the *Vindiciae* is contained in answers to four questions; there is much repetition in the answers. Ought subjects to obey when the King commands contrary to divine law? Brutus poses his first question, remarking that it never could be raised in Christian lands if monarchs, flattered by some and feared by others, had not arrogantly assumed unlimited power. " Holding the earth not great enough for their ambition, they will climb and conquer Heaven itself." [2] The answer to the question is contained in Scripture, which teaches that God alone has absolute authority; kings are his delegates, deriving certainly their power from him; but equally the people are the " Lord's inheritance ", and the primary condition of kingly authority is that the King shall so rule as to retain the people in the faith and worship of God. There is a covenant in which the King promises God that he will preserve his people; and the latter swear to obey the King in all causes divinely approved.

Here is clearly a feudal picture. The King is a mesne lord, who swears to be his Overlord's man; the conditions of service are expressed; should the conditions be broken, forfeiture is at once entailed, since to retain a fief in defiance of an Overlord is usurpation and treason.

This threefold solidary obligation is strengthened by a *pactum* between King and People, in which the former promises to rule justly, the latter to obey faithfully. But the King exists to defend his subjects in person and property; hence his commands can govern only their bodies and their goods; their souls are outside his appointed province. To attempt spiritual dominion in the sense of dictating to men what they shall believe in private and how they shall worship in public is usurpation of the Overlord's power, and therefore treason. " The exchequer of God takes nothing from that of Caesar, but each of them have their right manifestly apart." (Fiscus Dei Caesaris fisco nil adimat, sed cuique ius suum constet.)[3]

The answer to this first question is, he submits, obvious: a subject is bound to refuse to obey the King if else he must disobey God. Not the subject, but the King, is the rebel in such case; and so far from mutely refusing to obey, subjects should be active in resisting any command of this nature.

It is easy, of course, to criticize the position thus taken up by

[1] Sir Ernest Barker maintains that Huguenotism in its essence was not inimical to the unity of France (*Church, State and Study*, 1930, p. 75). In any event, it was the facts of the Huguenot position that dictated their political theory.
[2] *Vindiciae*, p. 2.
[3] *Op. cit.*, p. 28.

Brutus, but it is convenient to defer criticism until we have discussed the other questions, for not till then do we arrive at any complete picture of his theories, since, for example, he amplifies his " contract " teaching in two of the remaining subjects.

May a king be lawfully resisted, and by whom, if he infringes the Law of God or ruins his Church? Again Brutus says the answer lies in Scripture, and what was lawful for the Jews will be lawful for Christians. He proceeds to the first application of the covenant. Clearly he considers kingship did not originate at the same time as political society; monarchy was a later development. There was a direct covenant—before the days of Kings—between God and the people, whereby the latter undertook to be the avenger of His honour. When kings were inaugurated, this original two-sided covenant was embraced within the three-fold obligation already mentioned, since " the King being raised to so slippery a place might easily be corrupted ". Hence the people were as much bound to God as the King was; people and King were each respondents to God, pledged to see that the other party adhered to the covenant. Each party has a divine duty to fulfil its own respective parts of the covenant and divine right to see that the other does so.

Clearly, then, if the King fails to observe his conditions (the chief of which is to preserve the people as God's Church), who can punish him if not the whole people, since the latter have undertaken to God to keep the King in the right paths, to say nothing of the fact that the King has pledged himself directly to his people in the *pactum*? If the people have not this power there is no point in their being made by God a party to the three-fold covenant; nor in their entering into contractual relations with the King. Thus the people are not only justified in punishing the King, but are under a positive duty to do so, and are culpable of the King's crime if they fail to resist him.

He then defines the " people " who may so act. Not the whole rabble are so empowered, but those who represent the people; " Hujus vero foederis seu pacti, regni officiarii vindices et custodes sunt; "[1] the magistrates of inferior position to the King, but still established by the people to be consorts in power with him, like Spartan Ephors and Roman Tribunes, to restrain royal encroachments, and to stand for the whole body of the people. To these should be added " the Assembly of the Estates, which is nothing else but an epitome or brief collection of the Kingdom ". Just as the Conciliar Fathers taught that a General Council is of greater

---

[1] Op. cit., p. 294. " The Officers of the Kingdom are the guardians and protectors of this covenant or contract."

authority than the Pope, so a Chapter is superior to its Bishop, a University to its Rector; whoever is the chief official of a company is inferior to the whole, though superior to individual members. The King, holding office by the will and for the good of his people, is therefore less than his people: " . . . probavimus, reges omnes regiam dignitatem a populo accipere; populum universum rege potiorem et superiorem esse; regem regni . . . supremum tantum ministrum et actorem esse; populum vero, vere dominum existere ".[1]

But the *whole* people cannot move, so that resistance is to be undertaken by the chief persons in the State, since they are the " greatest " part; what is done by them and the Estates is the act of all.

At this point the *Vindiciae* becomes a *livre de circonstance*. Supposing a king, backed by the people and a majority of the princes, sets out to ruin the Church, and a minority, containing only a few princes and magistrates, wish to preserve it? What can lawfully be done? Not isolated individuals are postulated, but " some town or province, which makes a portion of a Kingdom " with its governing magistrate. He means plainly what can La Rochelle or Languedoc rightly do against a Charles IX, or Henri III, the Queen-Mother, the Guises and Catholic France? Scriptural authority is not too easy to produce, though the Maccabees afford an example. Well, then, suppose Antiochus (Charles IX, Henri III, and Catherine) abolishes true religion (in France), that Israel (i.e., France) connives, the Maccabaean (Huguenot) towns will say plainly that they will serve the Lord; and will rightly shut their gates when the King sends troops to force idolatry on them, driving out the King of France rather than the King of kings. Nor is this rebellion, since the King is a traitor to his Overlord, and not to resist is to take part in his treason. Whatever the King commands " in the quality of Caesar " the Huguenots will obey, but not when he arrogates to himself that spiritual dominion which can only belong to God, and Brutus indignantly denies that this is either sedition or rebellion.

He concludes, therefore, that all the people ought to repress such a king, but that, if they will not, the chief men, at least in towns and provinces, ought to do so. Magistrates, State officials, are guilty of negligence if they do not organize resistance. But until that happens let the private man wait, since the original covenant bound the whole people, and not individuals, and private men are in Scripture commanded to put the sword into its sheath.

[1] Op. cit., p. 264. "We have proved that all Kings receive their royal authority from the people; that the whole people is above and greater than the King; that the King is only the supreme governor and minister of the Kingdom; but that the people remain the absolute lord."

May lawful resistance be made, and by whom, to a king ruling oppressively? In answering this third question, Brutus relies less on Scripture and much more on the Law of Nature and of reason. This is a question that good kings will not object to being discussed, but evil rulers will, " for it is no marvel if those who receive no law but what their own will and fancy dictate to them, be deaf unto the voice of that law which is grounded upon reason ".

Kings, though appointed by God, are established by the people, who put the sceptre into their hands and approve their election by their suffrages. They have divine right in the sense of divine approval, but their authority is from the people, by election to office. In whatever countries custom of hereditary succession may exist, nevertheless the right of election underlies it, as is proved by historical precedent and prevalent coronation oaths and ceremonies.

Therefore the body of the people is greater than the King, even as in a ship the owners are superior to the pilot. " Populum universum rege potiorem et superiorem esse." [1] Obedience is to be paid to the King as long as he is " careful of the public good ", for this is the reason of his appointment. If he is profitless in his office he should be dispensed with, since (as Hotman had also pointed out) a people can subsist without a king, but no king can exist without people; which is in itself proof that the people are superior to their King.

He pauses to define again what is meant by the people. It is those who, in town or province, lawfully represent the people; " regni proceres "; " optimates " ; officers of the kingdom, whose offices in the nature of things must continue whether kings come or go (associated with the King in the administration of justice, sharing in the managing of the affairs of State, clothed with authority from the people, transmitted to them by the Estates) ; not, he points out, appointees of the King to personal and domestic posts, which by nature come to an end at his death or withdrawal, but the Elders of the Jews, the Ephors of the Spartans, the Senators and Tribunes of Rome—that is, the Constables, Marshals, Chancellors, Secretaries of France. In bygone days these officials, created by the Estates, and answerable to the " Parlement " of Paris, together with the twelve Peers of France, took oath to the people to preserve not only the King, but the Crown. Against the will of these men no king in French history could act as an irresponsible ruler; it was they who, in fact, decided if he performed his kingly function satisfactorily. They were—they are—the guardians of the public well-being.

[1] Pp. 116, 264.

Once a year the Estates used to meet, and with them lay the supreme control of all policy; a state of things which, he notes, still obtains in the kingdoms of England and Scotland. The fact that the Estates no longer meet gives the King no right by prescription to their ultimate supremacy; for they represent the State, and the State never dies. Neither is it defeasible by right of succession, since none can transmit a greater right than he himself possessed, and power unlawfully arrogated makes a king not a more lawful king, but a pirate. Nor yet can the people's supremacy be lost, should the peers and " regni proceres " join with the King in furthering tyranny.

For Nature itself dictates resistance to an oppressor. Men by nature prefer freedom to slavery, would rather command than obey; they have not given up their natural desire to somebody else except " for some special and great profit that they expected from it ". To govern means to provide for, and when a man who undertakes the burdensome office of a king rules so that his people are damaged and not profited, Nature urges his removal. As he is to rule for their good, he cannot then make laws at his own whim, since laws would be perpetually changing, and he would seek his own profit. Therefore every king is subject himself to the laws on which the life of the State depends—the fundamental laws of the State—whereby his personal profit and pleasures are restrained. The laws are anterior in time and importance to the King, who is their *Custos*, since kings are not admitted to their office until they have promised to do right according to the laws. From the same reasoning, no new laws may be added without the consent of the Estates, although Brutus admits a king has a natural equity to supply deficiencies where no law speaks. The King can therefore condemn none whom the law has not condemned, neither pardon those whom the law has found guilty. The King has no right, by nature, moreover, to the goods of his subjects, since they are to him rather brothers than slaves; nor has he a claim to the public revenue or landed wealth, for the kingdom belongs to the people; taxation, like the rest of the royal rule, is for utility's sake, and may be suffered no further than that. Not even an usufruct of the kingdom belongs to its Prince; he is much more an administrator of the kingdom's resources, for which he is liable to account, and he can no more alienate public wealth than a bishop can alienate property belonging to his see.

At this point Brutus again turns to his contract theory. Hitherto he has based it on religion; now he calls in the law of natural reason to support it, and the theses he has just enumerated in his third answer. The *pactum* between King and people is a stipulation,

an agreement requiring specific performance. The King makes the
first promise, that he will govern justly and according to the laws.
To this absolute promise the people (prior in time to the King)
reply conditionally that they will obey while he governs uprightly.
This is the basis of all governments, Brutus declares, even if the
agreement be tacitly understood; and the coronation oaths are
testimony. Further, apart from didactic proof of such contracts,
Nature herself teaches that kings were appointed conditionally on
ruling well; nothing else is thinkable. The mutual obligation
between King and people, be it civil or be it natural, or both, tacit
or expressed, cannot by any means be destroyed; [1] especially since,
as we see from the first answer, the people's obligation is really given
to God, whence in sacred duty they must keep the King to his just
work.

But while private people may not rise against their King, they
may readily do so against a tyrant, and are justified by the Law of
Nature, of nations, and of the State. A tyrant is an unjust ruler
with an unjust title. If his title be just, he is not a tyrant in the
sense that private vengeance may be taken on him.

The last question is: May and ought external Sovereigns lawfully to help subjects in other countries oppressed in religion or in
temporal affairs? Some princes have helped downtrodden subjects,
(he mentions Henry VIII among others), but in general that has
been where little danger and plenty of profit appeared. The
Church is a Universal Body, whose Head is Christ; consequently
the slightest harm to any part injures the whole. Therefore
religious oppression is the concern of all, and every king is charged
to preserve the Catholic Church inviolate. This Brutus justifies
by references to history and to Scripture, alleging that Christian
kings who will not aid the oppressed are morally murderers, per-
fidious traitors before God. If Brutus hoped by this means to exhort
Elizabeth to assist the Huguenot cause, he was destined to be
disappointed. Similarly, it is the duty of kings to interfere on
behalf of subjects civilly oppressed, in the name of common
humanity.

Such is the political theory of the *Vindiciae*, often confused and
illogical, indefinitely based in origins, heedless as to inevitable
consequences, yet supplying valuable material for philosophers of
other generations.

One of the drawbacks to his teaching is that Brutus cannot see
beyond the confines of the Jewish State. That is his model, the
perfect polity. He does not penetrate farther back than this into
the origins of political society, so that he confronts us suddenly

[1] P. 232.

with Israel, a non-monarchic people, governed in the first place directly by God, and contracted to Him. When kings arrive, they are no more than the leaders of the people, and the covenant now has three parties, not two. The chief point is the divine obligation lying on the people, making them responsible for their kings, and the obligation of the latter to rule rightly. The assumption, apparently, is that every State should be a reflex of the Jewish. Hence the only absolute sovereignty that Brutus has any idea of is that of God. The State must always be a theocracy, with a typical Calvinistic God, an earthly sovereign as a mesne lord, and people who are subjects to both. This picture would have sufficed at any time of the Reformation period, but Huguenot circumstances dictated strongly that room for rebellion *must* be found. It was found, not in Scripture, as all good Calvinists knew, but in the obligation of the people to God for their king, and in the nature of the thing from the utilitarian motive of kingly rule. But it is difficult to see how Brutus expected it all to work. His State must be a theocracy, yet he would accord the right of rebellion to towns and provinces, which, if successful, would set up their own régimes, and not merely in religion. By Huguenot teaching, the King was so limited in legislation and taxation that, beyond question, a province religiously independent would make a prompt bid for political autonomy as well. A State would consist of a bundle of feudal " imperia " and it scarcely seems possible to add " in imperio ". The only possible outcome could be a Confederacy of States, and, divided in religion and politics, it is inconceivable they could ever in the sixteenth century form a united whole.[1] So we are driven to the conclusion that Brutus had no conception of the modern, secular, omnicompetent State; unlike the Jesuits, who had. The latter, seeing existing circumstances clearly, approved the secular State, realizing that no identification of Church and State was possible. But for Brutus a State is still a Church-State, and the Church idea dominant, because God is its Sovereign and the people are his Church. He does not resemble Hooker in this identity, for the latter makes the State dominant, and " Anglican " follows " Englishman ", and for misrule the King is answerable to God alone. England is not in the primary Jewish sense a theocracy, though the State is divine; it is a State directed to make people good, and therefore religion is one of its concerns; there is nothing for which it is not competent.

The answer to the fourth question strengthens our conclusion that Brutus has no idea of the secular State. He is either a hopeless

---

[1] Yet, of course, something like this did take place with the Thirteen American Colonies.

idealist or a narrow class-bound feudal reactionary, ready to sacrifice his country for his party. In religious persecutions, and still less defensibly in civil oppression, he would have other States interfere. He says the Church is Universal, and the least harm in a part affects the whole; at a time when Europe was based on the principle of " cuius regio, eius religio ", he demands that national barriers be broken down; if an ideal, noble and great, how untrue to circumstances. He does not appear to see that each State has its right of self-determination—a glance across the Channel would have shown it him. In Papal Christendom, in the days of the " respublica Christiana ", Brutus' view was practicable, but not with a Europe now consisting of separate States, each conscious of its own nationality, and determining its own ends.

Brutus complicates his teaching by making religion no affair of the State; by putting a divine obligation on the people to control their King; and, paradoxically, allowing the King both a divine right and an earthly appointment. If the State, in the person of its Sovereign, can have no standing in religion, who can decide issues? Who is to decide between Caesar and God? Who shall settle what is " of conscience "? What is the Church? What is " divine law "? Who may proclaim that the moment for religious revolt has come? Who may decide these and similar questions? Not the King, certainly. We are not told that the " regni proceres " or the Estates are competent. There is no Protestant Pope. Where, then, is this tribunal of decision? It can only be answered, " Scripture ", which, in effect, is again the judgment of the indivi-dual; and logically Brutus cannot deny to the private rebel for conscience' sake the right to unsheathe his sword, since his view of " idolatry " may—for all any ultimate authority can say—be as sound as that of Brutus or of Calvin himself. Calvin denies the right of private revolt Scripturally, since kings rule by divine right. Brutus's view is really rationalistic and scholastic; the private man is not a true " part " of the State, and can only weep, not fight.

In this theocracy—that he would readily split into a Confederacy —where is the sovereignty placed by Brutus? He, as other Hugue-nots, not forgetful of mediaeval scholasticism, puts it by nature in the will of the people, even if kings reign by hereditary succession. Plenty of writers had made this point, and indicated that no people would have been so stupid as to give unrestrained power to one over themselves, from the nature of the case. Brutus hopes to strengthen this argument from nature by his contractual theory—parent of a fruitful offspring—of a three-fold covenant and two-fold *pactum*, the former of which he may have found in Aquinas. But under the covenant the King logically has divine right, up to which point absolutist and Huguenot would agree; yet whereas Hobbes would hold that by logic the King can answer only to God, the Huguenot urges, with less logic, that he is deposable by the people, who obey the King only in and for God—that is, they have divine right to depose him. We cannot say that the introduction of contracts (particularly a " tacit " contract) has clarified the theory of sovereignty put forward by Brutus. When, further, we understand that by the people our author really means a carefully defined class, the feudal nobility and great officials, we must conclude that in the last resort the sovereignty of the people is with him nonexistent, since the people have neither sovereign agency nor general will, and that, so far from developing the political freedom of the individual, Huguenotism is reactionary in favour of feudal privilege. Only in the vaguest sense are the people sovereign, in so far as government must be for the good and the needs of all, and rests on general recognition as a means to that end.

Moreover, Brutus would allow an appeal to be made by a minority to foreign States to interfere by force in the event of religious or civil oppression. Any Huguenot town might set itself up in judgment and invoke aid in resisting the King and the majority of France. It is difficult to see in his writings any genuine " sovereignty of the people ", any true " State-will ", while a minority can insist on its being alone in the right.

There is, moreover, no conception in the *Vindiciae* of any ultimate Sovereign who is above the law. The King is an official for utilitarian ends, restricted by laws. The legislative body is composed of the King and the Estates; the law itself has to be executed, and may be altered. The omission of this conception is a consequence from the emphasis placed on divine and natural law. We feel that for Brutus this is true law, positive law being a much less important affair. That being so, he is content with God as the Law-giver, and shirks the question of an earthly Sovereign who must logically be greater than his laws. An Austinian Sovereign, whose command is his law, would, according to Brutus's reasoning, be scaling Heavens for equality with God.

It is refreshing to turn to a smaller book, published about the same time as the *Vindiciae*, written by a Monarchomach who was no Calvinist. Born in 1506, dying in 1582, Buchanan (" Poëte célèbre, historien distingué, pamphlétaire bilieux ") was a Scot who spent much of his life in France; a humanist, whose *De Jure Regni apud Scotos* (1578) [1] has little *motif* in common with of those Huguenot monarchomachs and was too late in birth; a Protestant,

[1] Refs. to 1762 ed. (Aberdeen).

L

but of what type it is difficult to tell; a friend of the most learned among both Catholics and Huguenots. Though not published till 1578, the *De Jure* may easily have been accessible to other thinkers and, for all we know, it may have provided some of the lines on which Huguenot political thought was to run after the St. Bartholomew massacre. There is no Calvinism in the book from the religious or the political side; no Genevan State-Church; no passive obedience. Buchanan's theories have no Scriptural basis, though he may at times quote Scripture as evidence, but the Bible is a double-edged weapon, he points out,[1] and does not, in any event, contain all knowledge; a position which in itself marks this author out from those whose demand in all political controversy is, "Where groundest thou it in Scripture?" It is this wider outlook that enables Buchanan to give the most convincing of contemporary explanations of the Pauline doctrine of obedience to the powers that be. At once profounder than any of the Protestant Monarchomachs (though not always less confused), freed, too, from their Scriptural bonds, he goes more vehemently to his conclusions and enunciates with the doctrine of deposition a right of private as well as public vengeance unequalled (even in the *Réveille-Matin*) until Mariana's *De Rege* appeared. Buchanan's theory of political society and sovereignty is founded on Nature. Nature brings men together into States, and then teaches them that the general utility may be strengthened if they create the office of ruling magistrate; which members of the State proceeded to do, on condition that the magistrate governed for the prescribed end.

" The three great sources of a free spirit in politics, admiration of antiquity, zeal for religion and persuasion of positive right, which separately had animated La Boëtie, Languet (*i.e.*, Brutus) and Hottoman, united their streams to produce, in another country, the treatise of George Buchanan, a Scholar, a Protestant, and the subject of a very limited monarchy." [2] It is true that we find in Buchanan something of a consensus of the " Back to Nature " cry of the *Contr'un*, with the historical ideal of Hotman, but the religious fervour of the *Vindiciae* is absent. There is indeed truth in this quotation, but the source of the *De Jure Regni* is probably not so much in these authors as in the companionship of Buchanan with Monarchomach thinkers in general, and in his own classical and historical learning. But before further discussion, it is better to examine the outline of the book itself, in form a dialogue between Buchanan and one Maitland.

There was a time when men lived in a state of Nature, nomadic,

[1] p. 34, lxvi.　　　　[2] Hallam, *H.L.E.*, II, 38.

without laws or settlements.[1] Utility taught them to constitute a public society, but only as a secondary cause, since utility stimulates to private advantage, and would tend to dissolve a Society.[2] There was a much older link binding men together for safety, for mental pleasures, for the pursuit of knowledge, and that was Nature,[3] a light divinely infused into man, whereby he might discern good from evil. Some would describe it as Nature's urge, others as her law; it is nothing less than divine wisdom.[4] This is the origin of civil society, and Buchanan here makes an original contribution to political philosophy.

But the body politic must at times fall ill, and needs a physician called a king, though all histories " ostendunt Reges non sibi, sed populo creatos esse ".[5] The primary need for the State's health is justice,[6] and the people originally gave the kingship (a gift, since by Nature no one man can assume power over others) to one who seemed likely to be just. Nor can the art of ruling be learned in a day, and the precepts by which he should learn his office are the laws.[7] The law is at once his colleague and moderator.[8] It matters not what kind of Government is set up, as long as equity is the end in view.[9] But all kings are human, and when the pleasures of kings stood for laws, the people delivered laws to him to use.[10] " Multis enim edocti erant experimentis, melius libertatem legibus quam Regibus credi ",[11] since the former would keep one perpetual tenor, and by them was the royal administration bounded. Maitland rightly raises the question, Who is to legislate if not the King? and Buchanan proceeds to make it quite plain that the King is not the legislator. Laws should not be made " per vim ", but " communicato cum Rege consilio, communiter statuendum arbitror, quod ad omnium salutem communiter faciat ".[12] But Maitland reminds him that the "populus" is "bellua", full of rashness and inconstancy. Buchanan replies he did not mean that legislation should be entrusted to the multitude, but selected men of all ranks should meet the King in council; after which their proposals should be referred "ad populi judicium".[13] The King cannot be entrusted with this because two monsters, cupidity and self-will, exist in him. Maitland rather neatly rejoins that he does not see how adding a number of assessors will improve matters, since

[1] *De Jure Regni*, p. 4, viii.   [2] p. 5, ix.   [3] p. 5, x and xi.
[4] p. 6, xi.   [5] p. 6, xii.   [6] p. 7, xiv.
[7] p. 8, xvi.   [8] p. 9, xviii.   [9] p. 9, xix.
[10] *Ibid.*
[11] *Ibid.* " For they had learned by much experience that freedom is guaranteed better by laws than by Kings."
[12] p. 15, xxvii. " A Royal Council set up, I think that what makes for the common safety of all should be by the community decreed."
[13] *Ibid.*

they all partake of the same frailties. But many men, replies Buchanan, see and know more than one; a number will make abler judges than individuals, since their collected excellence is greater than that of any one man, and their opposing temperaments produce a healthy mediocrity.[1] Maitland complains that Buchanan has no notion of anything but written law; will he allow the King no judgment where laws conflict or are deficient? Has the King no " aequitas "? Could the " ius gentium " ever have come into existence on Buchanan's argument? The latter replies that it is the King's part to direct that laws shall not be obscure; where they are, the " responsa prudentium " will clarify them. But this is to give to inferior men what you deny to the King, the other points out; and the " prudentes " are more skilful and happy in legal quibbles than in searching for the truth. A perfect king, is the answer, would rule by nature, and there would be no need of law; anyhow, if you allow a king the interpretation of laws, you may as well allow him to direct legislation, and you have only to look at Europe now to see the results.[2] Maitland rather tamely is convinced, which seems unfortunate, as the logic of the argument is with him. Buchanan then paints a glowing picture of the ideal King, the father of his children, hushing their complaints, settling their quarrels, in such attractive imagery that he wins Maitland over sorrowfully to admit that no such king exists to-day. Thereupon they pass to the subject of tyranny.

A tyrant is one, in the first place, who rules against the people's will, a usurper,[3] governing for his own selfish ends: but a usurper whose rule the people later accept is no longer a tyrant.[4] The genuine tyrant is an enemy to God and man, and must be dealt with as such. " Qui occidit, non sibi modo sed publice universis prodest." [5] Maitland interposes the question of hereditary succession; how can that right be dissolved? [6] The ground of kingly rule is not succession by birth, Buchanan replies, but agreement with the subjects to rule for their good. The King is a trustee, and fraud or evil on his part gives to the *cestui que trust* the right to depose him. What beneficiary can more justly demand restitution than a whole nation? [7] The people would never have agreed to obey unless the King were to rule " utiliter ", nor would they have been so improvident as not to have made that a condition; they were neither driven by fear nor cajoled by flattery so as willingly to give themselves into slavery. Consequently, there is no such thing as hereditary right,[8] and remedies are open to the people for

---

[1] p. 15, xxviii. [2] p. 16, xxx. [3] p. 24, xliv and xlv.
[4] *Ibid.* [5] p. 25, xlviii. [6] p. 26, xlix.
[7] p. 28, liii. [8] p. 31, lviii.

violence, fraud, and sloth on the part of the King. A lawful king who rules for his own selfish pleasures instead of the people's good,[1] is a tyrant, and a public enemy. The summary of his contention is " populum a quo Reges nostri habent quicquid iuris sibi vindicant, Regibus esse potentiorem . . . quicquid iuris alicui populus dederit, idem eum iustis de causis posse reposcere ".[2] And he furnishes examples from Scottish and classical history of the public vengeance taken on unjust rulers. This is the reason why a king is not freed from the people's laws; for if he were, not one man, but two monsters within him are let loose.[3] Still Maitland is not happy as to how a lawful king can be a tyrant. Buchanan subjects him to questions, forcing the answers that the law is greater than the King, and the people than the law, since they are its author and parent;[4] the people as a society are prior in time to the King and greater, since able to subsist without him.[5] The utility of the people—i.e., the greater part—is aimed at, no man being able to satisfy every individual. To the obvious objection that a numerical majority may after all be corrupted by a tyrant, Buchanan rejoins that not all who live in a State are citizens. Only those are citizens who love their country above all else—the good, incorruptible, valorous patriots. Citizens are reckoned not by number but by worth. The " pars maior " is the " pars melior ". But Buchanan cannot feel too secure on this, for he hastens away with " non enim hic quid futurum sit, sed quid iure fieri possit quaerimus ".[6] He goes to the " mutua pactio " made between King and citizens.[7] Again he catechizes Maitland, obtaining the desired answers, that whosoever breaks the " pactio " first is an enemy to the other party; if it be the King, then he is a tyrant; if tyrant, then public enemy; against an enemy war is just, and most just against a tyrant, enemy of the human race; in war it is the duty of an individual as much as of the whole people to slay the enemy.[8]

The plain teaching of deposition and tyrannicide consequent on the sovereignty of the people is the clearest part of the " De Jure Regni ". Most of the rest is confused in thought. What is the legislative power? It is not the King, Buchanan declares, although, with both King and Society undegenerate, the King's natural equity would be all the law needed. As it is, laws are proposed in a council of the more important people, with the King present; their proposals have no binding force until the whole people agree. Appar-

---

[1] p. 35, lxvii.
[2] p. 37, lxxii. " The people from whom our Kings have whatever authority they claim for themselves is greater than Kings . . . whatever authority the people have given to anyone it can for just reason demand back."
[3] p. 39, lxxvi.   [4] p. 40, lxxvii.   [5] p. 40, lxxviii.
[6] p. 42, lxxx.   [7] p. 45, lxxxvi.   [8] *Ibid.*

ently Buchanan looks for a plebiscite, but he sets up no machinery
to that end. Bound up with this too is the " majority " question.
After frequent references to the whole people, he descends to admitting that this means the greater part. Here apparently he parts
company with Brutus, whose *Vindiciae* is based on the rights of a
minority. But perhaps the two are really in agreement. When
Maitland points out that a numerical majority is no safeguard,
Buchanan hastily replies that his majority is one of quality, only
" boni cives ". Of course he gives no criterion by which a citizen
is assigned to the major or minor part, and indeed there is nothing
whatsoever in his reasoning to prevent us from concluding that
Buchanan's majority of quality is a minority in number, and when
he comprehends in the " regia potestas " all degrees of magistrates [1]
we are perhaps not far from Hotman's " gens de bien " and Brutus'
" regni proceres ". Yet elsewhere he does indeed seem to be
counting heads ; the act of a majority is the act of all, of necessity,
since the people are never unanimous, and anyhow more heads are
better than one. " Non enim solum plus vident ac sapiunt multi
quam unus. . . . Nam multitudo fere melius quam singuli de rebus
omnibus iudicat. Singuli enim quasdam habent virtutum parti-
culas, quae simul collatae unam excellentem virtutem conficiunt." [2]
Each man has a virtue, and the accumulated virtues make a virtue
transcendent. It leaves us rather muddled ; a plebiscite, a
numerical majority, and a majority of the best quality.

Is the State divine? Only, he says, as it sprang from Nature ;
originally, when infused with the divine wisdom, human society
was divine, but after that the responsibility is not God's. This, too,
is dubious ; he clearly postulates some sort of organized Society,
naturally made for the mutual comfort of men, which at some
unspoken moment turns itself into a conditional monarchy. When
that moment comes, how men decide on the form of government,
the historic place of the " mutua pactio ", nothing of this he
mentions. The State suddenly arises from a divinely natural birth
into a man-made creation, from which God retires.

The writings with which we have dealt are the best known and
most important Monarchomach works written from positions other
than the Catholic. There is no fundamental unity of argument ;
they are clearly justifications of a point of view already held, and
had, as far as possible, to be syllogistically tenable. This is, of
course, true of the majority of books setting forward a particular

---

[1] p. 34, lxv.
[2] p. 15, xxviii. " For not only do many see and know more than one man. . . .
For a multitude judges almost better than individuals about everything, since
the united capacities of individual men furnish a pre-eminent capacity."

theory of government; the real ground is expediency, but when arguments are presented to which the argument of expediency is no reply, we are compelled to look for moral justification and prove, if we can, that what is expedient is also lawful. If we consider that unlimited monarchy is inexpedient, even if this be demonstrable it will be of no avail to inform the supporters of Divine Right of our conclusion. We must find some contrary doctrine in the same category as that of our opponents, and we shall hardly fail to bring forward one of Natural Right. But our adversaries are still able to produce Scriptural texts to appeal to the conception of " an anointed King ". We answer them by offering an original contract of some kind, the existence of which we take leave to assume by demonstrating that it would be unreasonable to assume its non-existence—truly a negative contention, and a poor one at best. But it is a contention which, in some form or other, lies at the back of all conceptions of government excepting that which is in a very special sense that of government by right divine. For it is well not to fall into the error of believing that a theory of contract excludes a belief in government by divine right—the authority for government is referred to the Almighty by monarchists and monarchomachs alike. The distinction is between a theory of mysterious, indefeasible divine right and a power obtained by contract and with divine authorization, but which ceases and loses its divine sanction when the contract is broken. The strength of the idea of Contract and, at the same time, how little it is to be identified with secularism, is shown by the covenant of the Pilgrim Fathers sailing in the *Mayflower*, " We do solemnly and mutually, in the presence of God and of one another, covenant and combine ourselves together into a civil body politic ".[1] To the American the Social Contract has its origin in verifiable history.

[1] " The Mayflower Compact ": Macdonald, *Select Charters*, p. 33.

CHAPTER VIII

THE RIGHT TO RESIST: THE JESUIT ANSWER

THE skill and devotion of the members of the Society of Jesus have been so great in every field of activity which they have invaded (and there are few from which they have been absent) that they have been rewarded by a superstitious awe and a superstitious hate. They share with one of their many opponents, Freemasonry, the fascination of a secret society, and they embody the cosmopolitan character of the Catholic Church. In fields so far apart spiritually as psychology and political theory, and geographically as Paraguay and Muscovy, they have exercised their devoted and highly trained talents. Rightly or wrongly, the ideal Jesuit has been taken as the type of Roman Catholic priest; so much so that, though no member of the Order has ever been Grand Inquisitor of Spain, Dostoevsky makes his Grand Inquisitor an acknowledged picture of a Jesuit.[1] Hunted priests in England and Mandarins in China each and all owed military obedience to the General of the Order, the commander of " the light horse of the Papacy ", the advance guard of the Catholic Church " in partibus infidelium ", the stay of the Counter-Reformation, the apologists and protagonists of the papal power among the faithful who might otherwise forget that Rome is, as always, to be considered particularly as " janua coeli ". Like most converts, St. Ignatius Loyola found in an extreme asceticism the surest refuge for his wounded spirit; what made him powerful was the ability to change his method in order the better to encounter circumstance. The adaptability that he showed has become a distinguishing characteristic of his followers, who have again and again exemplified St. Paul's wisdom of becoming all things to all men. The Jesuits are distinguished from the many diplomats and hypocrites, who pursue the same means, by the unswerving faithfulness to the ideal for which they contend and the close application of the highest ranges of the intellect in pursuit of their purpose.

Now, because the Huguenots, previous to the candidature of Henry of Navarre to the throne, had preached the doctrines of

---

[1] Fülop-Miller, *The Power and Secret of the Jesuits* (London, 1930), pp. 467 *et seq.*

deposition and tyrannicide and then abandoned them, and because the Jesuits apparently adopted them, they have been accused of insincerity, but this position is untenable. The Jesuit order as a whole was deeply imbued with the teaching of Aristotle and its interpretation by St. Thomas Aquinas. One of the principal deductions that St. Thomas drew, in the *De Regimine Principum*, from the *Politics* of his master, was that because, in the Aristotelian platitude, the State existed not for life only, but for good life, therefore the Pope might interfere " ad finem spiritualem ". Certainly it had been alike the theory and practice of the Papacy to depose heretical monarchs; Bulls of anathema against them involved the absolution of subjects from their obedience.[1] The " deposition " of Elizabeth, which, in the words of Professor Pollard, made " sedition a part of the religious duty of every English Catholic under Elizabeth ", was an up-to-date instance. Fortified by the teaching of St. Thomas and the age-long practice of the Papacy, the Jesuits propounded no new doctrine when they advocated the deposition of an heretical king in France. Not that we wish to exculpate— if exculpation it needs—the Society of Jesus from any innovation of teaching. We have already dwelt upon the adaptability of the minds and outlook of its members. The times had changed since, for instance, the publication of the Bull " Unam Sanctam ". The task of the Jesuits was the interpretation of the new conditions in the light of post-Tridentine Romanism and post-Reformation Nationalism. It is indicative of their realistic qualities that the Jesuits accepted the existence of the latter. Figgis has pointed out the significance of the fact that the most important Jesuit writers were all Spaniards, members of a new national kingdom, of which the very existence was a standing proof of the fall of the " universitas " of the Empire.[2] The fact of the existence of these kingdoms demanded a Catholic exposition of the relations of their Sovereigns with the Pope and with their peoples, and this explanation must be given in terms not conflicting with previous papal pronouncements. Just as freewill is a phenomenon requiring explanation in terms of ethics, of metaphysics, and even of physics, so this comparatively new phenomenon of the national kingdom as a " societas perfecta " required explanation in terms of the categories of political authority. It possessed clearly a double relationship, with the power of the Pope and the power of the people. It was this duality that was the opportunity of the new apologists of the Papacy. The Jesuits took advantage of it promptly by claiming the authority of the Pope

---

[1] For a modern Roman view, see P. Hughes, *Rome and the Counter-Reformation in England* (Burns & Oates, 1942).

[2] Figgis: *From Gerson to Grotius*, p. 146.

as immediately of God, and the power of the King only mediately through the people. The former contention accorded well with previous Catholic theory; the latter was the occasion of analysis of the means by which the people gave their authority to the King. In effect the protagonists of Divine Right in spiritual authority became the forerunners of the Jacobins in secular politics.

The emphasis of the Jesuit writings is rather upon the power of the people than the authority of the Pope, because the latter had been so often demonstrated, and to the good Catholic a refusal to acknowledge it was the result of a " stiff neck ". For example, Mariana in the *De Rege* scarcely mentions the Pope, but writes at length of the state of Nature and the duty of killing tyrants. Behind, above and within all things he sees Nature and Nature's Law.

> "Nor think, in Nature's state they blindly trod ;
> The state of Nature was the reign of God." [1]

He sees, in fact, little distinction between the different kinds of law ; all are founded upon that eternal principle of law—the Law of Nature. This conception of unity was the part of his work which most quickly perished. " Throughout these pages, long and tedious with dialectic, there runs the claim that law may be nullified because it embodies injustice as against the more modern view that anything that the lawgiver bids or forbids is good law merely by his fiat." [2] Again, he is so far consistent as to regard conscience rather as the voice of Nature, as the inherent knowledge of Nature's Law, than as the voice of God speaking privately to the individual.[3] And since every individual may be regarded equally as the repository of Nature's confidences, Mariana has more justification than most in accepting the decision of the majority as the publication of the law of Nature, and therefore of God, the Author of Nature.

We see, then, in this new scholasticism, of which we have by way of introduction taken Mariana as a type, a mingling of conceptions that would rule and develop with others that would droop and die. That the former so preponderate over the latter is a testimony to the youth and awareness of the Jesuitical writers. If we retain our suspicion, or even dislike, of the Order of Jesus, we must avoid the vulgar error of regarding it as superficial or insincere.

One principle the Huguenots and the Catholic League shared in common—namely, that religion was more important than monarchy. From the days of the first League (1576), at least, many zealous Catholics rated Church defence more highly than belief in royal absolutism and blind obedience. Zeal for the Church was the

---

[1] Pope, *Essay on Man*, Epistle III, lines 147-8.
[2] Figgis, op. cit., p. 153.   [3] Allen, op. cit., p. 366.

prime *motif* of the League, to which was later added the dynastic ambition of the House of Lorraine. When, with the murder of the Guises in 1588, a possible way to the throne was made for the heretic Navarre, the League theory reached its fullest expansion, and " le droit populaire " was opposed to the Salic law.[1]

It was easy for the Guises to use the " plebs ", and with the murders of 1588 the latter took matters into their own hands. It was then that emphasis was really laid on teaching that hitherto had seemed specifically Huguenot. The preachers and the mob helped themselves to the contract theory with its implications. Before the day of " mobocracy " the League had, in fact, struggled for the sovereignty of the Pope; now it was the sovereignty of the people that was claimed. Divine hereditary right,[2] the Salic Law, the absolutism of monarchs, the duty of obedience, they left to the Huguenots. The League thundered—mostly from the pulpit— that kings rule not by hereditary or natural right, but at the will of the people, who delegate their power and can resume it. There is a tripartite contract between God, King, and people, and if the King violates his faith towards either of the other two, the remedy lies with the people. He is the servant of God, graced by consecration to preserve the Church; he is the agent of the people in the performance of that function, pledged to it by yet another compact between them and himself. " Le principe religieux est placé avant le principe héréditaire "; in this lies the situation. At the first, and for most of its history, it was the Catholic Church of the Papacy which the League defended; but later, beyond question, the Gallican Church of France. And who were the " people "? None of those bodies that, with respect, might have claimed to be; not Estates, nor Parliaments—the people were the mobs of the towns. None the less, " Vox Populi " must be " Vox Dei ". On these foundations the Jesuits built.

The League had been both mediaeval in vaunting the power of the Pope to depose sinners and heretics, and modern in claiming later that prerogative for the people. What, then, was the purpose of the Jesuits in preaching " le droit populaire ", since the people were clearly less zealous in the papal cause? It has been said that they were indifferent to the claim of popular sovereignty, but, disguising indifference, caught as opportunists at this theory for dealing with heretical princes. That may be so, but it does not cover the whole situation. The Jesuits were no mere parochial intriguers. Unimpassioned thinkers, they saw the vision of

---

[1] Leaguers and Huguenots " pirouetted " on their former doctrines.

[2] As early as 1573 the *Réveille-Matin* states that it would as soon have the Guise as the Valois.

mediaeval Christendom always before their eyes. They knew as clearly as anybody that the Empire had long since gone, and that Europe was composed of secular, independent, national States. But the Church was still universal, and the aim of the Jesuits was to formulate a possible relationship between those States and the Catholic Church. Mediaeval in desire for unity, they perceived that the Church was, at the moment, the only possible unifying link; later the link was to be international law, but though this was brought nearer to actuality by the Society, it was incidental only to their main teaching.

The Pope's position must first be defined. He is the only Sovereign with immediate right, received direct from Christ, and, therefore, the only Sovereign legislator. He has no direct temporal power, but an indirect power [1]—that is, he can interfere if the Government in any State militates against the true end of that State, for that end is spiritual; he may not allow the souls of men to be imperilled. The State exists " ad finem spiritualem ", and the Jesuits write with this end always in view.

The civil power has a quasi-divine character. Society originated by Nature for the needs, preservation, and intellectual intercourse of men. Human society gave birth to political society, which is itself natural. But as Nature is divine wisdom, political society is in this sense divine, originating out of Nature, as Nature originates from God. Thus degrees and status in political communities are divine (there can be no Anabaptist equality), but the divine power rests in the whole people, and not in any one man. Taught by Nature, the people transfer their power to an elected delegate, for the temporal peace of the State. Thus the King can have only human and temporal authority, since first he is empowered by the people and, secondly, rules for a temporal purpose.

It follows that an unsatisfactory king may be deposed and even slain, though here the teaching of Bellarmine, according to his latest biographer, [2] is not that of the others. Bellarmine, like Hooker, states that once the people have accredited their ruler, they have no further control over him, and may not, without grave sin, rebel; and a strong passage declaring the exact opposite is stated to be a forgery. [3] But Bellarmine does seem to admit that for legitimate

---

[1] Bellarmine (vivebat 1542–1621) : De Romano Pontifice ; in the Disputationes (Rome, 1832), Lib. V, Caps. 4 and 6. Cologne ed. 1619–20: pp. 487 et seq. Tome i.

[2] Brodrick : Blessed Robert Bellarmine, 2 vols. (London, 1928).

[3] Op. cit., I, 229. But James I had little doubt about Bellamine's intentions! " The great and famous writer of Controversies the late Un-Jesuited Cardinall Bellarmine must adde his talent to this good worke, by blowing the Bellowes of Sedition, and sharpening the Spurre to Rebellion . . ." [Apology for the Oath of Allegiance, p. 27.]

reasons—which he does not define—the people may change the form of government. He is but little troubled with specific justifications of deposition, but much more concerned to show that the Pope may deprive kings who rule contrary to the spiritual end, for of this end the Church is guide and guardian. Be this as it may, however, the Society of Jesus, by sufficient representatives, allows deposition, and some members go farther; nor were their deductions illogical, if society and monarchy were not of immediate divine origin, as they said.

But the key to all their teaching lies in the fact that they still saw Europe a Christian unity, made up of national States. A State had a temporal head, a temporal origin, a temporal end, *qua* State, and with this the Church had properly no concern. As part of the Christian unity, it had a spiritual end, far grander than the temporal, because eternal and divine, and where this was jeopardized the Church (*i.e.*, the Pope) could move. The State as a political society was a secular creation. Now, this is where Jesuits, Independents, and Huguenots touched in agreement, and explains why loyal Anglicans could upbraid Cartwright and his fellows with being Jesuits in reality. Puritan and Jesuit argued that religion was not the affair of the State; the latter was going outside its province entirely in meddling with religion. It was the Two-Kingdom theory held by Independents, taught by Jesuits, rejected by Anglicans.

As all their ideas on politics were profounder than those of writers clouded with passion, so was the Jesuits' view of law incomparably nobler. The ethical aspect of law is never obscured; indeed it is the prominent notion. The idea of justice, of order, is with them both earlier and more important than the idea of command. Here they agree with Hooker; both see in law not an Austinian command, not the bare fiat of a Sovereign, but some part of the justice and the order of God himself. Justice is the essence of law.

The general importance of the Jesuit writers of this time, therefore, is that they developed and crystallized the doctrine of the sovereignty of the people, which hitherto had meant one thing with the Huguenots, another with the League. The sovereignty of the people lies in its duly authorized representatives. Therefore a general will could be understood with all its consequences, and the Jesuit completion of " le droit populaire " definitely helped to prepare the way for Rousseau's *Contrat Social.*

They crystallized, too, the conception of the State. By teaching that it is a complete entity, in no subordination on its secular side to Church or Pope, they paved the way unwittingly for the State to throw off religious burdens and responsibilities; to emerge, standing above the spiritual conflicts of its citizens, gazing good-naturedly or contemptuously and indifferently on them all; to become a Society sufficient in itself, by itself, and for itself, for all purposes of this world.

Yet they taught also that a national State should not live in isolation—cannot, in fact, as a member of the Christian unity. Even though the vision of Christian unity was not more than a vision, isolation was impossible. The need for international relationships, emphasized by Jesuit pens, was to be satisfied by the International Law of Grotius.

But although Catholic League, Jesuits, and Huguenots could picture religion as external to the State, not its concern, Hooker could not. He consecrates the State as the other aspect of the Church, divine in origin, in purpose, in function. The polity, existing certainly for temporal ends as the State, exists as the Church also, consecrated to divine ends. The Jesuits came to their conclusion because their idea was universal, greater than any State. The Huguenots reached their conclusion because they were a party smaller than the State. Hooker's conclusion is, as his outlook, precisely national; neither greater nor less than the national State, the State itself. His State is divine, omnicompetent, with its own religion; the Jesuits' is secular, temporary, for material ends, unconcerned with religion, save as a member—if it be one—of the Christian Commonwealth.

So Jesuits could teach that the King had no concern with religion; Huguenots and Leaguers exclaim that he must guard true religion or forfeit his place; Hooker is satisfied that the King's religion is the subject's religion—" Our Church hath dependency upon the Chief in our Commonwealth ";[1] from the right of the monarch comes the right of religion. " Is there any law of Christ's which forbiddeth Kings . . . to have such sovereign and supreme power in the making of laws, either civil or ecclesiastical? If there be, our controversy hath an end."[2]

We have noted a similar conception of law both in Hooker and the Jesuits. Further, both made Society originate in much the same way, but Hooker will give it and its works the full sanction of divine right; the Jesuits will allow at most a quasi-divinity, and that only to its origin, not to its form and functions. We need not pause to point out how unlike the Jesuit theory of " delegation " is Hooker's alienation of their power by the people to the King; and how, therefore, the Jesuit King is an office-holder, while Hooker's is the full-blooded monarch, who reigns and governs. Each side, profound, unimpassioned, logical, starting from similar foundations,

[1] *E.P.*, VIII, i, 7.   [2] *E.P.*, VIII, vi, 12.

and doubtless mutually influenced, could yet erect a building alike only in few features to the other.

In Juan de Mariana [1] the Society of Jesus had a fearless thinker. His book, *De Rege et Regis Institutione,* discloses both affinity with and, of course, dissonance from Hooker, and we shall see where their lines of thought run parallel and diverge. We cannot read the *Ecclesiastical Polity* without a conviction that its author lived in the presence of the Divine. For him God permeates both Nature and political society, and his treatment of his subject is suffused with reverence and godly fear. Everything in life subserves divine purpose; the world is a unity, an organic whole, and even political facts are lifted out of everyday and material existence to become expressions of the divine will. A student of Aquinas and Aristotle, Hooker is thus far a mediaevalist, in contrast with Mariana, whose teaching in some points is startlingly prophetic and modern. Both intensely national, the one affords a religious outlook, the other is frankly secular in his treatment of political institutions. The basis of all polity with Hooker is God's will as revealed in Nature and in Scripture; for Mariana it is a mere expression of the needs of man and exists solely by the will of men. Each to an extent worships his own country, and makes religion serve a utilitarian purpose, though one feels in reading Mariana very much in the company of Machiavelli. Thus Hooker views religion very largely as the spiritual expression of the State's very life; so much so that even recusants and Puritans must, for public unity's sake, agree to bow down in the House of Rimmon, notwithstanding their private beliefs. Critics who declared that he made the Church a State department, however nobly idealized, would have been wrong. There *could* be only one religion—that of the State, for the State was divine; and its religion was in fact the pure and primitive branch of Christ's Catholic Church in England.

Mariana similarly insists that there can be but one religion in any State, but solely on the ground that more than one will imperil its unity; and he really implies that it need not be the Roman Catholic faith—a false religion may equally well serve the State's purpose of preservation. Hooker maintains that all Englishmen must be Anglicans, not only because the laws of England require it, and dissent produces sedition, but because dissenters put themselves out of the stream of that divine life which sustains the State. Mariana demands adherence to one form of religion, since members of two religions would so distrust each other as to work the political down-fall of the State.

Far more vital difference lies between them in their treatment of

[1] *Vivebat* 1536–1624.

monarchy. We feel that Hooker is writing about a king who is King indeed; we seem to see at times the picture of Henry VIII or Elizabeth in his pages—idealized, perhaps, but still sufficiently true to history. The King is limited, indeed, by divine and natural law, and the original vague and forgotten compact; but quite decidedly in him, more than in any other part of the polity, lies the sovereignty. But Mariana's King is a closely-watched, suspect being, bound in by much stricter bonds, as we shall see, and sharing the government with nobles and bishops. "The people" is the real sovereign—that is, in its representative assembly; not so much an ultimate Sovereign, who once in time gave away its right never to be resumed, but an ever-present power, likely at any time (and thoroughly justified in certain circumstances) to regather into its hands that limited and qualified authority that conditionally it had given to its King.

Rebellion is never in Hooker's thought; granted a subject must not, even when ordered, act contrary to the divine or moral law; but revolt, deposition, regicide—sound, God-fearing, Church-and-State Anglicans in the reign of Elizabeth could not discuss such monstrous things; they had best be left to fanatical Scotch,[1] hotheaded English Puritans,[1] exasperated Huguenots and calculating Jesuits to weave into theories. And in Mariana we shall find one whose boldness followed where his logic led.

Mariana's *De Rege*[2] was published in 1598, and dedicated to Philip III. It started from the presupposition that before the Fall there was a Golden Age, in which men were morally perfect and naturally equal; "nullus locus fraudi, nulla mendacia, nulli potentiores . . . quibus assentari opus haberent".[3] After the Fall Man, distinct from brutes by speech and reason, insufficient by himself for material welfare, formed societies. "Hinc urbani coetus primum regiaque maiestas orta est, quae non divitiis et ambitu, sed moderatione, innocentia, perspectaque virtute olim obtinebantur",[4] since they found one for ruler and protector "iustitia fideque praestantem".[5] Thus the origin of civil society—"out of the weakness and needs of men civil society was born"[6]—had added to it a further occasion, to settle the quarrels that arose,

---

[1] Described by Sanderson as the "rigid, Scotised, through-paced Presbyterian on the one side, and the giddy Enthusiast on the other" (*Preface to Sermons*, 1657).

[2] Ref. to 2nd ed. (1641). But note, the pagination in that edition is often wrong.

[3] Op. cit., p. 13.

[4] "This was the origin of civil societies and royal authority, maintained in bygone days not by riches and strife, but by temperance, simplicity, and known virtue."

[5] p. 16.   [6] p. 18.

mostly about property: kingly power was added to be the guardian of the whole.[1] The ruler was to decide controversies by his " aequitas ", but, this coming into suspicion, laws were made which should speak always with one voice for all men. But evil grew and had to be restrained, consequently severer laws were passed. In these two requirements is found the origin of law; " Scribendi leges duplex causa extitit ".[2] By this time, he ironically remarks, a stage was reached " ut iam non minus legibus quam vitiis laboremus ",[3] and the labours of Hercules are not comparable.

The next development of political society is seen in territory-snatching and empire-building, not much removed from barefaced robbery. These were the stages in the growth of royal power following its inception.[4]

Monarchy seems to have been the original form of government, he thinks,[5] arising out of the family and family groups, probably because men found it more convenient in its unifying effect (" Res communes melius ab uno quam a multis curantur ").[6] The march of time, however, saw other forms, and there is something to be said for the government of more than one, since out of many the deficiencies of one may be made good,[7] and he adds, " There is a great poverty of truth with all princes ",[8] and one man is more likely to yield to bribes than many. A sole ruler is fawned on, blinded by flattery, can change laws at a nod, is difficult to restrain within legal limits, may thwart the laws of succession. But, on the whole, Mariana thinks monarchy is the best form, and it has the warrant of Scripture behind it. " Those drawbacks I see are out-weighed by greater advantages." [9] It affords unity at least, whereas in the government of many the " pars sanior " may be worsted in deliberations by the " pars peior ", since votes are not weighed, but counted.[10] Yet a monarch ought to call to counsel the best and wisest men,[11] and administer public and private affairs with their aid, for no graver harm can be imagined than the neglect of public business.[12]

In the third chapter Mariana discusses the principle of hereditary succession, pointing out the inconveniences that may arise when the heir is degenerate,[13] or a babe, or a woman, and of course a succession of good kings in one family will make a State risk a bad successor. But the advantage of heredity lies in its avoiding disputes about the succession [14] and, on the whole, it is likely to afford the State better service. " Demum res communes diligentius quasi propriae curantur ab eo, qui posteris relicturus est quam acceperit potestatem ;

---

[1] p. 18. [2] Ibid. [3] p. 19. [4] Ibid. [5] p. 20.
[6] p. 21. [7] Ibid. [8] p. 22. [9] p. 25. [10] Ibid.
[11] p. 26. [12] p. 27. [13] pp. 29-32. [14] pp. 31 and 34.

M

negliguntur ab aliis, qui exiguo vitae incertoque tempore circumscriptum principatum habent."[1] Beyond question, however, it is not a principle strictly necessary,[2] and as there may be many children, and the succession to the kingship is vastly more important than to private property, the law should regulate it. Primogeniture is the general rule, and is warranted in Scripture, though Solomon's succession to David makes against it. But where there is reasonable fear that the heir is less worthy than younger sons, one of the latter should succeed, "modo sine motu contingat contentioneque".[3] No existing King should be able to alter the law regulating succession, and women are unfit, unless a suitable consort can be found.[4]

He continues, in the next chapter, to insist that the great thing is to avoid uncertainty and disputation; therefore fix the succession, "successore in omne tempus per legem designato",[5] and do not allow a king to nominate any particular one out of his sons. No one can change the laws regulating succession to the throne without the assent of the people from whom the sovereignty of the State comes.[6] If the succession is not fixed there is bound to be trouble, because the less legal right a claimant has, the more by force will he strive for his end; this spells war and disaster in the State, for "silent enim inter arma leges".[7] There is neither divine nor natural right inherent in hereditary succession; it is purely a matter of convenience, and some States prefer it.

In the course of discussing the differences between a king and a tyrant,[8] Mariana defines kingly power thus: "Regia potestas, uni homini delata rerum omnium summa atque unius arbitrio constituitur".[9] A king will use it subject to limitations and for the good of all; a tyrant without bounds, and for his own ends. The king recognizes that he has received this power from his subjects[10] and exercises it therefore "singulari modestia", ruling over his people as if they were his children, not his slaves. Since this power comes from the people, his first care must always be to rule them with their consent.[11] Protected by his subjects' love, he has no need of guards, horses, armies; but the tyrant is a bloodthirsty monster, a robber on a large scale. The power he has seized, probably by violence, he exercises over his subjects heavily; "nullum scelus

[1] p. 32. "Finally, the public service is more carefully attended to—as if it were his own—by one who will leave to his descendants the power which he has received; and neglected by those who hold their supremacy limited to their short and uncertain length of life."

[2] p. 35.   [3] p. 36.   [4] p. 37.   [5] *Ibid.*
[6] p. 38.   [7] p. 41.   [8] Chap. 5.
[9] p. 43. "Royal power is established when the supreme control of everything is yielded to one man's decision."
[10] p. 45.   [11] *Ibid.*

sibi dedecori fore putat ".[1] (" He considers that no wickedness can shame him.")

Example is better than precept, and not less so because a man is king. " Longum enim iter per verba est, breve et efficax per exempla." [2] A good king will rule himself and his own family first. Neatly he sums up the differences between king and tyrant: " Timet quidem tyrannus, timet Rex: sed Rex subditis, ille sibi subditosque ".[3]

Very coolly, in the well-known sixth chapter, Mariana discusses whether it is right to kill a tyrant. He describes the murder of Henri III by the Dominican, Jacques Clément, in 1589, who made a great name for himself thereby.[4] He is so matter-of-fact that at first it is not easy to see if his sympathy is with the victim or the murderer, but later on we are left in no doubt. Opinions were divided, Mariana says, about this particular assassination. Some praised the monk highly and judged him worthy of immortality; others said it was a crime to slay even a tyrant " privata auctoritate ". The latter held up the examples of David with Saul, the young Amalekite, the early Christian martyrs obedient to St. Paul's teaching of non-resistance, and argued that at all costs sedition in a State must be avoided.[5]

But the " popular party ", he points out, have " non pauciora neque minora praesidia ". That party holds that, although the " regia potestas " has been conferred on a king, it is not " ut non sibi majorem reservarit potestatem ". A king was never instituted but that the people maintained a reserve of power over and above his. Thus the King cannot change certain fundamental laws— for example, of the succession, of taxes, and of religion—without the assent of the people; nor is any difference made by the fact of hereditary succession; the heir still holds from the people: his right to rule still rests on their assent.[6]

Therefore when a king becomes a tyrant by overstepping the bounds prescribed, lovers of their country, who, like Roman Brutus, rise against him, will be had in honour for their audacity, rather than reviled. Here Mariana is most interesting. What is it that prompts a patriot to attack his King? It is no low motive, no sordid desire, but a certain " voice of nature ", a real " common " sense speaking to men's minds, " auribus insonans lex ", which

---

[1] p. 44.   [2] p. 47.
[3] p. 50.
[4] p. 54. He omits in this edition the sentence that many people regarded Clément as an " eternal glory " of France. After the murder of Henri IV by Ravaillac in 1610 the Jesuits' " popular " theory roused such an outcry that the way was opened for royal absolutism.
[5] p. 57.   [6] Ibid.

convinces them that the King has become a tyrant, just as they, by
the same sense, distinguish right from wrong! [1]

The King has gone beyond his powers. Add to this that he is
like a beast, ravaging with horns and teeth to despoil and to slay;
is he not to be regarded as a cruel monster? Is not praise due to
him who risks his life to rescue the State? [2] Would a man avenge
on a tyrant the wrongs done to wife or mother, and yet allow his
fatherland (" to which we owe more than to parents ") to be
ravaged? " Apage tantum nefas, tantaque ignavia! " Life, laws,
fortune—all must be risked to free the State from danger and
destruction. This is his considered opinion. " Indeed I see that
philosophers and theologians alike agree that a Prince who seizes
the State by violence, with neither right nor public consent of the
people, can be dethroned and slain by anyone, for he is a public
enemy, rightly bearing the name and mark of tyrant." [3]

Where a prince has come to his throne by popular will or right of
heredity, his private vices and wrong-doing must be borne with,
since by changing rulers the State may incur greater danger; and if
his abdication is necessary, the procedure for enforcing it must be
carefully thought out, " lest evil pile on evil, and crime be avenged
by crime ".[4] The national assembly must come together, and
there fashion a plan. First they should warn the King to return to
sancr paths; if he pays heed, " sharper remedies " must not be
used. But if he will not amend, he must be deposed and attacked.
The State must defend itself by its own and more powerful authority.[5]
He must be proscribed as a public enemy, and it is lawful for any
private man, who is bold enough, to remove him altogether. Still
more desirable is this if the King prevents the Assembly from
meeting. It would be a just judgment, and in Mariana's opinion
anyone who attempted the task would be acting rightly.[6] But he
makes it clear that this right of private vengeance does not belong
to any one, or to any number " nisi publica vox populi adsit ",
except such tyranny as prevents the " publica vox " from ever
coming together. Such tyrants, then, as live in violation of all laws
of morals and the State can be slain not only by natural right, but
indeed to the praise and renown of the slayer.[7]

This right of vengeance will put a bridle on the madness of
kings, and will recall to them the first principle of all—that their
people are greater than they. That is the principle to be brought
home to a ruler: the authority of the realm is greater than his.[8]
But, of course, tyrannicide is a last step; it is liable to produce un-
settledness and tumult. Yet if no possible hope of reformation lies

[1] p. 58.   [2] *Ibid.*   [3] *Ibid.*   [4] p. 59.
[5] p. 60.   [6] *Ibid.*   [7] p. 61.   [8] *Ibid.*

elsewhere, who will be so wanting in sense as not to acknowledge it is proper by justice and law forcibly to overthrow a tyrant?[1] This is Mariana's sincere opinion; he is human and liable to err, but if anybody can show him a better way he will be grateful.

A whole chapter follows on the question whether a tyrant may be lawfully removed by poison. It is now agreed that it is a splendid work to exterminate this pestilential and destructive breed,[2] so what matters it, some ask, whether by poison or by steel? But Mariana is not too happy; he does admit that the removal may be thus made,[3] but points out that it is difficult to accomplish,[4] and in any case a tyrant ought not to be compelled to poison himself.

The eighth chapter introduces the crucial question—is the State or the King more powerful? It is not made easier to answer, Mariana says, since there is no third way out![5] When lawful kings were first instituted, the people circumscribed them with laws, lest they became pernicious rulers.[6] That is the first limitation. The second is that the " capita " of the State, the nobles and bishops, should have such wealth and power as to be able to check the King, for otherwise the State is weakened with the weakening of its noblest parts.[7] It is clear that for Mariana these classes constitute the people; theirs is the " publica vox ", and theirs is the reserve of power which the people have always retained, and by virtue of which an unsatisfactory king can be deposed, since he rules entirely conditionally. If these classes be reduced in influence, the stoutest props of the State are lost; one's mind is appalled at the evils that can come from this: the door is open to all mischiefs.

The King is not in the least " legibus solutus ". He is restrained by the law of God; then by the moral law,[8] "pudor atque honestas ", " modestia ", " decus ". This holds good whether the government is aristocratic[9] or democratic.[10] Then, whatever the government, there are fundamental laws (succession, taxation, religion) which cannot be touched except with the consent and known opinion of the whole realm.[11] Mariana concedes to the ruler a discretionary power in emergencies to make new laws, interpret old, and to supply deficiencies in the laws; but he may not invert existing laws, nor turn to private gain what was intended for all, and he must reverence custom and institutions.[12]

Thus bound, the King clearly has no power to interfere with religion.[13] Mariana agrees—as Hooker, too, points out—that in the most ancient times religion was the concern of secular rulers.[14]

---

[1] p. 62.　　[2] p. 64.　　[3] p. 68.　　[4] p. 66.　　[5] p. 68.
[6] p. 78.　　[7] p. 76.　　[8] p. 79.　　[9] p. 80.　　[10] p. 81.
[11] Ibid.　　[12] p. 80.　　[13] p. 85.　　[14] p. 86.

But it is clearly unlawful that religion should hang on the whim of one man, and he, perchance, lost in depravities. That state of things would mean that his followers and fawners (" aulici ") would practically dictate rites and ceremonies: " apage periculum grande "!

Such, in brief outline, is Mariana's conception of the State. It is purely natural, due to human needs and human will; it has no divine origin, nor yet purpose, since its only end is self-preservation. Law, so far from being a reflection of divine order, is rather a necessary nuisance, and his view of it clearly goes no farther than that it is essentially a command followed by punishment for any breach. The King is an officer of the people, appointed by them and removable at their pleasure, since he holds office only on condition. Whether that condition was ever expressed does not matter, since no people would be so stupid as to part with all their power. Certain fundamental laws are the people's concern alone; therefore they must have an Assembly of the wealthy and the wise, and this body is, in Mariana's eyes, the ultimate Sovereign, for it possesses the " publica vox ".

In 1613 another Jesuit, Francis Suarez [1] of Granada, published his *Tractatus de Legibus ac Deo Legislatore*,[2] a calm survey of the whole field of law and of government. It was written against James I's *Apology for the Oath of Allegiance*. Perhaps the greatest of the contemporary Jesuit writers on political theory, Suarez shares with them that faculty of unimpassioned, critical examination of human things. The *Tractatus* is a systematic work, in which every political question is held up for discussion and viewed from every possible angle. We do not seem to discover in these greatest writers the traces of partisanship visible in lesser men; their books are not *ivres de circonstance*, but possess an air of philosophic detachment not often found in English writers of the period—perhaps in none save Hooker and Bacon. As Hallam says, they do not write for the moment, and are free from local and contemporary prejudices apparent enough in the works of others.

The *Tractatus* of Suarez is wonderfully akin to the *Ecclesiastical Polity*, both in method and outlook. Both writers perceive that the nature of law must first be determined before any discussion of government can profitably be entered upon. Each is tireless in the patient fullness with which he writes on the theory of law, doubtless because each is closely indebted to their common master, St. Thomas Aquinas. Prolific as he is in his citation of authorities, Suarez makes it plain that St. Thomas holds the place of honour. He follows him closely where his teaching is clear, and attempts to

[1] *Vivebat* 1548–1617.   [2] Ref. to 1861 ed. (Paris).

clarify it where it is obscure. The other master shared in common is Aristotle, and so closely allied are their reasoning and their dependence that an epitome of the *Tractatus* would not, in essentials, be far different from an outline of the *Ecclesiastical Polity*. A marked contrast in one respect may be found, distinguishing Suarez alike from Hooker and Mariana. He is far less national than either. He is proud of his country, but not with the blind devotion of his compatriot; he will even venture to criticize the existing institutions of Spain. Again, he faces the question whether it may be lawful to resist an unjust ruler, which Hooker burked. The latter makes monarchy of divine right, although originating in the people's gift,[1] since what is natural is of God, and political society is natural. Suarez will not go so far. He agrees that political society is natural, but what form of government it establishes is its own concern, and cannot be said thereby to be truly of divine origin; because for him, as for other Jesuits, the State is secular, distinct now from the Church, which alone is a " Societas perfecta et divina ". But in their definition of law; in the grandeur of their conception of natural law, its breadth, its basic quality, its immutability; in their teaching that positive human law must accord with it; in their placing the ultimate sovereignty in the will of the people; still more in their insistence that, once the people have made a monarch for themselves, he must actually rule with a moderately free hand; in their teleological view of the State, these two men, Anglican and Jesuit, display a remarkable similarity. They must have been men of the same mind and soul, to whom in life theology, morality, and politics were as necessarily intermingled as they are in their books.

Suarez early defines law, following St. Thomas, thus: " Lex est commune praeceptum, iustum, ac stabile sufficienter promulgatum ".[2] All rational beings, capable of volition, must have their lives determined by law, natural, human, and divine; and underlying all is the Eternal Law—a classification taken from Aquinas and resembling Hooker's. This Eternal Law he defines: " Legem aeternam esse decretum liberum voluntatis Dei, statuentis ordinem servandum, aut generaliter ab omnibus partibus universi in ordine ad commune bonum, vel immediate illi conveniens ratione totius universi in ordine ad commune bonum, vel immediate illi conveniens ratione singularum specierum eius, aut specialiter ser-

---

[1] Burke felt much the same, and wrote: ". . . no power is given for the sake of the holder, and although government certainly is an institution of Divine authority, yet its forms, and the persons who administer it, all originate from the people " (*Thoughts on the Present Discontents*, p. 348).

St. Thomas Aquinas had held that the *principium* of political rule was divinely given, but the *modus* or form of that rule was from the people.

[2] *Tractatus*, I, xii, 5.

vandum a creaturis intellectualibus quoad liberas operationes earum ".[1] This is much the same as Hooker's conclusion that the throne of law is the bosom of God.[2] The will of God freely and eternally determines order in the universe, both generally for all parts of Nature, and specially for rational man. God is a God of order, not of confusion, as Hooker agrees. The Eternal Law is the divine will. Men, while they sojourn on earth (" viatores homines "),[3] cannot know this Eternal Law directly, but only in or through other laws, but it is the law by which the blessed in heaven are immediately governed. As second causes reveal the first, and creatures their Creator, so " human laws, which are part-sharers of Eternal Law, display the fount from which they flow ".[4] No rational being is without some knowledge of the Eternal Law, but many are not aware of it formally in a direct manner. Hence some men recognize it only " in inferioribus legibus ", but others, more gifted, also through those inferior laws.[5]

The Law of Nature, the greatest of the laws directly known to man, is not precisely Hooker's Law of Reason, or Pecock's moral law of kind, still less Luther's paltry conscience. Some hold " hanc legem nihil aliud esse quam ipsam naturam rationem ",[6] but Suarez, distinguishing the Law of Nature from pure reason and from conscience,[7] insists that it is a real law, resting on authority. Conscience is " dictamen de agendis ", orders in particulars,[8] and is necessarily wider in its scope even than the Law of Nature,[9] since that law, like any other, is a rule or measure " generaliter constitutam circa agenda ".[10] He insists that it is true law, since it has an author and subjects, and does not simply indicate right and wrong, but commands the one and forbids the other. It is both preceptive and imperative. " The Law of Nature is not only indicative of good and evil, but also contains its own prohibition of evil and command to do good . . . for the Law of Nature is genuine law." [11]

The Law of Nature is not known to all men equally; its most fundamental principles certainly are, such as the Decalogue, and they bind all men alike; [12] other rules drawn from these principles

---

[1] II, iii, 6. " Eternal Law is the free decree of the Will of God, establishing an order to be kept, either in general by all parts of the Universe with a view to the common good (to which this decree is directly appropriate either because the Universe as a whole is organized with a view to the common good or because the individual components are so organized) or in particular by rational creatures with respect to their free activities."

[2] E.P., I, xvi, 8.
[3] Suarez, op. cit., II, iv, 9.
[4] Ibid.   [5] Ibid.   [6] II, v, 1.   [7] II, v.
[8] II, v, 15.   [9] Ibid.   [10] Ibid.   [11] II, vi, 5 and 6.
[12] II, viii, 3.

are hidden from the more ignorant men, though known by intellectual deduction to others. Many of them in particular are unknown to the common people.[1] None the less, the Law of Nature constitutes an entire code for all, " hanc legem naturalem esse unam in omnibus hominibus, et ubique ".[2] It cannot be ignored, it is immutable,[3] and positive laws are not true laws if made contrary to the Law of Nature,[4] for no law contrary to justice or morality is law; no power of papal or human law can override the Law of Nature.[5]

The *ius naturale* dictates universal moral obligations in contrast to the *ius gentium*, which establishes what is commodious between nations.[6] The customs which nations use in their relations with each other need not be part of the natural law at all.[7] These customs are determined by what is expedient, and are human (" positiva et humana "),[8] whereas the principles of natural law are divine.[9] Disobedience to the *ius gentium* is not wrong, unless it is made part of the municipal law, but disobedience to the *ius naturale* is always wrong. But the *ius gentium* is to be held in esteem, since States are not individually self-sufficing and need the help of each other.[10] It is built up partly of natural precepts, partly of customary usage,[11] but corresponds rather to civil than to natural law, in that it is positive and human.[12]

In his treatment of the Law of Nations, and in his insistence on its necessity, since civil societies are naturally inter-dependent, Suarez goes farther than Hooker. The latter considers the Law of Nations desirable, but does not accord to it that degree of necessity that Suarez does. The Jesuit holds up a picture of a Europe once more united—not the *Respublica Christiana*, ruled by Pope and Emperor —but a confederacy of separate secular States, bound mostly (not all, he says) together by common obedience to the *ius gentium*. Here is the seed of that Internationalism which Grotius planted with the assistance of the Jesuits, possibly to be realized in the course of the twentieth century.

A positive municipal law must be a precept directed to the common good, established and promulgated, and this introduces the question of government, for the essence of government, Suarez agrees with Bodin, is the power to make law. He opens the Third Book—on positive law and government—with the question, Whence came the power of men to subject others by laws, since man is by nature free, and subject to none but his Creator?[13] His origin of society is familiar ground—it is simply that of Aristotle and Aquinas,

---

[1] II, viii, 7. [2] II, viii, 5. [3] II, viii, 11. [4] III, xii, 4.
[5] *Ibid.* " Nulla potestas humana, etiamsi pontificia sit, potest proprium aliquod praeceptum legis naturalis abrogare " (II, xiv, 8).
[6] II, xvii–xx. [7] II, viii, 5. [8] II, xix, 4. [9] *Ibid.*
[10] II, xix, 9. [11] *Ibid.* [12] II, xix, 5. [13] III, i, 1.

that social life is natural and implies regulation. The growth into civil society is first by way of the family, then the tribes in families, then the " communitas politica ", differing from the former groupings in that it exists for political as well as domestic regime.[1] This he calls a " civitas ", a real coalescence of families. The last stage is the " Societas plurium civitatum ", into a kingdom or principality of some sort. It is by Nature—since Nature abhors deficiencies—that a ruler is required,[2] for naturally men are not governed in political society either by angels or by the immediate action of God.[3] A supremacy being natural, is it naturally vested? Not in any one man, since all men are equally free;[4] nor yet in the lineal descendants of Adam[5] (here giving the lie by anticipation to Filmer's patriarchal theory), but in the whole community[6]— not indeed as a mere aggregate, but as a " societas " with a " communis sensus "; it is " unum corpus " mystically, morally, but none the less really, and it needs a head.[7] Government is posterior to political Society,[8] and is born entirely out of the will of that Society; its free-will is, as a man's free will, from the Author of Nature, and may to that extent be divine, but the immediate source of government is the community's " voluntas ", of political and not divine origin.[9] In proof of which, political government is at any time mutable, and transferable, according to the general will.[10]

Nor is any particular type of government dictated to men by Nature. They may set up what regiment they please.[11] Once this power is set up, it nevertheless still subsists in the people as a community, without whose consent it cannot justly be held, " because this power from the nature of the case comes immediately from the community; consequently if it is to reside in a single person it must be given to that person by the assent of the community ".[12] Such monarchs do not hold their power from God—it is not in point to cite Biblical kings like Saul and David, since their appointment was extraordinary and supernatural—but from the people, inasmuch as men enter on civil organization by natural reason, and in no sense by divine revelation.[13]

Nor can hereditary succession, however well established, confer the right of ruling upon any successor.[14] The will of the people is still in operation, even if not manifested, since it is clear that the actual succession cannot be the original root of royal power. The first monarch holds immediately from the State, his successor only mediately from him; yet radically from the State. This must be

---

[1] III, i, 3.   [2] III, i, 4.   [3] III, i, 5.   [4] III, ii, 3.
[5] Ibid.   [6] III, ii, 4.   [7] Ibid.   [8] III, iii, 6.
[9] Ibid.   [10] III, iii, 7.   [11] III, iv, 1.   [12] III, iv, 2.
[13] Ibid.   [14] III, iv, 3.

so, inasmuch as the second succeeds to the rights and duties of the first, and in those duties will be contained the conditions on which he took the sovereignty.[1]

The people have transferred their power, let us say, to a king. Suarez makes it quite clear that the transference holds indefinitely, unless he be guilty of injustice or tyranny. The transfer was not by way of delegation but alienation, " perfecta largitio totius potestatis, quae erat in communitate ".[2] He may rule as much or as little in person as he likes, and may delegate to others as he pleases.[3] " For the same reason a King cannot be deprived of his power . . . unless perchance he falls into tyranny, when the realm can with justice make war against him." [4] Short of injustice, tyranny and specific limitations, the King rules absolutely.

Possessing the total power of the community, the King obviously has the legislative as well as the executive authority, since originally legislative power lay in the bosom of the people.[5] Jurisdiction must include legislation and coercion.[6] Thus jurisdiction was what the people handed to him at the " conventio ", which may have been a written agreement; if not, custom will have dictated the mode of its exercise agreeable to the subjects. Undoubtedly, the consent of the people to proposed legislation will be required.[7]

Suarez proceeds to attack the teaching of Wyclif and Hus that wicked or heathen kings cannot possess true civil power; " sententia . . . erronea . . . et damnata ".[8] The Christian virtues of faith and hope are supernatural gifts; not being possessed by the law of nature, they can have nothing to do with civil power.[9] Granted an infidel king must not be obeyed in things contrary to faith and revealed religion, yet he can be a true king, and may exact obedience in all things which belong to the right governing of the State.[10] But what if the King be wicked, and not merely an unbeliever? The answer, replies Suarez, turns on the nature of his wickedness. He may in private life be evil, but yet make good laws; he is then a just king " tunc formaliter et in quantum rex ". But the evil may go beyond himself and cause him to prescribe evil for his subjects, in which case he must not receive obedience, " nam lex iniqua non est lex ".[11] Lastly, if the King be iniquitous as a usurper and a tyrant, obedience must not be paid to him.[12]

What, then, are the limitations by which a king is bound? The Law of God and the Law of Nature, of course, bind him. Further, the terms of the original agreement, which may have been in the

[1] III, iv, 2.   [2] III, iv, 11.   [3] *Ibid.*   [4] III, iv, 6.
[5] III, ix, 2.   [6] III, ix, 3.
[7] III, ix, 4; xix, 2; and xv, 3 and 4.   [8] III, x, 1.
[9] III, x, 2.   [10] III, x, 3.   [11] III, x, 7.   [12] *Ibid.*

form of a written contract, or expressed in custom, must be adhered to, prescribing the fundamental conditions of the transference. " It follows . . . that this power is in the supreme ruler in that measure and subject to that condition with which it was given and transferred by the community . . . because this is, as it were, a compact between community and prince, and the power received therefore does not exceed the measure of the gift or the compact." [1] Apart from this, a king cannot be hampered by querulous subjects; the opportunity of limiting his power was in the original agreement, and they should have taken it. " Fulness or limitation of Kingly power . . . cannot proceed from natural law, but depends upon human decision, and the ancient agreement or compact between King and the realm." [2] This is a strong reminder of Hooker's advice to the Puritan malcontents.

What is the great purpose of the State? It is to make men good. [3] Machiavelli has taught that its only end is increase and self-preservation, so that any immorality in laws or law-giver is justifiable to that end, and no king can be sufficient for his task if he allows himself to be subject to laws inculcating virtue. [4] Suarez laments this perverse opinion, but is forced to agree that there are often in the civil law things " quae in foro animae non possunt subsistere ". [5] But at all events Machiavelli's teaching is entirely false and erroneous, [6] since the law of nature prohibits whatever is disgraceful; and even if, by error of judgment, some wrong is by the magistrate prescribed in a law, it is in that law " potestate facti ", not " potestate iuris ". After his vigorous denunciation of Machiavelli, Suarez is, however, forced to admit that the civil law may at some time permit what is wrong—State-necessity may demand it; but it is one thing to permit, another to prescribe the wrong. [7] " Therefore the civil laws do not prescribe wrong; but sometimes they allow or tolerate what is wrong to avoid worse evils." [8]

The teleological teaching of Suarez is not that of Hooker and Aquinas. The latter taught that the end of the State is so to teach men to live as to help them to eternal bliss. But this is not the function of the State, according to Suarez, for the State is entirely secular. It must make men good citizens for its own sake, but to go farther is to trespass on the spiritual. " Potestas civilis et ius civile per se non respiciunt aeternam felicitatem . . . quia talis potestas est mere naturalis; ergo natura sua non tendit in finem supernaturalem." [9]

[1] III, ix, 4.   [2] V, xvii, 3.   [3] III, xii.   [4] III, xii, 2.
[5] Ibid.   [6] III, xii, 4.   [7] III, xii, 6.   [8] Ibid.
[9] III, xi, 4. " Civil power and the Civil law have not eternal happiness as their object . . . because such kind of power is purely natural, and its nature is not directed to a supernatural end."

An interesting question—not of much importance, except that Suarez's view conflicts with Mariana's, and shows us that he conceives of a king in an altogether more generous and far less suspicious manner than Mariana—is discussed in the Fifth Book, on Taxation. Is the consent of subjects necessary for the imposition of new taxes? [1] Assuming a threefold condition is fulfilled—" legitima potestas, iusta causa, ac debita proportio "—he sees no reason, and can find no authority, why a king should be obliged to obtain consent to proposed taxation.[2] The answer really depends on whether, in the " conventio ", monarchy was established limited in legislation by the people or a senate, or " simpliciter in solo principe ",[3] and Suarez makes no secret that this latter is the only form of monarchy that he approves.

If Suarez is a monarchomach at all, he is vastly different from the Protestant type, and even from his countryman, Mariana. It is true he places the ultimate sovereignty in the people, but he places over them a real king, as unrestrained as Bodin's, and almost identical with Hooker's. Suarez's King both reigns and governs. Let him rule according to divine and natural law, observing the limits of that original " conventio " (whereby the people alienated, not delegated, their power), and no voice can rightly be raised against such a monarch, be he infidel, an evil-liver, or even a woman. He grants rights of deposition and tyrannicide,[4] if necessary, distinguishing between a usurper and a lawful monarch. Between a usurper and a State there has never been a " conventio "; thus the former has no rights, and war can be made against him; [5] but if the usurper prevail as a *de facto* king, the people, unable to resist, may be deemed to have given tacit consent.[6] The lawful King becomes a tyrant if he oversteps his bounds, and rules iniquitously.[7] He may well be deposed and attacked, though he

---

[1] Mariana had fundamentally limited the right of the Spanish Crown to tax without consent; it was shortly to be a burning cause of strife between King and Parliament in England; yet Suarez dismisses the people's claim to assent as unnecessary.

[2] V, xvii, 1, 3 and 4.

[3] V, xvii, 4.

[4] Extract from a letter of Bishop King of Chichester to Izaak Walton (1664): " And it is worth noting, that when he had perfected the work . . . it was transmitted to Rome for a view of the inquisitors; who according to their custom blotted out what they pleased, and . . . added whatsoever might advance the Pope's supremacy, or carry on their own interest; commonly coupling together *deponere et occidere*, the deposing and then killing of princes; which cruel and unchristian language Mr. John Saltkell, the amanuensis to Suarez . . . often professed, the good old man . . . not only disavowed, but detested . . ." (Hooker, *E.P.*, I, 105).

[5] III, iv, 4.

[6] *Ibid.*

[7] III, iv, 6.

later adds that even a tyranny may be borne as a lesser evil,[1] and the rule of a tyrant may be better than no rule at all.[2]

It is impossible to combine all the teachings of these Jesuit Monarchomachs into a uniform and homogeneous system of political philosophy, but certain cardinal articles of opinion can be extracted from the welter of discussion. The sovereignty of the people is clearly defined, although the position of the titular Sovereign is not the same with each writer. The Jesuits agree in defining law as regulation of social life, necessitated by the growth of civilization; the affinity between Suarez and Hooker is remarkable when each makes the *ius positivum* a reflex of the *ius aeternum,* the will of God, which is the basic Law of the Cosmos. Lastly, the Jesuits regarded religion as external to, but not isolated from, the State. Mariana does not allow his King to interfere with religion, and Suarez declares that the τέλος of the State is to make men good citizens for its own sake, irrespective of the demands of religion; a cleavage is made between religion and politics; the Middle Ages have been left behind.

----

[1] III, xi, 8 and 9.   [2] III, x, 9.

CHAPTER IX

THE RIGHT TO RESIST: THE ANSWER OF SOVEREIGNTY

" In all governments," wrote Hume, " there is a perpetual intestine struggle, open or secret, between Authority and Liberty; and neither of them can ever absolutely prevail in the contest." [1] Sixteenth-century France was rent asunder by civil war, while in England the struggle was for the moment confined to paper. Each country produced a principal philosopher who attempted to resolve the conflict. In Bodin's view the cure for the ills of France was a Royal Absolutism, while Hooker asserted that the safety of the State lay rather in the unity of the people under a king supreme in all causes. Sovereignty is therefore Bodin's main thesis, while it is the Majesty of Law that permeates the pages of Hooker's *Ecclesiastical Polity*. Nevertheless, since he is a practical Englishman and Elizabeth sat upon the throne—the incarnation of the law—Hooker is obliged to consider the origin and nature of the sovereignty which that great Queen wielded.

Sovereignty, to Hooker, is God-willed, and must be exercised and accepted as such. That is probably a reasonable summary of what can be extracted from the *Ecclesiastical Polity* so far as a theory of sovereignty is concerned. Government may be the result of direct revelation to an individual, of indirect revelation through the success of arms, or of willing committal of sovereignty by the people in some form of contract. The contradictions and uncertainties in which Hooker is involved are inextricable and irreconcilable. Hallam may regard him as an original Whig,[2] Holdsworth can point to him as the ablest defender of Tudor rule among sixteenth-century philosophers.[3] No one could foresee what Elizabeth meant to do, and none can tell precisely what Hooker meant. This much we may say. So far as the distinction between the condition of men in a political society and in the State of Nature is concerned, he follows the great Greek philosophers rather than the Roman lawyers. For him the State of Nature was not the Golden Age,

---

[1] *Essays* (ed. Green, London, 1875), Pt. I, Essay v, i, 116.
[2] *C.H.*, I, 219–25; *H.L.E.*, II, 48.   [3] *H.E.L.*, IV, 212.

and for him the State was an association to provide a physical basis for a spiritual end.

Government is necessary, and there is a corresponding faculty in every independent multitude. They may appoint a Sovereign; they may then or later bind him by contract; but they may equally have a Sovereign imposed upon them by force of arms, or by another recognizable fiat of the Almighty. Whichever the case, even to " Kings by human right, honour by very divine right is due ".[1] Whatever his title, the Sovereign is bound by natural and revealed law, and if he happens to be a Sovereign appointed by contract, he has also to observe the articles of contract. But if he does not, there is no remedy; there is only the pious and ineffectual hope that he will not be " stiff in detaining " that power, the exercise of which is inconsistent with the public welfare. Hooker strongly objects to any idea of an elective sovereignty. He sees England as a feudal country, and the right of succession of heirs male is part and parcel of his mind. He is of opinion that, if there were a contract, it was made once and for all. He no more saw the difficulty of maintaining the contractual freedom of each generation, which Locke did, than he recognized the stipulation for conscious choice of baptism by each individual which is explicit in the Anabaptist position. All this is not to deny his outstanding importance as the unwitting parent of the future Liberalism, but how easily he can appear on the other side is to be seen in the considerable parallel that can be drawn between his work and that of Bodin. Indeed, no study of Hooker's political opinions could be complete without mention of his great French contemporary, for Jean Bodin [2] stands by himself amongst the French political thinkers of the sixteenth century alike in subject-matter and importance. Like Machiavelli, though in a different way, he exercised the most profound influence on contemporary and seventeenth-century political ideas, and deserves to be treated apart.

A professional student of jurisprudence and history, Bodin ranged over a much wider field than did Hooker—embracing as he did, among other things, a study of astrology, a defence of witchcraft and sorcery, and an original theory of the effect of climate upon politics; but he was at one with the Englishman in recognizing the need of the new national kingdoms to possess a strong royal government. Indeed, he saw clearly that the only way for France to save herself from perpetual civil war on the question of religion was for her to recognize the necessity for a king with powers unhampered by Estates, Parlements, Privileges, whose right to rule was by agnatic relationship, safeguarded by the Salic Law.

[1] *E.P.*, VIII, ii, 6.   [2] *Vivebat* 1529–96.

A completely-honest thinker, he continued to propound this thesis, undeterred alike by opposition from the League—of which he had once been a member—and indifferent to the displeasure of Henri III, whose attempts to alienate the royal demesne he roundly condemned.

The great work of Jean Bodin, the *Six Books of a Republic*,[1] published in 1576, is marked off from most other contemporary writings inasmuch as it is written for all time. True, nobody nowadays reads it with enjoyment, since it is vast, cumbrous, and ill-arranged; but at least every student of political theory must study it. Bodin, however much he kept his eye on contemporary politics, ranges over all history and considers most thought; whatever his religion may have been, the author himself is catholic enough in range and output.

The *Republic* was at once an important book from its publication in 1576, and became a text-book in lectures at Cambridge; most years down to 1583 saw new editions;[2] in 1586 Bodin himself translated the book into Latin, and before 1600 there were Spanish, Italian, and German renderings. Not till 1606 did an English translation appear, made by Richard Knolles, now a scarce and precious volume.[3]

Philosophers, ecclesiastics, statesmen had all contributed to the wealth of writings on political theory; but Bodin was remarkably qualified to write on political institutions and theory; he was the philosopher with experience. As his latest biographer writes: " C'est donc, dans sa pensée et dans celle de beaucoup, une excellente préparation à la composition de la République et un gage de competence, que d'avoir été juris-consulte, maître des requêtes, commissaire du roi, magistrat, en un mot d'avoir vu de près et par ses yeux la machine gouvernementale."[4] Consequently his book is vast in knowledge and heavy in fact, but marked by an intellectual honesty which insists on holding up facts and theories to the light. Immense thought and immense reverence (notwithstanding the author's unknown religious beliefs) characterize his writing.

It was, moreover, the book of and for the moment, gaining therefrom a reputation, launched on a French world torn and divided by

---

[1] His early work, the *Methodus ad facilem historiarum cognitionem*, published in 1566, was a sort of preliminary work to the *Republic*.

[2] There was a copy of Bodin's Latin translation in the Library at Corpus Christi College, which Hooker no doubt used. It is included in the manuscript catalogue of 1589 which is still extant. Hooker quotes from Bodin in *E.P.*, Book VIII, App., pp. 457-8.

[3] The text used here is the Latin edition of 1609, published at Frankfort, the pagination of which cannot always be relied upon. Hearne approved of Knolles' ability. [*Collections*, VI, 122.]

[4] Chauviré, *Bodin* (Paris, 1914), p. 277.

N

civil wars and massacre, the futility of the Estates, the feeble per-
sonalities of its monarchs, the ambitions of the House of Guise,
and the sure prospect of disputed claims to the throne.[1] The
Middle Ages, with their sense of unity and ordered life, had disappeared, and Bodin looked upon a Europe divided in geography,
in religion, in politics, and saw his beloved France, needing the
strongest of central monarchies, daily drawing nearer to chaos.
He had to speak with no uncertain voice, to set free the thoughts
of his last ten years, and to enunciate the doctrines of absolutism
and legitimacy, whereby alone France could again become a united
whole. A Sovereign was required who, except Almighty God,
saw no one greater than himself, and for his deeds was answerable
to none but God.[2]

Both Bodin and Hooker approached their tasks with deep respect
for their subject and profound reverence for the Deity. The statement of a modern writer on Bodin may not inappropriately be
applied to the other: " He sought to discover, in the midst of civil
strife disturbing to thought, not perhaps without contradictions, a
compromise between authority and liberty." [3] The lawyer, as the
priest, could see the Will of God working in human life; for him,
too, the natural is the divine; little wonder, then, that the works
of both strike a profound note; they are deep and learned, and are
not for the mere moment; a long preparation of reading and of
thought lies behind each; there are no marks of haste, though
inevitably confusions are made in a subject so widely treated and in
days of such bitter strife. Each saw his problem, and set out to
answer it with all the earnest learning he could bring to bear on it.
Neither is infallible; not only does confusion occur in plenty, but
the practical and existing conditions of political life did not in all
points accord with their theories; just as Bodin, for example, will
ascribe powers to the Estates which he elsewhere refuses, so Hooker
can omit the most essential element in the picture of Tudor England,
the Council. These two authors are possibly more closely related
in outlook than is sometimes imagined. There is no such clear-cut
antagonism between them as between Whig and Tory; they do not
stand in contradistinction to each other, as Hobbes and Locke; nor
yet is the gulf between them exactly that which divides the Con-
stitutionalist from the Royalist.

The origin of all society, civil and political, is the family, and the
characteristics of the family are property and patriarchal govern-

---

[1] England had had its " purge " in the Wars of the Roses, and the Ship of
State was in the 1590's in relatively calm waters. Bodin's manhood was passed
during the whole course of the French " purge ".
[2] Bodin, *Sex Libri de Republica* (Frankfort, 1609), p. 126.
[3] Chauviré, op. cit., p. 543 (cf. Weill, op. cit., cap. 8).

ment. Of a confederation of families is civil society born, and the addition of omnipotent sovereignty converts that civil society into a Commonwealth or State. " Respublica est familiarum rerumque inter ipsas communium, summa potestate ac ratione moderata multitudo ";[1] with this definition Bodin opens his book, varying it later: " Respublica est legitima plurium familiarum et rerum inter se communium cum summa potestate gubernatio ".[2] The ultimate " gubernator " has over his subjects powers of the same kind as, but greater in degree than, any man exercised under " patria Potestas ". This irresponsible dominion in a ruler is what marks a State off from mere civil Society.

Some Commonwealths originated in force and violence, since in the course of bloody wars families and tribes forfeited their liberty, becoming slaves to the vanquisher; which at once tended to emphasize his " absolutist " position, and the inferiority of subjects; *rex* and *cives subditi* constitute the State.

It is not easy to make out if Bodin looks on conquest as the normal method of founding a State; he seems to indicate that it is the most frequent mode.[3] But the most natural is by union of families, since a well-administered family is a true figure of the State itself.[4] Because of this, there must arise the question of property as well as of people, since property belonging to the family is as natural as the family itself.

When, then, a State is formed, by natural union of families or by conquest, or both, its functional purpose is the realization of the greatest good of each citizen, for that will be the good of the whole. Good of body, Bodin insists (as Hooker does), must come first, but more important is the knowledge and practice of virtues belonging to men; first, " opes corporis ", and then " animi bona ".[5] He reverts to this topic later in discussing the question of perpetual magistracies.[6] " Rerum omnium publicarum praecipuus idemque optimus finis est virtus; nec legislatori ac civium gubernatori optimo praestantior finis ad intuendum propositus est, quam ut virtutibus omnibus, quantum quidem fieri poterit, praestantes, et quam optimos cives efficiat." [7] Like any Utilitarian philosopher, he is sure

[1] Bodin, op. cit., p. 1.
[2] Op. cit., p. 18; cf. also p. 13. Translated by Knolles, 1606. " A Commonwealth is a lawful Government of many families, and of that which unto them in common belongeth, with a puissant sovereignty."
[3] II, ii, pp. 292 *et seq.*
[4] p. 13.
[5] p. 6.
[6] IV, iv, pp. 672 *et seq.*
[7] p. 673. " Of all public affairs the chief and best end is virtue; and there is no more excellent end set forth for any lawmaker or good ruler to observe than that he shall make his citizens (as far as he may) eminent in all virtues and as estimable as possible."

the State's greatest good is the good of the greatest number.[1]
The end of the State—in the sense of a Commonwealth " bien
ordonnée ", where the laws of Nature and natural justice prevail—
is properly the knowledge of virtue and all that it connotes. But he
implies that a State can exist without this purpose, since the one
requisite is a puissant sovereignty in the ruler over against the
subjection of the citizens. " Est autem civis nihil aliud quam
liber homo, qui summae alterius potestati obligatur ".[2] Sovereignty and protection [3] on the one hand, submission and service
on the other; it is well that this relationship should make for a life
of virtue, but that apparently can only be looked for in the best
kind of State.

His theory of Sovereignty (less clear-cut than is sometimes
imagined) is Bodin's greatest contribution to political thought.
He defines it as the highest, most absolute and perpetual power to
command citizens in a State. " Maiestas est summa in cives ac
subditos legibusque soluta potestas." [4] Unless power be perpetual it is not sovereign, for when a man who holds such power
for a period of time reverts to his original position he is no more
than a subject : he merely had sovereignty in trust or in pawn.[5]
By this definition no Roman Dictator was ever sovereign, for
sovereignty " cannot be limited by a superior power, neither by
laws nor time ".[6] Nor, again, is absolute power to be termed
sovereignty if it come by way of grant limited in condition or name
from the people; the power *is* the power of the State, vested
completely in the Sovereign by inheritance, conquest, or free gift,
and comes from no external source; no matter what wisdom,
what consent may help in furnishing laws, that which gives to a law
its force is " Quia sic nobis placuit "; [7] laws come from the will of
him who orders them. Therefore the first mark of Sovereignty is
the power to give laws to all subjects in general or particular without
consent; [8] and the logical corollary of this is that the Sovereign
has also full power to abrogate or dispense with existing laws.[9]
This law-making power is so vast as to include all other marks of
sovereignty—such as making war and peace; creating magistrates;
exercising the prerogative of pardon; the coining of money, and the
imposition of taxes. None of these rights can be alienated by a
King, nor does time run against him.

---

[1] p. 9.
[2] p. 71.   " A citizen is simply a free man subjected to the supreme power of
another."
[3] p. 167.
[4] p. 123.   " Sovereignty is supreme power over citizens and subjects, unrestrained by laws."
[5] p. 126.   [6] p. 123.   [7] p. 134.   [8] p. 240.   [9] p. 241.

Logically a King can bind neither himself[1] nor his successors by laws, although he may be bound in conscience[2] to perform his agreements on earth he is responsible to none, since he only is to be called Sovereign who next to God acknowledges none greater than himself.[3] He must give account only to the immortal God.

Later in the same great chapter on Sovereignty,[4] Bodin deals with the prevalent opinion that the power of the people is greater than that of the Prince. This he dismisses as absurd, since the Prince can have no protector unless he be an infant, a lunatic, or captive. Nor are Parliaments superior to him, for in all countries they approach the Prince with submission and requests, which he grants or refuses;[5] they have no existence till he summons them. Bodin gives as evidence the usages of the English Parliament, referring especially to that of 1566, when the Commons tried to make Elizabeth nominate her successor. He enjoys recalling her answer, " They were not to make her grave till she was dead," and notes that she did nothing of what they required. He sets up also the ancient claim of the English Parliament to control taxation, and the Act which, while recognizing Philip of Spain as King, yet deprived him of kingly power, rather as Aunt Sallies, to knock them down as not being in point; though not very convincingly. Parliaments, he admits, are convenient, but not necessary; even in England the King can reject laws without consent, and can levy taxes in emergencies.[6] The English Parliament has a certain authority, but Bodin insists that the sovereignty and legislative power are solely in the King. Then he summarizes, satisfied with his demonstrations, " Ex quibus efficitur, summum ius maiestatis in eo potissimum versari, cum non modo singulis, sed etiam universis leges dantur, iisque imperatur ".[7]

But he does, in fact, concede certain limitations on kingly power. The King is restrained by no human laws—he is entirely " legibus solutus "[8]—no temporal institutions can call him to account for public or private wrong; none the less, he is bound by the Law of God, the Law of Nature, and certain fundamental laws, nor can he levy taxes as he pleases. Thus he may not kill or rob, not because there are positive human laws forbidding crimes, but " ipsius Dei lex est, quam ab natura hausimus. . . ."[9] The Law

---

[1] p. 129.
[2] pp. 130 and 134–5.
[3] pp. 145, 152, and 230.
[4] Book I, Chap. viii.
[5] pp. 139–40.
[6] p. 143.
[7] p. 144. " From which it is shown that the supreme authority of sovereignty consists principally in giving laws not only to individuals but also to subjects in general and that by way of command."
[8] pp. 130, 134–5, 139 and 152.
[9] p. 152.

of Nature, as Pindarus taught, binds all rulers.[1] Kings who violate divine or natural law must be left to the judgment of God.

Yet also there may be certain fundamental laws concerning the state of the realm, such as the Salic Law in France. Princes can neither abrogate nor derogate from these.[2] But apart from this threefold limitation, the King has unbridled power—" princeps arbitrio suo ac voluntate omnia moderatur, et quaecumque decrevit, ac iussit, ea legum vim habent ";[3] he is more than God's lieutenant, he is the Divine " imago vivens ac spirans ".[4] None the less, he is not the absolute owner of the royal demesne; to alienate from it is not in his power, since he has only a life-interest in it.[5]

A Sovereign, then, is God's vicegerent, with powers to give laws to all; his will is the source of all law; " Lex nihil aliud quam summae potestatis iussum ".[6] His sovereignty can suffer no limitations in time, by law or in purpose; if conferred, it must be without condition, for "summum imperium conditione aliqua vel lege datum, summum non est ".[7] Legally, not morally, the sovereignty is incapable of limitation by any ruler, and it is immortal, since it is the enduring power of the State itself (" Maiestas est summa in cives ac subditos legisbusque soluta potestas "),[8] vested without condition in the ruler.[9]

Bodin gives the usual three types of commonwealth: monarchy, aristocracy, and democracy. Some people, he remarks, have endeavoured to construct a fourth, by a sort of confusion of these three, but such a feat is impossible. They call it a " mixed polity ", and some writers claim that France is so governed, which he indignantly repudiates;[10] the claim is that the Parlement of Paris is the aristocratic element, the three Estates represent democracy, and the King monarchy;[11] an absurd opinion, in his view. It is the work of theorists who follow Aristotle, who called such a mixture a πολιτεία, not knowing what else to call it, as he had never met such a constitution, nor knew how it could be worked. Bodin refuses to think that the sovereignty or legislative power may be divisible: but a little later he notes shrewdly enough (as did Hobbes) that he who is master of the forces is master of the men, of the laws and of all the Commonwealth.[12] This is well understandable, since both Bodin and Hobbes lived in a state of civil war and anarchy; both therefore offer the only solution of the problem of sovereignty which seemed capable of dealing with the situation.

Monarchy is unquestionably the noblest form of sovereignty in

[1] p. 159.
[2] p. 139.
[3] p. 140; cf. also pp. 230–1.
[4] p. 161; cf. p. 167.
[5] I, ix.
[6] p. 159.
[7] p. 130.
[8] p. 123.
[9] pp. 125 et seq.
[10] p. 274.
[11] p. 285.
[12] pp. 291 and 292.

Bodin's eyes,[1] and it may take one of three forms. The Monarch may be *Rex*, *Dominus*, or *Tyrannus*.[2] *Monarchia regalis*[3] is that state in which citizens enjoy their property and freedom, governed by a Prince himself obedient to divine and natural law; the *Dominus* (whom Bodin prefers to the *Rex*, since, though less noble, he is more effective) is a despot, although possibly a benevolent one, lord of his subjects' persons and goods, governing them as a paterfamilias his slaves; the Tyrant contemns alike the laws of Nature and of nations, and despoils his subjects,[4] " drinks their blood ". The ancients held that all tyrants (ruling well or ill) should be slain,[5] a discussion over which Bodin spills much ink, revealing that he is rather against tyrannicide in general, allowing it in particulars; but he affirms clearly that no lawful ruler—such as Kings of France or England—may be attacked, however severe his rule.[6] This view he bases on his theory of positive law, fortifying his argument with large extracts from Scripture as to the sacredness of the King's person, citing Luther to his aid.[7]

However firmly fixed in title a king may be, nevertheless there is shrewd practical advice given him by Bodin to enable him to retain his royal seat. Thus Parliaments may not be a necessary part of the constitutional machinery, but it is better to make use of them.[8] Again, changes in the form, or laws, or customs of a State should be avoided as far as possible. Ancient laws of essential nature especially are to be retained; but the first of all State laws is " Salus populi suprema lex ", and in the light of this there is no law so sacred that it may not be overthrown on urgent necessity.[9] But senile decay is preferable to sudden death! In the same way, too, a King should deal with ancient dependants and servitors; let them die off gradually, without replacement.[10] In appointments to offices, the wisest thing is to have some perpetual officers, and some for short terms; granting the perpetual office-holders little power, and the temporary magistrates more.[11]

The last part of the book Bodin devotes to the question of succession to the throne. Monarchy is the best form of government,[12] and should descend from one stock. He recalls a disputation in 1566 before Elizabeth of England that kings should be elective;[13] which he considers both a highly dangerous doctrine and an expensive method. There can be no assurance in a State whose throne goes by election, and he again reminds us of the English Parliament's anxiety in 1566.[14] Primogeniture is the safest method,

[1] pp. 292 *et seq.*; cf. VI, iv. [2] p. 295. [3] p. 303.
[4] II, iv. [5] p. 323. [6] p. 328.
[7] pp. 331 and 332. [8] p. 139. [9] p. 667; cf. p. 320.
[10] p. 670. [11] IV, iv. [12] VI, iv.
[13] VI, v. [14] p. 1132.

and is by divine warrant; and once more he mentions that the master of the forces is master of the State. He upholds the Salic Law—with an eye to the succession of Henri IV—and insists that descent must be through males only, since by Divine Law women have always been subject to men in all particulars; the marriage or non-marriage of queens cannot but breed complications. But, thanks be to God, the Salic Law has prevented Frenchmen from the disgrace of ever being ruled by a woman.[1]

In his great book Bodin provided the theory which he deemed rightly to fit the political situation. The facts of his day were making for absolutism, as they had in fifteenth-century England. The welter of confusion in France was bound to produce either continued anarchy or absolutism, and the enfeeblement of constitutional machinery made directly for the latter. Consequently Bodin erects a king, free from all duties, fettered by no laws or conditions, possessing the supreme virtue and power of the State itself; a position more than half-way towards the identification of the King with the State. Much as he dislikes the teaching of Machiavelli, and often as he insists that the King has moral obligations and the court of conscience to face, Bodin is obliged to allow the doctrine of State necessity. His work purports to be, and is, a scientific treatise, but it seldom loses sight of the practical object in view— the vindication of absolutist and legitimist rule. Thus we read nothing of contract or mutual duties—there can be no rights against the King. If Bodin's theory be a generalization from the facts of his day, the King will be definitely high and lifted up above all other parties and interests. The old theory of the State with divine sanction for its existence, and the King as guardian of its law, is gone. No longer is law a rule of operation; it is the fiat of the King; no more a measure of conduct, but a peremptory command. It is a logical situation, demanded by the times; a necessity seen clearly by Bodin, just as he was the first to examine precisely the nature of sovereignty.

Matters on which criticism may be made are obvious. We have already seen that Bodin does not state how and when his union of families became a State; it could hardly be the moment when such a union decided to live as an ordered whole for the purpose of a life of virtue, since Bodin allows that a State can exist without such end. This is due to the fact that he often has in mind two sorts of States, and does not always distinguish them. There is the State consisting of its supreme monarch and subjects, and the State " bien ordonnée ", where the ruler lives in obedience to God and Nature, and the Commonwealth lives for virtue.

[1] VI, v.

Then he will not hear of a mixed polity. He contemns it as a mere Aristotelian theory, impossible in fact, since sovereignty is indivisible. But he had only to cast his eyes across the Channel to see something in England which at least resembled this mixed polity; and there was undoubted sovereignty in England. Bodin vitiates his reasoning on this point, because he can only conceive of a legislative Sovereign; the position in England was easier because the Sovereign was in fact the executive.

Estates and Parliaments have no existence save by the King's decree, and no power when they do meet except to advise. Yet Kings are strongly recommended to rule by their means, and in the eighth chapter of Book I Bodin states that they are obliged to proceed in taxation by means of Parliament. In emergencies the doctrine of " salus populi " will cover imposts levied by the King, but the trend of this part of the chapter is clearly in favour of Parliamentary control of direct taxation. It is a difficult point, and full of confusion; nobody can say exactly what Bodin meant to teach; but it does remain that he quotes de Commines with approval to the effect that it is no more right to levy taxes without consent than it is to rob subjects. It is at least evident that in the realm of taxation the King is not irresponsibly supreme. It is amusing to imagine what would have happened if a French Hampden had been prosecuted in a Ship-money case. Bodin would have had to listen to extracts from his own book, and would doubtless have approved Mr. Justice Berkeley's dictum, " The Law knows no such King-yoking policy ", but would have substituted the " State " for the " Law ".

It has to be remembered that, whatever theories they weave, Bodin and Hooker have their eyes fixed on the political facts of their day. Hooker saw the Tudor Monarchy, emphatically sovereign in executive, if not in legislative power; Bodin, passing over the wreckage of Henri III, envisaged his ideal on the French throne in the person of Navarre, Sovereign in law even if the facts made against it. Both saw that the only solution for order in a State was authority. In England it existed, in France scarcely so; in the former it was sheer fact, in the latter a royalist theory. The explanation of the difference lies in the word " recognition ". The fact of the Tudor supremacy, dictatorship, sovereignty—by whatever name it is called—was acceptable to the bulk of Englishmen. The King functioned as Sovereign; the Council executed the royal will; Parliament assisted that will; the whole machinery of government was dominated by the *volo* or *nolo* of the Tudor monarchs, but they were endowed with the tact which taught them when to refuse or consent. If Henry wished to eject the Pope, to treat the

Crown as private property, to make laws by proclamation, to settle the faith of Englishmen; if Mary determined to subject England to Rome; if Elizabeth treated Parliament as a convenient instrument; whatever their will, it was carried into effect; often enough by " constitutional " means, but that was a thin veil through which observant folk could see. In a word, they were Sovereigns—almost in the Bodin sense—because their sway was agreeable, which is the ultimate basis in fact of any enduring rule. When this recognition was withdrawn, " free " sovereignty, in the shape of the monarch's will, failed, as happened to the Stuarts.

Hooker was endeavouring to make a philosophic basis for this fact of Tudor supremacy, and it is not therefore surprising that the parallels between him and Bodin are striking, though the theoretical differences are marked: yet it is possible they are often formal rather than real. It must be admitted that Bodin divides his State into " rex " and " cives subditi "; that he wrote, " The Prince governs everything by his decision and will, and whatever he decrees has the force of law : " [1] that he will not bind the Sovereign, save in conscience, to keep his own contracts, and certainly not those of his predecessors; a " mixed " constitution is abhorrent; his King is utterly " legibus solutus ", and this the very *differentia* that, as with Austin, divides the State from any other condition of civil society. All this most decidedly sets Bodin on the contrary side to the Contractualists. Further, undoubtedly, a first impression gathered from the perusal of the two books would be an entire antagonism in the matter of the consent of the people to legislation. Hooker declares this an essential element, while Bodin defines sovereignty as the power to make laws for all without consent. Yet the two are not poles asunder. Hooker's King is fully King, and though ordinarily he will legislate by means of Parliament, yet his veto or approval is, as Hooker confesses, the ultimate essence of a law. Moreover, the " consent " of the people is to an extent a fiction; at best it is a majority vote in Parliament, and Hooker was well enough aware of the unrepresentative character of Tudor Parliaments. Again, the Sovereign, with the Council, enacted a vast amount of the laws under which Englishmen then lived and were governed, by proclamations, injunctions, and orders to the Justices of the Peace. Henry VIII and Bodin's King would not be noticeably dissimilar. There is little doubt, in fact, that both writers dogmatized on sovereignty from the person of Elizabeth; but while Bodin looked on sovereignty as before all things legislative, and *sic nobis placuit* as the essence, Hooker saw it as executive power, possessing a legislative veto as potent as the other's *sic placuit*. Bodin

[1] Bodin, pp. 140; 230–1; 253–4.

certainly regards Elizabeth as filling the required position, but because she did before the eyes of all men actually reign and govern, he, ignoring the executive aspect, and under-estimating the place of the English Parliament, elevates the legislative power of the Crown to a degree which, in England, it did not at law possess.

It is true that Bodin declares the King *legibus solutus* which English kings never had been from before Bracton's time. But what if Hooker's King freed himself from the restraints of the law? He is answerable to God—there is only the Court of his own conscience, whatever it be worth; the subjects have no remedy except force, which Bodin denounces and Hooker refuses to consider; the latter can only piously hope that an undesirable ruler will not be " stiff in detaining " the people's power, but the people must wait his good pleasure, and rest content with refusal to obey tyrannical decrees. Hooker shirks further answer to this question always; if his problem had been as acute as Bodin's, he might have faced this situation more frankly.

A serious flaw in Bodin's arguments is that he omits mention of the real source of sovereignty. It is not in the people, as the *populus*, for they must in that case be greater than his King. It is not conferred by contract or donation, nor does it come by the will of God. Valuable as Bodin's analytical philosophy of sovereignty is, it fails as a working scheme unless it possesses a basis philosophic as well as actual, and Bodin provides that basis neither in law nor fact. Hooker, with greater wisdom, lays its legal foundation in an original compact, which comes to look surprisingly like an alienation, and its factual basis in the recognition of Englishmen. Consequently we are on surer ground with Hooker, and Bodin leaves us in the air. The cleavage between the two seems most marked at this point. Bodin did not live to see the day of Absolutism in France—Louis XIV is the monarch of the " Republic " *par excellence*—a sovereignty based on recognition on the part of privileged classes, and on the impotence of the residue of the nation; had he done so, Bodin would have been forced, like Hooker, to examine the basis in fact and in law of such extravagant claims.

These authors are further broadly distinguished by their conceptions of the State and its ends; which is much the same as to say their attitude towards God. The State, in Hooker's view, is a society of people organized for material welfare, but for a spiritual end; a reflex of the State on high, permeated by the principle of divine order. It is an essentially religious conception, monarch and laws existing to direct men to their true end; it is a theocracy in the vaguer sense; the people are meant to be a people of God, and even if the King is responsible only to God, it is a fearful responsibility. A frankly National State, admitted, but in subserving its national ends, the State subserves divine purpose, too. Hence law is a directive rule; the King, representative of God and depository of the people's power, is not a sharp commander, but a paternal guide. Bodin was a man obviously imbued with the religious spirit, but God is not in any sense immanent in Bodin's State. It is true he admits what is natural to be divine, and the family is therefore divine; but since the purpose of his State is not God-wards, he cannot find a divine origin for the State in his union of families. His conception of the State is secular and like Mariana's, for the latter agrees that the exact form of religion is immaterial as long as it is a generally accepted form, and Bodin considers any reasonable form of Christianity might be allowed. At all events, the State originated in force and depravity, and law is in consequence a sharp command, issuing from the unrestrained will of the Sovereign, who is the totalitarian embodiment of his people's wills and powers. While Hooker's law will guide into truth, Bodin's command represses aggressive wills. Bodin would tolerate religions, since religions should not affect the legal relationship between *rex* and *civis subditus*; but Hooker cannot admit toleration, for the unity of the State would be destroyed; and the ruin of the State is the ruin of God's purpose.

Perhaps the real cause of the divergence between the views of these two men is to be found in the fact that whereas Bodin saw the State through the eyes of a modern man, Hooker was forced to buttress the powers of the Tudor monarchy with arguments still mainly mediaeval in character. It is, indeed, from this fact that most of the inconsistencies and uncertainties that we have found in the *Ecclesiastical Polity* arise. Hence he cannot recognize the existence in England of religious minorities, or consider the problem educed by them, except to provide an argument for a strictly limited liberty of conscience—though not for its exercise—which was in effect that allowed by More in his *Utopia*. Hence also it is that he nowhere faces up to the full implications of his doctrines of the unity of Church and State and of the Royal Supremacy, which in the hands of the Jesuits had become a two-edged weapon. For if Church and State were one, and the secular head also the spiritual head, did a refusal to recognize the one provide a justification for the denial of the other; in short, provide a right to rebel? This was a question which Hooker could not answer, for the mediaeval answer was in favour of the right of resistance—were not the subjects of an excommunicated Prince absolved from their allegiance?—and the modern answer of toleration which Bodin had given was foreign to his system of thought and hateful to him as a loyal son of that land and Church encompassed by fierce enemies.

As a matter of fact, we shall find Hooker's most extreme statement of his doctrine of sovereignty and of the nature of civil obedience, not in the *Ecclesiastical Polity* so much as in the " Sermon of Civil Obedience " appended to it by Keble in his edition of the *Ecclesiastical Polity*. The fragment of the sermon that remains begins by asserting that " God himself doth authorize " the laws made by the Sovereign, and that " to despise them is to despise in them him ". Hooker admits that there is force in the argument that the conscience should be inviolate from the laws of the Sovereign, that " men are not able to make any law that shall command the heart "; but to those who made such a show of distinguishing between God's law and man-made law he urges " for their better instruction " the reminder that " the law of God himself doth require at our hands subjection ", and that " we are in conscience bound to yield it even unto every one of them that hold the seats of authority and power in relation unto us ". All which is a gloss upon the text " the Powers that be are ordained of God ". Rulers were " of God's own institution, even when they were of man's creation ", so that " he that resisteth them, resisteth God ".

Thus far Hooker might seem to be rivalling Bodin, if not Hobbes, in the statement of his theory of sovereignty; but in fact he is very far from doing so. He is doing no more than restating, with a new clarity and certainty in the presence of the Tudor monarchy, the Imperialist claims on lay sovereignty which had been repeated since the thirteenth century, and generally with the aid of the same text of St. Paul (Romans 13. 1). And Hooker's mystic claims for sovereignty carried with them, not the implications which Bodin attached, but the limitations which were always implied in similar mediaeval statements. Thus he argued that " usurpers of power " were not those who had won their authority by force—how could the loyal subject of a grand-daughter of Henry VII argue otherwise? —but those who " *used more authority than they did ever receive* ". This was the mediaeval proviso that the King was subject to the fundamental law and customs of his realm, and it imposed limits on the sovereignty of a ruler as great as any which the seventeenth-century experiments were to evolve.

In so far, then, as Hooker produced any complete statement of a theory of sovereignty, it is found to reside not in the *Laws of Ecclesiastical Polity*, but in this sermon, this intellectual exercise on Civil Obedience. The divergence between such a theory and what he knew to be the implications of his belief in the force of custom and tradition, as well as in the need for the consent of the governed—had he not written, " What have we to induce men unto the willing obedience and observation of laws but the weight of so many men's judgment as have with deliberate advice assented thereunto? " [1]—was, it may well be, too wide for his formal treatise. Hooker could not reconcile extreme claims for Tudor sovereignty with what, with his profound historical sense, he knew to be the main lines on which the English polity had been developing for a thousand years. Nor could his age reconcile them; and therein lay the incompatibility which made the Civil War inevitable.

[1] *E.P.*, IV, xiv, 1.

CHAPTER X

THE POLITICAL INFLUENCE OF HOOKER

BEFORE we can make an assessment of Hooker's subsequent importance, his relationship with two of the most remarkable and original
thinkers of the sixteenth century—namely, Machiavelli [1] and Sir
Thomas More [2]—calls for consideration. Both were dead before
he was born, but they cast a spell upon the men of their day, and no
view of the current of political thought is complete without them, for
they represent the note of pessimism and despair which gathered
force as the century proceeded, and which culminated in England in
sentiments like those uttered by Prospero in the Epilogue to the
Tempest.

The *Prince* of Machiavelli, who shares with Bodin the distinction of being the most original and powerful thinker of his age, was
published posthumously in 1532. [3] In it he demonstrated to the
princes of Europe how they could best maintain themselves in
despotic power. Although designed chiefly to fit the situation in
Italy, the book became a handbook on government for all absolutists.
In its advocacy of " Staatsraison " and " Machtpolitik " the book
marked a total divorce between politics and morality, and a complete breach with the ideas of mediaeval Christendom. Its influence
was immediate, profound, and lasting.

Hooker nowhere refers to the great Florentine by name, but
he was exceedingly well aware of his writings. [4] Dr. von Meyer
has traced no fewer than three hundred and ninety-five references
to Machiavelli in Elizabethan literature, [5] and Hooker met the
political principles of *The Prince* in the practices of Catherine
de Medici in France—Machiavelli had dedicated his book to her
father—and to a lesser degree of Elizabeth in England. The two
writers were completely in opposition, for to Hooker the law,
proceeding from God through the human reason, is the touchstone

[1] *Vivebat* 1469–1529.
[2] *Vivebat* 1480–1535.
[3] It was written in 1514, and was Cromwell's textbook (Constant: *Reformation
in England*, I, 261 and n.).
[4] *E.P.*, VIII, viii, 5; cf. V, ii, 3 and 4. " Political literature of the sixteenth
century is characterized by opposition to, or agreement with, Machiavelli " (*Richard
Hooker als politikischer Denker*, G. Michaelis, Berlin, 1933, p. 104).
[5] *Machiavelli and the Elizabethan Drama* (Weimar, 1897), p. xi.

of political behaviour, not reasons of state which claimed to be
independent of, and superior to, both the law and morality. When
Machiavelli taught princes that they were unrestrained by the
Moral Law of Nature, it seemed, as Gierke says, to the men of his
time " an unheard of innovation and also a monstrous crime ".[1]
But the difference goes farther. Hooker is shocked and moved even
to wrathful language that certain people should regard religion as a
mere political device, forged to serve the State's purposes. It is
clear that he has Machiavelli in mind. "Wise malignants" he calls
them, and "this execrable crew", who can so debase religion as to
make it a mere political weapon.[2] There is thus no meeting ground
between the radical Machiavelli and the conservative Hooker, and
the disciple of Aquinas has nothing to do with the disciple of Satan.

With Sir Thomas More, Hooker [3] has much more in common,
for they both combine a veneration for the past with a high degree of
moral earnestness; both exalt the place of reason in religion; and
both are Idealists. The religious principles of the people of Utopia,
" though, these be pertaining to religion, yet they think it meet that
they should be believed and granted by proofs of reason ",[4] and
they held that " virtue to be life ordered to nature, and that we be
hereunto ordained of God. And that he doth follow the course of
nature, which in desiring and refusing things is ruled by reason.
Furthermore that reason doth chiefly and principally kindle in
men the love and veneration of the divine Majesty ".[5] It has been
said that More was " isolated not only, or chiefly, by time ", [6]
and it is true that his famous book *Utopia*, published in 1516, belongs
to pre-Reformation thought, being in fact a product of the Renaissance, and scarcely touches many of the issues which faced the
contemporaries of Luther and Calvin. Yet it has enshrined for all
subsequent ages, wherever men have become enslaved and insecure,
a vision which has kept hope alive. Much of More's unique reputation depends upon the exalted position he held, the charm and
simplicity of his life and manners, as revealed by Roper, his son-in-
law, and above all on the tragic conflict with his master, Henry VIII,
over the nature of the Royal Supremacy, and his death as a political
and religious martyr. Unlike Machiavelli, he is the complete
idealist, in bitter opposition to the new capitalist and commercial
forces whose triumph coincided with the triumphs of Luther and

[1] Maitland's *Gierke*, p. 86.
[2] *E.P.*, V, ii, 3, 4.
[3] Hooker refers to More in *E.P.*, VIII, iv, 8, and in Sermon II (Keble's ed.,
III, 537–8) and to " Utopians " in V, xxxvi, 4.
[4] More's *Utopia* (London: intro. by H. G. Wells), p. 128.
[5] *Utopia*, p. 129.
[6] J. W. Allen, op. cit., p. 135.

Calvin.[1] He looks back to the theocentric nature of mediaeval society, if not to the communist ideas of Plato, for salvation, and thus stands apart from the main currents of the political thought of his day. Hooker shares his strong conservative feeling for the vanished world of the past, but his reverence is paid to Aquinas and the mediaeval system of natural law, whereas for More it is the whole manner of life of the mediaeval world that is the attraction. Hooker possesses ideals as lofty as More's, and though he is not realist enough to translate them into the Tudor scheme of government, he is sufficient realist to know that he cannot and dare not do so! He is as much alive to the practical situation of the day as was Machiavelli.

An examination of Hooker's subsequent influence reveals two facts: that it was at first confined to England, and that, though it is not conspicuously marked until we come to Harrington, Sidney, Locke, and the later seventeenth century, he all unwittingly, through these men, helped to furnish the political philosophy of Liberalism (e.g., the political principles of the American Colonists), while, strangely enough, he is not without importance in the history of the development of the modern Sovereign State.

That Hooker's influence should at first be confined to England is not perhaps strange. He had dealt primarily with an English situation; and also it so happened in the seventeenth century that England was the real home of political speculation.[2] Such speculation was not encouraged in the France of Richelieu and the Bourbons or in the countries where the Counter-Reformation had triumphed. There was, however, one European figure whose thoughts Hooker might have been expected to influence, and that was the Dutchman, Hugo Grotius (1583–1645), whose immense, but methodical and erudite book—*De Jure Belli ac Pacis*,[3] published in 1625—was concerned with, and laid the foundations of, modern International Law. Of the philosophers whose works have been reviewed in this present book, Mariana is in Grotius' mind from first to last, and hardly less so is Bodin. Contrary to the statement that Grotius does not even name Suarez,[4] frequent reference is made to him,[5]

[1] " Therefore, when I consider and weigh in my mind all these commonwealths which nowadays anywhere do flourish, so God help me, I can perceive nothing but a certain conspiracy of rich men procuring their own commodities under the name and title of the commonwealth " (*Utopia*, p. 199).

[2] Holland, with Grotius and Spinoza, was its only rival, and the destinies of the two countries were closely linked throughout the century.

[3] Ed., 1689, Amsterdam.

[4] Hugo Grotius: Lecture by F. J. C. Hearnshaw, London, 1926, printed in *Social and Political Ideas of some Thinkers of the Sixteenth and Seventeenth Centuries*, p. 136.

[5] Ref. to Suarez, e.g., Lib. I, cap. iv, s. 15; Lib. II, cap. iv, s. 5; Lib. II, cap. xiv, s. 5.

O

as well as to Hotman.   Selden finds mention, as does the good Sir
Thomas Smith.   But the prime English author in the eyes of Grotius
is Camden—" optimus Camdenus ", he calls him [1]—to whom he
refers again and again.   With the facts and principles of the
Elizabethan Settlement Grotius shows himself familiar; he knows
its chief historian, but ignores the principal apologist.   The
omission at first sight seems strange—yet, perhaps, not so strange.
For one thing, the whole of the *Ecclesiastical Polity* was not at the time
published; in particular, the Eighth Book was unknown.   Then,
again, it was with the domestic condition of England that Hooker
was concerned, while Grotius gazes on the international situation
and says, " I saw through the Christian world a licence in making
war that would shame barbarians." [2]   Even if Hooker's name be
omitted from the authorities given in the Prolegomena (an " obviously
incomplete " list, Professor Hearnshaw notes),[3] we can remain proud
and content that two such men in successive generations saw the
majestic conception of law to be the answer to the problems of their
times, and the guarantee against rebellion and barbarism; and
believe that the Englishman gave something to the Dutchman.

The intellectual atmosphere of England in the early part of the
seventeenth century was not favourable to Hooker's thought; for
he represented a compromise politically and theologically which
neither of the principal protagonists was prepared to accept.   With
the accession of James I the theory of Divine Right took complete
possession of the field on the one side, whilst on the other there was
emerging the doctrine of the sovereignty of the people.   With neither
side was Hooker quite at home, and it is no surprise to find Fuller
lamenting that " his book in our late times was beheld as an
almanack grown out of date ".[4]   The Church of England came to
identify itself with the doctrine of Divine Right because it was the
only answer that dealt equally well with Roman and Puritan
opposition alike, but there were not many weapons it could draw
from Hooker's armoury to support this position.   The controversial
Seventh and Eighth Books had not yet been published, and Hooker's
reputation with the Caroline divines rested mainly on his theological
and devotional worth.   Here he received praise at the hands of
Lancelot Andrewes and Archbishop Laud, both of whom acknowledge their debt to him.   The *Ecclesiastical Polity* made favourite
reading with everybody throughout the century.[5]   Charles I

[1] *De Jure Belli ac Pacis*, Lib. II, cap. III, s. 10 (n).
[2] Op. cit., Prolegomena, p. xviii.
[3] Hearnshaw, op. cit., p. 136.
[4] *Worthies*, I, 423 (ed. Nuthall, 1840).
[5] Hallam states that the Preface to the *Ecclesiastical Polity* influenced James II to
return to the Roman Church (*C.H.*, I. 218).

recommended it to his daughter, because it " would ground me against Poperie ",[1] whilst Pepys read it because his friend Mr. Chetwind declared it to be " the best book, and the only one that made him a Christian "; [2] and the Latitudinarian Bishop Burnet admitted " no book pleased him more ".[3]

But the political thinkers were less open in their praise. On the royalist side, Sir Robert Filmer (died 1653) in his *Patriarcha*,[4] whilst professing a high regard for Hooker as a divine—placing him in Divinity on a level with Aristotle in Philosophy [5]—is not afraid to disagree with him. Both Hooker and Aristotle, he points out, " are but men " and " the profoundest Scholar that ever was known hath not been able to search out every Truth that is discoverable." [6] Filmer, with skill and tact, likening himself to a dwarf beside giants, appears to turn the tables on them by professing himself " beholding to their Errors " in that what he found amiss in their opinions guided him " in the discovery of that Truth which (I persuade myself) they missed." [7]

Filmer is careful, therefore, never to attack Hooker outright, and, indeed, twice quotes him to support his own arguments. He cites him first of all to support the view that Scripture affords no example of the people's choosing their own king,[8] and secondly to clinch his argument that in Parliament the King alone makes the Laws, " as His Majesty King James, of happy Memory, affirms in his true Law of free Monarchy; and as Hooker teacheth us, That Laws do not take their constraining force from the Quality of such as devise them, but from the Power that doth give them the Strength of Laws: Le Roy le Veult, the King will have it so, is the Interpretative Phrase pronounced at the King's passing of every Act of Parliament." [9] Both quotations are of doubtful value to Filmer, for both are taken out of their proper context.[10] From the first it would be made to appear that hereditary birthright is Hooker's title for sovereign power, whereas he admits the right of conquest and elaborates a theory of contract that Filmer elsewhere denies. The second quotation is more questionable still, for the next sentence, which Filmer does not quote, goes on: " That which

---

[1] *The Works of King Charles the Martyr* (ed. 1687), p. 206.
[2] *Diary* (ed. Wheatley, London, 1928), II, 61; cf. II, 84; VI, 273, 325.
[3] Burnet: *History of his own Times* (London, 2 vols., 1724), II, 675.
[4] Remained in MS. till published 1680.
[5] *Patriarcha*, p. 7.
[6] *Ibid.*
[7] *Ibid.* and 8.
[8] Op. cit., pp. 46–8.
[9] Op. cit., p. 127.
[10] Sidney accuses Filmer of "vilely abusing Hooker" (*Discourses*, ed. 1750, I, 151).

we spake before concerning the power of government must here be applied unto the power of making laws whereby to govern; which power God hath over all: and by the natural law, whereunto he hath made all subject, the lawful power of making laws to command whole politic societies of men belongeth so properly unto the same entire societies, that for any prince or potentate of what kind soever upon earth to exercise the same of himself, and not either by express commission immediately and personally received from God, *or else by authority derived at the first from their consent upon whose persons they impose laws*, it is no better than mere tyranny.[1] Laws they are not therefore which public approbation hath not made so." [2] Which earns Sidney's dry comment, " The humour of our age considered, I should not have dared to say so much." [3]

Thus the whole temper of Filmer's arguments runs in an opposite direction to those of Hooker,[4] despite the attitude of outward respect he pays him. Filmer is writing against the " Vulgar Opinion " that " mankind is naturally endowed and born with Freedom from all subjection, and at liberty to choose what Form of Government it please: And the Power which any one Man hath over others, was at first bestowed according to the discretion of the Multitudes ", which he finds both in the Jesuits, Parsons, Suarez, and Bellarmine; and the Puritans, Calvin, and Buchanan. He has no use, therefore, for any compact or contract, denies all rights to the people [5] and places the King above all laws—*solutus legibus*. His monarch, although altogether differently established in power from Hobbes' Leviathan, enjoys the same complete sovereign rights.

On the extremer Puritan side Hooker is even more suspect and the conspiracy of silence better maintained. He was much too Anglican for them, and they were no doubt aware that the *Ecclesiastical Polity* was a double-edged sword. For the Puritan William Prynne (1600–69), to whom, with Hugh Peters, the Long Parliament entrusted the unpublished books of the *Ecclesiastical Polity*, made no use of the material for his own pamphlet *Sovereigne Power of Parliaments and Kingdomes*, published in 1643.[6] He had suffered persecution at the hands of Archbishop Laud, and was filled with

---

[1] Though Hooker admits an *absolute* monarch's edict has the force of law (*ibid.*).

[2] *E.P.*, I, x, 8 (italics mine).

[3] *Discourses on Government* (ed. 1750), I, 151.

[4] Natural Law or Natural Liberty was the issue Filmer mentions when first disagreeing with Hooker (*Patriarcha*, p. 7).

[5] Chapter II of *Patriarcha* is entitled, " It is unnatural for the People to Govern, or choose Governours ".

[6] Possibly he feared the accusation of using Hooker's political views only where they suited him, particularly as they are so closely bound up with his Church views.

rancour against the teachings of " Court Prelates and Chaplaines "
who " have for sundry yeeres inculcated into our Kings and People
(who preach little else but Tyranny to the one, and Slavery to the
other, to support their own Lordly Prelacy, and hinder an exact
Church Reformation) a new Utopian absolute Royall Prerogative,
unknown to our Ancestors, not bottomed on the Lawes of God or the
Realm." [1]   His work breathes a fierce and bitter hostility towards
" the opposite Royall and Malignant party " as he calls it, made up
of " Court parasites, Lawyers and Theologues " [2]—a set of " Un-
naturall Vipers and Traytors " [3] engaged with the Pope and the
Jesuits in " the most execrable conspiracy . . . to extirpate the
Protestant Religion, subvert the Government and Parliament, and
poison the King himself (if he condescend not to their desires, or
crosse them in their purposes) whom they have purposely engaged
in these warres." [4]   To such a man as Prynne, therefore, an appeal
to the " judicious " Hooker was out of the question, and although
he has a wealth of quotations from the Scriptures, from classical
history and contemporary writers, he never mentions Hooker,
alive though he is to the importance of Marsiglio of Padua.[5] He
prefers the spirit and writings of the continental Monarchomachs to those of the apologist of the Church of England, whose
writings must have been at least as well known to him as Jewel's
Apology and Bilson's *True Difference*, which receive frequent
mention.

A more reasoned statement of the doctrine of the sovereignty of
the people is to be found in the writings of Samuel Rutherford
(1600–61). He was a Scottish Presbyterian minister, and one of
the Commissioners of the General Assembly of divines held at
Westminster in 1643. He published his *Lex Rex* in the following
year. The book, which takes the form of answers to forty-four
questions about the nature and powers of monarchy, is strongly
anti-Roman in tone, being most careful to point out that views of
constitutional monarchy were held long before the advent of the
Jesuit Monarchomachs and owed nothing to them.[6] All government is held to be by divine law, but authority comes not from God
alone, but through the people.   In his language about the supremacy
of Law, Rutherford at times echoes Hooker, though he never quotes
from him; but in his stress on the elective aspects of monarchy and

---

[1] *An Appendix to the Sovereign Power of Parliaments and Kingdoms* (ed. 1643),
p. 1.
   [2] Op. cit., Ascription to the Reader.
   [3] Op. cit., Fourth part, p. 36.
   [4] Op. cit., p. 33.
   [5] Op. cit., p. 78.
   [6] *Lex Rex*, ed. 1846, pp. 204–10.

the frank acceptance of it on the grounds of mere convenience [1] he is a true child of the seventeenth-century Puritans.

To what extent did Milton [2] draw on Hooker? This is a difficult question to answer with much precision, for Milton seldom quotes precise authorities, and most of his political writings are *livres de circonstance*. Yet it cannot be questioned that Hooker's *Ecclesiastical Polity* was extremely familiar to the passionate defender of the Commonwealth. For example, when he writes on the iniquity of tithes in his *Likeliest means to remove hirelings out of the Church*, Milton seems to have the Fifth Book of the *Ecclesiastical Polity* (and especially section 79) before him. [3] Again, his *Tractate on Education* suggests his familiarity with particularly the sixteenth chapter of the First Book. [4] In his *Reason of Church Government*, Milton refers by name to Hooker and disputes with him as to what precisely was " the commandment " to Timothy, [5] although in that pamphlet, as also in his *Prelatical Episcopacy*, [6] he appears by no means to regard him as a defender of the Divine Right of bishops, but rather Andrewes and Ussher. But his short book, *The Tenure of Kings and Magistrates*, [7] written to justify the Independents' treatment of Charles, reveals a careful scrutiny of the *Ecclesiastical Polity*. In this pamphlet he harks back for a moment to the origin of Society, and a comparison of the few pages devoted to this topic shows a very close resemblance to the line of argument taken by Hooker in the First Book of the *Laws of Ecclesiastical Polity*. Indeed, it may not be extravagant to say that Milton appears to have made a précis of Hooker's famous tenth chapter. He reasons (here and there in language strikingly similar to Hooker's) that men were by nature free; that after Adam's sin they wrought such mutual harm that they agreed " by common league " to a Society. They saw it was needful to ordain some authority with executive force to ensure peace and common right. This power, inherent in them all, they derived into the hands of a ruler, who governed well for a time, but later yielded to the temptation to practise injustice and partiality. Consequently, the people invented laws, consented to by all, in order to confine and limit the ruler; law was set above the magistrate. [8] The original establishment of a magistrate took place,

---

[1] Such veiled republicanism as " I am not against it that monarchy well-tempered is the best government, though the question to me is most problematic " is completely alien to Hooker (p. 38).

[2] *Vivebat* 1608–74.

[3] *Prose Works* (ed. St. John, London, 1848), Vol. III, esp. pp. 9, 10, 16, 18.

[4] Op. cit., pp. 462 *et seq.*

[5] Op. cit., II, 448.

[6] Op. cit., II, 420 *et seq.*

[7] Op. cit., II, 1–47.

[8] Op. cit., II, 8–10.

says Milton, " lest each man should be his own partial judge ",
which is not strikingly dissimilar to Hooker's opinion that men
ordained a public government and yielded themselves subject to it,
" inasmuch as every man is towards himself . . . partial ".[1]
Again, in his Preface to *A Defence of the People of England*,[2] a passage
on the origin of civil society reflects Hooker's view and almost his
words in the same chapter of the First Book. Further, Milton
insists that covenants must be interpreted according to the Laws of
Nature,[3] which he identifies (with Hooker) as the Law of Reason.
Here and there may be found other parallels, and it seems certain
that Milton must have known his Hooker well. Of course he relied
on many another author, particularly upon the Monarchomachs.
But whatever fundamental premisses he took from Hooker, Milton
reasoned to different conclusions. He was as radical in his attitude
to life as Hooker was conservative, and firmly held that all tyrants—
those who ruled for themselves as against law and the common
good—should be deposed and put to death. His justification of
regicide—even of tyrannicide—would have shocked Hooker.
About Milton there is a touch of Rousseau, as has been well said.
When he writes, " No man, who knows aught, can be so stupid to
deny that all men naturally were born free ",[4] we cannot but
think of the opening words of the *Contrat Social*.

It was by the moderate Puritans that Hooker was most appreciated.[5] The poet Andrew Marvell (1621–75), who was at one
time, like Milton, Oliver Cromwell's secretary, although he was
opposed to episcopacy and in his book *Rehearsal Transposed* (published
1672) attacked the High Anglican position, speaks of Hooker
throughout in terms of the greatest respect. " I have a great
reverence for Mr. Hooker." [6] Hooker is always " the Reverend Mr.
Hooker " or simply " Master Hooker ", whose modesty and
candour are contrasted with the ignorance and prejudice of those
who quote him without having always read him.[7] The extreme
upholders of prelacy are bidden not to use his name continually as

---

[1] *E.P.*, I, x, 4.
[2] Milton, op. cit., I, 16.
[3] *Tenure of Kings*, I, 30.
[4] Op. cit., I, 8.
[5] Though he shocked Baxter. " But when, at his (i.e., Bishop Morley) persuasion, I revised them (i.e., the *Laws of the Ecclesiastical Polity*) I admired at their
Infatuation, that ever they suffered such Books as Hooker's Eighth Book . . . to
see the light; when Hooker goeth so much further than the Long Parliament
went, as to affirm that the Legislative Power is so naturally belonging to the
whole Body; that it is Tyranny for a single Person to exercise it . . . with
many more Antimonarchical Principles " (*Reliquiae Baxterianae* (London, 1696),
Pt. II, 375).
[6] Marvell, op. cit., p. 125.
[7] Op. cit., pp. 408, 485.

a " piece of inchantment " to upbraid Nonconformity.[1] Marvell, indeed, saw that there were two sides to Hooker and that " in some things he did answer himself " [2] and was an example of moderation as well as the champion of a definite position.

Likewise, the Presbyterian theologian, Edward Gee (1613–60), in his *Divine Right and Original of the Civil Magistrate from God* (published 1658), appreciates Hooker enough to quote him six times— using not only the First Book but the Eighth as well—and some of his definitions—such as the equation of the law of Nature with the dictate of right reason—are echoes of Hooker's own words.[3] He perceived clearly that—to quote his own words [4]—" The great subject of debate, difference, exagitation, and contrivement in the late commotions, that which the most stir hath been about is the matter of Authority "—and his own book is in the nature of a commentary on the text (Romans 13. 1). " The powers that be are ordained of God ", in which he argues that " power is originally in God, and from Him passeth by means of the people's consent to the Magistrate ".[5] He asserts that his view " hath had before these times the approval of some of our learnedst men (as Mr. Richard Hooker, and Mr. Banes) " [6]. And from it he draws the conclusion that mere possession does not of itself give an unquestioned title to power. This constitutional limitation can of course be used against the Protectorate as much as against the Stuart Monarchy, and it is not surprising that Gee ended his life as a moderate royalist.

Somewhat apart from the orthodox Royalists and Republicans stood the most original political philosophers of the seventeenth century—James Harrington [7] and Thomas Hobbes.[8]

Harrington's *Oceana*,[9] published in 1656, was an essay in practical Utopianism, outlining a model constitution. We know that Harrington esteemed Hooker, since he acknowledges his debt to him in a quotation from the *Ecclesiastical Polity*. In this passage [10] he has adopted one of Hooker's basic ideas—that reason is a governing principle in all physical life: there is a Law of Natural agents whereby Nature teaches men their common interest—as Reason teaches men that their true interest is communal. But though there are no other direct traces of Hooker in the *Oceana*, it is not fanciful to conclude that Harrington is further in his debt. On the contrary, he stresses that the whole purpose of government is the public utility—" The wisdom of the few may be the light of mankind;

---

[1] Op. cit., pp. 429–30.   [2] Op. cit., p. 125.
[3] Gee, *Divine Right*, p. 32.   [4] Preface, sec. 2.
[5] Op. cit., p. 295.   [6] *Ibid.*
[7] *Vivebat* 1611–77.   [8] *Vivebat* 1588–1679.
[9] Morley's ed., 1887.   [10] Ed., 1887, p. 28; cf. Hooker, *E.P.*, I, iii, 2–5.

but the interest of the few is not the profit of mankind, nor of a commonwealth." [1] Government is that art which preserves political society in being on the foundation of common interest; no party interests may be permitted to overbalance the whole, as against Hobbes, whose idea of government is sheer, naked force. [2] Government and people being bound together for public utility, the executive must rule according to the laws passed by the legislative sovereign, which is the Senate and the people [3]—and here he reminds Hobbes that the executive's sword is *in* and not above the law. [4] The heart and core of every government is the civil society's fundamental laws. [5] All this is in the spirit of Hooker, although the latter would not, as Harrington does, claim that the executive is answerable with his head for misrule! But while Harrington may well have drawn his ideas of Reason, Public Utility, Balance and Unity, the Supremacy of the Law, from Hooker, in other important matters he diverges sharply. Thus he argues for liberty of conscience and toleration, [6] and holds that religious minorities are possible; [7] he would not have clergy in political office (" an ounce of wisdom is worth a pound of clergy ") [8] and seems to think that ecclesiastical power is *in toto* derived from the civil power. [9] Again, he makes no reference whatever to social contract or covenant, and agrees rather with Filmer that paternal power is natural and original, and the parent of the commonwealth. [10] Lastly, he thoroughly approves of Machiavelli (" whose books are neglected "), [11] " the only politician of later ages ", who, in Hooker's eyes, is one of an " execrable crew ". [12] Harrington " is curiously aloof from his contemporaries; he will not fit into any category, nor adopt any known label of his own day. Consequently, he appears more original than he really was." [13]

Very different was Thomas Hobbes, whose two books, *De Cive* (1640) and *The Leviathan* (1651) aroused great controversy in both Royalist and Republican camps, and proclaimed him the most original thinker of his day. Hobbes was the complete rationalist, with a strong dislike of the Church and the whole apparatus of revealed religion and an even greater horror of anarchy. Largely indifferent to forms of government, what he wanted to see was the Absolute State, the great Leviathan, irremovable and all-powerful. The principal ingredient of man's nature was, according to Hobbes, fear; and he pictured a state of nature in which there was " continuall feare, and danger of violent death: And the life of man,

---

[1] p. 30.   [2] pp. 18–23.   [3] p. 31.   [4] *Ibid.*
[5] p. 103.   [6] pp. 45, 84.   [7] p. 67.   [8] p. 216.
[9] pp. 214–5.   [10] p. 82.   [11] p. 16.   [12] *E.P.*, V, iii, 1.
[13] F. J. C. Hearnshaw, *Social and Political Ideas of some Great Thinkers of the Sixteenth and Seventeenth Centuries* (ed. London, 1926), p. 193.

solitary, poore, nasty, brutish and short ".[1] To escape this men surrendered their natural rights in favour of a Sovereign Person or Power; they formally contracted away their authority to this Someone, who became thereby the absolute controller of their wills and persons, and was in fact indued with their personality. No State can be secure where such contract has been imperfectly made; where the Sovereign enjoys less than absolute power; where subjects claim rights of conscience or of property; where the Sovereign is limited by law; or where Corporations or other societies claim real personality, " like wormes in the entrayles of a naturall man ".[2] The State consists of an Absolute Sovereign and a number of individuals or atoms.

It would at first sight seem incredible that there could be common ground between Hooker and Hobbes. Yet the former was certainly the earliest writer on political theory in this country to formulate the doctrine of contract, derived from his conception of Nature and its law, while Hobbes was the most original exponent of the natural law and the theory of contract. Certainly Hobbes nowhere quotes Hooker, but it is inconceivable that he should not have been familiar with the *Ecclesiastical Polity*, and there are points of common interest between them. Both advance the contract theory; distinguish two ways to the knowledge of truth, Revelation and Reason; and hark back to the union of kingly and priestly power in Israel to justify the Erastian State.

But although Hooker and Hobbes share the terminology of the social contract, their conceptions of it are as different as are their ideas of the Law of Nature. To Hooker, as we have seen, the contract is two-fold—first the social compact which actually forms society from a group of individuals, and then the contract of sovereignty, by which Society sets up its government. The first is irrevocable, the second is open to modification. On the other hand, Hobbes sees one contract only. By it each individual enters into agreement with every other individual to surrender his natural rights in favour of a third party, the Ruler. This surrender is incapable of revocation, and since the community was never invested with those rights abandoned by separate individuals, it can never question or challenge the power of the Sovereign Ruler. He is outside and above the original contract, for ever. In passing, we should note that Hobbes is not here arguing in favour of the Divine Right of kings, for he is indifferent as to who rules, so long as his rule is supreme and unchallenged. Thus, while Hooker has

---

[1] *Leviathan* (Oxford, 1909), p. 97. Cf. " De Cive ", Hobbes' *Works* (ed. Molesworth, London, 1839), II, cap. 1, sects. 2–4.

[2] *Leviathan*, p. 257.

his idea of a double contract to safeguard, in the last extremity, the rights of subjects against tyrants, and to assert the Government's responsibility to the people, Hobbes utilizes his view of a single contract for the reverse purpose : to safeguard the Sovereign power against any attempt on the part of the commonwealth to limit its authority or insist on its responsibility. The one is looking at the Constitutional Monarchy of Elizabeth, the other at the anarchy produced by the Civil War. They are really alike only in their insistence that there can be no legal sovereignty without contract, and in their agreement that a kingdom established by conquest can qualify to become legal if it proceeds to develop along stable and orderly lines.

The difference between these two writers is equally sharply marked in their attitude to the Law of Nature, which is the most important problem of the doctrine of law. Hobbes distinguishes between right and law, between *Jus* and *Lex*; Hooker never does. Hobbes, following Roman Law, admits that natural men are by nature equal, but are also by nature utterly selfish beings whose actions are caused by simple passions. They are brutish, impulsive creatures, living in a state of Nature and therefore in a continual state of war. For a state of Nature *is* a state of war, " an irregular jostling and hewing of one another, of every man against every man, homo homini lupus ". This is a result of every man having a right to everything, and the sole arbiter being force. But natural man seems to have two natures :—

(i) The selfish brute who desires everything.
(ii) The reasoning brute who discovers that he can only get part.

It is this reasoning side of man's nature which is important, because it leads him to discover the Laws of Nature, which Hobbes defines as " maxims found out by reason "; these lead men to a code of conduct whereby they can live together in a state of peace. It is clear that Hobbes' Laws of Nature are strictly utilitarian in their basis, and the difference between them and Hooker's Law of Nature (the Moral Law of Reason) is the substitution of personal advantage for moral obligation. He avoids the ethical point of view, emphasizing the purely political side of his arguments. Thus he would secure all the virtues for his natural man without admitting that man has more than an objection to war and a desire for comfort. We have to acknowledge that Hobbes' view of the State, like Hooker's and Aristotle's, is teleological, but it differs from theirs in that with Hobbes the ultimate end of all human actions, and therefore of the State itself, is self-preservation. Hooker's *Lex*

Naturalis is the Law of Reason, evident to all, of divine origin, imposing moral obligations, and consequently engendering order, harmony, unity and freedom. Hobbes' Law of Nature knows nothing of ethics, militates against order and freedom, and its supersession by an unbreakable contract is therefore a necessity. Hooker, as we have seen, had likewise no illusions about the state of Nature, from which his double contract is also a deliverance, but the idea that law was not organically connected with order and freedom was wholly abhorrent to his outlook and to the classical and Thomist philosophy from which it developed. In brief, the whole difference is one of outlook between the theocentric religious man and the pure rationalist.

It may well be, however, that Hobbes did deliberately follow Hooker in the belief that there are two methods by which truth may be apprehended—namely, Revelation and Reason. A comparison of a passage [1] from the Preface to the *Ecclesiastical Polity* with the fifteenth chapter of the *De Cive* suggests this.[2] There Hobbes speaks of the natural kingdom and the prophetic kingdom, and follows Hooker in stressing the place of reason in human knowledge. He is speaking of the different ways in which God makes his laws known—that is, by reason, or by revelation (which may be through the voice of some outstanding man). This is reminiscent of Hooker's words: " There are but two ways whereby the Spirit leadeth men into all truth; the one extraordinary, the other common; the one belonging but unto some few, the other extending itself unto all that are of God: the one, that which we call by a special divine excellency Revelation, the other Reason." [3]   True, Hobbes alters the emphasis, reversing the order; but we can hardly help thinking that as Hooker was the first Englishman (if we ignore Pecock) to ascribe such importance to Reason—transcending Scholastics and Reformers alike as to the relationship between Reason and Revelation—so Hobbes was the first to draw the full consequences from this teaching. A further point of common interest between the two philosophers is that they both turn to the Old Testament for historical evidence to support the view that the Church and the State are properly controlled by the Sovereign power. This, of course, is common to all sixteenth- and seventeenth-century political philosophers. They might despise the individual Jew, but the early history of his race was essential. Hobbes cannot exempt the Church from Leviathan's control. To avoid the objection that in a State Church sacred and profane elements would

---

[1] *E.P.*, Pref., iii, 10.
[2] Hobbes' *Works* (ed. Molesworth, London, 1839), II, 333-4.
[3] *E.P.*, *ibid.*

be impossibly confused, he separates natural from revealed religion, as he had divided natural from revealed knowledge. Natural religion is the concern of the State, revealed religion is for the individual.[1] Hooker and Hobbes are both in this respect Erastians, but Hooker develops his arguments to deal with the claims of the Puritan opposition, whereas Hobbes cannot tolerate the idea of personality in any community, society or corporation. The former is thinking of the welfare of the English Church and of the divine purpose of the State, *bene vivere*; the latter is bent on preserving the State in its omnipotence, *vivere*.

Hobbes is the first representative of purely rational thought in this country, and Hooker undoubtedly is his most important fore-runner. It is possible that in answer to Puritan, Huguenot and Jesuit philosophy Hobbes developed his own ideas originally and independently; but if he did not do so, it is reasonable to conclude that some degree of inspiration was drawn by him from the writings of Hooker.

Like Milton, Hobbes does not cite his authorities, and it is there-fore difficult to prove that he ever had the *Ecclesiastical Polity* in mind when he wrote his books. The same cannot be said of the two Whig writers, Algernon Sidney (1622–92) and John Locke (1632–1704), for they both frequently mention Hooker by name, often quote from the *Ecclesiastical Polity*, and the connection between them both and Hooker is obvious and intimate. Sidney, who was an active Republican during the Commonwealth, and suffered execution in 1683 for alleged complicity in the Rye House Plot, wrote his *Discourses concerning Government*[2] (published 1693) as a reply to Filmer's *Patriarcha*.

Sidney brackets Hooker with Aristotle as having correctly established the fundamental truth that man is by nature free.[3] Men surrendered their right of self-determination solely for their own good, and as a consequence every Government exists for the people, and not (as Absolutist writers would maintain) the people for the Government. Since men voluntarily formed political societies, whatever be the mode of government, it rests upon the consent of the people,[4] Sovereign and subject being bound together by covenant.[5] If a ruler governs for his own ends, the people may resume their power, which was entrusted to him for the public good,[6] and logically may depose him.[7] Inasmuch as the mass of the people can seldom or never act together, they elect representatives who possess the people's power.[8] In England this representative

---

[1] Cf. *E.P.*, III, xi, 14; *De Cive*, II, 345–6.   [2] Ed. 1750, 2 vols.
[3] I, 19.   [4] I, 62–64, 67, 151.   [5] I, 450; II, 34 *et seq.*
[6] I, 134.   [7] I, 450.   [8] I, 138–9, 146.

body is the Parliament, the legislative Sovereign.[1] The executive powers of a ruler are encompassed by the laws which the representative assembly makes; law establishes the Ruler and is superior to him, as even Queen Elizabeth found.[2] As against the monarchical writers, Sidney, following Hooker, holds that law is essentially directive rather than coercive.[3] In all these fundamentals—the Nature of Law, the Origin of Society, Contract and Covenant, Consent and Representation, the Supremacy of Law—the disciple follows his master. But he presses his arguments to logical ends from which Hooker would have shrunk. For example, Sidney has no belief in the doctrine of hereditary right [4] which, if true, would make nonsense of the Coronation oaths [5] so much stressed by his opponents. He maintains that, so far from obeying a bad king,[6] subjects have a duty of revolt.[7] Filmer may argue that successful usurpation is a valid title to rule—" We are to look upon the power," complains Sidney, " not the ways by which it is obtained . . . though gained by violence, treachery or poison " [8]—and Hooker is quoted by Sidney to the effect that tyranny can create no right.[9] True, but even against a tyrant Hooker could not envisage rebellion, whereas Sidney argues that revolt may well be plain duty. " When things are brought to such a pass, the boldest counsels are the most safe; and if they must perish who lie still, and they can but perish who are most active, the choice is easily made." [10] The mere idea of a passive obedience is folly.[11] Hooker, dazzled by the personal magnetism of his Tudor sovereign, the undoubted (and much needed) executive, and influenced by his conceptions of unity and " the public good ", could not at such a moment of English history have worked out his fundamentals of government to their logical conclusion, a constitutional Monarchy. Sidney, a realist with experience of the Civil Wars, the Commonwealth, and the corruption of Charles II's Government, was able to press them to their end. His departure from Hooker's side is an indictment of Stuart rule. In the sixteenth century the King reigned and governed; the Monarchy was personal. The seventeenth century saw a Republic, after which it was impossible a king should ever govern; Monarchy was an office. This is the explanation of the divergence between the two authors—the King, a man of flesh and blood, the divine agent; the King, an office-holder, the Agent of the people's sovereignty. Two passages describe their respective

[1] II, 168–9.   [2] II, 195, 233, 356.   [3] II, 93.
[4] I, 57–8; II, 41.   [5] II, 163.   [6] I, 364.
[7] I, 324.   [8] I, 92.   [9] I, 155.
[10] II, 339.   [11] II, 180.

"Ideal Kings" and illustrate Sidney's development from Hooker's century:—

Hooker: *E.P.*, V, lxxvi, 8.

> . . . the chiefest happiness for which we have some Christian Kings in so great admiration above the rest is . . . if so be they have virtuously reigned, if honour have not filled their hearts with pride, if the exercise of their power have been service and attendance upon the majesty of the Most High, if they have feared Him as their own inferiors and subjects have feared them . . . if revenge have slowly proceeded from them and mercy willingly offered itself, if . . . they have tempered rigour with lenity, if . . . they have been . . . careful not to do anything but that which is commendable in the best . . . if the true knowledge of themselves have humbled them in God's sight no less than God in the eyes of men hath raised them up."

Sidney: II, pp. 354–5.

> "The King that renders justice is indeed always there: he never sleeps; he is subject to no infirmity; he never dies unless the nation be extinguished, or so dissipated as to have no government. No nation that has a sovereign power within itself, does ever want this King. He was in Athens and Rome, as well as at Babylon and Susa; and is as properly said to be now in Venice, Switzerland, or Holland, as in France, Morocco or Turkey."

Finally we come to the name of Locke, through whom Hooker's ideas passed directly to the eighteenth-century political malcontents in America and France. Indeed, Hallam, as we have seen, levels the charge against Hooker of being an original Whig, whose doctrine of contract, consent, and sovereignty of the people led not only to Locke, but also to Rousseau and red revolution.

"A good portrait of Locke", it has been remarked, "would require an elaborate background. His is not a figure to stand statuesquely in a void ".[1] The change of background had, indeed, been considerable. For one thing,

> "William was our King declared,
> To ease a nation's grievance",

and that provided the immediate cause for the Essay on Government; but the discoveries in natural science and the different conclusions at which philosophers had arrived, independently of

[1] Santayana: *Locke and the Frontiers of Commonsense* (Cambridge, 1933), p. 1.

revelation, provided a different intellectual ἦθος. Spinoza had written in favour of toleration, upon one excellent ground, among many, that we can never be quite sure of our conclusions. Before the optimism of the perfectibility of man became fully established the optimism of the comprehensibility of the universe, and with it much pride in assured conclusions, was passing. In politics England had suffered the Stuart despotism and the military tyranny of the Commonwealth, neither of which possessed any element of consent. In the one the King, in the other the Army, was always right.

Now the full-blooded doctrine of the consent of the people is to be preached, and beyond doubt Locke's admiration for Hooker is sincere and genuine. It is expressed on every page, and quotations from Hooker are innumerable. But if some of Locke's foundations are taken from parts of the *Ecclesiastical Polity* which argue for contract and the consent of the people, the building is a new one. He speaks in the name of Hooker, but the words are the words of Brutus. Locke is saturated with the spirit of the *Vindiciae*, but embodies it in the phrases of Hooker. We cannot accuse the disciple, as we certainly can the master, of maintaining what Pope called " the right divine of Kings to govern wrong ".

Locke agrees that man originally lived in a state of Nature, a state of freedom and equality; it was from this that Hooker had deduced the obligation of men to mutual love, and the duties of justice and charity.[1] Men owned property in that state by reason of any labour bestowed on natural things; whence property is primitive and natural. The law that governed men then was the Law of Nature or Reason,[2] each man being his own executive of that law " for reparation and restraint ".[3] This State existed, Locke affirms, till political societies were formed, by men's mutual consent,[4] in order to avoid war, which was the outcome of un-restrained freedom.[5]

This power which men by nature possessed they resigned into the hands of the community which by agreement they had formed,[6] for protection of property (which includes a man's person and liberty and all belonging to him). Thus private wills and judgment gave way to settled rules and impartial judges, of necessity embracing all members, since, as Hooker remarks, " No man in civil society can be exempted from the laws of it ".[7]

So consent, and consent alone, gave birth to political society, and the power of the community thus established is understood to be

---

[1] *E.P.*, I, viii, 7.
[2] Locke, " Treatise on Government," *Works*, 10 vols. (London, 1812), p. 341.
[3] Op. cit., p. 342.   [4] p. 347.   [5] p. 350.
[6] pp. 388, 412.   [7] p. 394.

that of the majority.[1] " And this is that, and that only, which did, or could give beginning to any lawful government in the world." [2] Absolutism (the opposition of one man's will to the community's) is consequently impossible in any civil society, for it brings back the conditions of insecurity and war; a return to the state of Nature, the only condition of absolutism.[3]

The political Society possesses political power; that is, a right to make and execute laws for the preservation of men's " property ", and for protection from foreign enemies; the one criterion of legislation being always that it must be for the public good.[4] " And this power has its original only from compact and agreement, and the mutual consent of those who make up the community ",[5] and is entrusted, expressly or tacitly, to those governors whom the society has set over itself.[6] All subsequent governors rule by the terms of the original compact. The theory that a Prince rules by God's direct authority he dismisses as untrue, and never having been heard of till lately; [7] if Filmer's patriarchal theory be true, then all Kings should be priests, and the only priests, indeed, as heads of families were originally both.[8]

He distinguishes a separation of powers in the rule of political Society: the Legislative from the Executive. The Legislative is the supreme power of the Commonwealth, " sacred and unalterable in the hands where the community have once placed it ".[9] No edict, proclamation or anything else can be a law which has not been enacted by the chosen and appointed Legislature.[10] Legislation must accord with natural law, since " the law of nature stands as an eternal rule to all men, legislators as well as others ".[11] Extemporary, arbitrary decrees are not laws; both laws and judges must be rightly established and known.[12] No ruler can have any arbitrary power over men's persons and estates, nor legislate arbitrarily; since this would put subjects into a state worse than that of Nature, wherein at least they had liberty to defend themselves from injuries.[13] Nor is the legislative power able to transfer its rights, since itself is only a delegated power of the people.[14]

While the form of government endures, the Legislative is superior to the Executive, " for what can give laws to another, must needs be superior to him ".[15] But there is always a residuum of power in the people, who may retake what once they conditionally gave— " the community perpetually retains a supreme power of saving themselves from the attempts and designs of anybody, even of their

---

[1] p. 395.	[2] p. 306.	[3] pp. 390, 398.	[4] p. 339.
[5] p. 441.	[6] Ibid.	[7] p. 405.	[8] p. 382.
[9] p. 415.	[10] p. 417.	[11] p. 418.	[12] p. 419.
[13] p. 420.	[14] p. 423.	[15] p. 427.	

P

legislators ";¹ " for the society can never . . . lose the native and
original right it has to preserve itself. . . ."² But in the absence
of the Legislative, the Executive is ruler. If the executive rule
illegally (as by hindering the assembly of the legislature), " the true
remedy of force without authority, is to oppose force to it ".³ The
mere fact of convenience that the Executive summons and dismisses
the Legislative is no sign of superiority.⁴

But the Executive is always present and the Legislative not so;
hence the former must have power to meet possible emergencies.
This is often called " prerogative ", which Locke happily defines as
" the power of doing public good without a rule ".⁵ He admits
the need, and says that " salus populi suprema lex " is a just and
fundamental rule; if sincerely followed, the ruler cannot err. There
is always one and that an easy criterion of prerogative rule—" is it
for the good or hurt of the people? " ⁶ It is the misuse of this
prerogative that is the cause of all evils in Kingly government.⁷
He admits that England's greatest monarchs enlarged the prerogative freely, without protest from the people, since their rule
was dominated by one point of view, the public good.⁸ Perhaps
Locke is here helping Hooker out of a difficulty; he knew the
Tudor era was the time of prerogative rule *par excellence*, and his
master had nowhere criticized it.

In the event of strife between Executive and Legislative, and of
attempts of the former to rule independently, the sovereign people
must go to arms to assert its right of self-preservation, and oust the
usurper.⁹ Likewise, in the event of tyranny, which is " the exercise of
power beyond right ", recourse must be had to force, which " though
it hath the name of rebellion, yet is no offence before God ".¹⁰

This outline suffices to show that it is freedom from arbitrary
authority far more than from mere authority that men seek, and
which Locke determined they ought to have—" the community perpetually retains a supreme power of saving themselves from the
attempts and designs of anybody, even of their legislators ".¹¹ The
whole purpose of government is to protect the property, and that
includes the life and freedom, of those subject to it. ¹² In consequence, the only safeguard that they can have is that the Government should be removable, and the people are, as it were, holders
of eminent domain over it. He will not, as Hooker did and later

---

¹ p. 427.   ² p. 468.   ³ p. 430.   ⁴ p. 432.
⁵ p. 438.   ⁶ p. 435.   ⁷ p. 436.
⁸ But cf. Dicey (*Privy Council*, 1887, p. 118). " The rule of the Tudors was in
the main a selfish rule. Where the interests of the Crown and of her people
coincided the government acted with patriotism. Where they differed, everything
was sacrificed to the interest of the King."
⁹ p. 439.   ¹⁰ p. 455.   ¹¹ p. 427.   ¹² p. 396.

Burke would do, represent the social contract as at most a deed past and made once and for all. Every new generation, every person newly subject to government, must consciously and freely enter into contract with it. So insistent is he as to the eminent domain of the people that Tucker was able to twit him with a marked similarity to his great opponent, Filmer. Tucker maintains that this similarity exists because both contend for an indefeasible right of *de iure* sovereignty, although in different subjects, a right which not even the lapse of time can destroy.[1]

Locke has, moreover, focused the relative functions of the Legislature and the Executive, which Hooker did not do. The latter lived under the shadow of the great Elizabeth, and her visit to the House of Commons (her ever-faithful Commons) in 1566 was confusing to the Englishman and a cause of triumph for such an exponent of unmixed constitutions as Bodin. But in the subsequent struggle between Legislature and Executive the Legislature had won, and now the only remnant of arbitrary authority to be left to the Executive was " the power of doing public good without a rule ".[2] Indeed, in times of emergency arbitrary action may be taken by every member of the Commonwealth, including the members of the Executive, for " necessity knows no law ", but woe to those who meant well if the law should know no Act of Indemnity.

But in the conception of Natural Law there is some affinity between Hooker and Locke, though they lead to diametrically opposite political conclusions. To both of them the Law of Nature is the discovery of reason, and may in fact be equated with the reasonable principle of the universe.[3] " What all men have at all times learned, Nature herself must needs have taught "[4] is a good statement alike of the foundation of the *ius gentium*[5] and of Locke's conception of the over-ruling Law of God. This, together with consent, is the one check upon government; it involves, which we shall see is dangerous, what Maitland calls " the jural conception of morality ",[6] with which a conflict between civil and natural law, between the State and morality, becomes likely. This issue Hooker always shirked. He will go no farther than to allow that where State Law conflicts with law natural or divine men may not be forced to obey. But the consequences that may well flow from such conflict, and the whole right of resistance on the basis of natural or divine right, he ignores completely. Here, as so often with him, the

[1] Tucker: *On Civil Government* (London, 1781), pp. 81 *et seq.*
[2] p. 438.
[3] *E.P.*, I; Locke, *Human Understanding*, II, xxviii, 8–11.
[4] *E.P.*, I, viii, 3.
[5] Maitland, *Collected Papers*, I, 23.
[6] Maitland, *ibid.*

factual situation prescribes the philosophy. His idea of natural rights differs completely from Locke's. Locke understands the natural right of the individual, as something of which he can never be deprived, and to permit which is the purpose of government, with a remedy against the Government where it fails. This is a revolutionary principle, the basis of a political philosophy totally distinct from Hooker's. The latter admits a social compact, though it is not necessarily the basis of political society. He accepts the traditional dogma of human depravity as necessitating some political organization. This, however, does not mean that the State has a sinful origin; nay, rather it is a blessing and an instrument of progress, a remedy originating in God to curb the evil tendencies of men. It is this aspect which Locke totally ignores, and he conceives of the State only in terms of a rigid contract; a contract whose purpose is to recognize the natural rights of the individual over and against the State; an artificial creation wherein the rights of the individual may be systematically constructed within the terms of the State. Hooker is providing a rational basis for the concrete constitutional facts, indicating the various ways in which consent can be shown to be the foundation of political authority. The State and its institutions, though human, are natural, and therefore divine, since the Laws of Nature are part of the eternal laws which govern all creation. Hence legitimate authority is divine in itself, and its worth is never dependent on the will of human beings alone; there is always a " divine right ". It is thus that he balances human institutions and the divine sanction of lawful authority. On the other hand, his immediate Anglican successors, in propagating the doctrine of the Divine Right of Kings, will deny any validity to the people's will as the foundation of authority; while Locke and the Contractualists will insist that the origin and nature of political authority are entirely human. Both types are therefore hostile to Hooker's view of the Law of Nature, by means of which he had successfully harmonized a religious conception of the world, as governed by divine providence, with a rational justification of political life, as the free sphere of human activity.

Hume, when he set out to prove that the Original Contract was historically an inaccurate account of the establishment of government, stated very precisely the position of his opponents when he wrote, " No party, in the present age, can well support itself without a philosophic or speculative system of principle, annexed to its political or practical one ".[1] Henceforth, England was to be ruled by a Parliamentary majority, and Locke provided the philosophic basis for the divine right of majorities to rule.

[1] *Essays* (ed. Green and Grose, London, 1875), I, 443, Part II, Essay XII.

A test case whereby to estimate the liberalism of master and soi-disant disciple may be found in the American controversy with George III's Government. Whatever be his teaching as to consent and natural law, it is certain that Hooker would have asserted the authority of the British Parliament; the interests of unity and order, and the sacred principle of authority would demand the submission of the Colonists. Any contract to which George III could be deemed a party belonged to a remote period, anterior to the factual British Constitution, possessing a mere archaic interest for philosophers. King and Parliament ought certainly to act in obedience to law itself, but no power existed to compel their obedience. On the other hand, Locke would set up a Fundamental Law—the principle of the good and security of all men—as the Constitution itself; which, in fact, the Americans did in pursuit of his teaching. What with Hooker was at best a counsel of perfection, entailing a moral obligation on the Sovereign, became to Locke a legal obligation to administer the Sovereign Law. His Fundamental Law, embracing both the contractual terms and the Law of Nature, was at once the instrument of government, supreme over Legislature and Executive, and the guarantee of the people's security in person, property, and liberty. Translating his philosophy into fact, the Americans created their fixed and rigid Constitution, of which Executive and Legislature were the mere servants, purposing to possess for all time that personal security, freedom and happiness to which by the Law of Nature every man is of right entitled.[1]

So when, on July 4th, 1776, Congress published the Declaration of Independence, whose second paragraph runs: "We hold these truths to be self-evident, that all men are created equal, that they were endowed by their creator with certain inalienable rights, that among these are life, liberty and the pursuit of happiness.[2] That to secure these rights governments are instituted among men, deriving their just powers from the consent of the governed. That whenever any form of government becomes destructive to these ends, it is the right of the people to alter or abolish it, and to institute new government, laying its foundation on such principles and organizing its powers in such form, as to them shall seem most likely to effect their safety and happiness . . ." they were enunciating the pure doctrine of Sidney and Locke, who had twisted Hooker's ideals, forcing them out into the arena of realist politics.

[1] See Morison and Commager, *Growth of the American Republic* (Oxford, 1942), Vol. I, chap. 7.
[2] Thomas Jefferson substituted " the pursuit of happiness " for Locke's " property ".

CHAPTER XI

THE FINAL ASSESSMENT

THE closest friend of Hooker's last years was Adrian Saravia, a Prebendary of Canterbury. He was also his confessor, and it was from him that Hooker received absolution and Communion on his death-bed, when there appeared " a reverend gaiety and joy in his face ".[1] His thoughts were upon that hierarchy of being and of laws that had been the occupation of his life, for he said that " he was meditating the number and nature of angels, and their blessed obedience and order, without which peace could not be in Heaven; and oh, that it might be so on earth ".[2] His last words were, " I could wish to live to do the Church more service, but cannot hope it, for my days are past as a shadow that returns not." [3] He died in the afternoon of 2 November and the Register at Bishopsbourne records, " Mr. Richard Hooker late parson of Bishopsbourne buried yᵉ 4 of November."

Though his wish to live longer in the flesh that he might further serve the Church Militant was not granted, yet his writings are a perpetual service, and " they shall last till the last fire shall consume all learning ".[4] They are the text of all those who value the Anglican Via Media, written with such broadness of conception and condescension to the " imbecility " of men, that members of various schools of thought can appeal to them, and learn that controversy may be directed to the discovery of truth and not to the humiliation of an opponent. The heart and core of them is to uphold the eternal principle of law, and to recall to humble and rational adoration him " Who actually and everlastingly is whatsoever He may be, and which cannot hereafter be that which now He is not ".[5] The title " judicious ", applied to Hooker, has been ridiculed as " ludicrously inadequate ".[6] But it is the proper quality of a judge to be judicious, and the essence of his fitness is skill in the laws. That Hooker, pre-eminent in the latter, should be reverenced as possessing the former quality is surely apt, and the

---

[1] Walton, op. cit., I, 85.
[2] *Ibid.*
[3] Op. cit., p. 86.
[4] Op. cit., p. 71.
[5] *E.P.*, I, v, 1.
[6] Allen, *Political Thought*, p. 184.

PAGE FROM THE BISHOPSBOURNE REGISTER SHOWING ENTRY OF RICHARD HOOKER'S DEATH.

[*To face page 222.*]

title may be a guide to us in the study of those laws which he loved, followed, and expounded.

This book is a study of Hooker and his thought against the background of the current political ideas of the sixteenth century. An attempt has been made to show what the major political issues of the time were, and how contemporary philosophers endeavoured to solve them. Some questions were brought into prominence by the religious upheavals of the Reformation, but few were created. They were old problems in new guise.

We have examined Hooker's own answers to these problems as he gives them in the *Ecclesiastical Polity*. We have seen something of what he owed to the past, what he borrowed from the present and what he passed on to the future. It remains to attempt some final estimate of his importance. Why is the *Ecclesiastical Polity* still read? And who reads it? Will it, indeed, last till all learning shall be consumed? Has Hooker any but a purely antiquarian value? Do any of the problems of his times still affect us and, if so, how? What are the qualities in Hooker that call for present-day admiration?

To most people Hooker is remembered solely as the author of the *Ecclesiastical Polity*. This is not unnatural, for it was not merely his *magnum opus*, but almost his only work, and it is on the *Ecclesiastical Polity* that he must, in the end, be judged. Many, from the days of Walton's biography, have been attracted by the charm and simplicity of his life. His modesty, his freedom from self-seeking, his perception of where his duty lay and his conscientious performance of it, his single-minded devotion to the Church, have all been singled out for praise, and properly he has been held up as an example of how a Christian could live in an age of strife and controversy. But Hooker's life, though an undoubted inspiration, had nothing uncommon about it. There have been scores of such humble scholars of the Church, and there will be many more. The *Ecclesiastical Polity* itself, however, is a rarer gem, and would still be prized if we were ignorant how Hooker lived or what manner of man he was. For the *Ecclesiastical Polity*, although not now a " popular " book, is certainly very great.

In the first place, it is a masterpiece of English prose, possessing the signal advantage of being the product of a great literary age.[1] Hooker's lifetime was the age of Shakespeare and Marlowe, of Spenser and Bacon; the Authorized Version was scarcely a generation away. There is a balance and lucidity about Hooker's style

---

[1] Johnson included very many quotations in his *Dictionary*. " I shall not think my employment useless or ignoble . . . if my labours . . . add celebrity to Bacon, to Hooker, to Milton and to Boyle." (Folio ed. 1755: last page of the *Preface*.)

that is the hall-mark of great writing. The book is full of passages of persuasive dignity, exhibiting a note of spaciousness which reflects the Elizabethan Age in which the pages were written. The author is described by Hallam as " the finest, as well as the most philosophical, writer of the Elizabethan period ", the book " one of the masterpieces of English eloquence." [1] The opening sections of the First Book, in which Hooker sets out the difficulties of defending an established cause, and the famous closing paragraph of the same book, where he extols the power and place of Law with an almost lyrical note, are but examples of what may be found almost anywhere in the long pages of the *Ecclesiastical Polity*. It is difficult to forbear including at least one favourite excerpt, surely among the most beautiful words ever written on the Nature of the Eucharist. " He which hath said of the one sacrament, ' Wash and be clean ', hath said concerning the other likewise, ' Eat and live ' . . . what moveth us to argue of the manner how life should come by bread, our duty being here but to take what is offered, and most assuredly to rest persuaded of this, that can we but eat we are safe? When I behold with mine eyes some small and scarce discernible grain or seed whereof nature maketh promise that a tree shall come, and when afterwards of that tree any skilful artificer undertaketh to frame some exquisite and curious work, I look for the event, I move no question about performance either of the one or of the other. Shall I simply credit nature in things natural, shall I in things artificial rely myself on art, never offering to make doubt, and in that which is above both art and nature refuse to believe the author of both, except he acquaint me with his ways, and lay the secret of his skill before me? " [2]　The verdict of a contemporary admirer runs thus : " So to express what he conceived, in the eloquence of a most pure style, was the felicity almost of himself alone." [3]

But while the *Ecclesiastical Polity* is rightly hailed as a masterpiece of literature, it is a no less notable contribution to English theology. It covers a wide range of subjects, and there is scarcely an aspect of classical theology on which it does not touch. Not only does Hooker concern himself with Church order and Church discipline, not only does he expose the weaknesses of his opponents' case, but he discourses, in the least political but most noble part of his book, on the doctrines of the Incarnation and the Person of Christ, he examines the Liturgy and the Creeds, and sets forth the Anglican teaching on prayer and the Sacraments. Biblical exegesis moves side by side with quotations from the Fathers, and nowhere is there a division between matters of administration and matters of doctrine.

---

[1] *H.L.E.* (1873), II, 200.　　　　　[2] *E.P.*, V, lxvii, 12.
[3] Covel : *Just and Temperate Defence* (1603), p. 148.

Theology, however, is no longer the queen of the sciences, and even students of literature are perhaps in the minority. But Hooker has two principal claims on the public, the first of which lies in his contribution to political philosophy. His was not an original genius; as we have seen, he owes much to his predecessors, and even his own ideas were often contradictory and in need of elucidation and development. Like Burke, he had a vivid sense of the process of history, and esteemed it his duty to preserve the best of one age and pass it on to the next. In nothing was he more truly English; he was not a comet unexpectedly streaking across the sky and commanding our whole attention till it sinks to oblivion. He was rather a known constellation which sheds an understanding light about it, and at which we do not too often look because we know it is always there, a symbol of the clear order of Eternity, above our fever and malice. It was Hooker's function to link the political theory of an intense age with the past and the future, and with the eternal laws which underlay it.

His first contribution, then, to political philosophy is his conception of the Natural Law, which leads to his contractual theory. If here, again, he is not entirely original, these ideas, with their corollaries of " consent " and the " rights of the people ", were to form a main stream of political thought, flowing from him to Hobbes, to Locke and America, to Rousseau and France, with world-shaking consequences.

The Reformation struggle was, at heart, political as much as theological. On the one hand was the genesis of the " omni-competent State ", on the other the claim of corporations to act freely within it. It was characteristic of the century that the corporations which took up the struggle were religious—the Puritans, the Huguenots, the League [1]—and so, as Figgis puts it, " political liberty is the residuary legatee of ecclesiastical animosities ". But even while Hooker pleaded and argued for unity and obedience to the Sovereign Power as of God, he was furnishing the minorities with an armoury by which ultimately they would triumph. The Law of Nature taught that anterior to political association there was a contractual arrangement: hence a Sovereign had duties as well as rights, and subjects rights as well as duties. That which was contentious—however unknowable the Law of Nature, and however unhistorical any social contract—came to exist in the instinctive bases of human thought, and was to triumph over the other conception of the sole and absolute sovereignty of the State, at least until the twentieth century. It is ironical that Hooker, mediaevalist, conservative, the champion of the Tudor despotism, contributed

[1] *From Gerson to Grotius* (Cambridge, 1923), p. 18.

dynamic conceptions which were to become the basis of that political thought which is termed "Liberalism". As Abednego Seller [1] later put it, "In this Reign, Mr. Hooker published his judicious Books of Ecclesiastical Polity: from the first of which it must be confessed, it is observed, that he lays the Foundation of Government in Agreement, he herein following the Schoolmen too strictly, who had brought in the Terms and Notions of the Aristotelian Philosophy into the Christian Church, while Aristotle is known to be a great lover of *Democracy*: but whatever he laid down in *Thesi*, I am sure he hated the Deductions that some men make from him, that because Government arose out of Compact, therefore the People may call their Princes to an account."

Then, in the second place, he assists us in defining the doctrine of sovereignty and foreshadows the Sovereign State. Less bold and clear than Bodin, less practical than Sir Thomas Smith, nevertheless he is sufficiently imbued with the practice and precept of Tudor Government to perceive the full importance of sovereign power. A less position than the "highest uncommanded commander" would make for anarchy. There must be a force, as Bodin also saw, which holds the political society together. The national community is a true Empire, sole and independent, sovereign and omni-competent. All obedience is due to this *regnum superiore carens* whose symbol is the Monarch. The whole body is the ultimate Sovereign, for it is immortal, transcending always the sum total of its individual members. This united, living organism delegates the exercise of its sovereign power. Hooker may theorize but it is always from the concrete example of the Tudor Constitution. He has to reconcile the principle of Monarchy with popular sovereignty in the sense that the whole people are ultimately possessed of the sovereign power. His solution is found in the principle of representation, for his philosophy is made to accord with the machinery of the Constitution under which he lived. It is true that he often speaks in exalted language of the supremacy of law, the great mediaeval conception, but that law has become the expression of the conscious sovereign will of the whole people, as declared in their representative assemblies. Thus far it is completely true that he does furnish a philosophic explanation and defence of the Tudor rule: but, more important for subsequent history, he has given birth to an idea of tremendous importance—the idea of the State's own personality and sovereignty. Thus it is that, for all he may say of consent and the original rights of the

---

[1] *The History of Passive Obedience since the Reformation* (Amsterdam, 1689), pp. 29, 30. Written by Abednego Seller (Hearne's *Collections* I, 86.)

people, these ideas could never with him lead to their practical assertion by force, as they were to do in the century that followed him.

It has therefore to be admitted that Hooker is not one of the most consistent thinkers, and that there are two voices often to be heard. What change of tone there is between the early and later books may in part, perhaps, be due to revision by subsequent hands—though, as far as present certain knowledge goes, this must remain unproved. It seems indubitable that in some places the indecision of view is Hooker's own. After all, he is typically English in the desire not to push things to an extremity. Nor is he a casual opportunist, producing a *livre de circonstance*. He is defending the Elizabethan Settlement, which, in any event, was a compromise, and it is not unnatural that one aspect should sometimes be more present to his mind than another. Yet in all the process of contemporary history he has a vivid conception of Divine Providence, and sees the English Reformation *sub specie aeternitatis*. For Tudor England was no place for clear-cut theory, and when, as with James I, logic dominated the field, disasters came apace. But books, like the aggregation of not wholly consistent legal decisions, make precedents and sow seeds. More than he realized, Hooker had his feet in two camps—that of Divine Right and that of Contractual Theory. A contemporary tract describes him, with great discrimination, as a " solid Hooker, so skilful that, with only one hook, he fisheth of both sides ".[1] To take another example, he undoubtedly did, in various passages, emphasize the importance of consent—as when he writes, " The assent of them who are governed seemeth necessary " [2]—though any real exercise of that consent would have horrified him; but Maitland holds that in so writing he " was doing what was of more importance to the world than he can have been aware of ".[3]

In the course of time James II disappeared, and with him heredity as a principle of the right to rule. The substitute was the consent of the people for the time being, who contracted to be governed, but only so far and by whom they should be willing. To challenge the right of Parliament to alter the succession is to this day high treason; [4] and he who argues that Parliament does not represent the people is liable to be committed for contempt. The legal position is unusually clear. Henceforward England was to be

---

[1] *Treatise of Ecclesiastical and Political Power* (London, 1612). This tract is a translation of Edmond Richer's *Libellus de ecclesiastica et politica potestate*; the translator, who signs himself : Δ_1 is unknown.

[2] *E.P.*, I, x, 4.

[3] *Collected Papers*, I, 14.

[4] 6 Anne, c. 41.

ruled by a Parliamentary majority, and Locke (Hooker's disciple) provided a philosophic basis for the divine right of majorities to rule. Now, Maitland had no difficulty in showing that a man continually in the minority was no more free from obeying laws to which he had not consented than one under the rule of the most absolute despot; [1] nor, although in Sir Thomas Smith's day every man had been " intended " to be present in the Parliament, could the eighteenth-century Parliament be said to represent the whole people. Indeed, if England was then a democracy, it was something of the Athenian kind, and not of the " American " variety, which so startled the gentry of the next century, but which was implicit in the teaching of the contractualists. It was implicit in their teaching because any theory of original contract demands an admission of the equality of man. Hooker might have held it upon the ground of men's equal facility for discovering the Law of Nature, Hobbes might base it upon the equal capacity of men to harm each other, Rousseau and the Romantics upon an equal facility for pain; but with the contract theory it was an axiom. The continual tendency in politics was to be the enfranchisement of more and more of the population, on the ground of the equal right of all to consent to laws by which they should be bound. Gladstone's declaration is the logical outcome of the contractual position—" I contend that it is on those who say it is necessary to exclude forty-nine fiftieths of the working classes that the burden of proof rests. Every man who is not presumably incapacitated by some consideration of personal unfitness or political danger, is morally entitled to come within the pale of the Constitution ". [2] This again is closely consistent with the Third Article of the Declaration of the French Revolutionaries—" The principle of every sovereignty resides essentially in the nation. No body of men, no single individual can exercise authority which does not expressly issue from thence." Maitland believes that " if this had been presented as a naked proposition . . . even Hooker would have accepted it ". [3] Though he would doubtless have qualified his acceptance, the probability that may be drawn from his works that he would have accepted it gives him an undoubted share in the responsibility for the slow but steady approach to the present position of our constitution. It is precisely this—the position of democracy as we know it—that is directly challenged in our day. That the challenge might well come was foreseen by Sir Henry Maine as long ago as 1885. In

---

[1] " Essay on Liberty " in *Collected Papers* (Cambridge, 1911, Vol. I).
[2] Quoted Trevelyan's *British History in the Nineteenth Century* (Longmans, 1937) p. 343.
[3] Maitland, " On Liberty," *Collected Papers*, I, 68.

the heyday of our national prosperity and pride, when the peoples of Europe were admiring and copying the English Constitution, he sounded a note of warning.[1]   In delivering the Rede Lecture at Cambridge in 1901, at the height of Imperialistic zeal only little abated by the South African War, Maitland spoke of the dangers and difficulties which might arise from diverse development of the Common Law in different colonies.   The challenge and the danger have come.   There is a finality in the last extension of the franchise, as though of the natural completion of a struggle of 700 years. It was accepted with little excitement, a move in the weary party game;   the crowds did not cheer, and very few books were written about it.   But it was the last triumph, the ultimate extent of the franchise, the freedom to choose the laws by which one will be governed.

Democracy thus reached its logical completion in a universal franchise, but not its perfection in an ideal State.   It has produced bitter enemies in the totalitarian Governments which have restored the reign of fear to Europe;   their principles have been inhumanity and ruthless expedience for the glory of the nation.   These despots asked, as it were, the same question as Maine put: " To what end, towards what ideal state, is the process of stamping upon law the average opinion of an entire community directed? " [2]   While even Maitland considered that democratic government is less oppressive and capricious only because it is unwieldy.[3]

These present years are therefore fraught with considerable danger to the British Constitution as it has been handed down and developed by various generations.   Issue was joined in war with the totalitarian States, but it is not impossible that some of their principles may subtly invade Britain's post-war constitution, as making for greater efficiency.   In the economic sphere of our national life this has now come about: there is considerable regimentation of industry and commerce, typical of the twentieth century, but well enough known to the men of early Tudor England.[4]

But it is with law, not economics, that we are here concerned, and if all that has been won at so much cost is not to be abandoned to the fury of theorists, dangers and difficulties must be faced.   Our democracy has developed into its present shape by the influence of the Law of Nature—the principle of reason—and of the principle of consent.   These have been the real checks on Government; but there is involved what Maitland calls " the jural conception of

[1] *Popular Government* (London, 1885).
[2] Op. cit., p. 35.
[3] Maitland, op. cit., p. 85.
[4] E.g., Froude, *H.E.* (Longmans, 1870), Vol. I, chap. 1.

morality ",[1] the likelihood, that is, of conflict between civil and natural law, between the State and morality.

" The most certain token of evident goodness is, if the general persuasion of all men do so account it." [2]   Now, as the system by which the general persuasion of all men makes itself felt has improved, as the doctrine of government by consent has taken a stronger hold, there has been an increasing tendency to regard the legislature as voicing " the general and perpetual voice of men " and, therefore, " as the sentence of God Himself ".[3]   Professor Dicey summed up the legal conclusion in these words: " The plain truth is that our tribunals uniformly act on the principle that a law alleged to be a bad law is *ex hypothesi* a law, and therefore entitled to obedience by the Courts." [4]   The vulgar conclusion is that moral law and statute law cannot conflict. Figgis has pointed out how aggrieved constitutionalists are at the suggestions that the State may sanction or order anything which may reasonably be regarded as morally wrong.[5]   This is undoubtedly one of the dangers to which Christian morals are exposed under any kind of government other than the united temporal and spiritual sovereignty which Hooker envisaged. And in its development it is, as we have seen, due in part to the increased weight given to a decree of the Government because it is taken to be an embodiment of the persuasion of the people. To another danger closely allied—that of Church and State—we shall have occasion to refer later. The danger of a renewed ascendancy of the Executive over the Legislature, contrary to the principles of Locke and of 1688, is clearly set forth in a book written by the late Lord Hewart, Lord Chief Justice of England.[6] But difficulties of such nature are to be dealt with in the traditional English manner, by persuasion, not force, in reform, not revolution; for they are infinitely less than the problems thrust upon us by the totalitarian States.

Hooker's second claim on the public interest lies in his position as the greatest apologist of the Church of England, supreme in his own day and unchallenged ever since. For Hooker England was itself a *Respublica Christiana*, both omnipotent and sacred, and its main purpose was the preservation of true religion. He would maintain that this identification is possible only where a State accepts this end, and required uniformity to secure it. Consequently, he would, with Marsiglio, admit that when a State is not thus professedly Christian, the Church—that is, those who boast

[1] *Collected Papers*, I, 23.   [2] *E.P.*, I, viii, 3.   [3] *Ibid.*
[4] *Law of the Constitution* (London, 1893), p. 60.
[5] *Churches in the Modern State*, Lecture I.
[6] *The New Despotism* (Benn, 1919).

the true religion—will regard itself as an independent and self-governing body, a *societas perfecta*. But, if the State be Christian, the true religion will be established and uniform, permitting no religious liberty save *in foro conscientiae*. It is logical, therefore, for Hooker to deny a right of real existence to any merely human organization, though he was arguing realistically, upholding the Settlement in difficult times. But beyond doubt he was in line with the Statute of Appeals, and was unconsciously assisting to lay the foundation of the modern omnicompetent State—his logical position is not far off that of Hobbes. From Gardiner to Hooker the question was made one of sovereignty and obedience. John, asks Gardiner, is subject to his King, as a citizen; is he not still subject as a Christian? " Our question," says Hooker, " is of dominion. . . . Suppose that to-morrow the power which hath dominion in justice require thee at the court; that which in war, at the field; that which in religion, at the temple; all have equal authority over thee." [1] It was the answer to Roman and Puritan alike. There was no place for divided allegiance in the Tudor State, and these writers unconsciously make the argument one of politics, in the name of national unity, against those who demanded independence for the Church; and unwittingly they were foreshadowing the modern Sovereign State. In Hooker, as F. D. Maurice said, as little as in Elizabeth, was there any inclination to a mere balance of opinions. " Both were alternately intolerant, and the best and most effective champions of toleration against those who would have made the existence of it impossible." [2] Whitgift had begun the Anglican defence by revealing the virtual identity of Roman and Puritan outlook, and could bring a charge against them in common that they were obstructing national sovereignty. Bancroft followed this lead, but Hooker went beyond them all in portraying a Sovereign State, united and one, possessing a national conscience, faithful to the Christian fundamentals. In his hands the State becomes the sole *persona*, but he has reconciled Christian ideals and the political conscience.

The Church in England before the Reformation had been in no real sense national. It was in the nation but not of it, being an organic part of the Western Church, and independent of the secular State. This Church, which possessed the Vicegerent of God as its head, claimed dominion over kings, and precisely in this lies the origin of the rivalry between Church and State. There was no ecclesiastically organized body, as Maitland points out,[3] answering

[1] *E.P.*, VIII, ii, 18.
[2] F. D. Maurice, *Moral and Metaphysical Philosophy*, II, 192.
[3] *Canon Law in the Church of England* (London, 1898), e.g., p. 100.

to the name of the Church of England; the tie which linked bishops in England together was that which likewise bound them to French and Spanish bishops—there was no other. Had there been a Church of England it would have been an *imperium in imperio*—no Thomas Becket could have challenged a King of England, and a national Church would have been unsuccessful in its pretensions against such monarchs as Henry II and Edward III. The Western Church was a theocratic State of which the Church in England was a vital part and branch, but with the independence of the whole. This Western Church was a State possessing its own laws, law courts, lawyers and law-givers; it could compel men to obedience, for it had police and prisons, and was able by excommunication to deprive men of their civil status; it could even pronounce sentence of death; its financial income was derived from tithe and taxation; its Supreme Appellate Court was "foreign", and its highest officers were appointed by this same foreign central Power.[1] All this factual situation is declared right and proper in law by Bracton, who writes: "Among men there are differences in status because some men are pre-eminent and preferred and rule over others. Our Lord the Pope, for instance, is pre-eminent in matters spiritual which relate to the priesthood, and under him are Archbishops, Bishops and other inferior prelates. Also in matters temporal there are Emperors, Kings and rulers in matters relating to the Kingdom, and under them Dukes, Counts, Barons, magnates or vavasours and Knights." Now Maitland and Bracton were lawyers, and it has to be admitted that their clear-cut legalistic view is in need of qualification. We are bound to recall the sturdy refusal of earls and barons to change the law of England and legitimatize bastards, even though the Bishops urged that English law on this matter was directly against the common order of the Church;[2] and, for another example, the royal influence in nominating bishops. Yet even if the independence of the mediaeval Church in England is by the legal mind to some degree overstated, the picture would appear, in the main, true enough.

At the Reformation, therefore, the Church in this country was violently and decisively removed from membership of this theocratic State by the hands of King and laity, most probably against the will of the mass of the clergy.[3] The strife of laity and clergy was of ancient

[1] Maitland, *ibid.*
[2] 1235. 20 Henry IV. cap. 9.
[3] The Jesuit Robert Parsons, writing in 1596 (*Jesuit's Memorial*, ed. Edward Gee (1690), p. 193), quotes from Tertullian to show the antiquity of the distinction between clergy and laity, and " the antiquity of that hatred and emulation which our times have received between these two States, to the infinite hurt and prejudice of God's Catholic Church ".

date and may, indeed, not yet be wholly extinct. Froude is perhaps guilty merely of over-emphasis when he writes: "The original Reformation was a revolt of the laity against the clergy, a revolt against a complicated and all-embracing practical tyranny . . . based on an assumption . . . that the Church was the source of all authority, secular as well as spiritual." [1] The decisive nature of the cleavage is seen in the fact that the Supreme Head of the Church was dethroned, and another—a layman—took the Pope's place; that much of the Church Law was abrogated—although a good deal remained and remains in force—and future legislation forbidden; that its Courts paled before the Courts of the King, even though for limited purposes, chiefly matrimonial and testamentary causes, they were to continue to function till 1857; that the secular National State became the Law-maker and Law-giver for the severed Church, even if Convocation retained a restricted power of legislation; that the higher officers of the Church were appointed by the State, and its doctrine came within the purview and control of the State. Thus the independence of the Church in this country was removed —it became an *imperium* within the State, and in law and constitution completely subject to it. Consequently, legally and constitutionally (though not spiritually nor historically), there emerged a new institution; and the motivating forces were national consciousness (which was so potent that the organization of the mediaeval Western Church could not stand before it), the will and personality of the Monarch, and economic capitalism. The severity of the break with the past was concealed by the skill of Tudor Sovereigns and statesmen, who appeal in magnificent phrases in the preambles of various Statutes to bygone history when English kings had been independent Sovereigns, reigning over Church and State alike, until much of their power had been subtly filched from them by the Popes. This falsification would not of itself have secured the historic continuity of Christianity in this country; but the retention of the Scriptures, of the decrees of the first Four Councils, the Sacraments, the three orders of the Ministry, with the declaration that the Reformed Church was now on all fours with primitive Christianity, was now again what once it had been, purged of abuse—all this, beyond question, both softened the blow of secession and assured the continuity of Christian faith and worship in this land as the desire and purpose of the people. The historic succession did not depend on the Papacy or on any mechanical theory of Apostolic Succession, nor was it inherent in the clerical estate; it was inherent in the people (the argument both of Marsiglio and of Jewel) under their godly Prince. This is

[1] Froude, *Lectures on the Council of Trent* (1896), pp. 4, 5.

Q

really the opinion of Hooker also, who declared that the Church is a
" politic society ", a perpetual corporation with " power of providing for itself " ; [1] and his Church meant the people of England,
and the people meant the Church.

For the sixteenth-century divines rejected as unhistorical the
claim that acceptance of the Papacy was necessary to the Catholic
Church. Papal supremacy was a late development in Christian
history, unknown to the Great Councils. Obviously, if the Papacy
is the *esse* of the Church, then Rome was and is right—though it is
her weakness to be at once plaintiff and judge in her own cause.
But if it is not so, as Jewel and Hooker insisted, then the English
Reformation is historically justified, and Anglicans to-day need not
fear to maintain the Catholicity of the Church of England on the
bases laid down in the sixteenth century. This led Anglican writers
to the allied opinion that the laity were justified in insisting that they
were an active and effective part of the Church, competent to ignore
and override a hostile Convocation, as they did in 1559. This
position—as against the papal claim of supremacy and the claim of
the clergy to be the Church—was reinforced by appeal to the Old
Testament on behalf of the godly Prince and his authority over the
Church; a view that lay at the basis of sixteenth-century thought,
and not only in Protestant countries. For Spanish monarchs like
Philip II and Isabella were fully convinced of their royal authority
over the Church, and the French concordats with Rome are
evidence that a similar view prevailed in France.

No narrower view was tenable; the continuity of the Church in
this country was not in essence, therefore, dependent on Parker's
consecration [2] and the retention of bishops. Indeed, it is well known
that such prelates as Cranmer [3] and Barlow held that, in case of

---

[1] *E.P.*, VII, xiv, 3.

[2] An interesting book has been recently published by a Catholic writer, J. C.
Whitebrook (Mowbrays, 1945), to which a reply has been made by the present
writer (S.P.C.K. 1948) *sub titulo* " Elizabeth's First Archbishop."

[3] Cf. Strype: " One of the very first things that was done in young King
Edward the Sixth's reign, in relation to the Church, was, that the bishops, who
had the care of ecclesiastical matters, and the souls of men, should be made to
depend entirely upon the King and his Council, and to be subject to suspension
from their office, and to have their whole episcopal power taken from them at his
pleasure. . . . In this I suppose the Archbishop had his hand; for it was his
judgment, that the exercise of all episcopal jurisdiction depended upon the Prince;
and that, as he gave it, so he might restrain it at his pleasure. And therefore he
began this matter with himself, petitioning, ' That as he had exercised the
authority of an Archbishop during the reign of the former King; so that authority
ending with his life, it would please the present King Edward to commit unto him
that power again.' For it seemed that he would not act as Archbishop, till he
had a new commission from the new King for so doing." (*Memorials of Cranmer*
(Oxford, 1832), Vol. I, Bk. ii, pp. 201-2. And see further, op. cit., II, Appendix,
pp. 744-51. " The Solution of some Bishops to certain Questions about the
Sacraments.")

necessity, the King could of himself validly appoint bishops without consecration. Political opinion argued that Elizabeth could have established the Church without Episcopacy, and none could have challenged it.[1] Jewel nowhere claims that bishops are essential, and Hooker would surely content himself to describe Episcopacy as of human institution with divine approbation,[2] a formula which would cover equally State officials and Civil Servants.[3] Moreover, the Tudor Church of England had friendly and warm relations with the Continental Reformed Churches, and in the Treaty of Berwick (1586) between Elizabeth and James VI the religions of the two countries are regarded as being in agreement.[4] Men like Whittingham, Dean of Durham, Travers, Saravia,[5] and Casaubon[6] could hold office in the Anglican Church with non-episcopal ordination.[7] During Elizabeth's reign the English Embassy at Paris possessed no chaplain, Mark Pattison notes, and English Ambassadors attended the Reformed Church.[8] John Morrison, a minister of the Reformed Church of Scotland, was in 1582 licensed to officiate throughout the Province of Canterbury, the licence taking express notice of his Presbyterian ordination.[9] The licence was issued by Dr. Aubrey, a civilian, who then exercised the office of Vicar-General, nominated by the Queen, in the time when Archbishop Grindal was under a sequestration. Bancroft, Archbishop of Canterbury, deemed it unnecessary to ordain first to the diaconate and priesthood the Scottish presbyters who in 1610 were consecrated bishops. Andrewes may have desired the preliminary ordinations, as Burnet says, but was overruled by King James, " who thought it went too far towards the unchurching of all

---

[1] Strype: *Whitgift*, III, 222.

[2] *E.P.*, VII, xi, 10.

[3] *Ibid.* The cynical Smectymnus says episcopacy "was not of Apostolical intention but of Diabolical occasion." [*Answer to Remonstrance*, p. 29.]

[4] Makower, *Constitutional History of the Church of England* (Sonnenschein, 1895), pp. 113-4, 178, 181.

[5] " It has been said that Saravia was, contrary to the usual practice of the time, re-ordained when admitted to benefices in England. Diocesan registers have been examined and all likely sources of information explored for some notice of his having received episcopal ordination, but without success. Had he done so, it could scarcely have escaped comment from friend and foe. . . . Further, if Saravia had been re-ordained, Morton, Bishop of Durham, an intimate friend of Hooker, could not have written, as he did in 1620, that re-ordination under like circumstances ' could not be done without very great offence to the reformed Churches, and that he did not choose to be the originator of such a scandal ' " (*D.N.B.* Article (*sub.* Saravia)).

[6] Mark Pattison: *Isaac Casaubon* (Oxford, 1892).

[7] For a full discussion of this, see Child, *Church and State under the Tudors* (Longmans, 1890), pp. 293-304.

[8] Pattison, op. cit., p. 420 n.

[9] Strype's *Grindal* (Oxford 1821), pp. 402-3; Collier, *Eccles. Hist.* (London, 1840), VI, 639.

those who had no Bishops among them ".[1] The Thirty-Nine Articles nowhere require Episcopacy as of the *esse* of a Church, but are satisfied that the Anglican Orders of ministry are agreeable to Scripture.

All contemporary evidence goes to prove that the Anglican Church was built upon King and people; and retained all that was ancient and venerable and agreeable to English custom and usages— " to avoid as far as possible the appearance of innovation and to draw all imperceptibly into the new camp ".[2] Any emphasis upon Episcopacy was due to a desire to strengthen the Anglican position against the Puritans, not to erect it as the *esse* without which a Church would forfeit its title to validity.

The vital and creative factor was the Royal Supremacy symbolizing the unity of the National English State in its secular and spiritual aspects. The Supremacy was as proper to Kings of England as to Kings of Israel. History guaranteed it, reason demanded it; against powerful enemies none but the King could supply the unifying force. It inhered in him personally by virtue of his office, and Acts of Supremacy but affirmed a fact which the Word of God had declared of kings long centuries before.

Doubtless to opponents it might appear as stated by Dr. Burn, " There was no branch of sovereignty with which the princes of this realm . . . were more delighted than that of being the Supreme Head of the Church, imagining (as it seemeth) that all that power which the Pope claimed . . . was . . . annexed to the imperial crown of this realm . . . and those princes . . . seem to have considered themselves plainly as popes in their own dominions." [3] But to the Anglican it was every way most consonant with history, for, as Hooker wrote, " That which as Kings they might do in the matter of religion, and did in matter of false religion . . . the same they are now even in every respect as fully authorized to do in all affairs pertinent unto the state of true Christian religion." [4]

If you could assume—as was assumed—that Englishmen were Anglicans, then the nation was a theocracy, soul and body intertwined. Critics might call the resultant Church Erastian, and point out that its establishment rested on the cynical principle of *cuius regio eius religio*, but the authors of the English Reformation defined it proudly and with sound reason as Anglican; neither Eastern, nor Western, nor Protestant Reformed, but in doctrine and order primitive, sanctioned by the laws of the land (which are *ex hypothesi* within the laws of God), maintained, defended, and

---

[1] Burnet, op. cit., I, 139.　　　　[2] Makower, op. cit., p. 177.
[3] Quoted by Browne, *History of Congregationalism*, p. 5.
[4] *E.P.*, VIII, vi, 13.

corrected by the Sovereign Lord of those millions who formed at once Church and State, in accordance with the will of God. As John Sprint,[1] Vicar of Thornbury, conforming to Anglicanism to escape deprivation after a thorough-going Puritan career, wrote in his *Cassander Anglicanus*[2] to persuade others to a like prudence: " The Church of England is the whole society of Englishmen compact in one entire body, visibly possessing the religion of Christ distinguished from the bodies of Scotland, France, Germany and other countries. . . . For the doctrine and practice of the Church of England I take to be that which by common consent of the whole State, King, Nobles, Bishops, Judges, Commons in Parliament, is taught and commanded; whatsoever cometh hence, cometh from the complete body of the Church of England."

But with all its strong foundation and vigorous protection, it is contended that the Anglican Church of the sixteenth century contained grave seeds of disruption within it. Any alliance between Church and State had been condemned by Milton in cruelly hard words. " When the Church without temporal support is able to do her great works upon the unforced obedience of men, it argues a divinity about her. But when she thinks to credit and better her spiritual efficacy, and to win herself respect and dread by strutting in the false vizard of worldly authority, it is evident that God is not there, but that her apostolic virtue is departed from her, and hath left her key-cold; which she perceiving as in a decayed nature, seeks . . . to worldly help . . . to hatch a counterfeit life with the crafty and artificial heat of jurisdiction. But it is observable, that so long as the Church, in true imitation of Christ, can be content to ride upon an ass. . . in her humility all men with loud hosannas will confess her greatness. But when, despising the mighty operation of the Spirit by the weak things of this world, she thinks to make herself bigger and more considerable, by using the way of civil force and jurisdiction . . . instead of hosannas every man pelts her with stones and dirt."[3] In less harsh frame an Anglican Archdeacon expressed a not dissimilar view. One hundred and fifty years ago Paley reasoned, " The making of the Church an engine, or even an *ally* of the State; converting it into the means of strengthening or of diffusing influence; or regarding it as a support of regal in opposition to popular forms of government have served only to debase the institution, and to introduce into it numerous corruptions and abuses."[4] In our own day Toynbee has argued that considerable spiritual impoverishment has befallen

---

[1] Died 1623.   [2] (London, 1618), p. 265.
[3] *Reason of Church Government*, Prose Works (ed. St. John), II, 489.
[4] Paley: *Moral Philosophy* (1790), Vol. II, Bk. VI, p. 305.

Churches in those countries where they became subservient to political power. "We are still re-acting against a subordination of Religion to Politics which was the crime of our XVIth and XVIIth century forebears. The policy of *cuius regio eius religio* is avenging itself up to the hilt." [1] And Sturzo denounces this political principle as " an offence both to the personal right of every man not to be forced to accept a religion as a legal duty sanctioned by punitive laws, and to that of the Christian religion in its Catholicity to expand in every place." [2] This " monstrous " doctrine was itself in part an outcome of the gathering to themselves by National Kings of the Pope's authority as the Vicar of God, known to history as the Divine Right of Kings. But perhaps the results in this country have been less disastrous than elsewhere, less debasing and enfeebling than Milton or Paley feared, neither of whom could ever have foreseen how the genius of Englishmen could cause their national institutions to develop and evolve, innocent for the most part of violent pangs either of birth or death. It may not be denied that in the reigns of Henry VIII and Elizabeth the Anglican Church was by Crown with the assent of Parliament established in accordance with this principle. But it was a very wise and wide Church that was set up, adherence to which can have violated the consciences of relatively few. It was not a harsh tyranny unless and until religious dissent could be equated with political disloyalty. Its " Articles " might be in Calvinistic strain, but its Prayer-book was Catholic, and down the centuries room has been found within it for many types of religious genius. Moreover, the inbred sturdiness of the English character would never for long accept the attempted tyranny of a Laud, though Anglican Church-manship would for the time be sapped of some of its vigour in the quietude and subservience of the eighteenth century, when cynical politicians would utilize the Church for their political purposes. From the days of Elizabeth the *Ecclesia Anglicana* has been a Church of compromise in doctrine as in jurisdiction, but an eminent authority has told us that compromise (so odious to passionate and intellectual natures alike) may well be both just and profitable in religion. The Englishman has found it so. " The Englishman finds that he was born a Christian, and therefore wishes to remain a Christian; but his Christianity must be his own, no less plastic and adaptable than his inner man; and it is an axiom with him that nothing can be obligatory for a Christian which is unpalatable to an Englishman." [3]

[1] Toynbee, *Study of History*, V, 671.
[2] *Church and State* (London, 1939), p. 242.
[3] Santayana: *Soliloquies in England* (New York, 1923), pp. 83, 84.

It must be admitted that in this present day over the whole of Europe the influence of the Church has notably diminished under the sway of the intense nationalism of the twentieth century. Yet at all events it is not in England, but in those countries most historically connected with the Empire of the Papacy, that the cruellest despotisms of this century have flourished. It is this grim fact that destroys the blandishments of such writers as Christopher Dawson [1] and Algernon Cecil [2] when they invite men to return to the bosom of the Pope as the sole hope for the salvation of Europe. In the Middle Ages the Roman Church was totalitarian, it denied freedom to individuals and to minorities, and there is no reason to think matters would be much otherwise to-day.

For it is the individual and the corporation whose existence is at stake to-day. The Christian view is that the individual is a free *persona*, the recognition of his value as an eternal being; he has real existence independently of the State, and possesses rights that may not be invaded. What is true of him is true of the Church itself, and of minorities. The duty of the Christian Church is to struggle to preserve those freedoms. Certainly Hooker never faced the question what was to be done with this particular " seed of disruption "—namely, the existence of the individual and of religious minorities. The Anglican Church of his time rested upon the hypothesis that all Englishmen were Anglicans, and that therefore dissent indicated treason. The hypothesis was not true, or anywhere near the truth, even then, and became less and less true. But dissent was at least as potent a seed of disruption as the principle on which the Anglican Church was established. Hooker's citizens were Papists, Presbyterians, Independents, and yet proved their political loyalty. He avoided the problem, and ultimately history provided the only possible answer in toleration; [3] religious tests were by degrees abolished, until to-day their sum total consists of the prohibition of Roman Catholicism to the King and the Lord Chancellor. In our day it is realized that the breakdown of the Elizabethan Church—the work of Independency and Cromwell—was in fact salutary; had it been otherwise English history might have known enduring ecclesiastical tyranny, a Charles I and Laud the equivalent of Louis XIV and Maintenon. Later generations have come to perceive that these religious minorities are precious

---

[1] See, e.g., *Religion and the Modern State.*

[2] See, e.g., *Metternich* (Eyre and Spottiswoode, 1943), and *A House in Bryanston Square* (Eyre and Spottiswoode, 1944).

[3] When in 1689 Nonconformity secured its right to exist, receiving at the hands of Wesley and Whitfield in the eighteenth century a host of new recruits. Political equality was extended to Nonconformists in 1828, to Roman Catholics in 1829, and to Jews in 1858.

in the life of a nation, while Hooker would have compelled them to
outward conformity to ensure the undisturbed oneness of the State,
for he never foresaw the dangers of the State Leviathan.[1] But
such minorities proclaim by their very existence that they are real
" persons ", that societies can live within the larger Society of the
State by virtue of inherent right to live and grow, that the State
itself is not therefore a unique fact, the supreme and sole object
of its members' worship and devotion, able to exact blind obedience
and unquestioning subservience. And, from the other angle, the
State's recognition of the Free Churches has destroyed once and for
all that identification, in any numerical sense, of the Church with
the State of England, which Elizabethan apologists regarded as
vital.

The other twin pillar on which Hooker's argument was based was
the personal Supremacy of the Monarch. The existence of religious
minorities and the growth of unbelief have removed the first pillar,
while the transfer to Parliament of the Crown's prerogatives has
varied the second. The Royal Supremacy up to the date of the
abolition of the Court of High Commission enjoyed and exercised
ecclesiastical powers as wide as those exercised by the Royal prerogative over the secular State. The seventeenth century found so
extensive a prerogative hostile to liberty, with the result that the
same century saw the Crown's dispensing power limited at the
Revolution. Finally the growth of Parliament and the evolution of
the Cabinet have placed the ecclesiastical supremacy in the hands of
the Ministry of the day. The " godly Prince " could be defended
by Scripture, history and reason as the paramount ruler of the
Church; but the Fathers of the Church of England of the sixteenth
and seventeenth centuries might argue—as Gardiner and Bonner
protested that the Council of Edward VI could not wield his
ecclesiastical supremacy—that the Lordship of the House of
Commons is sheer usurpation, indefensible on any ground. Yet
the Supremacy which was once the personal prerogative of Henry
and Elizabeth—and in virtue of which even William III issued
injunctions—is still a real fact of the Constitution, however unseemly
its present repository may be deemed. This topic has furnished
recent history. In 1927 and 1928 proposed revisions of the Book
of Common Prayer were rejected by the House of Commons, and
much was made of the fact that that body included Nonconformists,
Papists and Atheists. These rejections, not unnaturally, accelerated
the demand for Disestablishment. It is both interesting and
incumbent upon us to consider what position Hooker would have
taken up, but before doing so it is to be noted that it is at least

[1] E.g., *E.P.*, V, lxviii, 7.

arguable that Parliament by this action did the Church a service. For it now seems clear that neither proposed Book would, in fact, have ultimately gratified the members of the Church of England as a whole. Revision in the main then tended to one direction, due to causes which no longer obtain, while to-day there would not be that same emphasis. The Church of England possesses weaknesses enough, but it is conceivable that it would be weaker at this moment had Parliament accepted either proposed book. The debates in Parliament on those occasions reached a high order, and revealed that the Houses took most seriously their position in relation to the Church. Lay opponents of the Revised Prayer Book have been abused [1] for scrutinizing matters of doctrine alleged to be contained in the book, but they were acting in accordance with their constitutional rights, and if there were in fact changes of doctrine proposed in the book, then, both by the Elizabethan Act of Supremacy and by the Enabling Act of 1919, members were justified in causing them to be discussed.

Hooker was, as we have seen, a realist, and his philosophy in largest measure was derived from the facts of his day. He had also a consummate sense of historical process and development, as when he writes, " In these things the experience of time may breed both civil and ecclesiastical change from that which hath been before received, neither do latter things always violently exclude former, but the one growing less convenient than it hath been, giveth place to that which is now become more." [2] It is conceivable that on these grounds he would defend the present Supremacy, and resist the demand for Disestablishment. He might well argue that the Church is the abiding witness to the nation of its eternal destiny, and that as the State still professedly embraces Christianity, the Church of England is the Church of the nation; [3] if now less a reality, still something of a symbol of " the religious consecration of social life ".[4] Let it be admitted that the active members of the Church may be but some five million or so; none the less, he would point to the fact that there is a nominal adherence of five or six times that number, very many of whom hold the Christian faith at least " in gross ". At all events, the Church is not the Church of those five millions only; its history, the widespread national interest at the time of the Revised Prayer Books, its nominal membership, and its Churches overseas are all evidence to prove a wider loyalty. Further, the State is still professedly Christian, and still possesses a godly Prince, who must be a member of the Church;

---

[1] Henson, *Retrospect of an Unimportant Life* (Oxford, 1944), II, 173.
[2] *E.P.*, VII, xiv, 7.   [3] Cf. *E.P.*, VIII, i, 2.
[4] Sturzo, op. cit., p. 68.

the Church of this State is still therefore inherent in the Prince and the People, until formally rejected. Again, in the sixteenth century it was in Hooker's eyes a fundamental fact that in Parliament was the Assembly of the whole people, and that all laws affecting any part of the national life must be passed by Crown in Parliament. If in the sixteenth century every man could be " intended " to be present in Parliament, how much more so may he be thought to be there in the twentieth, when democracy has furnished the adult vote? The mere fact that the process of history has transferred to the Cabinet what was once the ecclesiastical prerogative of Elizabeth no more destroys the nature of the Church of England than the transfer of the prerogative of mercy to the Home Secretary jeopardizes the life of any individual. The ultimate sovereignty of the realm is in the whole people, a united living organism, which delegates the exercise of its sovereign power. In the sixteenth century that power was delegated to the Monarch, who recognized the ultimate sovereignty of the people by co-operating in legislation with their representatives. In the intervening centuries, and with the development of the historical process, the people have delegated the exercise of sovereign powers to the Cabinet, and among those powers is the right of jurisdiction over the Church of England. Hooker would realize, of course, that the omnicompetent State has emerged into reality; if it purposed to dethrone Christianity, then the Church must withdraw itself as a *societas perfecta*. But until the State determines to act in that manner, Hooker would conclude that the Church must remain the Church of the State, for the purpose of keeping the latter true to its moral and religious purposes. Deliberately to forsake it, because the flow of history has wrought constitutional changes, would be escapism on the part of the Church, and might well doom the State to pursue only material ends, to its ultimate destruction.

Or it may well be that Hooker, having regard to the diminution in numbers of the Church of England and the toleration of Free Churches, would support the view advanced by Warburton [1] in 1736.[2] Warburton saw that the sixteenth-century fiction of the identity of Church and State could no longer be maintained. They were not composed of the same people; England was no longer one Society under two aspects, each controlled by its respective officers. But nevertheless he insisted that the Church possessed its own inherent sovereignty, as did the State; and he accordingly argued that the true relationship between these sovereign and independent societies should be a free alliance for the advantages of both. The State could claim the right to make alliance with that Church

[1] *Vivebat* 1698–1779.   [2] *Alliance between Church and State.*

whose membership was the largest; in England that would be the
Anglican Church, in Scotland the Presbyterian. This may seem a
realist suggestion, but Warburton would argue that it is defensible on
the ground that the Church of the greatest number would be that
most in accordance with the religious genius of the people. The
Church, being a sovereign body, would be free to initiate legislation
for its internal affairs, while the sovereignty of the State would be
displayed in the right of Parliament to veto such proposed legislation.
This particular theory, in actual fact, became accepted when, in
1919, the Church was permitted by the Enabling Act to legislate
for herself, subject only to the assent or veto of Parliament. Of
course, Warburton did not live to see Parliament thoroughly
secularized, or he might have hesitated to ascribe any degree of
control to it. It was this very secular control of the Church which
shocked the Tractarians and gave such impetus to the Oxford
Movement. Yet even a secular Parliament has a conscience, and
may be deemed capable of respect for the Church. The utter
impossibility of enforcing the Public Worship Regulation Act of
1874 indicates that the State cannot and would not impose its will
against the conscience of the Church. The danger therefore of
Parliamentary tyranny over the Church is negligible compared
with the anarchic dangers of Disestablishment, and seen in the light
of the relations of Parliament with the Church Assembly since 1919.

It is, indeed, highly probable that Hooker would have approved
the Enabling Act of 1919, whereby the Church obtained some
measure of legislating for itself, but he would surely have equally
approved the proviso that such legislation must obtain the consent
of Parliament, on the ground that the Church of England is still the
Church of the people, and the people are present in Parliament with
the right to be consulted and the claim to give assent. " It is a
thing most consonant with equity and reason ", he wrote, " that
no ecclesiastical law can be made in a Christian commonwealth,
without consent as well of the laity as of the clergy." [1] He might
properly feel that even if the Church is now but a minority, and
its supreme Head a " monster ", none the less it is historically the
spiritual life of the nation, something which may well be vital and
precious to millions of nominal Churchmen or even non-Anglicans,
who realize that but for the Church of England the people of
England would not have contributed what they have in fact given
to the world, and would not be what in fundamental character
they are known to be the world over.

This is neither to deny the seriousness of the Church's problems,
nor to suggest that solutions be not pursued. Conflict has arisen,

[1] *E.P.*, VIII, vi, 8.

for example, between Church and State in matters affecting moral conduct. We have seen that what Maitland calls " the jural conception of morality " can produce conflict between the State and the individual. The Established Church cannot hope to escape similar conflict. Thus, to take one example, it is the law of England that where Canon Law conflicts with the Law of the Land the latter shall prevail. It was contrary to Canon Law that a man should marry his deceased wife's sister, and that was the law of the Church of England until in 1946 Convocation promulgated a revised Table of Kindred and Affinity, permitting such a marriage. But as far back as 1907 Parliament had legalized that kind of union, and refusal to recognize its validity on the part of Church authorities gave ground for legal action in the Courts.[1]

Again, the Laws of the Church and the Law of the Land are not in accord on the subject of divorce and remarriage. Admitted that this question bristles with difficulties, it is not impossible that the innocent party, divorced and legally re-married, would have a right of action against those who refused him participation in Anglican religious worship, since a man can hardly be in the eyes of the Law an open and notorious evil liver who does what Statute Law permits and obeys the findings and direction of a High Court judge. And time alone will show whether the decision of the House of Lords in the recent case of *Baxter* v. *Baxter* (December 1947) has or has not furnished a new cause of conflict, arising from a divergence between Church and State as to grounds of nullity. On all grave moral issues the Established Church is faced with clear choices: it can equate its laws with those of the State, as it has tardily done in the matter of the Deceased Wife's Sister Act, though it can hardly do so if it considers that its own laws affirm divine standards; or it can insist on its own law and risk persecution; or it can decide that the subordination of Church Law to State Law in the event of conflict is humiliating to such an extent that the Church must sever itself from the chains that bind it to the policies and expediences of the State.[2]

[1] (Thomson *v.* Dibdin, L.R. 1912. A.C. p. 533.)

[2] Since these words were written in 1943 an Archbishops' Commission has issued (1947) a Report on Canon Law and Proposals for a Revision. Even so it is difficult to see that such Revised Canon Law would remove ground of conflict. Indeed, the Commissioners recognize that any subject of His Majesty aggrieved by proceedings in an Ecclesiastical Court may apply to the High Court for remedy (Canon CXII, *Report*, p. 195, S.P.C.K.). The Commissioners' Proposals cannot become operative without Parliamentary sanction, e.g., *re* Marriage, the new Ecclesiastical Courts, and " lawful authority ", and it is improbable that Parliament would grant such wide powers to Convocation in which there is no House of Laity at all. The Report may therefore prove to be but a step towards Disestablishment, a progress difficult to arrest once any Canon Law Bill is set in motion.

Again, it is an admittedly grave fact that the Church of England, reckoned by the number of " active " members, is but one more minority in the State. The idea of comprehension, for which Hooker strove, has not survived save as a distant and as yet unattainable ideal. Since the time of Dr. Arnold it has found no outstanding advocate. Political nationalism has swept all before it, while religious nationalism has suffered a continuous decline. If we may estimate the Church's numerical adherence by those who are annually baptized and confirmed in it, together with those who make their Easter Communion, its effective membership is not much more than some 5,000,000, as against nominal membership of twenty-five or twenty-six million.[1] Roman Catholics, reviving in the nineteenth century, are said to number about 2,120,000,[2] and Methodists nearly 3,000,000.[2] It may be reasonably debated that a Church thus membered cannot with any accuracy be described as a National Church, even though at its establishment in the sixteenth century it was regarded as comprising the nation, when, nevertheless, penal laws had to be invoked to compel people to come into uniformity, where interest, glory, or conviction failed to persuade.

Can, therefore, a religious minority be said to be national in the sense of reflecting either the Christian or the " educated " outlook of the nation on national or international problems? Does the Established Church, it is asked, *as such*, " enshrine Christian qualities in the life of the nation " more than a Church " free " to determine and proclaim what those qualities are? Is the witness of the Roman Church or of the Free Churches of less value than that of the Anglican? No one can deny the difficulty of the Church of England at once " national and established ", and yet a numerical minority, to provide answers to these questions. But even if it can be no longer described as national from the point of view of numbers, it may still be reasonably maintained to be the National Church in very true sense. Warburton would claim its title was fair on the ground that it is the largest of all Churches. Hooker would reason that whatever its present numerical membership, it is the Divine Society, " with power of providing for itself ", which has existed in this country since Christianity came to our shores. In this sense it is more truly and wonderfully " national ", and down all the ages has been the soul of the nation. It is certain that Hooker would remind the Church of its inherent right to spiritual function, since for this end it exists and is divinely commissioned, especially if with increasing State deification there were

[1] Vide *Official Year Book of the Church of England*, 1939.
[2] Figures taken from *Whitaker's Almanack*, 1939.

danger of the Church's being regarded as the mere ecclesiastical department of the State, inferior to it in time and dignity: but historically and spiritually it has been organically connected with the State as soul with body, and so in Hooker's eyes would remain to-day, irrespective of numbers. He would thus disagree with Thorndike that a national Church is a misnomer unless true in numerical fact.[1] It is the birthright of every Englishman, and continues such unless and until the Englishman is so dead to history that he chooses to exchange his birthright for membership of another communion or lapses into atheism. If the Church of England witnesses, at this moment, no more powerfully for Christ than the Roman Catholic or Free Churches, that is the fault of the Church members themselves, Hooker would properly argue. Lack of vitality cannot be attributed to the *form* of the Church—which was what the State secured in the sixteenth century—but to unawareness of its spiritual origin and spiritual power. Another Reformation may be due—the clergy may be here too wealthy, there too poor; bishops may exhibit too much of the character of " diocesan inspectors "; the parochial system may be out of date; this innovation of a " Church Assembly " may be too completely aristocratic; [2]

---

[1] Thorndike asserted that a National Church is a misnomer unless true in fact. That Erastianism which holds that the Church and its rights exist only by the laws of the land, and that an Englishman is *ipso facto* a member of the Catholic Church is " accursed doctrine ". (He has Hobbes, not Hooker, in mind.) Thorndike advocates toleration of religious minorities, but is all against Comprehension, due to his views on the necessity of Episcopacy. The State is scarcely a *persona* at all for him; hence his assent to Toleration. In so far as the State exists, it is as the handmaid of the Church. The Church is the real *persona*. His ideas are valuable in our day when the tendency is to regard the State as the only *persona*, and nothing else to exist save individuals. (See his *Works*, Oxford, 1844, especially " True Principle of Comprehension ", " The Church's Power of Excommunication ", " Right of the Church in a Christian State ", and " Plea of Weakness and Tender Consciences ".)

[2] It may not be out of place here to point out that the Church of England has had a definite " upper middle-class " character since the Reformation. Brewer (*Reign of Henry VIII*, II, 479), writing in the third quarter of the nineteenth century, remarks, " It is only when political power shall have been transferred to new hands, and new classes shall have supplanted the old, that the Church of England will . . . be called upon to modify its teaching and enlarge its sympathies." Archbishop Benson (see his *Life*, by A. C. Benson) expressed his concern that the Church was so little in touch with the working classes. Political power has now been transferred to the great mass of Englishmen, and it is a matter for regret that the Church's representative machinery is still limited almost exclusively to the leisured, wealthy, and professional classes. For example, an examination of the membership of the House of Laity in the Church Assembly (*Official Year Book of the Church of England*, 1939) shows approximately twelve Lords, seventeen titled ladies, twenty-seven Baronets and Knights, thirty-five Navy and Army officers, fifty professional gentlemen (lawyers, doctors, M.P.s, etc.), fifteen J.P.s, eighty-two who can fairly be described as University or Public School class, sixty-one ladies (some of whom have relations in the Houses of Bishops and of Clergy), out of a total membership of 336. Only about half-a-dozen seem to be of elementary school origin. If working-class people attend the church in any large quantities, this

the Church may have disregarded social evils for all too long, and may be blind to its opportunities; but, Hooker might well ask, will vital reformation of these and other weaknesses be secured merely by disestablishment? Does the historic connexion of the Church with the State embarrass Anglicans to such extent that they are crippled and hindered from desired reformations? If the Church Assembly presented to the Supreme Head a programme of reform, is it conceivable that it would be rejected? So far from its being refused, it is all the more probable that the searching scrutiny and the cordial approval of Parliament would mightily strengthen the hands of the Church. At all events, until the State rejects Christianity the Church of England is still the soul of England's people, Hooker would with propriety conclude; and, sever body from soul, neither shall long remain. "It is no peculiar conceit," he writes, "but a matter of sound consequence, that all duties are by so much the better performed, by how much the men are more religious from whose abilities the same proceed. For if the course of politic affairs cannot in any good sort go forward without fit instruments, and that which fitteth them be their virtues, let Polity acknowledge itself indebted to Religion." [1] In fact, the very safety of all estates in any realm depending upon religion, all well-ordered States will love her as their chiefest stay.[2] Of such a Commonwealth the priest is a pillar.[3]

As there are seeds of weakness within the Church, lessening its spiritual force, so there are problems in its external relations with other Churches. In the sixteenth century the *Respublica Christiana* of Europe yielded to the National States in the vigorous efficiency of their new birth; with the rise of these States, their national Churches and vernacular literatures, mediaeval unity became only a feature of the historic past. For 500 years these States have now endured, no longer "natural" in the Aristotelian sense, but each composed of people of many diverse origins. But with modern scientific discoveries the world has shrunk, and nations realize their interdependence; they can no longer live to themselves, the fortunes of one may affect the fortunes of many. This is obvious in war, and it seems clear that an economic unity or oecumenicalism must come into existence in the not distant future. Political internationalism may be a vision of far-off days, but even from this aspect certain large sections of the world may

---

"representation" is sheer fiction. Possibly this obvious fictitious representation was a prime factor in the rejection of the Revised Prayer Books. The Church must "enlarge its sympathies" and avail itself of the good sense and ability to be found in the non-leisured members.

[1] *E.P.*, V, 1, 2.   [2] *E.P.*, V, i, 5.   [3] *E.P.*, V, lxxvi, i.

come together into some defined degree of accord, although there may seem small ground for considerable optimism in this matter. At all events the need for unity is widely felt, and probably for this very reason the Roman Church will gather considerable accession of strength.

Now, in the Middle Ages political oecumenicalism was possible because there was the fact of religious unity. In the present day the rise of totalitarian States and the paganism of State worship dictate the lively need for Christian Churches to draw together into united strength. It would seem that if non-Roman Christendom is to survive in this century as a spiritual force, the various Churches must come into concord. What separates the Churches cannot be compared in importance with that which ought to unite them. They have one great enemy in common—the cynical materialism of the age.

There are two factors that withhold the Church of England from union with the Free Churches of Britain—those spiritual societies to which so much is owed—and the Protestant Churches of Europe which once were the Church's friends. Episcopacy presents the first difficulty, yet the Anglican Church can hardly in this century, which is full of menace to Christianity's very existence, deny the validity of the Reformed Churches which it acknowledged in the sixteenth. It extended then the hand of fellowship, and for a century welcomed Ministers into its own ranks; [1] not less friendship is required now. Writers like Jewel and Hooker might regret that the Swiss, French, and Dutch Churches were not episcopally administered, but nowhere did they or Anglican formularies insist that episcopacy is the " esse " of a Church.[2] The Elizabethan Fathers deeply regretted the Separatist Movement in this country, where extremists—while admitting the soundness of Anglican

---

[1] Child, op. cit., pp. 293–304.

[2] Stillingfleet cites Hooker to prove that Episcopacy may be primitive, but is not *iure divino*; and is in any State only lawful because established or tolerated. " Those who please but to consult the third book of learned and judicious Mr. Hooker's *Ecclesiastical Polity*, may see the mutability of the form of Church Government largely asserted and fully proved " (*Irenicum* ed. 1661, p. 394). Calamy notes with satisfaction that Hooker asserts no complete particular form of Church polity is fixed in Scripture, and that Episcopacy can be said to be divinely ordained only in the sense that " any kind of government in the world is of God (*Life and Times*, 2 vols., London, 1830, I, 235–46). While these pages were being revised in MS. the enthronement of the present Archbishop took place at Canterbury. The Dean and Chapter felt themselves honoured by the attendance of several ministers of the Reformed Churches. Among them were men who had witnessed and suffered at the hands of the Gestapo for the Christian Faith, such as Bishop Arne Fjellbu of the Norwegian Church, and Pastor Harald Sandbaek of the Danish Church. Ought not the Anglican Church to regard reunion with the Reformed Churches as an honour and glory to itself, so far from its being simply a Christian duty?

doctrine—had unnecessarily weakened the national front on the less important cause of Church government; and seventeenth-century history amply bore out their gloomy prophecies that rebellion in religion would come to revolution in politics. And it was on the ground of national unity and prosperity, not for reason of its essential need, that they implored their Puritan opponents to yield to the episcopal government of the Church as by law established.

The sum of all Hooker's teaching on episcopacy can be thus contained: the Anglican Church is justified by history in retaining that government for herself, as being of an Apostolic origin, and further that this government has been declared part of the Laws of the Realm to be obeyed by loyal Englishmen, but that this is not to say that non-episcopal Churches are not in the full sense of the Church of Christ. Hooker's teaching as to Episcopacy is that of the " middle way " of the Anglican tradition; he declares its value as historic and primitive, but declines to assert an exclusive position for it with the consequent un-churching of non-episcopal bodies. Thus Hooker would welcome those who held the faith " in gross ", all " soldiers of the same Army, enlisted under Heaven's Captaincy " against Wrong, as Carlyle would say,[1] whatever their difference in uniform. So Ussher, twenty-five years after, would define the Catholic Church as " the communion of all nations " [2] united in the three Creeds. It is perhaps unwise in our own day to press as that *esse* something which is incapable of proof in the Primitive Church.[3] Particularly may this be thought to be so when the method of Anglican Episcopal appointment renders it impossible to many minds to accept any *ius divinum* in its Episcopate. A clergyman is nominated by the Prime Minister; the Dean and Chapter of a cathedral are ordered under penalties to " elect " and an Archbishop to consecrate him. To invoke the Holy Spirit in such circumstances might even seem to thoughtful people to take his

[1] *Heroes* (ed. 1897), p. 120.
[2] *A Brief Declaration of the Universality of the Church.* A Sermon preached before the King, 1624.
[3] Cf. Hoadly, Bishop of Bangor, writing to the Lower House of Convocation. He states the harm to the Church in " making the eternal salvation of Christians to depend upon that uninterrupted succession, of which the most learned must have the least assurance, and the unlearned can have no notion, but through ignorance and credulity " (*Answer to the Representation by the Committee of Convocation* 1717, pp. 89-91).
Cf. Alford, who says in reference to the power of the Keys, " This gift belongs to the Church in all ages, and especially to those who by legitimate appointment are set to minister in the Churches of Christ: *not by successive delegation* from the Apostles—*of which fiction I find in the New Testament no trace*—but by their mission from Christ, the Bestower of the Spirit for their office, when orderly and legitimately conferred upon them by the various Churches " (*New Testament for English Readers* (1863); cf. Westcott on St. John, 20. 23).

R

Name in vain, or to imply that the Holy Spirit is bound to accept the Prime Minister's choice. On the other hand, if the State is divine in origin and purpose, and the march of history has transferred ecclesiastical power from King to Minister, the latter may reasonably look for as much divine approbation on his Church appointments as Plantagenet or Tudor kings expected for theirs.

But it is improbable that Hooker would find difficulty in accepting the Prime Minister's nominations as thoroughly valid. He stoutly defends the King's right to appoint, on the common-sense ground that bishops are peers of the realm, and that the King ought properly to enjoy what profits may be derived from appointments and in vacancies, since he, or his predecessors, went to considerable expense in originally establishing episcopal sees.[1] In support of his case he adduces evidences from foreign history.[2] The Capitular election is, in his eyes, entirely nominal and could be omitted; and while he admits a right of the laity in ancient times to approve nominations, that right became too inconvenient for retention. He entirely repudiates the view that justification for royal appointments lies in some " quasi-ecclesiastical " character pertaining to a king crowned and anointed. The King nominates simply because he is supreme over all causes. It is not the nomination but consecration which gives " divine impress ", and this comes from the Church, not from the King. Now, in the process of history and by the will of the people he would recognize this power of nomination as rightly entrusted to the Prime Minister, with the consequence that Anglicans are bound in conscience to submit to this power. For " the power of all sorts of superiors, made by consent of commonwealths within themselves . . . such power is of God's own institution in respect of the kind thereof ".[3] Yet this is not to say that Hooker would insist on *monarchical* Episcopacy as essential. He himself enjoyed the spiritual ministrations of the non-episcopally ordained Saravia, and never denied full validity to the Reformed Churches. On his premisses he would certainly have supported the " Comprehension " schemes of the seventeenth century had they met with Parliamentary approval.

The second obstacle to a wider unity is considered to be the fact of Establishment itself, breeding in many Anglicans a reluctance to surrender a privileged position, redolent of superiority and condescension. Disestablishment is recommended on the ground that it would cure the internal evils of the Church, and would promote

---

[1] *E.P.*, VIII, 7, i–iii.
[2] *E.P.*, VIII, 7, iv.
[3] " Sermon on Civil Obedience," App. to *E.P.*, VIII, p. 458; cf. *E.P.*, VII, xi, 10.

a considerable degree of non-Roman oecumenicalism. Bishop
Henson became the most formidable protagonist of Disestablishment.
He argues that the loss involved in it would be "material and
sentimental . . . the gains would be moral and religious. The
Church would at last be free to direct its own course in spiritual
policy; it would be able to determine its own rules of discipline and
to enforce them; it would be able to cut itself free from the degrading
tradition of clerical ill faith which . . . has in the past done so
much to enfeeble the influence of the clergy, and to alienate the
public conscience; and it would be relieved from the embarrass-
ment and disadvantage of the State connexion when it seeks by
negotiation with other Churches to restore the broken fellowship
of the Christian Society. Disestablishment would inflict on the
Church of England the strain and sacrifice of the difficult transition
from Erastian subordination to spiritual independence, but it would
restore the Church's self-respect, and once more secure from the
nation an audience for its message." [1] The loss would certainly
be material if disendowment followed disestablishment, and there
is much to be said for a thorough investigation of the Church's
endowments and their better and more proportioned distribution.
But for this purpose disestablishment is not itself needed. In the
bishop's view all the evils from which the Church suffers are due
to the Establishment. But this seems altogether too sweeping.
Beyond doubt the Church has inherited difficulties from its State
connexion, but they are susceptible of less drastic remedy. The
better proportioned distribution of property and income is within
the power of the Church Assembly, as is also the subject of clerical
discipline. These and other problems are already engaging the
attention of the Church's leaders. But to describe the Establishment as the sole cause of clerical ill faith, clerical idleness, the
alienation of the laity, and of the feebleness of Christianity in the
country is so gravely to over-emphasize a case as to make of it
nonsense. It may well be asked if the Church of England is more
conspicuously endowed with idle and dissolute clergy than other
Churches, or if the parson's freehold imperils religion more than the
minister's dependence on his congregation? It is not noticeable that
Free Churches are thronged by the devout while the parish churches
of England are empty. Neither is it easy to comprehend what is
particularly meant by the phrase "Erastian subordination". It
scarcely appears to be a burden of which the average parish priest
or diocesan bishop is aware. The State certainly refused the Revised
Prayer Books, and it retains from its kingly predecessors the right
to nominate bishops. There is no evidence that better and abler

[1] H. H. Henson, *The Church of England* (Cambridge, 1939), pp. 55-6.

men would be elevated to the Episcopate were the power of nominating them transferred from Downing Street to Canterbury. It is
not impossible that were that transference made, Lambeth and
Canterbury might witness such clerical intrigue for promotion as is
now admittedly non-existent. " The decease of the former bishop "
might again be " an alarum to such as would labour for the room ".[1]
To argue that the fact of Establishment has lessened the power of
the Church's Gospel message can only mean that individual clergy
have temporized on the message because of preferment they have
secured or hope to secure or because security of tenure has bred
idleness.[2] If that be at all true, the particular clergy are worthy
of condemnation, but scarcely the Established Church itself; in a
disestablished Church the same kind of men would seek whatever
loaves and fishes were to be had, and idleness can be effectively
dealt with by a reformation in discipline. Clerical idleness and
clerical ambition are peculiar neither to the Church of England nor
to the twentieth century. " There are ", Hooker notes with ironic
humour, " that make an idol of their great sufficiency, and because
they surmise the place should be happy that might enjoy them,
they walk everywhere like grave pageants observing whether men
do not wonder why so small account is made of so rare worthiness,
and in case any other man's advancement be mentioned they either
smile or blush at the marvellous folly of the world which seeth
not where dignities should offer themselves." [3] There is therefore
no sound basis to the call for Disestablishment in order that the
Church may effectively preach its message. Rather is it for the
Church to recover that intimate fellowship with the people of
England that it once had, for if the Anglican Church should fail
herein, no other Church can save the nation from paganism.
The Church has displayed vigour enough in this century, but un-
fortunately over liturgical matters and " things indifferent ". Its
prime duty is to teach the Christian faith, in season and out of
season, lest, failing in its trust, the people of this country become
completely secularized.

The only loss, beyond that of property, would be a sentimental
loss, Bishop Henson insists. Apparently the history of the centuries
bears no permanent meaning. What Bishop Henson would call
sentimental, Hooker would describe as vital—the tearing of soul
from body, and the last impetus given to the State to go headlong
to materialistic ruin.

[1] *E.P.*, VIII, 7, vi, quoting from Sidonius.
[2] Burnet warns the clergy that they are the idlest he has met and that unless a
better spirit animate them, " Laws and Authority "—i.e., the Establishment—
will not be strong enough to preserve the Church (op. cit., II, 640–2).
[3] *E.P.*, V, lxxvii, 14.

The Church's internal problems will not be solved by the one stroke of disestablishment. They are remediable by the reformation in life and zeal of the clergy themselves in the first place, followed by reformation in such matters as property distribution, discipline and Church order, the parochial system, a democratic reorganization of the representative Assemblies and so forth. Reformation of all such matters is essential, the spirit of the age demands it, and the Church on the whole is alive to the need. It may well be that the task calls for more urgent attention than is being given to it, and this is undoubtedly so if there is the least truth in the Bishop's condemnation, and if the Church rejects the opinion of Professor Toynbee that its present vitality varies inversely with the degree to which it has been subordinated to State control in the last 400 years. For the enfeeblement of Christianity presents an infinitely more serious danger to the world than economic or political ills, since the battle is not properly between Church and State, but Christianity and paganism. From the middle of last century Kingsley [1] could foresee that the real struggle of the future would not be between Popery and Protestantism, but between " Atheism and Christ ". The triumph of paganism would destroy both Church and State. For this supreme reason the historic connexion of the two Societies calls for preservation, and requires, indeed, to be made a more vital factor in the life of Englishmen. True, where the State threatens to become Leviathan with menace to the freedom of individual or corporation, the Church will resist the State: as the State will deny to the Church extravagance in its own claims. Each is imperfect, fallible and spotted, affording but temporary shelter to pilgrims marching to Eternity: no more than that. Each Society has treasure, but the vessel is earthen.

Yet just as disestablishment will not, of itself, provide any short cut to all necessary reformation, so there is no reason to conclude that it would inevitably promote reunion among non-Roman Churches. The resultant disestablished Society might itself quickly be split into distinct bodies, and the prospect of reunion pushed into the hopelessly remote future. Rather is it for the Established Church of England, secure in its divine origin, its age-long history, in its vital integration with all that is English at its best, to extend its arms in welcoming back to itself those children who once were her own; and in the judicious and Christian spirit of Hooker to restore the friendly and warm relations with the Reformed Churches that obtained in the sixteenth century. We have already seen evidence for the latter fact, and it is timely to recall that friendlier relations have existed between the Church of England and English

[1] *Life and Letters* (London, 1883), p. 58.

Nonconformists in the past. The goodwill of the Nonconformists is essential not so much because politically they are powerful enough to bring about disestablishment, but because the Church of England is by history and design comprehensive, and union among Christians was never so much needed as now. In 1688 Sancroft [1] issued Articles of Instruction to the Clergy, in a spirit that may well be emulated to-day. He urges them to " have a very tender regard to our brethren the Protestant Dissenters; . . . visit them at their houses, and receive them kindly . . . and treat them fairly. . . . And, in the last place, that they warmly and most affectionately exhort them to join with us in daily fervent prayer to the God of Peace, for the universal blessed union of all reformed Churches both at home and abroad against our common enemies ". [2] Nor did the Archbishop's efforts stop at exhortation; he set on foot such measure of revision of the Book of Common Prayer as should make it possible for Nonconformists to rejoin their Mother Church, which the events of history unhappily brought to nothing. If fear of Rome could induce Sancroft to this conciliation, fear of paganism should lead the Church of England to open its doors to its former children while it is yet to-day. " I apprehend it my duty ", said the then Dissenter Ralph Thoresby, " to go as far as I can, possibly, in a national concord in religion." [3] In this moment this is the duty of Anglicanism.

Some real and not-long-delayed degree of reunion is demanded by the circumstances of these days, if not by Christian charity, including worship at the Altar, the place of Fellowship for Christians with their Lord and each other. In the seventeenth century it was a not uncommon practice for Dissenters occasionally to communicate at Anglican altars. " We told his Lordship ", [4] writes Calamy, " that the communicating with the Church of England, was no new practice among the Dissenters, nor of a late date, but had been used by some of the most eminent of our ministers ever since 1662, with a design to show their charity towards that Church ", [5] and proceeded to show him that if the " Bill for preventing Occasional Conformity " passed, the breach between Church and Noncon-

---

[1] *Vivebat* 1617–93.

[2] D'Oyley, *Life of Sancroft* (London, 1840), p. 196. Twenty years earlier Bishop Wilkins (1614–72) had proposed a " treaty of comprehension " for Dissenters who would come into the Church; those who already had Presbyterian ordination were not to be " re-ordained " but admitted to serve in the Church by the imposition of hands with appropriate words. Parliament, learning of this, voted that no such Bill should be received (Burnet, op. cit., I, 259).

[3] Thoresby, *Diary and Corr.*, I, 285.

[4] Bishop Burnet.

[5] Calamy, op. cit., I, 473 (sub anno 1702) (Cf. Thoresby: *Diary and Corr.*, I, 285; III, 321, 439).

formity would be wider than ever. In the House of Lords the Archbishop (Tenison) vigorously opposed the Bill, arguing that the Dissenters had a right and a duty to communicate in the Church of England. His words are no less applicable to the affairs of our own times. " At a time that all Europe is engaged in a bloody and expensive war ", he said . . . " at a time that the Protestant Dissenters . . . are heartily united with us against the common foes to our religion and government: what advantage these, who are in earnest for defending these things, can have by lessening the number of such as are firmly united in this common cause, I cannot for my life imagine." [1]

For, though written three hundred years ago, the words of a Chaplain in Ordinary to His Majesty King Charles I are appropriate. " In points essential to the Nature and Being of a visible Church, no Christian Churches are distinct; and in points not essential all do differ. And therefore the distinction of Christian Churches can be but circumstantial at most in points of Doctrine not simply necessary unto every man's salvation; for if any particular Church shall come to differ from the rest in Fundamentals directly, it must thenceforth cease to be a visible Church, as wanting those essentials that do constitute the Church and Church's visibility. These essential Fundamentals are at once delivered by St. Paul; One Lord, One Faith, One Baptism." [2] With the same thought in his mind, in every probability originating with Hooker, Sherlock points out that " all true Churches are Members of the One Mystical Body of Christ, as being all united to Him, as to their Head . . . in what the Apostle makes essential to this One Body: One Lord, One Faith, One Baptism." [3] Where this is so there is but one Church—the Catholic Church—into however many distinct Communions it may be divided. As Chillingworth said, reunion is possible only either by removing difference of opinion (which would be a miracle) or by showing that these differences ought not to hinder communion. " Christians must be taught to set a higher value upon these high points of faith and obedience wherein they agree, than upon these matters of less moment wherein they differ. . . . For why should men be more rigid than God? " [4]

---

[1] *Life of Tenison*, pp. 103–4.

[2] Dr. Walter Raleigh: *Certain Queries proposed by Roman Catholics and Answered* (ed. 1719), p. 33.

[3] *Discourse concerning the Nature, Unity and Communion of the Catholic Church* (London, 1688), p. 30.

[4] Chillingworth: *Religion of Protestants, A Safe Way to Salvation* [" that admirable Book", Hearne's *Collections*, VI, 118], p. 201. Cf. the devout Matthew Henry, writing to Thoresby in 1703: " To the general assembly and church of the first-born, which are written in Heaven, we are already come in faith and hope; by virtue of which we meet daily at the same throne of grace, and have comfort in a

In combating the exclusive claims of the Roman Church Hooker summed up the position proper to be adopted by all Non-Roman Churches. " *Church*," he wrote, " is a word which art hath devised thereby to sever and distinguish that society of men which professeth the true religion from the rest which profess it not . . ." (that is) . . . " Christian belief which yieldeth obedience to the Gospel of Jesus Christ, and acknowledgeth him the Saviour whom God did promise . . . the *only object* which separateth ours from other religions is Jesus Christ, in whom none but the Church doth believe and whom none but the Church doth worship. . . . If we go lower, we shall but add unto this . . . accidents, which are not properly of the being . . . of the Church. . . . This is the error of all popish definitions that hitherto have been brought. They define not the Church by that which the Church essentially is, but by that wherein they imagine their own more perfect than the rest are." [1] From any similar error it is urgent the Church of England free itself, in the words and spirit of Hooker: " I take no joy in striving. . . . There can come nothing of contention but the mutual waste of the parties contending till a common enemy dance in the ashes of them both." [2]

It would seem, then, that the modern democratic citizen, alike with the admirer of the modern Supreme State, may look back to Hooker as in some degree his political parent, while the Anglican regards him as the father of the Church of England. But it is to be feared that Hooker would not be entirely happy in assenting to so much responsibility. He would have small pleasure in a democracy based purely on numbers, in which one man was the worth of any other, in which his own noble, religious, and spacious conception of Law has been desiccated into the mere fiat of popular will.

The modern omnicompetent State, the object of so much worship

---

spiritual communion with all that in every place call on the name of Jesus Christ our Lord, both theirs and ours: this is an earnest of that blissful state in which we shall be with all the saints, none but saints, and saints made perfect; where Luther and Calvin are both of a mind " (Thoresby, *Diary and Corr.*, III, 439).

[1] *E.P.*, V, lxviii, 6.

[2] Three years after these pages were written, the present Archbishop is reported to have spoken to the Free Church Federal Council thus:—" Reunion, when it comes, if by God's grace it does, will be reunion of the Church of England. It will not be reunion with the Church of England by you. I want you to weigh that phrase. It will not be reunion with the Church of England; it will be reunion of the Church of England, for you and I were in origin the Church of England in this country, and in a real sense we still remain the Church of England in this country. When we come together we become again the Church of England." He goes on that when this day of reunion comes, the various Free Churches must retain their traditions, their identity with the past, their customs and methods, each Church functioning with its own identity (*The Times*, March 28th, 1946). His Cambridge sermon on reunion was preached in the same year.

in this century, would seem to him an idolatrous monster if its sole purpose should ever become the assurance of material existence for its citizens rather than the " good life ". He would lament that the sovereign power of to-day—the result of the historical process— is conscious of responsibility primarily towards the electorate, when it ought first to have the fear of God before its eyes. But, finally, he would no more rend the Church from the State in deference to the onslaughts of cynical materialism than he would have yielded up his Elizabethan Church to the attacks of Papists and Puritans. For the Church of England was to him the spiritual society of all Englishmen—conscious or not of their heritage—the very soul of that national body which had, in his own lifetime, passed out of adolescence into fierce and passionate manhood.[1]

" In every kind of things that is best which is most one." [2] So Dante, the protagonist of the imperial claim, quotes from that " arch-philosopher ", Hooker's greatest master; and with patient argument and measured prose Hooker asserts the mediaeval doc- trine of imperial unity and magisterial supremacy for a smaller, but more real, Empire. The State was the vehicle of salvation for its members. Salvation, union with God, must ever be that true end purposed for the State by those who refuse to regard their political association as intended only to satisfy their bellies. " But if all communities aim at some good, the State or political com- munity, which is the highest of all, and embraces all the rest, aims, and in a greater degree than any other, at the highest good." [3] So wrote that master " whose eye scarce anything in nature did escape ", but it is undeniable that, two thousand years after Aristotle, and three hundred and fifty after Hooker, we are more than ever in danger of regarding the State as a means of " filling our mast ", and, finally, of relieving us of the necessity of doing anything else. Not that material progress as such is evil, " because happiness is perfect, and therefore the happy man needs as an addition the goods of the body and external good and fortune that in these points he may not be fettered ".[4] But the acquirement of material well-being is the removal of an impediment, not the attainment of an end. As Carlyle was never wearied of pointing out,[5] a man can only truly live by believing something; a depth of tragedy

---

[1] Hooker was no mere champion of the Church of England, but " was possessed and penetrated by her highest life " (F. D. Maurice: *Moral and Metaphysical Philosophy*, II, 195).

[2] Dante: *De Monarchia*, I, xv. Quoted from Aristotle, *Metaphysics*, I, 5, and *Politics*, I, 5.

[3] Aristotle, *Politics*, I, i.

[4] Aristotle, *Nichomachean Ethics* (ed. Bywater, Oxford, 1942), VII, xiii, 152.

[5] Op. cit., p. 174.

has been reached when he believes in nothing but what he can put into pocket or stomach: " lower than that he will not get ". In the day of rationalization and technocracy, we need the reminder of a high law and a high end, lest we fall, not by rational process but by the blindness of appetite, not by mere enjoyment of " things " but by moral slavery to them, into an insipid atheism, " the fountain and well-spring of which impiety is a resolved purpose of mind to reap in this world what sensual profit or pleasure soever the world yieldeth, and not to be barred from any whatsoever means available thereunto." [1] Hooker assumes in England the co-extensiveness of Church and State. Even in Elizabeth's day that assumption was not perfectly correct: in our own it is indefensible. But Hooker in this connexion refers to the Church as the invisible body, whose members agree in essentials in the doctrine of Christ, leaving out of account that broad mass of " things indifferent " which we shall hardly limit more closely than he.[2] What to Hooker was an assumption must be to us a lively hope. Until the State more vividly realizes that it is a spiritual as well as a material body, until a spiritual orientation is universally adopted, economic conferences, tariff walls, arbitration boards and Government controls are capable only of the limited success proportionable to the limited nature of their end. It is alike the privilege and the duty of the Church of England to hold the State to its true purpose.

Sometime in 1933 Herr von Papen referred to riches and poverty as " the touchstones of human virtue ", and the drift of the world since has been in the direction of endorsing that view. In this country of Hooker, we of our day evidently need a scheme of moral values more than of social security—needful and desirable though that is—and we shall find it only by reference to the laws of being, human and divine, the law of reason, and the law of God. To such a search Hooker is a director, and in it a guide. In a world as full of physical and intellectual complication as our own, Hooker thought deeply and wrote with a sincerity which is a measure of the depth of his own perception. Some of the rough places that he had to make plain are plain enough now, but others are not, and new crookednesses have been realized which call to be made straight. A study of the thought of his age and of his own system of philosophy has the double advantage of giving us direct guidance in those of

---

[1] *E.P.*, V, ii, 1; cf. *Wisdom*, ii, 21.
[2] Cf. Arnold: " I would unite one half of the Archbishop of Dublin's theory with one half of Mr. Gladstone's: agreeing cordially with Mr. Gladstone in the moral theory of the State, and agreeing as cordially with the Archbishop with what I will venture to call the Christian Theory of the Church, and deducing from the two the conclusion that the perfect State and the perfect Church are identical " (*Lectures on History* (Oxford, 1842), pp. 65–6).

our problems which were also his, and of presenting to us the example of a man striving for truth. And he strove for it humbly, a man for ever with his eyes upon the ground, as we are told, but seeking as much as any astronomer for knowledge of that eternal Principle of Law which retains the stars in their courses, and man " a little lower than the angels ".

BIBLIOGRAPHY

ADMONITIONS TO PARLIAMENT. *Puritan Manifestoes.* Ed. Frere and Douglas, S.P.C.K., 1907.
AINSLIE, J. L. *The Doctrines of Ministerial Order in the Reformed Churches.* T. & T. Clark, 1940.
ALFORD, H. *New Testament for English Readers.* London, 1863-6.
ALLEN, J. W. *Political Thought in the XVIth Century.* London, 1928.
ALMACK, E. *Bibliography of the King's Book.* London, 1896.
ALSTON, L. Ed. *De Republica Anglorum.* Cambridge, 1906.
ANON. *The Princely Pellican.* 1649.
AQUINAS, ST. THOMAS. *De Regimine Principum. Opera* ed. Venice, 1787.
         Summa Totius Theologiae. Cologne, 1604.
ARBER, E. *Tracts : English Scholar's Library.* 1878-82.
ARMSTRONG, E. *French Wars of Religion.* London, 1892.
ARNOLD, T. *Lectures on History.* Oxford, 1842.
AUSTIN, J. *Lectures on General Jurisprudence.* 3rd ed., 1869.
BANCROFT, R. *Sermon Preached at Paul's Cross,* 1588.
         Dangerous Positions and Proceedings, 1593.
         A Survey of the Pretended Holy Discipline, 1593.
BARKER, E. *Church, State and Study.* Methuen, 1930.
         Gierke : Natural Law and the Theory of Society. Cambridge, 1934. 2 vols.
BARRY, A. *Masters in English Theology.* London, 1877.
BARWICK, J. *Vita J. Barwick.* London, 1721.
BATESON, M. *A Collection of Original Letters.* Camden Society, 1893, 1895.
BAXTER, R. *Reliquiae Baxterianae.* London, 1696.
BAYNE, R. *The Ecclesiastical Polity : The Fifth Book.* Macmillan, 1902.
BEARD, C. *The Reformation of the XVIth Century.* London, 1927.
BELLARMINE, R. *Opera, Rome* 1832; or *Cologne* 1619-20, Tome i, *De Romano Pontifice.*
BENSON, A. C. *Life of Archbishop Benson.* London, 1899-1900.
BEZA, T. *Praefatio de Presbyteris et Excommunicatione.* J. Norton, London, 1590.
BILSON, T. *The True Difference between Christian Subjection and Unchristian Rebellion.* 1585.
BIRT, H. N. *The Elizabethan Religious Settlement.* Bell and Sons, 1907.
BLACK, J. B. *The Reign of Elizabeth.* Oxford, 1937.
BODIN, J. *Six Books of a Republic.* Trans. Knolles, 1606.
         De Republica Sex Libri. Frankfort, 1609.
BRACTON, H. DE. *Notebook :* ed. F. W. Maitland. London, 1887. 3 vols.
BREWER, J. S. *Reign of Henry VIII.* London, 1884. 2 vols.
BRIDGES, J. *A Defence of the Government established in the Church of England for ecclesiastical matters.* London, 1587.
BRODERICK, J. *Blessed Robert Bellarmine.* London, 1928. 2 vols.
BROOK, B. *Lives of the Puritans.* London, 1813.
BRUTUS, JUNIUS. *Vindiciae contra Tyrannos.* Latin ed., Amsterdam, 1660. English ed. by H. J. Laski, London, 1924.
BRYCE, J. *Studies in History and Jurisprudence.* Oxford, 1901. 2 vols.

BUCHANAN, G. *De Jure Regni apud Scotos.* Aberdeen, 1762.
BURKE, E. *Reflections on the French Revolution, 1791.* Ed. Everyman.
　　　　Thoughts on the Causes of the Present Discontents. Works. Bohn
　　　　ed., 1902.
BURNET, G. *History of his own Times.* London, 1724. 2 vols.
　　　　History of the Reformation. Oxford, 1829. 6 vols.
CALAMY, E. *Life and Times.* London, 1830. 2 vols.
CALVIN, J. *Institution de la Religion Chrestienne.* Ed. Lefranc, Paris, 1911.
　　　　Lectures on Amos. Edinburgh, 1846.
CANON LAW OF THE CHURCH OF ENGLAND. S.P.C.K., 1947.
CARDWELL, E. *Documentary Annals.* Oxford, 1844. 2 vols.
CARLYLE, R. W. and A. J. *Mediaeval Political Theory in the West.* Blackwood,
　　　1928.
CARTWRIGHT, T. *Admonitions to Parliament.*
　　　　　　Full and Plain Declaration (see Travers).
　　　　　　Reply to Whitgift's Answer 1574.
CHAMBERS, R. W. *Sir Thomas More.* Cape, 1942.
CHARLES I, KING. *Works.* London, 1687.
CHAUVIRÉ, R. *Jean Bodin.* Paris, 1914.
CHILD, G. W. *Church and State under the Tudors.* Longmans, 1890.
CHILLINGWORTH, W. *Religion of Protestantism a Safe Way to Salvation.*
　　　London, 1846.
CHURCH, F. J. *The " De Monarchia " of Dante.* London, 1879.
CHURCH, R. W. *Introduction to Hooker, Book I.* Oxford, 1882.
CLARENDON PAPERS in the Bodleian Library.
COLERIDGE, S. T. *Literary Remains.* London, 1836–9. 4 vols.
COLLIER, J. *Ecclesiastical History.* London, 1840. 6 vols.
CONSTANT, G. *Reformation in England.* Sheed & Ward, 1939–41. 2 vols.
CONTR'UN. *See* La Boëtie.
COOPER, T. *Admonition to the People of England, 1589.* Ed., Arber, 1882.
COULTON, G. C. *The Mediaeval Village.* Cambridge, 1931.
COVEL, W. *Just and Temperate Defence of the Five Books of the Ecclesiastical
　　　Polity.* London, 1603.
CREIGHTON, M. *Queen Elizabeth.* Longmans, 1899.
CROCE, B. *On History.* London, 1921.
　　　　Aesthetic. London, 1922.
DANTE. (See CHURCH, F. J.). *De Monarchia.* Florence, 1879.
DAWSON, C. *Religion and the Modern State.* Sheed & Ward, 1935.
D'ENTRÈVES, A. P. *Ricardo Hooker.* Turin, 1932.
DICEY, A. V. *Privy Council.* Macmillan, 1887.
　　　　Law of the Constitution. London, 1893.
DIXON, R. W. *History of the Church of England, 1878–1902.* Oxford. 6 vols.
DOCUMENTS. *See :* Gee & Hardy; Kidd; Macdonald; Prothero; Stubbs;
　　　Tanner.
DOWDEN, E. *Puritan and Anglican.* London, 1901.
D'OYLEY, G. *Life of Sancroft.* London, 1840.
DUNNING, W. A. *Political Theories :—*
　　　　　　Ancient & Medieval. New York, 1923.
　　　　　　Luther to Montesquieu. New York, 1923.
EINSTEIN, L. *Tudor Ideals.* London, 1921.
FIGGIS, J. N. *Churches in the Modern State.* London, 1913.
　　　　Divine Right of Kings. Cambridge, 1922.
　　　　From Gerson to Grotius. Cambridge, 1923.
FILMER, R. *Patriarcha.* London, 1680.
FISH, S. *Supplication for the Beggars, 1529.* Ed., Arber.
FOSTER, C. W. *State of the Church.* Lincoln Record Society, 1926.

FOWLER, T. *History of Corpus Christi College.* Oxford, 1898.

FREEMAN, E. A. *Historical Essays.* London, 1898. 4 vols.

FRERE, W. H. *History of the English Church.* Macmillan, 1924.

FRERE, W. H. and DOUGLAS. *Puritan Manifestoes.* S.P.C.K., 1907.

FRERE, W. H., and KENNEDY, W. P. M. *Visitation Articles 1536-75.* Alcuin Club, 1930. 3 vols.

FROUDE, J. A. *History of England.* Longmans, 1870. 12 vols.
    Lectures on the Council of Trent. Longmans, 1896.

FULLER, T. *Worthies of England.* Ed., Nuttall. London, 1840. 3 vols.
    Church History of Britain. Ed., Nichols. London, 1842. 3 vols.

FÜLOP-MILLER, R. *The Power and Secret of the Jesuits.* London, 1930.

FUNCK-BRENTANO, F. *The Renaissance.* Bles, 1936.

GAIRDNER, J. *Lollardy and the Reformation.* London, 1908. 4 vols.

GARDINER, S. R. *History of the Commonwealth and Protectorate.* Longmans, 1901. 3 vols.

GARDINER, S. *De Vera Obedientia.* Ed., P. Janelle. Cambridge, 1930.

GAUDEN, J. *The Love of Truth and Peace.* London, 1641.
    Three Sermons preached upon Several Public Occasions. London, 1642.
    Hieraspistes, or a Defence for the Ministry of the Church of England. London, 1653.
    Ecclesiae Anglicanae Suspiria. London, 1659.
    Slight Healers of Public Hurts. 1659.
    Considerations touching the Liturgy of the Church of England. 1660.
    Loosing of St. Peter's Bands. London, 1660.
    Sermon at the Funeral of Dr. Brounrigg, Bishop of Exeter. London, 1660.
    Anti-Baal-Berith. 1661.
    The Eight Books of Hooker's "Ecclesiastical Polity". London, 1662.
    Eikon Basilike, 1648. Printed in Works of King Charles, 1687.

GEE, E. *Divine Right and Original of the Civil Magistrate from God.* London, 1658.
    Ed., *Jesuits' Memorial of Robert Parsons.* London, 1690.

GEE, H. *Elizabethan Clergy.* Oxford, 1898.
    The Reformation Period. Methuen, 1909.

GEE, H., and HARDY, W. J. *Documents illustrative of English Church History.* Macmillan, 1896.

GENT, T. F. P. *The Life and Character of Mr. John Locke.* Trans. from the French of Le Clerc; London, 1706.

GIBSON, E. *Codex Juris Ecclesiastici Anglicani.* Oxford, 1713. 2 vols.

GIERKE, O. *Political Theories of the Middle Ages.* Trans. F. W. Maitland, Cambridge, 1938.
    Natural Law and the Theory of Society. Cambridge, 1934. 2 vols.

GOOCH, G. P. *History of English Democratic Ideas in the Seventeenth Century.* Cambridge, 1898.

GOODMAN, C. *How Superior Powers ought to be Obeyed.* 1558.

GRINDAL, E. *Remains.* Parker Society, 1843.

GROTIUS, H. *De Jure Belli ac Pacis.* Amsterdam, 1689.

GWATKIN, H. M. *Church and State in England, to the Death of Queen Anne.* Longmans, 1917.

HADDAN, A. W. *Works of Thorndike.* Parker, 1844-6. 8 vols.

HALLAM, A. H. *Constitutional History.* Murray, 1867. 3 vols.
    Europe during the Middle Ages. Murray, 1868. 3 vols.
    History of the Literature of Europe. Murray, 1873. 3 vols.

HANBURY, B. *Hooker's Ecclesiastical Polity.* London, 1830. 3 vols.

HARLEIAN MISCELLANY. London, 1808. 10 vols.

HARRINGTON, J. *Oceana*. Ed., Morley. London, 1887.

HARRISON, G. B. *The Elizabethan Journals, 1591–1603*. London, 1939.

HEARNE, THOMAS. *Remarks and Collections*. Oxford Hist. Society. 13 vols. 1885– .

HEARNSHAW, F. J. C. *Social and Political Ideas of the Middle Ages*. Harrap, 1923.
    Social and Political Ideas of the Renaissance and Reformation. Harrap, 1925.
    Social and Political Ideas of the XVIth and XVIIth centuries. Harrap, 1926.
    Some English Thinkers of the Augustan Age. Harrap, 1928.

HENSON, H. H. *The Church of England*. Cambridge, 1939.
    Retrospect of an Unimportant Life. Oxford, 1944. 2 vols.

HEWART, LORD. *The New Despotism*. Benn, 1919.

HOADLY, B. *Answer to the Representation by the Committee of Convocation*. London, 1717.
    Works. London, 1773. 3 vols.

HOBBES, T. *De Cive. Works*. Ed., Molesworth. London, 1839.
    Leviathan. Oxford, 1909.

HOLDSWORTH, W. S. *History of English Law*. Vol. I. Methuen, 1903; Vol. II. 1909; Vol. IV. Methuen, 1924.

HOOKER, RICHARD. *The Laws of Ecclesiastical Polity*. Ed., Keble and Paget. Oxford, 1888. 3 vols.

HOTMAN, F. *Franco-Gallia, 1573*. English Translation, 1738.

HUGHES, P. *Rome and the Counter-Reformation in England*. Burnes & Oates, 1942.

HUME, D. *Essays*. Ed., T. H. Green and T. H. Grose. London, 1875. 2 vols.

JACOB, E. F. *The Register of Archbishop Chichele*. Oxford, 1943–47. 4 vols.

JAMES I. *Apology for the Oath of Allegiance*. London, 1607.

JANELLE, P. (ed.). *De Vera Obedientia*. Cambridge, 1930.

JELLINEK, G. *Allgemeine Staatslehre*. Berlin, 1905.

JEWEL, J. *Apology for the Church of England*. Ed., Isaacson, London, 1829.
    Works. Parker Society, 1845–50. 4 vols.

JONSON, BEN. *Timber; or, Discoveries made upon Men and Matter*. London, 1641.

KEBLE, J. *See* Richard Hooker.

KENNEDY, W. P. M. *The Interpretations of the Bishops*. Alcuin Club, 1908.
    Parker. Pitman, 1908.
    Studies in Tudor History. Constable, 1916.
    Elizabethan Episcopal Administration, 1575–1603. Alcuin Club, 1924. 3 vols.
    See also Frere, W. H., and Kennedy, W. P. M.

KENNETT, W. *Register*. London, 1728.

KINGSLEY, C. *Life and Letters*. London, 1883.

KIRK, K. E. *The Study of Theology*. London, 1939.

KNAPPEN, M. M. *Tudor Puritanism*. Chicago University Press, 1939.

KNOLLES, R. *The Six Bookes of a Commonweal*. London, 1606.

KNOX, JOHN. *Works*. Ed. Laing. Woodrow Society, 1846–64. 6 vols.

LABITTE, C. *Démocratie de la Ligue*. Paris, 1865.

LA BOËTIE, S. *Contr'un*. 1576. English edition, *Discourse of Voluntary Servitude*. 1735.

LAGARDE, G. DE. *Recherches sur l'esprit politique de la Réforme*. Douai, 1926.

Lane Poole, R. *History of Medieval Thought and Learning.* London, 1920.

Laski, H. J. *Foundations of Sovereignty.* Harcourt, Brace & Co., 1921.

Lattey, C. *St. Thomas Aquinas.* Cambridge, 1925.

Laud, W. *Conference with Fisher.* Parker, 1844.
    Life and Trial. London, 1695.

Lives of the Bishops. London, 1731.

Locke, J. *Works.* London, 1812. 10 vols.

Luther, Martin. *Address to the Nobility of Germany.* Ed., Wace: Murray, 1883.
    The Ninety-five Theses. Ed., Wace: Murray, 1883.
    Werke. Ed., Weimar.
      Vol. VIII. 1889. Eine Treue Vermahnung zu allen Christen, 1522.
      Vol. XVIII. 1908. Ermahnung zum Frieden, 1525. Widder die sturmenden Bawren, 1525. De Servo Arbitrio, 1525.
      Vol. XIX. 1897. Ob Kriegsleute auch in selingem stande sein Können, 1526.
      Vol. LVI. 1938. Divi Pauli apostoli ad Romanos Epistola.

Macdonald, W. *Select Charters.* New York, 1899.

Machiavelli, N. *The Prince.* Ed., World's Classics.

Machyn, H. *Diary, 1550–1563.* Camden Soc., 1848.

McIlwain, C. H. *High Court of Parliament.* Yale Press, 1910.

Maine, Sir H. *Popular Government.* London, 1885.

Maitland, F. W. *Canon Law in the Church of England.* London, 1898.
    Elizabethan Gleanings. *English Historical Review,* Vol. XV. 1900.
    English Law and the Renaissance. Cambridge, 1901.
    Collected Papers. 1909. 3 vols.
    Constitutional History. Cambridge, 1926.
    Gierkes Political Theories of the Middle Ages. Cambridge, 1938.

Makower, F. *Constitutional History of the Church of England.* London, 1895.

Mallet, C. E. *History of the University of Oxford.* Methuen, 1925. 2 vols.

Mariana, J. de. *De Rege et Regis Institutione.* 2nd ed., 1641.

Marprelate, Martin. *Hay any Worke for Cooper.* London, 1845.
    The Epistle, 1588. Ed., Arber, 1880.
    Tracts. Ed., Arber, 1895.

Marsden, J. B. *The History of the Early Puritans.* London, 1853.

Marsiglio of Padua. *Defensor Pacis.* Ed. C. W. Previté-Orton. Cambridge, 1928.

Marvell, A. *Rehearsal Transposed.* 1672.

Maurice, J. F. D. *Moral and Metaphysical Philosophy.* London, 1873. 2 vols.

Merriman, R. B. *Life & Letters of Thomas Cromwell.* Oxford, 1902. 2 vols.

Meyer, A. O. *England and the Catholic Church under Queen Elizabeth.* Kegan Paul, 1916.

Meyer, E. *Machiavelli and the Elizabethan Drama.* Weimar, 1897.

Michaelis, G. *Richard Hooker als politikischer Denker.* Berlin, 1933.

Micklethwaite, J. T. *The Ornaments of the Rubric.* Alcuin Club, 1898.

Milne, J. G. *The Early History of Corpus Christi College, Oxford.* (Blackwell, 1946.)

Milton, John. *Prose Works.* Ed. St. John, London, 1848. 5 vols.

Minute Book of the Dedham Classis. Ed. for the Royal Historical Society, 1905.

MONTAIGNE. *Essays*. Trans. Cotton. Bell & Sons, 1930. 3 vols.
MORE, SIR THOMAS. *Utopia*. With Introduction by H. G. Wells. London, 1908.
MORISON S. E., and COMMAGER, H. S. *Growth of the American Republic*. Oxford, 1942. 2 vols.
MULLER, J. A. *Stephen Gardiner and the Tudor Reaction*. S.P.C.K., 1926.
MURRAY, R. H. *Political Consequences of the Reformation*. Benn, 1926.
NASH, T. (? LYLY, J.). *Pappe with an Hatchet*. London, 1844.
NEAL, D. *History of the Puritans*. London, 1822. 5 vols.
NEALE, J. E. *Queen Elizabeth*. Cape, 1934.
NEVILLE, H. *Plato Redivivus*. London, 1763.
OGLE, A. *The Canon Law in Medieval England*. Murray, 1912.
ORR, R. L. *The Free Church of Scotland Appeals*. Edinburgh, 1903.
OSBORNE, F. *Memoirs of Queen Elizabeth*. London, 1658.
PAGET, F. *An Introduction to the Fifth Book of Hooker's Treatise of the Laws of Ecclesiastical Polity*. Oxford, 1907.
PALEY, W. *The Principles of Moral and Political Philosophy*. London, 1790. 2 vols.
PARKER, J. *Did Queen Elizabeth take " other order "?* Parker, Oxford, 1878.
PARKER, M. *Correspondence*. Parker Society, Cambridge, 1853.
PARKER SOCIETY. *Zurich Letters*. 1842, 1845. 2 vols.
            Original Letters. 1846–7. 2 vols.
PARSONS, R. *Jesuits' Memorial, 1596*. Ed., Edward Gee, 1690.
PATTISON, M. *Isaac Casaubon*. Oxford, 1892.
PECOCK, R. *Repressor of Overmuch Blaming the Clergy*. Rolls Series. 1860. 2 vols.
PEEL, A. *The Seconde Part of a Register*. Cambridge, 1915. 2 vols.
            The Note-book of John Penry. Royal Historical Society, 1944.
PENRY, J. *Humble Motion*. London, 1590.
            Public Wants and Disorders 1588. London, 1861.
PEPYS, S. *Diary*. Ed., Wheatley. London, 1928. 10 vols.
PETERS, H. *Dying Father's Last Legacy*. London, 1660.
PIERCE, W. *An Historical Introduction to the Marprelate Tracts*. Constable, 1908.
            The Marprelate Tracts. Clark & Co., 1911.
POLLARD, A. F. *England under Protector Somerset*. London, 1900.
            Henry VIII. Longmans, 1905.
            Political History of England. Longmans, 1910.
            Wolsey. Longmans, 1929.
POLLOCK, F. *History of the Science of Politics*. Longmans, 1919.
POLLOCK, F., and MAITLAND, F. W. *History of English Law*. Cambridge, 1898. 2 vols.
PONET, J. *Short Treatise of Politicke Power*. London, 1566. Ed., 1642.
POWICKE, F. M. *The Reformation in England*. Oxford, 1941.
PREVITÉ-ORTON, C. W. (ed.). *Defensor Pacis of Marsiglio of Padua*. Cambridge, 1928.
PROTHERO, G. W. *Statutes and Constitutional Documents, 1588–1625*. Oxford, 1906.
PRYNNE, W. *Sovereign Power of Parliaments and Kingdoms*. 1643.
PULLAN, L. *Religion since the Reformation*. Oxford, 1923.
RALEIGH, W. *Certain Queries proposed by Roman Catholics and Answered*. London, 1719.
RATCLIFF, E. C. *See* Kirk, K. E.
Réveille-Matin, Le. French ed., Edinburgh, 1574.
RICHER, E. *Libellus de ecclesiastica et politica potestate*. 1612.
RICKABY, J. *Aquinas Ethicus*. London, 1896. 2 vols.

S

ROBERTS, J. *Memoirs of the Life and Times of T. Tenison, late Archbishop of Canterbury.* London: ?1716.

ROUSSEAU, J. J. *Le Contrat Social.* Ed., H. J. Tozer. London, 1909.

RUNCIMAN, S. *Byzantine Civilisation.* London, 1932.

RUTHERFORD, S. *Lex Rex.* London, 1846.

SANDERSON, R. *Sermons.* London, 1657.

SANTAYANA, G. *Soliloquies in England.* New York, 1923.
  Locke and the Frontiers of Commonsense. Cambridge, 1933.

SCOTT-PEARSON, A. F. *T. Cartwright and Elizabethan Puritanism.* Cambridge, 1925.
  Church and State. Cambridge, 1928.

SELLER, ABEDNEGO. *The History of Passive Obedience since the Reformation.* Amsterdam, 1689.

SHELDON PAPERS. Bodleian Library.

SHERLOCK, W. *Discourse concerning the Nature, Unity and Communion of the Catholic Church.* London, 1688.

SHIRLEY, J. *Elizabeth's First Archbishop.* S.P.C.K., 1948.

SIDNEY, ALGERNON. *Discourses on Government.* Edinburgh, 1750. 2 vols.

SISSON, C. J. *The Judicious Marriage of Mr. Hooker.* C.U.P., 1940.

SMECTYMNUS. *An Answer to a Book entitled an Humble Remonstrance.* London, 1641.
  Vindication of An Answer, etc. London, 1641.

SMITH, A. L. *Church and State in the Middle Ages.* Oxford, 1938.

SMITH, T. *De Republica Anglorum.* Ed., Alston, Cambridge, 1906.

SPRINT, J. *Cassander Anglicanus.* London, 1618.

STILLINGFLEET, E. *Irenicum.* London, 1661.

STRONG, T. B. *Christian Ethics.* Longmans, 1897.

STRYPE, J. *Annals of the Reformation.*
  Ecclesiastical Memorials.
  Life of Aylmer.
  Life of Grindal.
  Life of Parker.
  Life of Whitgift.
    Oxford, 1821–28.

STUBBS, W. *Lectures on Medieval and Modern History.* Oxford, 1887.
  Select Charters. Oxford, 1905.

STURZO, L. *Church and State.* London, 1939.

SUAREZ, F. *Tractatus de Legibus ac Deo Legislatore.* Paris, 1861. 2 vols.

SYKES, N. *Church and State in the XVIIIth century.* Cambridge, 1934.

TANNER, J. R. *Tudor Constitutional Documents.* Cambridge, 1922

TAWNEY, R. H. *Religion and the Rise of Capitalism.* Murray, 1927.

TAYLOR, H. O. *Thought and Expression in the XVIth Century.* Macmillan, 1920. 2 vols.

THORESBY, R. *Diary and Correspondence.* London, 1830. 4 vols.

THORNDIKE, H. *Works.* Ed. A. W. Haddan. Parker, 1844–46. 8 vols.

TOLAND, J. *Amyntor, or a Defence of Milton's Life.* London, 1699.

TOYNBEE, A. J. *A Study of History.* Oxford, 1939. 6 vols.

TRAVERS, W. *Full and Plain Declaration.* 1575.

TREATISE OF ECCLESIASTICAL & POLITICAL POWER. *See* Richer, E.

TREVELYAN, G. M. *British History in the XIXth Century.* Longmans, 1937.

TREVOR-ROPER, H. *Archbishop Laud.* Macmillan, 1940.

TUCKER, JOSIAH. *On Civil Government.* London, 1781.

TYNDALE, W. *Obedience of a Christian Man.* Parker Society, 1848.

UDAL, JOHN. *The State of the Church of England, 1588.* Ed., Arber, 1879.
  A Demonstration of the Truth of the Discipline, 1588. Ed., Arber, 1880.

USHER, R. G.　*Presbyterian Movement.*　Royal Historical Society, 1905.
　　　　Reconstruction of the English Church.　Appleton & Co., 1910.
　　　　2 vols.
　　　　The Rise and Fall of the High Commission.　Oxford, 1913.
USSHER, J. (ARCHBISHOP).　*A Brief Declaration of the Universality of the Church.*　London, 1624.
WALTON, IZAAK.　*Lives of Donne, Wotton, Hooker, etc.*　London, 1825.
　　　　Life of Hooker.　Keble's edition of the *Ecclesiastical Polity,* Vol. I.　Oxford.
WARBURTON, W. M.　*The Alliance between Church and State.*　London, 1736.
WEILL, G.　*Pouvoir Royal en France.*　Paris, 1892.
WESTCOTT, B. F.　*Commentary on St. John's Gospel.*　London, 1919.
WHITEBROOK, J. C.　*The Consecration of Matthew Parker.*　Mowbray, 1945.
WHITEHEAD, A. N.　*Adventures of Ideas.*　Cambridge, 1943.
WHITGIFT, JOHN.　*Works.*　Parker Society, 1851–53.　3 vols.
WHITTINGHAM, WILLIAM.　*A Brief Discourse of the Troubles at Frankfort, 1554–58.*　London, 1908.
WOOD, ANTHONY À.　*Athenae Oxonienses.*　Ed., Bliss, 1817.　4 vols.
WOODRUFF, C. E., and CAPE, H. J.　*Schola Regia Cantuariensis.*　London, 1908.
WORDSWORTH, C.　" *Who wrote Eikon Basilike ?* "　London, 1824.
ZWINGLI, ULRICH.　*Opera.*　Tomes 3.　Zurich, 1581.

INDEX

PRINTED IN GREAT BRITAIN BY RICHARD CLAY AND COMPANY, LTD.,
BUNGAY, SUFFOLK.